The Financial Times Guide to Personal Tax 2010–11

Sara Williams and Jonquil Lowe

Financial Times
Prentice Hall
is an imprint of

Harlow, England • London • New York • Boston • San Francisco • Toronto • Sydney • Singapore • Hong Kong
Tokyo • Seoul • Taipei • New Delhi • Cape Town • Madrid • Mexico City • Amsterdam • Munich • Paris • Milan

PEARSON EDUCATION LIMITED

Edinburgh Gate
Harlow CM20 2JE
Tel: +44 (0)1279 623623
Fax: +44 (0)1279 431059
Website: www.pearsoned.co.uk

The Financial Times Guide to Personal Tax was previously published as the *Lloyds TSB Tax Guide*

First published by Pearson Education in Great Britain 2006
Second edition published 2007
Third edition published 2008
Fourth edition published 2009
Fifth edition published 2010

© Vitesse Media Plc 2006, 2010

ISBN: 978-0-273-73569-4

British Library Cataloguing in Publication Data
A catalogue record for this book can be obtained from the British Library

10 9 8 7 6 5 4 3 2 1
14 13 12 11 10

Typeset in 9pt Stone Serif by 3
Printed and bound in Great Britain by Henry Ling Ltd, Dorchester, Dorset

Contents

The authors / viii
Acknowledgements / ix
Dear Reader! / x
Tax changes after the General Election / xi
Introduction / 1

PART I HOW TO PAY LESS TAX / 5

1 Tax changes for 2010–11 / 7

2 An overview of income tax / 15

3 Paying and reclaiming tax / 27

4 Dealing with tax problems / 47

5 Tax and your household / 57

6 Tax and your home / 71

7 Savings, investments and pensions / 79

8 Making the most of fringe benefits / 107

9 Minimising capital gains tax / 127

10 Gifts and passing your money on / 159

PART 2 FILLING IN YOUR TAX RETURN / 177

11 Getting started / 179

12 Income / 191

13 Reliefs / 223

14 Allowances / 247

15 Employment / 253

16 Share schemes / 285

17 Self-employment / 303

18 Partnership / 345

19 UK property / 349

20 Foreign income / 367

21 Trusts / 381

22 Capital gains / 389

23 Non-residence / 401

APPENDICES / 407

A Tax-free income / 407

B Converting net income to gross / 411

C The short tax return / 414

D Tax deadlines / 417

E Useful leaflets, forms and contacts / 420

Index / 425

The authors

Sara Williams is a former investment analyst and financial journalist. She has contributed many articles on tax and finance to national newspapers and for a number of years wrote for *Which?*, including the *Which? Tax-Saving Guide* and the *Which? Book of Tax*. She is also the author of the *Financial Times Guide to Business Start Up*. Sara is now the executive chairman of AIM-listed Vitesse Media, an online, events and print media business. Its titles include *What Investment, Business XL, Growth Company Investor, Information Age, The AIM Guide*, SmallBusiness.co.uk and GrowthBusiness.co.uk. She is a qualified investment manager and adviser.

Jonquil Lowe started out as an economist and worked for several years in the City as an investment analyst. She is a former head of the Money Group at Which?, a past editor of *The Which? Tax-Saving Guide* and was for many years a regular contributor to *Which? Way to Save Tax*. Jonquil now splits her time between being a Lecturer in Personal Finance with The Open University and working as a freelance researcher and journalist. She holds the Diploma in Financial Planning and writes extensively for a diverse range of clients, including Which?, the Financial Services Authority and LexisNexis Butterworths. Jonquil is the author of more than 20 books, including *Be Your Own Financial Adviser*, published by Pearson, *Giving and Inheriting, The Pension Handbook, Finance Your Retirement* and *Save and Invest*, all from Which? Books, and the *Personal Finance Handbook*, published by the Child Poverty Action Group.

Acknowledgements

A tax guide of this type cannot appear without the help and hard work of a multitude of people too numerous to mention. However, we would like to give special thanks to Keith M Gordon MA (Oxon) FCA CTA (Fellow) Barrister and Ximena Montes Manzano BSc Barrister, who have helped us on the technical side.

Thank you,

Sara Williams and Jonquil Lowe

Note

Both of us – along with everyone at Vitesse Media plc – have made strenuous efforts to check the accuracy of the information. If by chance a mistake or omission has occurred, we are sorry that neither we nor the publisher can take responsibility if you suffer any loss or problem as a result of it. But please write to Sara Williams and Jonquil Lowe, *FT Guide to Personal Tax*, Octavia House, 50 Banner Street, London, EC1Y 8ST if you have any suggestions about how we can improve the content of the guide. Bear in mind that the UK tax system is complex. The general guidance given in this book may apply differently in your own particular circumstances. If you are in any doubt, you are strongly advised to seek professional advice (see Appendix E).

Dear Reader!

The *FT Guide to Personal Tax* is fully updated for the Budget that took place in March 2010 and went to press shortly after the General Election in May 2010. We have included a summary of the main manifesto tax pledges of the coalition parties (see opposite). A second Budget was scheduled to be held on 22 June 2010, in which some of these pledges or other measures were expected to be implemented. If you want to keep abreast of any further developments, you can contact us in either of two ways:

- send for our free update, which will be issued in the autumn – see below for instructions on what to do

- log on to the Tax Guide website – at www.pearson-books.com/FTtaxguide

To get the paper version send an A4-sized self-addressed envelope with a 66p stamp on it to: Sara Williams and Jonquil Lowe, *FT Guide to Personal Tax*, Octavia House, 50 Banner Street, London EC1Y 8ST.

Yours sincerely,

Sara Williams
Jonquil Lowe

Tax changes after the General Election

This book went to press soon after the General Election 2010. No party had an overall majority and, after a few days of intensive negotiation, a coalition government of the Conservative and Liberal Democrat parties was formed. The new government pledged to hold an emergency Budget within 50 days (see p. 3 for how you can get an update) and issued a statement of agreement that indicates some of the tax measures that the Budget might contain (see below). What other tax changes may emerge over time depends on compromises the two parties may reach and their respective manifesto pledges. Therefore, this section also summarises the tax intentions contained in the manifestos of the coalition parties.

Tax measures expected in the second 2010 Budget

- **Income tax and allowances** The personal allowance will be raised substantially from 2011–12, targeted at people on low and middle incomes. There will be a longer term commitment eventually to raise the allowance to £10,000. The Conservative 'marriage tax break' is unlikely to go ahead.
- **Tax credits** Tax credits for higher earners will be reduced.
- **Capital gains tax** The tax rate on non-business gains is to rise to more closely match income tax rates. There will be exemptions for 'entrepreneurial business activities'.
- **Savings and investments** For higher earning families, the Child Trust Fund scheme will be cut back. On pensions, the obligation to buy an annuity at age 75 is to be scrapped – some commentators suggest this change might be limited to people with large pension savings (say, £100,000 or more). The default retirement age of 65 will be phased

out. The date at which state pension age starts to rise is likely to be reviewed and probably brought forward.

■ **Inheritance tax** The tax-free threshold is unlikely to rise.

■ **National insurance** The previously announced 1 per cent rise in rates from 2011–12 will go ahead. There will no longer be any increase in the primary threshold at which contributions start so employees – and the self-employed – will feel the full impact of the rise. However, there will be an increase in the threshold at which employers start to pay to offset the rise.

■ **Other** Air passenger duty will shift to a per-plane basis from the current per-passenger basis. Tackling tax avoidance will be a high priority.

Tax pledges in the Conservative manifesto

■ **Income tax and allowances** A person who is married or in a civil partnership to be allowed to transfer up to £750 of their personal allowance to their partner and this would allow tax relief up to the basic rate in the recipient's hands. This would save a couple up to £150 tax a year.

■ **Tax credits** to cease to be paid to families with incomes over £50,000. The tax credits system to be reformed to reduce overpayments and fraud.

■ **Homes and property** Permanent increase to £250,000 in the threshold at which stamp duty on a property purchase starts, but this would apply only to first-time buyers.

■ **Savings and investments** Government contributions to child trust funds to stop, except for children from low-income families and children with disabilities. Green individual savings accounts to be introduced to help fund a low-carbon economy. On pensions, abolish obligation to buy an annuity at age 75 and look at how to end the default retirement age (currently 65). When resources allow, start to remove 'the effects of the abolition of the dividend tax credit for pension funds' – the previous abolition of the credit means that, at present, the return from pension fund investments is not completely tax free because income from shares and share-based income is taxed at 10 per cent.

■ **Inheritance tax** Inheritance tax threshold to be raised to £1 million.

- **Small businesses** Exemption from employer's national insurance on pay to your first ten employees during your first year of trading. Small business rate relief to become automatic. Local councils to be given the power to introduce further business rate discounts. Cut in small business rate of corporation tax to 20 per cent initially and possibly more later, funded by reductions in 'complex reliefs and allowances'. Reduction in the number of forms required to start up a business.

- **National Insurance** The Conservatives would go ahead with Labour's pre-announced increases from 2011–12, but increase the primary threshold further so that anyone earning under £35,000 would be protected from the increase.

- **Other** Council tax to be frozen for two years and plans for a council tax revaluation to be scrapped. Consultation on a 'Fair Fuel Stabiliser' which would cut fuel duty when oil prices rise and vice versa. Air passenger duty to be reformed to encourage fuller, cleaner planes. Non-domiciled UK residents to have to pay a flat-rate levy. The government would meet the student loan repayments for top maths and science graduates who take up work as teachers. Scotland to be given more responsibility to raise the money it spends.

Tax pledges in the Liberal Democrat manifesto

- **Income tax and allowances** Personal allowance for everyone, regardless of age, to be £10,000.

- **Tax credits** restricted and likely to include abolishing child tax credit for wealthier families. Tax credit awards to be fixed for a period of six months at a time to reduce the problem of overpayments.

- **Reliefs** Tax relief on pension contributions to be restricted to the basic rate only. Tax relief on Gift Aid to be given at a single rate of 23 per cent, abolishing higher rate and additional rate relief. New 'easy-giving accounts' to be available through the publicly owned banks.

- **Homes and property** New 'mansion tax' on homes worth over £2 million at a rate of 1 per cent a year on the value above that threshold. Local councils to be given the power to increase council tax on second homes. If you have an empty property, you could be eligible for a grant to renovate it for use as social housing or a loan if it is to be used privately. Measures to prevent the avoidance of stamp duty on house purchase through the use of offshore trusts.

■ **Savings and investments** Government payments to child trust funds (CTFs) to cease. Early access to personal pension funds to be allowed, for example, in case of financial hardship. Scrap requirement to buy an annuity at age 75. Compulsory retirement ages would also be scrapped. Private investors to be able to invest through a new UK Infrastructure Bank (UKIB). This would fund major transport and energy projects and offer savers stable, long-term returns. UKIB investments could be suitable for funds that aim to produce annuity income.

■ **Capital gains tax** Capital gains to be taxed at the same rates as income.

■ **Small businesses** Business rates to be based on site value rather than rental value.

■ **Other** Tighter measures to tackle tax avoidance, including giving HM Revenue & Customs additional powers. Domicile rules to be reformed with automatic UK-domicile after seven years' residence meaning worldwide income would be subject to UK taxes. Replace Air Passenger Duty (APD), charged per person, with a new per-plane duty (PPD) that would apply to air freight as well as passenger travel. PPD would be increased for domestic flights where alternative, less-polluting forms of travel are available. Prepare for introduction of road pricing offset by the abolition of vehicle excise duty and a reduction in fuel duty for drivers in rural areas. National minimum wage to be set at the same rate for all ages (except apprentices).

Introduction

Following the global financial crisis of 2007 and 2008, the government launched a huge programme of spending and, to a lesser extent, tax cuts to stave off a major economic depression. This pushed government debt from around 36 per cent of the UK's national income in 2007 to a forecast 77 per cent by 2013–14. Measures to reduce this debt mountain start in 2010–11 and become more severe from 2011–12 onwards. Never has it been more important to understand how the tax system works and what you can do to ensure you do not pay more tax than you should.

While paying tax may hurt, the collection process is often fairly painless with tax automatically deducted through the Pay As You Earn (PAYE) system. But around 9.5 million people have to complete either a short or full tax return each year under the self-assessment system. And PAYE taxpayers need to check that the correct amount of tax is being collected, especially – the Chartered Institute of Taxation warns – since a change in the HM Revenue & Customs computer systems was causing wrong PAYE codes to be sent to many taxpayers and their employers in spring 2010.

However your tax is collected, you are ultimately responsible for ensuring that all your income and any other taxable sums are declared and the correct tax paid. You have strict obligations to declare your income within time limits and pay the tax due. Since April 2009, HM Revenue & Customs (commonly just called the Revenue) have increased powers to check that you are meeting your obligations. Despite this, over a million taxpayers every year pay their tax late and even more deliver their tax return late. Remember there are:

- dates by which you have to send in your tax return (p. 31)
- rules about records that you must keep (p. 28)
- dates to pay your tax bill (p. 34)
- rules about which income you will pay tax on (p. 18)
- dates for reporting income (p. 27)
- penalties you have to pay if you don't stick to all the rules (p. 52).

The taxes you might pay

There are several ways in which the government raises money from tax-payers. Some of the taxes are as follows:

- income tax – some of your income is taxed at varying rates
- capital gains tax – some of the gains you make on investments or possessions may be taxed at varying rates
- inheritance tax – when you die, some of the money you leave to others could be taxed, and some lifetime gifts are taxable too
- pre-owned assets tax – an income tax on the benefit you are deemed to get if you still use or enjoy something you have given away
- national insurance – this is compulsory only for people who are earning: employees and their employers, the self-employed or business partners.

Other taxes include council tax, corporation tax, business rates, value added tax, stamp duty land tax and excise duties.

The tax returns for the tax year ending 5 April 2010 should have landed on your doorstep during April 2010. These will cover your income and gains, reliefs and allowances for the year ended 5 April 2010 (the 2009–10 tax year). The information you provide will be used by you or your tax office to work out your income tax and capital gains tax bills and any pre-owned assets tax due.

How tax rules are changed

Strangely enough, income tax is a temporary tax and a new Act of Parliament is required each year to allow the government to go on collecting it. This provides the ideal opportunity for the government to ask Parliament to approve changes to the tax rules, so there is an annual cycle:

October/December before the start of the next tax year: Pre-Budget Report (PBR)

The government announces complicated or tentative proposals to change the rules, often inviting experts and the public to comment. Recently the PBR has been used to announce major changes (such as increases to income tax and national insurance contributions) that would normally have been made in a Budget.

March/April: Budget

The government announces changes. Many apply from the start of the tax year. Other changes may take effect from different dates. 2010–11 is an unusual tax year because there are likely to be two Budgets. Following the General Election, the coalition government was expected to announce further changes to the tax system.

6 April: start of the new tax year

March/April: Finance Bill published

This is the draft legislation to implement the changes from the Pre-Budget Report and the Budget. Sometimes other last-minute government changes are slipped in too. Parliament sets about debating and amending the draft rules. If unusually (as in 2010–11) there are two Budgets in one year, there will be two Finance Bills as well.

July (usually): Finance Act passed

The measures in the act become law – many are backdated to the start of the tax year, Budget Day or even earlier.

What is in this guide?

This tax guide explains the rules for the main personal taxes: income tax, capital gains tax, inheritance tax, pre-owned assets tax and national insurance. It covers most of the rules which the majority of taxpayers need to know, but it may not cover very specialised cases.

In Part 1, the guide gives a broad outline of the rules and helps you to plan your affairs to minimise your tax bills. It covers what you need to know for the current tax year ending 5 April 2011 (the 2010–11 tax year). It includes the changes proposed in the Budget announced in March 2010. By following its advice you should be able to save tax in the current and future tax years.

The guide went to the printers just after the General Election in May 2010. Its guidance is based on the Finance Act that followed the first (March 2010) Budget. We have included a summary of the tax proposals contained in the Conservative and Liberal Democrat manifestos and a second Budget was scheduled for 22 June 2010. You can receive notice of these later changes by either visiting our website, www.pearson-books.com/FTtaxguide, or sending an A4 stamped (66p), self-addressed envelope to Sara Williams and Jonquil Lowe, *FT Guide to Personal Tax*, Octavia House, 50 Banner Street, London EC1Y 8ST.

In Part 2, the guide helps you to fill in your tax return and has the information and figures for the tax year ending 5 April 2010 (the 2009–10 tax year).

The guide includes nearly 240 tax-saving ideas to help you cut your tax bill for this year, last year and, in some cases, even more distant tax years.

How to pay less tax

1

Tax changes for 2010–11

In 2010–11, public finances continue to be dominated by the aftermath of the global financial crisis and recession, with a pressing need to cut government borrowing. A mixture of tax rises and spending cuts are being programmed in for future years. But no government wants to swing the axe too heavily just ahead of a General Election, and so the tax climate in 2010–11 remains relatively benign except for higher-rate taxpayers.

This chapter summarises tax changes up to and including the March 2010 Budget. This book went to press immediately after the General Election and the main manifesto tax pledges of the coalition parties are set out towards the start of this guide. A second 2010 Budget, probably in July, seemed likely – see p. 3 for how to get an update.

Income tax and allowances

Allowances and thresholds are usually uprated in line with price inflation up to the previous September. As the figure for September 2009 was negative, the allowances and thresholds for 2010–11 are unchanged from 2009–10. Therefore allowances remain at £6,475 (under-65s), £9,490 (65 to 74) and £9,640 (over-75s). The limit at which the higher age-related allowances start to be lost is £22,900. From 2010–11, personal allowance is reduced for people of all ages with income over £100,000 a year: £1 of allowance is lost for each £2 of income over the £100,000 threshold.

The threshold at which higher-rate (40 per cent) tax starts remains £37,400. This threshold is to be frozen in 2012–13 at the 2011–12 level. As previously announced, a new 50 per cent additional tax rate is introduced from 2010–11 for people with incomes of £150,000 or more.

Reliefs

From 'later in 2010' (date to be announced), relief for giving to charity through Gift Aid and payroll giving is extended to cover charities and community amateur sports clubs in the EU, Norway and Iceland as well as the UK. This follows an EU court ruling and back claims for tax relief on donations to charities in these countries from 27 January 2009 to 1 April 2010 will be considered on an individual basis.

As previously announced, the lifetime limit and annual allowance for pension benefits and savings are frozen at £1.8 million and £255,000 from 2010–11 to 2015–16 inclusive. This also affects the trivial commutation rate which is set at 1 per cent of the lifetime limit.

Further restrictions apply in 2010–11 to tax relief on pension contributions for people on high incomes (over £130,000 a year) – see p. 226. Details have also been announced of how the 2011 system for clawing back relief will work, including:

- Clawback will apply to individuals with gross income of £150,000 or more. 'Gross income' means income before deducting pension or Gift Aid contributions and including the value of pension benefits from the employer (or other sources). But you will be outside the rules if your income excluding employer pension benefits is less than £130,000 (called the 'income floor').

- The value of the employer benefit in a defined benefit scheme will be calculated according to government scales of age-related factors that vary with age now and normal pension age (but not sex). The factors will be reviewed every five years. Your schemes will tell you the value.

- If you are within the clawback rules, tax relief on your contributions will be reduced by 1 per cent for every £1,000 of gross income over £150,000. This continues until relief is reduced to 20 per cent from £180,000 upwards.

- The clawed back relief will be collected through self assessment. But, where the clawed back amount exceeds £15,000, you can elect for the pension scheme to pay, in which case your benefits from the scheme will be reduced by an appropriate amount.

Tax credits

The child element of child tax credit (CTC) has risen by £20 more than earnings indexation in 2010–11. Families with children aged 1 and 2 will receive an extra £4 a week CTC child element from April 2012.

Working tax credit (WTC) is to be available from 2010–11 to over-60s working 16 hours or more per week (previously 30 hours). From April 2011, people moving from employment and support allowance into work will automatically qualify for the disability element of working tax credit. The government will review the 'disadvantage test' used in the WTC rules.

From 2011, the government will pilot an online renewal service for tax credits.

Paying and reclaiming tax

The arrangements allowing small businesses to request extra time to pay their taxes (Business Payment Support service) is to continue for now.

From autumn 2010, increased penalties will apply to people who fail to comply with the disclosure of tax avoidance schemes rules.

From 1 April 2011, penalties for offshore tax evasion will be scaled up depending on the tax jurisdiction involved: twice the UK penalty if the jurisdiction does not share information with the UK; one-and-a-half times UK amounts if the jurisdiction will share information but not automatically; and the same as the UK amounts if the jurisdiction automatically shares information.

Homes and property

For first-time buyers only, the nil-rate threshold for stamp duty increases to £250,000 for a period of two years from 25 March 2010 to 24 March 2012 inclusive. There will be a new 5 per cent rate on residential property purchases of £1 million or more from 6 April 2011 onwards.

Schemes to help home owners have been extended. The HomeBuy Direct scheme (which helps first-time buyers) is being extended to 2010–11.

Under the Support for Mortgage Interest scheme, the standard interest rate is frozen at 6.08 per cent until 31 December 2010.

HMRC is discussing with lenders a possible new income verification system where lenders could check against data held by HMRC for tax purposes.

The furnished holiday letting rules (see p. 353) were due to end on 5 April 2010, but the proposal was withdrawn from the Finance Act at the last minute. It is not clear whether it will be reinstated.

Savings and investments

The individual savings account (ISA) limit rises to £10,200 (£5,100 for the cash ISA) from 6 April 2010. From 2011–12 and for the life of the next Parliament, the limit is due to be increased in line with price inflation, with the cash ISA limit set at half the total limit.

From 2010–11, the government will pay an extra £100 each year to the child trust funds of disabled children (or £200 if severely disabled).

The Saving Gateway, a matched funding scheme to encourage low-income households to save, goes national from July 2010. The government is exploring options for other matched schemes, for example, for basic rate taxpayers aged 18 to 30.

From mid-2010, real estate investment trusts are to be allowed to pay out stock dividends and these will count towards the 90 per cent distribution requirement (see p. 85).

From mid-2010, the rules for venture capital trusts (VCTs) and the enterprise investment scheme are being extended to include shares in businesses trading mainly in the EU as well as the UK. VCTs will be able to include preference shares as well as ordinary shares.

Life insurance deficiency relief (see p. 220) is being amended to allow additional rate (as well as higher rate) relief for surrenders from 6 April 2010.

Capital gains tax

The tax-free allowance is unchanged at £10,100 for 2010–11 and the rate remains at 18 per cent.

The lifetime limit for entrepreneurs' relief is doubled to £2 million (was £1 million) from 2010–11.

Inheritance tax

The nil-rate band is frozen at the 2009–10 level of £325,000 from 2010–11 to 2014–15 inclusive.

Employees

Changes to the taxation of company cars aim to encourage greater take-up of energy-efficient vehicles. From 6 April 2010 to 5 April 2015, the appropriate percentage in the benefit calculation is set at 0 per cent for 'zero-emission' vehicles (which includes but is not limited to electric cars) and 5 per cent for vehicles emitting 75 g/km CO_2 or less. The flat rate charge for zero-emission vans will be £0.

A change to rules for childcare vouchers and employer crèches provided through salary sacrifice means that schemes no longer have to be open to employees at or near the minimum wage. This is backdated to 2005–06.

The enterprise management incentive rules are to be relaxed so that the scheme is no longer restricted to businesses carried out wholly or mainly in the UK. They will merely need a permanent establishment in the UK.

Effective from 24 March 2010, anti-avoidance measures aim to stop employees receiving more than £30,000 of shares through company share option schemes via 'geared growth' arrangements.

Businesses

The main rate of VAT returned to 17.5 per cent from 1 January 2010. The threshold for registrations rises to £70,000 (was £68,000) from 1 April 2010. The threshold for deregistrations also rises to £68,000 (was £66,000).

The VAT exemption for Royal Mail postal services is to be removed for non-statutory services (e.g. Parcel Force) from 31 January 2011.

The Annual Investment Allowance (AIA) is doubled to £100,000 (was £50,000) for expenditure from 6 April 2010. Where your accounting period straddles this date, the two rates are time-apportioned but relief for spending before 6 April 2010 is restricted to £50,000.

There have been some changes to the items eligible for 100 per cent first-year capital allowances for environmentally beneficial spending (see www.eca.gov.uk). A new 100 per cent first-year allowance is introduced for new zero-emission goods vehicles purchased between 6 April 2010 to 5 April 2015, inclusive – but firms in the following industries are excluded: fisheries, aquaculture, waste management.

See 'Capital gains tax' above regarding entrepreneurs' relief.

From October 2010, there is a temporary (one-year) relief from business rates through the small business rate relief scheme. This means firms with premises whose rateable value is up to £6,000 will pay no rates. Up to a £12,000 rateable value, there will be a tapered reduction.

Employers operating PAYE with a history of serious non-compliance can be asked to put up security and face criminal fines of up to £5,000 if they refuse. This is with effect from 1 April 2011.

The government intends to introduce single integrated online services for starting up a business and checking tax liabilities.

National insurance

The level of earnings (primary threshold) up to which no Class 1 national insurance contributions are paid is unchanged at £5,715 (£110 a week) in 2010–11. The upper earnings limit is also unchanged at £43,875 (£844 a week).

In 2010–11, Class 2 contributions paid by the self-employed are unchanged at £2.40 a week and the threshold below which payment is optional remains at £5,075. The lower and upper profit limits for Class 4 contributions are also unchanged at £5,715 and £43,875, respectively.

Voluntary class 3 contributions remain at £12.05 a week.

Rates are unchanged in 2010–11, but an additional ½ per cent increase is now due on top of a previously announced increase. This means, from 2011–12, that rates are due to rise as follows:

■ employees (Class 1): main rate 12 per cent (currently 11 per cent) and additional rate 2 per cent (currently 1 per cent)

■ self-employed (Class 4): main rate 9 per cent (currently 8 per cent) and additional rate 2 per cent (currently 1 per cent).

The primary threshold at which Class 1 contributions start to be paid (and the lower profit limit at which Class 4 contributions start) is to be raised by an extra £570 from 2011–12. This will protect anyone with earnings below

£20,000 from the additional ½ per cent rise (but not the original ½ per cent rise that had already been announced).

Trusts

For settlor-interested trusts (where the settlor is liable for tax on the trust income), from 6 April 2010, if the settlor reclaims tax on the income because his or her personal tax rate is lower than the tax deducted by the trust, the tax refunded must be paid to the trustees. This does not count as a gift for inheritance tax.

Trusts for asbestos victims set up before 24 March 2010 as part of an arrangement between a company and its creditors will be exempt from capital gains tax, income tax and inheritance tax backdated to 6 April 2006.

Other

Guardians and carers looking after children under Special Guardianship Orders and Residence Orders are to be exempt from tax on related payments from parents and local authorities from 2010–11.

From 1 April 2010, households that install a low-carbon electricity generating system, such as solar panels and small wind turbines, can claim a payment (feed-in tariff) for the electricity generated even if used by the household itself. This is on top of any resulting fall in fuel bills and reduces the pay-back period for installing such systems. Income from the feed-in tariff is tax-free provided the energy you produce is mainly for your own household use.

2

An overview of income tax

Broadly speaking, income tax is a tax on the regular sums that you receive – for example, earnings from a job, profits from your business, pensions, interest from savings, rental income and so on.

Quick guide

There are many complexities and exceptions in the way that income is taxed. What follows is a broad brush outline. It gives some important relationships:

Adjusted net income = (Income – Reliefs)
Taxable income = (Income – Reliefs – Allowances)
Income tax = Taxable income × The rate(s) of tax

Example

Jessica Jones has income from employment of £28,000. She pays £1,000 into an occupational pension scheme and she can claim a personal allowance for 2010–11 of £6,475. Her taxable income is: *other or top rate.*

	£
Income	28,000
Less reliefs: pension contributions	1,000
Total income	27,000
Less personal allowance	6,475
Taxable income	20,525
Tax at 20%	**4,105**

Income is made up of what you earn from your job or self-employment and what you receive as income from other sources, such as pensions and investments. But not all the money you receive is income and some income you receive is tax-free (p. 407). Some income you receive has had tax deducted (called *net* – pp. 21 and 79) and some income is paid without tax deducted (called *gross* – pp. 21 and 82). Note that this use of the word 'net' is different from its use in the term 'adjusted net income' which means net of reliefs. Adjusted net income is the new Revenue name for what previously was called your 'total income' and is important when working out how much personal allowance you can claim (see pp. 24, 60 and 247).

Reliefs are amounts which you pay out and on which you get tax relief, such as pension contributions and donations to charity. Relief may be given in different ways (p. 21).

Allowances are amounts to which you are entitled because of your personal circumstances. Personal allowance and blind person's allowance reduce your income before your tax bill is worked out, giving you relief at your highest rate of tax. But with married couple's allowance (available only to older people), relief is restricted and given as a deduction in your tax bill. From 2010–11 onwards, the personal allowance for people on high incomes will be reduced (see p. 24).

Taxable income is the figure on which your tax bill is based. The amount of income tax depends on how much taxable income you have and what rate of tax is paid on it (see below). From this initial tax bill you then deduct any reliefs and allowances that are given as a reduction in the bill. The maximum reduction is the amount needed to reduce your tax bill to zero.

The rates of tax

There are different rates of tax:

- starting rate tax (10 per cent for 2009–10 and 2010–11). Only savings income can be taxed at the starting rate. (In 2007–08 and earlier years, any type of income could be taxed at this rate.)
- basic rate tax (20 per cent for 2009–10 and 2010–11) (Between 2000–01 and 2007–08, the basic rate was 22 per cent.)
- higher rate tax (40 per cent for 2009–10 and 2010–11)
- additional rate tax (50 per cent) which is new from 2010–11 onwards.

The income levels at which these rates apply can vary from year to year. Here are the levels of income for each of these rates for 2009–10 and 2010–11:

2009–10 tax year

Income tax band £	Size of band £	Tax rate %	Tax on band £
0–2,440	2,440	10[1] or 20	244[1] or 488
2,441–37,400	34,960	20	6,992
Over 37,400		40	

2010–11 tax year

Income tax band £	Size of band £	Tax rate %	Tax on band £
0–2,440	2,440	10[1] or 20	244[1] or 488
2,441–37,400	34,960	20	6,992
37,401–150,000	112,600	40	45,040
Over 150,000		50	

(1) The 10 per cent rate applies only when this band is set against savings income (see below). If it is set against any other type of income, tax is charged at the basic rate.

Different tax rates apply to dividends from shares and distributions from share-based unit trusts and similar investments. These are paid with tax at 10 per cent already deducted. Non-taxpayers cannot reclaim the tax. There is no further tax to pay unless you are: a higher rate taxpayer, in which case you pay an extra 22.5 per cent of the gross dividend; or an additional rate taxpayer, in which case you pay an extra 32.5 per cent of the gross dividend.

You set your tax allowance(s) and tax bands against your different types of income in a set order: first against non-savings income (such as earnings, profits, pensions and rents), next against savings income (for example, interest from bank and building society accounts), then against dividend income. This means that you can benefit from the starting rate on savings income only if your non-savings income is low enough not to use all of your starting rate band – see Examples overleaf.

Example   16ihq>.

> Jenny and Ruth are sisters, both in their late 60s and retired. They each have an income of £16,030 in 2010–11 but Ruth pays £244 more tax than Jenny because Ruth is unable to use the 10 per cent starting rate. — savings
>
> Jenny's income is made up of state pension of £5,490, an occupational pension of £4,000 and interest from savings of £7,000. The pensions just use up her personal allowance of £9,490 (p. 25). She can set the full starting rate band against her savings, on which tax is (£2,440 × 10%) + (£4,560 × 20%) = £1,156.
>
> Ruth's income comprises £5,490 state pension, occupational pension of £7,000 and interest of £4,000. Her pensions uses up her personal allowance (£9,490) and all of the starting rate band (£2,440). This leaves her savings income to be taxed at the basic rate. Her tax bill for the year is £1,400.

Example

> Brad, aged 55, does not work and lives off income from his savings which comes to £30,000 a year. After deducting his personal allowance of £6,475, he has taxable income of £23,525. His tax bill in 2010–11 is worked out as follows: £2,440 × 10% + £21,085 × 20% = £4,461.
>
> Don, aged 55, works and earned £30,000 in 2010–11. After deducting his personal allowance of £6,475, he has taxable income of £23,525. All of this is taxed at the basic rate, giving him a tax bill of £4,705.

Tax credits

Since 6 April 2003, two state benefits – the working tax credit and child tax credit – are integrated into the tax system, with the amount you get based broadly on your adjusted net income (see p. 15). For details see p. 66.

Tax-saving idea 1

> If your income is low, tax that starts at 20 per cent, together with national insurance contributions (see p. 12), takes a large chunk out of any earnings and can make it look as if taking a job would not pay. Make sure you also claim working tax credit which is designed to integrate with the tax system and partially offset the impact of taxes on your take-home pay.

Income

Your income will be made up of money or goods you receive or anything you get in return for a service – but not all payments you receive count as income (see below). The following *will* all normally be considered as income:

■ what you earn from your work, including a job, a partnership or self-employment, including salary, tips, fringe benefits and business profits

■ rent from letting out property

■ income from investments, such as interest, dividends and distributions

■ pensions (from the state, your previous employer or your own plan)

■ casual, occasional or miscellaneous income, such as freelance earnings, income received after you close a business, income from guaranteeing loans, dealing in futures, income from underwriting, certain capital payments from selling UK patent rights, gains on many discounted securities, accrued income in bond and gilt strip prices

■ social security payments, such as jobseeker's allowance

■ income from a trust.

Main types of income for 2010–11 tax year

Type of income	Tax deducted?	At what rate?	More tax to pay?
Earnings from a job	yes	BR, HR	no[1]
Taxable fringe benefits	yes, from earnings	BR, HR	no[1]
Occupational or personal pension, retirement annuity contract	yes	BR, HR	no[1]
Bank, building society interest from UK account	yes[2]	BR	yes – HR, AR
Bank interest from offshore account	often, no		yes
Gilts and most other bonds	no[3]		yes
Income from annuity (other than pension annuities)	yes[2] [4]	BR	yes – HR, AR
Dividends from shares	yes[5]	10%[5]	yes[6]
Distributions from share-based unit trusts and oeics	yes[5]	10%[5]	yes[6]
Distributions from real estate investment trusts	no		yes

▶

Type of income	Tax deducted?	At what rate?	More tax to pay?
Income from an executor before a will is sorted out	yes	10%[5] and BR	yes – HR, AR
Income from a trust	yes	varies[5][7]	yes/no[7]
Income from self-employment or a partnership	no		yes
Social security benefits	no[8]		yes
Rent from property	no		yes
Pre-owned assets	no		yes

Key: BR = basic rate; HR = higher rate; AR = additional rate

(1) There could, of course, be more tax to pay if insufficient has been deducted.

(2) Non-taxpayers can have this income paid without tax deducted – see p. 81.

(3) But you can choose to have interest paid with tax deducted at the basic rate.

(4) Tax is deducted from the part of the annuity which counts as income, not the part which counts as a return of the capital.

(5) Non-taxpayers cannot claim back the tax deducted.

(6) Higher rate taxpayers pay at a rate of 32.5 per cent; additional rate taxpayers pay at a rate of 42.5 per cent.

(7) Depending on the type of trust – see p. 382.

(8) But if you return to work, tax, if due, will be deducted from your earnings.

Payments that are not income

Some payments you receive are not income. For example:

- loans
- presents and gifts (but occasionally inheritance tax may be due later)
- lottery prizes
- gambling winnings (if you are a gambler rather than a bookmaker)
- proceeds from selling assets unless this is how you make a living (but capital gains tax may be due)
- maintenance from an ex-spouse or former partner
- money you inherit (though inheritance tax may have been deducted).

Tax-free income

Some other payments you receive are income but are specifically tax-free, including premium bond prizes, interest on National Savings Certificates and income from savings held in a cash individual savings account (ISA). There is no capital gains tax either on items that are income. A comprehensive list is given on p. 407.

How income is paid to you

Income which is taxable can be paid to you without any tax deducted (*gross*) or with tax deducted (*net*). In 2010–11, the tax can be deducted at the basic rate and/or some other rate. The table on pp. 19–20 lists types of income, whether or not they are paid with tax deducted and if any further tax will be due.

If you need to give a figure for gross income when you have received net income, there are ready reckoners which help you to gross it up in Appendix B.

Tax-saving idea 2

Look for opportunities to arrange your income to be tax-free. (See p. 407 for a comprehensive list.) In the case of a couple, seek to distribute income between the two of you to the greatest advantage (see Chapter 5).

Reliefs

You make certain choices in life but sometimes the government gives a helping hand to encourage particular courses of action, such as saving for retirement or giving to charity. It does this by letting you have tax relief on what you pay. The items which qualify for this tax relief are known as reliefs, outgoings or deductions.

You can get a double boost from making some payments if they reduce your 'adjusted net income'. This may save extra tax if you qualify for age allowance (pp. 24, 60 and 247), would otherwise lose personal allowance (p. 24) or entitle you to extra tax credits (p. 66).

How you get tax relief

Tax relief may be given in one of three ways, depending on the type of spending involved:

▨ by deducting basic rate tax relief from the payment before handing it over. Any higher rate relief is given by raising the threshold at which you personally start to pay tax at the higher rate. Examples include contributions to personal pensions (including stakeholder schemes) and Gift Aid donations. For example, in 2010–11, if you want £100 to go into your personal pension, you hand over just £80. For Gift Aid, there are some transitional rules to help charities adjust to the fall in basic rate tax relief from 22 to 20 per cent since 6 April 2008. For the three years 2008–09, 2009–10 and 2010–11, although you will get 20 per cent tax relief on your contribution, the charity can claim back 22 per cent. For example, if you are a higher rate taxpayer and donate £80, this is treated as a gross donation of £100 and you can claim a further £20 relief through your tax return. But the charity claims £22.56 from the Revenue

Tax-saving ideas 3 and 4

When you pay into a personal pension or stakeholder scheme, you get tax relief at the basic rate even if you are a non-taxpayer or your top rate of tax is the starting rate.

Rules applying in 2010–11 let you make especially tax efficient donations through Gift Aid. If you are a higher rate taxpayer and you want a charity to receive £100 in total, you donate £78 which after higher-rate relief costs you just £58.50.

- a reduction in your income before tax is worked out. This gives relief up to your highest rate of tax. Examples include contributions to an occupational pension scheme and payroll-giving to charity. (However, if your income before deducting pension contributions and charitable donations is more than £130,000, some of the relief on pension contributions may be clawed back – see p. 226.)
- as a reduction in your tax bill. This applies, for example, to maintenance payments (available only to older people) and enterprise investment scheme investments. Relief is restricted to a percentage of the eligible payment.

Any relief not automatically given by deducting it from the payment is given either through the PAYE system (so less tax is deducted from your salary) or by a claim through your tax return (in which case the appropriate deduction is made when working out your tax bill).

Example

Peter Atwell wants to put £2,400 into a stakeholder pension scheme. He makes the payment net – in other words, after deducting tax relief at the basic rate which comes to 20 per cent × £2,400 = £480. Peter is a higher rate taxpayer, so can claim extra relief of (40 per cent × £2,400) − £480 = £480. His income is well below £130,000, so none of the relief is clawed back. His pension contribution of £2,400 has cost him only £2,400 − £480 − £480 = £1,440.

Tax-saving ideas 5 and 6

If, say, you have forgotten to claim a relief or allowance, you can go back to correct the past and claim a refund of tax overpaid. You must make your claim within four years of the end of the relevant tax year. So, provided you make your claim by 5 April 2011, you can go back as far as the 2006–07 tax year.

Some reliefs, such as some ways of using business losses, have to be claimed within shorter time limits than the general limit given above. Make sure you claim in time. For a summary of the most important deadlines, see Appendix D.

The table below lists the main types of reliefs and how you get them. There are more details about reliefs in Chapter 13.

Main types of relief for 2010–11 tax year

Type of relief	Amount of relief	How do you get tax relief?
Business losses not already set against profits	BR, HR or AR	through your PAYE code or tax bill
Charity[1]: Gift Aid[2], gifts of shares, land or buildings	StR, BR, HR or AR	BR: make lower payments HR/AR: either PAYE code or tax bill
EIS (up to limits)	20%	through your PAYE code or tax bill
VCT (up to limits)	30%	through your PAYE code or tax bill
Community investment tax relief	5%	through your PAYE code or tax bill
Home income scheme[3]	23%	lower payments through MIRAS[3]
Interest on some loans to invest in business	BR, HR or AR	through your PAYE code or tax bill
Job expenses	BR, HR or AR	through your PAYE code or tax bill
Maintenance payments[4]	10% of £2,670	through your PAYE code or tax bill
Mortgage interest on a property you let	BR, HR or AR	lower tax bill on rental income
Landlord's energy-saving allowance (up to £1,500)	BR, HR or AR	lower tax bill on rental income
Pension contributions to employers' schemes	BR or HR[5]	through PAYE system

▶

Type of relief	Amount of relief	How do you get tax relief?
Personal pension payments (including stakeholder pensions)	BR or HR[5]	BR: make lower payments HR: through PAYE code or tax bill
Retirement annuity contract payments	BR or HR[5][6]	through your PAYE code or tax bill (or as for personal pensions)

Key: StR = starting rate; BR = basic rate; HR = higher rate; AR = additional rate
(1) And community amateur sports clubs that meet certain conditions.
(2) You make lower payments by deducting relief at the basic rate. If your tax bill is less than the relief deducted, the Revenue may claw back some of the relief.
(3) Relief not available for loans made on or after 9 March 1999 (p. 71).
(4) Available only where one or both parties was born before 6 April 1935.
(5) If your income before deducting pension contributions and charitable donations is £130,000 or more, some relief may be clawed back (see p. 226).
(6) Providers can choose to treat payments in the same way as those to personal pensions.

Allowances

Most people are entitled to an allowance to deduct from their income to ensure some of it is tax-free. This is called the personal allowance. The amount of the allowance varies with age and also your adjusted net income (see p. 15).

The higher personal allowance for people aged 65 and over and the personal allowance that anyone may get are both reduced if your adjusted net income is more than a set threshold:

- **Age-related personal allowance (age allowance).** You lose £1 of allowance for each £2 by which your adjusted net income exceeds £22,900 in 2010–11. But the reduction stops when your allowance has been reduced to the standard £6,475 that someone under 65 gets. If your income is in the region where you are losing age allowance, the combined effect of tax at 20 per cent and the loss of personal allowance is an effective tax rate of 30 per cent

- **Personal allowance (for anyone, whatever your age).** If your adjusted net income exceeds £100,000, you lose £1 of allowance for every £2 of income above that level. If your income is £112,950 or more in 2010–11, you lose the whole allowance and all of your adjusted net income is taxable. If your income is between £100,000 and £112,950, the combined effect of tax at 40 per cent and the loss of personal allowance is an effective income tax rate of 60 per cent.

There are a few other allowances that you may be able to claim – but these depend on your personal circumstances. There are details of allowances in the table overleaf and in Chapter 14. Usually, allowances are increased each year in line with price inflation as measured by changes in the Retail Prices Index up to the September preceding the start of the tax year. In September 2009, inflation was negative and the government decided to freeze allowances for 2010–11 at their 2009–10 level.

Example

Lily Crabtree, 71, has a total income of £24,000. This is higher than the £22,900 limit. Her personal allowance is reduced to £9,490 − 1/2 × (£24,000 − £22,900) = £8,940.

Example

Karamu has an adjusted net income of £105,000 in 2010–11. This is £5,000 more than the £100,000 threshold at which personal allowance starts to be lost. Therefore her personal allowance is reduced as follows: £6,475 − (1/2 × £5,000) = £3,975 and her tax bill is £32,930. If Karamu pays a gross contribution of £5,000 into a pension scheme, this would reduce her adjusted net income to £100,000, in which case she would get the full personal allowance of £6,475 and her tax bill would fall to £29,930. In effect, Karamu gets tax relief of £3,000 on the £5,000 pension contribution.

Tax-saving ideas 7–10

From 2010–11, once your income exceeds £100,000 for the year, you lose £1 of personal allowance for each £2 of excess income until the allowance has been lost. Thus, if your income is in the region where you are losing personal allowance, your effective top rate of income tax will be 60 per cent. This means that any spending that qualifies for relief at your top rate, such as Gift Aid donations and pension contributions, will be especially valuable, since each £100 you pay will save you £60 in tax.

In 2010–11 you will be losing age allowance if your adjusted net income is in the range £22,900 to £28,930 if you are aged 65 to 74 and £22,900 to £29,230 if you are aged 75 or more. (The upper limits will be higher if you also qualify for married couple's allowance – p. 60.) Income for this purpose does not include any tax-free amounts (such as, your winter fuel payment). If you are losing age allowance, you can cut your total income and so increase the allowance by switching from taxable to tax-free investments – for example, from an ordinary savings account to a cash ISA.

Making pension contributions and Gift Aid donations will be especially tax efficient because they also cut your adjusted net income and so increase your age allowance. In effect, you will get tax relief at 30 per cent on such payments.

If you are 65 (men) or around 60 (women) or older, you might consider deferring your state pension to earn a state pension lump sum (p. 206). The lump sum does not count as part of your total income and so does not reduce your age allowance.

Details of allowances

Allowance	Age[1]	Tax year	Amount
Personal	under 65	2009–10	£6,475
		2010–11	£6,475
	65–74	2009–10	£9,490[2]
		2010–11	£9,490[2]
	75 plus	2009–10	£9,640[2]
		2010–11	£9,640[2]
Married couple's[3]	75 plus	2009–10	10% of £6,965[2]
		2010–11	10% of £6,965[2]
Blind person's	any	2009–10	£1,890
		2010–11	£1,890

(1) On birthday falling within the tax year.

(2) The amount of these allowances is reduced if total income is above a certain amount. In 2009–10 and 2010–11 the income limit is £22,900. For more details see pp. 24, 60 and 247.

(3) From April 2000, this allowance was abolished for people born on or after 6 April 1935. Where the allowance received by an older person is restricted because of income – see note 2 above – it will not be reduced below £2,670 in 2009–10 and 2010–11.

3

Paying and reclaiming tax

Self assessment started in 1996. It puts the onus on you to report any sources of income and gains, provide a figure for the tax due (though in practice you can ask the Revenue to crunch the numbers for you) and ensure that you make timely payments of the tax due. There are a range of rules and sanctions to discourage cheating and these have recently been revised and strengthened. This chapter sets out your obligations; Chapter 4 looks at the sanctions, together with your rights to challenge any Revenue actions and penalties.

Not everyone has to operate self assessment. Over two-thirds of taxpayers have their tax calculated and collected through PAYE (p. 39). But even they need to be aware that a change in their circumstances or a change in the tax system (such as the introduction of the pre-owned assets tax – see Chapter 10) can trigger an obligation under self assessment with the onus on the taxpayer to realise when this occurs.

In addition to policing the system, the Revenue also tries to help its customers (taxpayers) to understand the system and operate it correctly. In this role the Revenue tries to put on a friendly public face. Normally a single tax office deals with your affairs, sending you returns, issuing your tax code and so on. But, if you have a query or problem, increasingly you will deal with a website or remote call centre (see Appendix E).

Your obligations

New source of income or capital

If you don't receive a tax return, you must notify your tax inspector of any income or capital gains, which have not been previously declared, within six months from the end of the tax year in which you make the income or gain (i.e. by 5 October). This applies even if you don't yet know the amount of the income or gain and even if previously you have received a letter from the Revenue saying you do not need to complete a tax return.

There are certain circumstances in which you don't have to notify your tax office. This applies, for example, if all the income comes under the PAYE system or if the income is paid with tax already deducted and you pay tax at no more than the basic rate.

If you fail, within the time limits, to tell the Revenue about your untaxed income or gains, you are liable to a penalty based on the amount of tax owed (see Chapter 4).

A shorter time limit applies if you become newly self-employed, in which case you must register with the Revenue without delay. There is no precise time limit, but you can be fined if not registering results in tax being paid late and you are deemed to have been careless or dishonest in delaying your registration (see Chapter 4).

Records

In general you do not have to send in any documents and workings with your tax return. The exception is where you owe capital gains tax (CGT), in which case you do have to include your calculations and the tax return notes provide worksheets for this purpose (see Chapter 22).

However, you must have and keep records to back up the figures you have reported in your return. To date, this has been a general requirement and it has been up to you to decide which records are relevant, but they will certainly include, for example, end-of-year statements of your employment income (P60s), bank statements, interest certificates, dividend vouchers, and so on. Normally you should keep the originals, but if you don't have them, you can complete your tax return using information that can be verified by an external source. You should also keep any working papers that you have used to make your calculations. Under a recent change in the law, the Revenue has new powers to specify exactly which records you must keep. At the time of writing, the Revenue had not yet drawn up any such lists, but it seems likely that it will.

You must normally keep these records for one year from the 31 January following the end of the tax year covered by the return. But, if you run your own business or have letting income, the period is five years. The Revenue can override these rules and specify an earlier date.

This period is extended if there is an enquiry into your affairs. Records must be kept until the enquiry is complete. The period to keep records is also extended if you send in your return late or need to correct it after you have sent it in. The documents need to be kept until one year after the end of the quarter in which you amended the return or sent it in late. Quarters end on 31 January, 30 April, 31 July and 31 October.

The failure to keep records can result in a heavy penalty (see Chapter 4).

Tax-saving idea 11

Make sure you keep all your records and your working papers. If you don't, you may end up paying more tax than you should because you can't provide the evidence to back up your tax return. And don't forget you can be fined for not keeping your records. If you are in business or letting, for the tax year 2009–10, you must normally keep your records until 31 January 2016. Other taxpayers must keep records for that year until 31 January 2012.

Example

Roger Rose (a basic-rate taxpayer) is an employee paying tax under the PAYE system. He buys some shares in a UK company in October 2009 and receives a dividend of £84 some two months later. He also decides to do some freelance consulting on the side, as well as his job. He doesn't know how much income that will bring in, since part of his payment will be in the form of commission.

As a basic-rate taxpayer, Roger has no further tax to pay on the dividend. So, if this had been his only extra income in 2009–10, he would not have needed to take any action. But he also has the freelance income on which tax will be due. Even though he does not yet know how much the income will be, he must tell his tax office about it by 5 October 2010 (that is within six months of the end of the tax year). His tax office will then send him a tax return which he has three months to complete.

The tax return

Your current tax return asks for details of your income, deductions and allowances for the 2009–10 tax year just ended, that is the year ending on 5 April 2010. Roughly 1.5 million people with straightforward tax affairs are sent a short four-page tax return – see Appendix C. If your affairs are more complex, you will receive the full return comprising a six-page main return accompanied by additional forms and supplements (see Chapter 11). It is your responsibility to check that you have received the correct tax return and supplements and to obtain the right form and any other supplements you need.

Example

> For years, Helen Hickie has lived on her pensions and modest income from invest-ments. On this basis, the Revenue sends her a short tax return for the 2009–10 tax year. But during that year, Helen's sister who lived abroad died leaving Helen some foreign shares which now provide Helen with around £1,000 of extra income a year. The short return is not suitable and Helen needs to contact the Revenue Orderline (p. 180) to request a full return including the foreign supplement.

You must provide precise figures throughout your return. This means getting hold of the documents you need. If you are an employee, these include forms P60 (summary of income from a job and tax already paid), P45 (summary of income and tax paid where you have left a job), P11D or P9D (taxable fringe benefits and expenses). Your employer is responsible for supplying you with these forms by certain dates (see Appendix D). Where precise figures are not available (for example, where you are self-employed and the relevant accounting period has yet to end), give a provisional esti-mate and say when the final figure will be available. With subjective figures (for example, the value of an asset you have given away or received from your employer), get an independent valuation and give details in the *Any other information* sections of the return.

If figures on returns from taxpayers like you are commonly subject to errors, or based on previous years your figures seem out of step with those for similar taxpayers, you may receive a letter from the Revenue suggesting you take particular care in completing that section of your return. Where applicable, give extra details (for example, the basis on which you are claiming a proportion of a part-private/part-business expense) in the *Any other information* sections.

In general, you do not need to send supporting documents with your tax return. If you wish to draw the Revenue's attention to an item or explain the basis of you figures, it is normally best to make a note in the *Any other infor-mation* boxes provided on the main return and its supplements. If you do send supporting documents, it is unlikely that they will be read unless your tax office decides to open an enquiry into your return (see Chapter 4).

Deadlines for your tax return

For your 2009–10 tax return, there are two key dates. Which one is important for you depends on how you file your return:

▪ **31 October 2010.** This is the date by which you must send in a paper tax return. The Revenue will work out your tax bill for you. If you file a paper return after this date, you normally incur an automatic fine (see Chapter 4)

▪ **31 January 2011.** This is the final deadline for the return and there is an automatic fine if you miss it (see Chapter 4). To take advantage of this later date, you must file your tax return online (see opposite) and the software will automatically calculate your tax bill.

If you receive the short tax return, you can either file it in paper form by 31 October 2010 or use online filing based on the full return.

If the amount of tax you owe for 2009–10 is less than £2,000, you can agree to have it collected through PAYE during the course of 2011–12, provided you file a paper return by 31 October 2010 or an online return by 30 December 2010.

Tax-saving idea 12

If you are paying tax under the PAYE system and have some other income, for example from investments, on which you will need to pay tax, send in your 2009–10 tax return by 31 October 2010 or 30 December 2010 if you file by internet. If you do this, and the amount of tax due is less than £2,000, you will not have to pay tax on this extra income by 31 January 2011. Instead, it will be included in your PAYE code for the 2011–12 tax year, thus spreading out and delaying the payment.

Where a tax return has been issued after 31 October, you are given three months to complete it and send it back to your tax office. If the return is issued after 31 August and you want your tax inspector to calculate the tax due, it must be returned within two months.

Tax-saving idea 13

If you prefer to complete a paper tax return, make sure you send it in by 31 October following the end of the tax year to avoid paying a fine. However, for your 2009–10 tax return, the fine for delivering a paper return after 31 October 2010 is reduced to zero provided you have paid all the tax due by 31 January 2011.

Filing by internet

Around 5.8 million taxpayers filed their 2007–08 returns by internet. This is expected to increase further, partly in response to government policies to promote online filing.

Filing by internet is free if you use the Revenue's own software, which is based on the full return. The Revenue software covers the following supplements: employment, self-employment, partnership, UK property, capital gains tax and foreign. If you need the trusts or residence supplements, you will either need to use commercial software instead or file a paper return by 31 October. You can use the Revenue software to file your current return and, if applicable, past returns going back to tax year 2007–08.

The main advantages of online filing are that the software prompts you to correct common errors, immediately tells you the amount of tax you owe, immediately states whether your return has been received and gives you the option to pay tax in instalments by direct debit (see p. 38). Also, the 'any other information' sections are part of the electronic return and so definitely passed to your tax office, whereas such details on a paper-based return are not transferred to the Revenue's computer system and sometimes get overlooked. You can attach supporting documents as PDFs (maximum file size 5Mb) but these are unlikely to be read unless the Revenue is opening an enquiry into your return. Therefore, if you especially want to draw the Revenue's attention to extra information, it is best to type it into the *Any other information* sections.

To file online you must first register, which can take up to seven working days. Follow the instructions supplied with your return or on the Revenue website. You can also pay tax electronically – see the Revenue website for details.

In 2009, the Revenue warned of a big increase in fraudulent claims for tax repayments, often using passwords and other information obtained from taxpayers. Beware of so-called 'phishing' emails that purport to be from the Revenue and ask for sensitive information or instruct you to click on a link. The Revenue will never ask you for passwords or request bank details in this way. If you receive such emails, do not open them or click on any links (which may activate the download of malicious software to your machine). Forward such emails to phishing@hmrc.gsi.gov.uk and then delete them.

Tax-saving ideas 14 and 15

Online filing gives you an extra three months to sort out your tax return and is free if you use the Revenue's own software. Commercial software prices start at around £25 for the full tax return.

If you are new to the Revenue's online filing software, do not leave sorting out your tax return to the last minute. It will be too late to send in a paper return and you must register before you can use the online service. This takes around seven working days, so, for the 2010 return, apply by 20 January 2011 at the latest. There is normally an automatic penalty if you file your return late. If you run a business in partnership with others, note that you can use the free Revenue software to file your own partnership supplement online but not the partnership return itself.

If you don't send in your tax return

Failing to send back your completed tax return means you can be charged a penalty (see Chapter 4) and allows the Revenue to issue what's called a determination. This is an estimate of the tax you might owe and is often deliberately on the high side. The tax shown on this determination is payable; you cannot appeal against it or postpone it. The only way you can overturn this estimate is to complete your tax return and tax calculation. From 1 April 2010 onwards, you must do this within three years of the date by which you should have filed the return (before 1 April 2010, the time limit was five years) or, if it is later, within a year of the determination by your tax inspector.

If you miss this deadline, you must normally pay the amount of tax stated in the determination. However, if you can show this is excessive compared with what you would have had to pay had you sent in a return on time, you may be able to get the tax bill reduced to the amount that would have been payable under a process called 'equitable liability'. If you think this may apply in your case, contact your tax office or a tax adviser (see Appendix E).

The Revenue must normally issue a determination within three years (was five years) of the normal filing date for the missing return. But if there is reason to think that the failure to file is due to carelessness, the limit is extended to six years or, if due to deliberate attempt to avoid paying tax, 20 years.

Tax calculation

After you have sent in a paper tax return, the Revenue checks it for obvious errors, such as arithmetical mistakes or failing to copy figures correctly from one part to another. You will be sent a tax calculation form (SA302), unless you have opted to calculate your own tax bill (and we recommend you don't). The form sets out the tax the Revenue thinks you owe and the amount of any payments you have to make. Check this carefully as soon as it arrives. If there is anything you do not understand, or you disagree with the figures, write to or phone your tax office – otherwise you will be expected to pay the amounts shown on the form. If you file online, the software will immediately tell you the amount of tax you owe and when it is due to be paid.

Tax-saving idea 16

> Always check tax forms, such as a tax calculation or coding notice (p. 40) to make sure your tax office has got the sums right. Under new rules that apply to tax returns for 2008–09 onwards, you may be charged a penalty if the Revenue make an error that results in you paying too little tax and you fail to alert your tax office to the error within 30 days (see Chapter 4).

Tax payments

Self assessment is used to collect income tax, capital gains tax and, if you are in business, class 4 national insurance contributions (NICs). You, your adviser or your tax inspector works out the total amount due. The tax is usually paid in three instalments.

Interim and final payments

Self assessment requires two interim payments on account. The first is due on 31 January during the tax year; the second on 31 July following the tax year. Each payment is normally half the amount of your income tax and class 4 NICs bill for the previous year less any tax paid through the PAYE system, dividend tax credits and so on. There is no adjustment for changes in tax rates and allowances from one year to the next. However, if you expect your income to be lower this year than last, you can ask for a reduction in the payments on account (see opposite) – but, if you turn out to be wrong, you'll have to pay interest on the tax paid late.

The final balancing income tax payment or repayment will be made on 31 January following the end of the tax year after completion of the tax return. Any capital gains tax due will also be paid with this third instalment.

Working on the basis of the tax due for the previous tax year, if the total tax payable, net of tax deducted at source (including PAYE), is less than a set amount (£1,000 for tax due for the 2009–10 tax year onwards) or if tax deducted at source (including PAYE) is more than 80 per cent of the total income tax plus class 4 national insurance due, then interim payments won't be required.

Employees can put off paying a final tax bill of less than £2,000 by agreeing to have it included in next year's PAYE code. If filing a paper return, this happens automatically unless you opt out (p. 187). If filing online, your 2009–10 tax return must be submitted by 30 December 2010 for the tax to be collected in this way.

An effect of the self assessment payment system is that, if your income increases from one tax year to the next, you may face a hefty tax bill in the following January. This is because the jump in income produces a final payment to scoop up tax underpaid in the last tax year plus an increased payment on account for the current tax year – see Example on p. 38.

Conversely, if your income falls from one year to the next, there may be a large drop in your January tax payment if you stand to get a refund of tax overpaid and a lower first payment on account.

Tax-saving ideas 17 and 18

Payments on account are based on last year's tax bill. If you expect your income to be lower this year or your allowances and reliefs to be higher, you can make reduced payments – see below.

If your income is increasing year on year, expect a large tax bill in January comprising your final payment and an increased payment on account. Make sure you set aside enough money to pay this bill, otherwise you risk interest charges on tax paid late and possibly penalties too.

Self assessment statement

Shortly before a payment on account falls due, you will usually receive a self assessment statement (form SA300) showing the amount to pay and with a pay slip attached. If you are registered for the Revenue's internet service, you can view recent statements online.

These statements are personalised and will look broadly like the example overleaf. The key figure is the 'Amount due by . . .', which shows what you must pay and when. Paying late means paying interest, so it's vital to check your statements.

How to reduce your payments on account

If you think your tax bill this year, for the types of income covered by your self assessment statement, will be lower than in the previous year, you can claim to make lower payments on account than the Revenue is asking for. This can happen because your income has dropped – for example you are getting less in profits or rents. Or maybe you have become newly eligible for a tax allowance or extra relief, for example because you have reached age 65 or increased your pension contributions.

If this is the case, carefully work out your expected tax bill for this year (including class 4 national insurance if you are self-employed – see p. 341). Halve the total to find the amount for each payment on account. Then fill in form SA303, which you can get from your tax office or the Revenue website at www.hmrc.gov.uk or make your claim for a reduction online. To reduce a forthcoming payment, return the form before the 'due by' date on the self assessment statement. If later you realise you will owe even less tax, you can make another claim, again using form SA303.

What your self assessment statement might look like

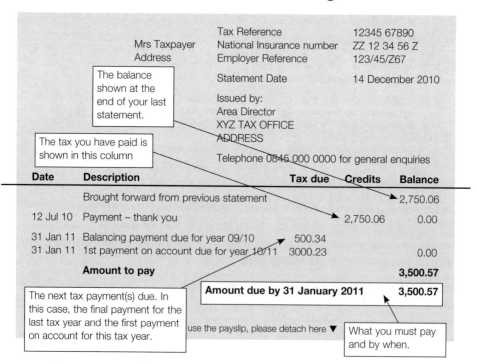

Tax-saving idea 19

Always check your self assessment statement to see if you can claim a reduction in the interim payments on account. But, if in doubt, it is better to pay slightly more than to ask for a reduction. You will be charged interest if you pay too little, whereas tax you have overpaid may earn interest. The interest charged on underpaid tax is much higher than that added to overpaid tax (in early 2010, 3 per cent on underpayments compared with 0.5 per cent on overpayments). You can also be fined if you knowingly reduce your payments on account by too much.

Interest and surcharges

Provided you pay the original payments on account demanded on time, no interest is normally charged even if your tax bill for the year turns out to be much higher. In other cases, interest is payable on tax paid late. On the other hand, any tax you have overpaid usually earns interest. Any interest charged or received will be shown on your self assessment statement.

From mid-2009 onwards, interest is set by the Revenue in line with the Bank of England base rate:

■ on tax paid late, interest is set at the Bank of England base rate plus 2.5 per cent

■ on tax overpaid, the rate is the Bank of England base rate minus 1 per cent but subject to a minimum rate of 0.5 per cent.

Interest is automatically charged on any tax left unpaid after the 31 January or 31 July payment deadlines.

From 6 April 2010 onwards, where any tax due is unpaid 30 days after the due date, you will have a surcharge added to the bill equal to 5 per cent of the tax outstanding. Further surcharges of 5 per cent each are added if the tax remains unpaid five and then 11 months after the first penalty. Interest is charged on any surcharges paid late. The surcharges may be suspended if you contact the Revenue and agree a schedule for clearing your tax debt.

Example

> Shalini Edwards is self-employed. Her profits are usually around £32,000 but, for 2009–10, they jumped to £40,000. During 2010, her tax bills are £4,000 in January and £3,659 in July. Of these, 2 × £3,659 = £7,318 are payments on account for 2009–10. But due to the profit increase, the total bill for the year is £9,448. Shalini must make a final payment on 31 January 2011 of £9,448 − £7,318 = £2,130. The increased total bill feeds through to a higher first payment on account for 2010–11 (1/2 × £9,448 = £4,724), also due on 31 January 2011. Her total tax bill for January 2011 is £6,854. This is two-thirds more than the previous January's bill, even though her profits increased by only a quarter.

How to pay

The Revenue has been expanding the methods available for paying tax. To pay a tax bill that is already due, you can choose between:

- sending a cheque by post
- paying cash, cheque or debit card at any Post Office or your own bank or building society branch
- using phone or internet banking to transfer the payment direct from your own to the Revenue's bank account. The payslip or payment reminder you receive includes the Revenue bank account details that you will need
- paying by internet using a debit or credit card. For how to do this, see https://www.billpayment.co.uk/hmrc/scripts/index.asp. If you use a credit card, you must also pay a transaction fee (1.25 per cent in 2010) and of course if you do not pay off the credit card debt in full you will have to pay interest on the outstanding balance
- paying over the internet by direct debit, provided you are registered for the Revenue's internet filing service (see p. 32).

If you use the Revenue's online filing service, you also have the option of setting up a budget payment plan which is a direct debit to make regular weekly or monthly payments that reduce your next tax bill. To be eligible your current tax payments must be up to date. You cannot withdraw the advance payments you have already made but you can, at any time, alter the amount of your future payments, suspend them for up to six months or cancel the plan. Your advance payments do not earn interest.

Another option for paying your tax bill in advance is to buy certificates of tax deposit (see www.hmrc.gov.uk/payinghmrc/cert-tax-deposit.htm). These work rather like buying savings stamps. The minimum you can have saved with certificates of tax deposit at any time is £500 and you can buy further certificates in amounts of at least £250. You can use the certificates either to pay a tax bill or cash them in. Unlike the bill payment plan, certificates normally do pay you interest, though the rate you get is lower if you cash in the certificates than if you use them to pay a tax bill and in either case less than you would get from most bank or building society savings accounts. Moreover, in early 2010, with the general level of interest rates in the UK still low, certificates of tax deposit were paying nil interest on deposits under £100,000. An advantage of certificates of tax deposit is that they can be used to prevent an interest charge for late payment of tax following a Revenue investigation into your tax affairs – see p. 50.

Tax-saving ideas 20–22

A budget payment plan or buying certificates of tax deposit can help you plan for future tax bills and so avoid late payment penalities. Financially you may be better off setting up a direct debit to pay regular savings into a bank or building society account that pays interest on your savings, but you need to be confident you would not withdraw the money to use for anything other than your tax bill.

Failing to pay tax on time results in interest charges (see p. 37) and penalities (see Chapter 4) and the Revenue is quick to chase late payments. If you are having problems paying your tax bill, contact your tax office straight away. You may be able to negotiate an agreement, for example to pay by instalments and avoid penalty charges.

To help businesses affected by the 'credit crunch' and resulting recession, the Revenue launched a new Business Payment Support Service. If you anticipate that you will not be able to pay your tax on time, the Revenue may agree a tailored package to pay the tax owed on dates or in stages that match your cash flow. Interest will be added to tax paid late, but no penalties or surcharges will be incurred. To find out more, see www.hmrc.gov.uk/pbr2008/business-payment.htm or call the Business Payment Support Line on 0845 302 1435.

The PAYE system

Your employer or private pension provider is an unpaid tax collector for the Revenue using the PAYE system – Pay As You Earn. Every time employees or pensioners are paid, income tax and national insurance contributions (NICs) are deducted from the earnings or pension and sent in a batch to the collector of taxes. Your employer is also responsible for collecting student loan repayments on behalf of the government (p. 265) through your pay packet.

Your employer or pension provider needs various bits of information to operate the PAYE system, in particular a PAYE code for each employee or pensioner. This is issued by the Revenue and tells the employer or pension provider how much tax-free pay to give you each month or week. The Revenue also sends you a notice of your PAYE code, for example in January or February in time for the coming tax year or when your circumstances change. You will not necessarily get a notice every year. You can request a coding notice at any time.

PAYE is used to collect tax on other income, not just the earnings or pension from a particular employer or provider, and to give you any reliefs and allowances that are due. Because other income, reliefs and allowances may vary from year to year, your tax office may send you a tax review form P810. This is like a mini personalised tax return that you fill in to tell the Revenue about any changes that need to be reflected in your tax code. You might get a P810 only once every three years, in which case, the Revenue will estimate the amounts of your other income, reliefs and allowances for the intervening years. Later there may be an adjustment to your tax code to collect or refund any under- or overpayment of tax. If you would prefer an immediate adjustment, so that your PAYE code accurately reflects your current tax position, you can opt back into the self assessment system by voluntarily submitting a tax return.

Tax-saving idea 23

According to the National Audit Office (a body that keeps a watch on the government's money management), around three out of ten coding notices contain errors. If your PAYE code is wrong, you may pay too much tax and have to wait for a rebate. And, although paying too little tax might seem attractive, you will have to make up any underpayment in the following tax year – often in one go if it is £2,000 or more. So it makes sense to check your PAYE code carefully whenever you receive a notice of coding.

The coding notice

The coding notice (form P2) sets out the Revenue's calculations to arrive at your PAYE code. Your employer uses the code in conjunction with tax tables supplied by the Revenue to work out how much tax to deduct from your pay.

If you work for two employers, you should have two PAYE codes – one for each job – and two coding notices. If you are retired and receive an occupational and/or personal pension, you will also have tax deducted through PAYE. If you have just one main pension, you'll get one PAYE code. If you have two or more substantial pensions, you may get a code for each one.

Your PAYE code reflects the amount of allowances your tax inspector estimates you can set against your earnings in the current tax year. It may be adjusted to collect tax on fringe benefits and income, such as freelance earnings and savings interest. The amounts are based on information in your tax return (if you get one), P810 (if you get one), from your employer or from other organisations that send details of payments to the Revenue.

Your employer usually makes various other adjustments to your gross salary to arrive at your take-home pay. These can include deduction of national insurance, student loan repayments, pension contributions and donations to charity through payroll giving. None of these is reflected in your PAYE code.

Checking a coding notice

Your coding notice is a short, personalised form with relevant notes on the form itself.

The main figures on the coding notice are in two columns. The column on the right is the main sum, which starts with your allowances and reliefs and then subtracts the total of any adjustments. The column on the left details the adjustments. For example, if you will have taxable fringe benefits (such as a company car) in the current year, their value will be listed in this column. So will the amount you are expected to get from other sources of untaxed income, such as freelance earnings, taxable state pensions and benefits, and savings income that has not already been taxed.

Tax-saving idea 24

You do not have to agree to have untaxed income taxed through PAYE. You can opt for it to be taxed, instead, through the self assessment system described in the first part of this chapter. Self assessment means you pay the tax later (through payments on account and any final payment) but does involve more admin than PAYE.

Checking the entries on your coding notice is very straightforward. Start by making sure that you have all the allowances and deductions to which you are entitled in the right-hand column. Some allowances and deductions are not included if you have already been given the correct amount of tax relief at source – for example, where a basic rate taxpayer makes contributions to a personal pension or Gift Aid donations to charity. If you pay tax at the higher rate, there will be an entry on your coding notice to give you the extra relief due (see Example below).

Example

Gerry Walker puts £5,000 gross (before tax relief) into a stakeholder pension scheme in 2010–11. Since the basic rate of tax is 20 per cent, he gets relief at source of 20% × £5,000 = £1,000. So he actually hands over just £4,000. But Gerry is a higher-rate taxpayer so he is entitled to relief of 40% × £5,000 = £2,000. The extra £1,000 relief is given by increasing his tax allowances by £2,500 since 40% × £2,500 = £1,000.

Next check the amounts in the right-hand column that are to be taken away. Most are straightforward. The main complications are:

- **Allowance restriction** if you get married couple's allowance and/or qualify for tax relief on maintenance payments (both now available only for people born before 6 April 1935). These give tax relief only at a rate of 10 per cent. If your top rate of tax is expected to be just 10 per cent (the starting rate), then the full amount of the allowance will be added to your personal allowance. But, if your top rate of tax is higher than 10 per cent, an adjustment is needed to prevent PAYE giving you too much relief. The Example on p. 44 shows how this is done.

- **Higher rate tax adjustment** collects extra tax due at the higher rate on interest, dividends and some other sorts of income which are paid after deduction of tax that covers any basic rate tax due. See the second Example on p. 44.

- **Tax underpaid** is an adjustment to collect any tax of less than £2,000 outstanding from a previous tax year. For example, if you owe £500 and pay tax at the basic rate of 20 per cent, £2,500 will be deducted from your allowances so that 20% × £2,500 = £500 tax is collected.

 HM Revenue & Customs

PAYE Coding Notice

Tax code for tax year

2010–11

Please keep all your coding notices. You may need to refer to them if you have to fill in a tax return. Please also quote your tax reference and National Insurance number if you contact us.

010000:00000080:001   491/1

MR B ANDREWS
MATHESON HOUSE
GRANGE CENTRAL
SOMERSET STREET
TELFORD
SHROPSHIRE   TF3 4HQ

H M INSPECTOR OF TAXES
NORTH WEST MU1
5 ABBEY FOREGATE
SHREWSBURY
SALOP
SY2 6AD

Inland Revenue office phone	Date of issue
01567 3456789	19 January 2010

Tax reference	National Insurance number
491/G7070/HD	CE 00 00 30 A

Dear MR B ANDREWS

Your tax code for the year 6th April 2010 to 5th April 2011 is 297T

You need a tax code so Giveus Abreak can work out how much tax to take off the payments they make to you from 6th April 2010. We have worked out your tax code but need you to check that our information about you is correct. The wrong tax code may mean you pay too much, or too little tax. Please keep your Coding Notices, you may need them if we send you a Tax Return.

Here is how we worked it out

your personal allowance		£6,475	(see Note 1 below)
car benefit	- £1,500		(see Note 2 below)
car fuel benefit	- £1,500		(see Note 3 below)
interest without tax taken off (gross interest)	- £501	- £3,501	(see Note 4 below)
a tax free amount of		£2,974	(see Note 5 below)

If we have got it wrong, or if your circumstances have changed and you think it could affect the tax you pay, please tell us. Our telephone number and address are above. We turn £2,974 into tax code 297T to send to Giveus Abreak. They should use this code with the tables they receive from HM Revenue & Customs to take off the right amount of tax each time they pay you from 6th April 2010. Giveus Abreak do not know the details of 297T or how it is worked out - that is confidential between us.

Notes

1   The law allows everyone who lives in the UK to receive some income before tax has to be paid - a "tax free amount" of income. That tax free amount starts from a "personal allowance" that depends on your circumstances. Our records tell us you are entitled to £6,475 for this tax year, the standard personal allowances for people who will be under 65 at 5th April 2011.

2   We have to see if anything should reduce your tax free amount. We understand you have a company car from Giveus Abreak. You have to pay tax on the benefit of using that car for your private motoring. By taking into account the car's cost...

P2(New)   Page 1   Please turn over

Example

Bill Svensen is married and was born before 6 April 1935. He gets £6,965 married couple's allowance in 2010–11. This amount is shown in the right-hand column on his coding notice. But he is a basic rate taxpayer and if £6,965 of his income were tax-free, this would give him 20% × £6,965 = £1,393 in tax relief. This is £696.50 too much because the married couple's allowance gives relief only at 10 per cent (10% × £6,965 = £696.50). Therefore an allowance restriction of £3,482 is deducted in the left-hand column. Since 20% × £3,482 = £696.40, this claws back virtually all of the excess relief.

Example

Betty Pinder pays tax at the higher rate and receives £800 of interest from which tax at 20 per cent (£200) has already been deducted. But Betty should have paid tax at 40 per cent on the gross amount, which means she owes a further £200 tax. To collect this, a higher rate adjustment of £500 is deducted from her allowances, since 40% × £500 = £200.

Calculating your PAYE code

All the adjustments are subtracted from the allowances and reliefs to find the net amount of tax-free pay for the year. This is converted into a PAYE code, normally by knocking off the last figure and adding one of the following letters, depending on your allowances and tax rate:

- L – personal allowance at the rate for those aged under 65
- P – personal allowance for those aged 65–74
- Y – personal allowance for the over-75s.

So, if your only tax allowance is the single person's allowance for people under 65 of £6,475 and you have £3,501 deductions to collect extra tax, your total tax-free amount for the year will be £6,475 − £3,501 = £2,974. Your code is found by knocking off the last figure to give you 297 and adding L. Your PAYE code will be 297L.

When it comes to deducting tax from your pay, the employer's tax tables say that an employee with a code 297L is entitled to £2,979 of tax-free pay and this is spread equally over all the pay periods in the year.

The letters after the number enable your tax bill to be adjusted automatically when tax allowances change without a new code being issued.

T and K codes

If your code ends in the letter T, your tax position is more complicated – you may be getting other allowances (such as blind person's allowance), have fringe benefits (such as a company car) or you have asked for the T code because you do not want your employer to know what allowances you are entitled to. Your tax bill can't be automatically adjusted if you have this sort of code and you will have to wait for your tax office to tell your employer what adjustment to make.

If, in working out your code, the deductions come to more than your allowances, you will have a PAYE code starting with the letter K. This tells your employer to add an extra amount to your pay before working out tax – see Example below. K codes have to be recalculated every time the tax allowances change or there is some other alteration in your circumstances.

Example

Rasheed Patel gets the personal allowance of £6,475. However, he has a company car with a taxable value of £6,600, so his tax-free amount for the year is £6,475 − £6,600 = −£125. His PAYE code is found by dropping the last digit to get 12. Then he subtracts 1 to get 11, giving a code of K11. This means, Rasheed will have £119 added to his pay for the year before tax is worked out (instead of having some allowances deducted).

More than one source of income

There are special PAYE codes that don't have numbers or have numbers that don't stand for tax allowances. These are mainly used for deducting tax from second or third sources of income:

■ BR – this income is all taxed at the basic rate: this is where other sources of income have used up all your allowances

■ DO – this income is all taxed at the higher rate because other sources of income have used up your allowances and basic rate band

■ NT – you are not entitled to any tax-free pay but this income is to be taxed at the basic rate and then, if necessary, the higher rate.

Claiming a tax refund

If you have paid too much tax through PAYE because you have stopped doing a job part way through the tax year, a refund will be arranged automatically by your new employer or the Jobcentre Plus office handling your benefit claim. But, if you are neither going to a new job nor getting benefit, claim a tax rebate using form P50.

In other cases where you have paid too much tax – for example, because tax has been deducted from your savings income but you are a non-taxpayer

– claim a refund using form R40. Do not send any documents, such as certificates of tax deducted, with the form but keep them safe in case your tax office asks to see them. The Revenue normally aims to process your claim within 28 days. Refunds are based on the information you provide, but the Revenue can open an enquiry either before or after paying the refund. You do not have to wait until the end of the tax year to make a claim but repayments of less than £50 are not usually made mid-year.

Either ask your tax office for the relevant claim form or download it from www.hmrc.gov.uk. You can't submit these forms online.

Take care when claiming tax back. If you make an error, you are liable for the same penalties as apply to mistakes made in a tax return (see p. 53).

PAYE and students

Increasingly, students take on some paid work to help finance their way through college. If you expect to earn less than your personal allowance and will be working only during the holidays, you may be able to arrange to be paid gross by completing form P38(S), available from the Revenue website. However, the employer does not have to agree to this and can opt instead to pay you through PAYE in the normal way.

You cannot use the P38(S) system if you work during term time. The Revenue is consulting on ways to ensure that students in this situation do not overpay tax unnecessarily, and changes are expected from April 2011.

Being taxed through PAYE means you can pay too much tax. There are ways to get it back:

- if you take another job during the tax year, you may get a refund through PAYE operated by your new employer. This is most likely if you can give the new employer a P45 (a form you should be given when you leave a job, summarising your tax and pay from that job)

- you can claim a refund once the tax year has ended by contacting your tax office (which will be shown on your tax or pay documents)

- you may be able to claim one or more refunds during the course of the tax year using form P50 available from the Revenue website.

Tax-saving ideas 25 and 26

Students can check whether they may be due a tax refund by using the Revenue calculator at www.hmrc.gov.uk/calcs/stc.htm.

Make a point of asking for a P45 when you leave a job. If you take another job, giving your new employer the P45 will help to ensure that you get a refund of any overpaid tax and do not overpay in the new job.

4

Dealing with tax problems

Given the complexity of the UK tax system, it is hardly surprising if your tax affairs do not always run smoothly. Here are some ideas on how to cope with the most common problems you are likely to face.

Changes to your tax return

Estimates, mistakes and corrections

There are several reasons for wanting to alter a tax return after you have sent it in. If a change results in extra tax being due, you will be charged interest on the tax paid late and you may have to pay a penalty if you have been careless or fraudulent (p. 52).

If you have put a provisional figure in your return (p. 30), you must supply the final figure as soon as it is known.

You might make a mistake when you complete the return. You have 12 months from the filing date within which you can amend your return with a minimum of fuss. Simply phone or write to your usual tax office explaining the amendment required. If, within nine months of the date you sent in the return, the Revenue picks up any obvious errors, it too can amend the return.

You also have an additional time period to correct any mistakes and claim back any tax overpaid as a result. From 1 April 2010, this period is four years following the end of the tax year. This means, for example, you will have only until 5 April 2013 to correct your 2008–09 tax return and 5 April 2014 to correct your 2009–10 return. You should notify your tax office in writing. However, you can't use this route to make a back claim for a tax relief where the time limit for making the claim has expired. (This applies, for example, to some types of loss relief if you run a business.)

Any tax due as a result of a revised self assessment should be paid either by the normal payment date or 30 days after the making of the self assessment (but this does not put off the date from which interest is charged).

Interventions

Since July 2006, the Revenue has been using a range of informal methods to help taxpayers get their tax right where the Revenue suspects there may be problems. These 'interventions' can take the form of letters, phone calls or visits. The Revenue may ask you to review the way you keep your business records, fill in a questionnaire to review the tax-compliance risks you face, or reconsider particular entries on your tax return. Where it has third party information, the Revenue may correct your tax return and ask you to explain the perceived error and to take steps to avoid it happening again. So far, it is up to you to choose whether to take part in these interventions.

Enquiries

Your tax office has the right to open a formal enquiry into your tax return. A small proportion of all returns is selected at random for enquiry. But most are chosen because the Revenue thinks there is something wrong or a risk assessment analysis suggests there is a high chance of this. Your tax office must tell you if the enquiry is into your whole return or just some aspect of it (such as a particular expense you have claimed).

Your tax office must give you written notice of an enquiry. For your 2009–10 return, the enquiry must normally start within one year of the date on which you filed your return. If your return was late or you amended it, the enquiry deadline is extended to one year from the end of the calendar quarter in which you sent in your late or amended return.

In effect, the enquiry window can be extended if your return includes a valuation, some other value judgement or you have interpreted tax law in a different way from the Revenue and you are deemed to have given insufficient information about this on your return. In this situation the Revenue is allowed to make a discovery assessment (see opposite) following the ruling in a case called *Langham* v *Veltema*. You can find guidelines on the Revenue website (www.hmrc.gov.uk) on the information you should supply in your tax return to avoid a discovery assessment.

Your tax office has the right to demand that you produce certain documents as part of the enquiry. When you receive a notice of an enquiry, you may also receive a notice to produce these within 30 days. You can provide copies, but your tax inspector may insist on seeing the originals. You can appeal within 30 days against this notice to produce documents.

You can also appeal to the First-Tier Tribunal (p. 54) if you consider that an enquiry should not have been undertaken or is being continued unnecessarily. If it agrees, the tribunal can issue a notice to the Revenue requiring it to close the enquiry.

When the subject of an enquiry is complete, your tax office will issue you with a formal notice telling you so, how much tax you are considered to owe (if any), any penalty charge (p. 52), and requiring you to amend your self assessment. You can appeal against it, if you don't agree. The result of a tax enquiry may also lead to a revision of any tax credits you claim (p. 66). Once the enquiry is closed, no further enquiry can be made into the same return but a discovery assessment (see below) is possible. For more information about enquiry procedures and your rights, see Revenue booklet IR160 *Enquiries under self assessment* or www.hmrc.gov.uk/pdfs/ir160.htm.

Discovery assessments

The aim of the enquiry process was to give you, the taxpayer, certainty about when the assessment for a tax year had become final and could be consigned to the archives. However, the Revenue can reopen a past return even after the enquiry window has passed, if it discovers that more tax should have been paid and either you are deemed to have acted carelessly or dishonestly or your tax office could not reasonably have known on the basis of the information available at the time that extra tax was due. In these situations, the Revenue can send you a discovery assessment setting out the amount of extra tax it thinks you now owe.

Currently, the Revenue must normally make any discovery assessment within four years after the end of the tax year. However, the limit is extended to six years if you are deemed to have been careless, and 20 years if you deliberately withheld information.

A discovery means that your tax office has discovered that some income or gain on which you should have paid tax has not been included in your self assessment, or the assessment is too low, or the amount of relief given is too much. A discovery assessment is issued to collect the extra tax due and a penalty charge may be imposed (p. 52). You can appeal against a discovery assessment (p. 54).

A discovery assessment cannot be made if full and correct information was sent with your tax return to the Revenue and it should have been possible to work out the correct tax. If the tax lost results from an error in the taxpayer's return but the return was made in accordance with prevailing practice at the time, no discovery assessment can be made.

Tax-saving idea 27

If the outcome of an enquiry or appeal against a discovery assessment is that you have to pay extra tax, interest will be added to reflect the fact the tax is being paid late. However, at the start of the enquiry or appeal, if you buy a certificate of tax deposit to cover the amount of tax in dispute, interest stops accruing from the date you buy the certificate. If the dispute is settled in your favour, you can exchange the certificate for cash.

Information checks

Since 1 April 2009, you can be asked to provide a tax officer with any information and documents reasonably required for the purpose of checking your tax position. This is an extremely wide power that can mean virtually any type of information or document and can relate to your past, present or future tax liabilities. The information need not be linked to a tax return, so can focus on how adequately you are maintaining your records on a day-to-day basis. It can also apply not just to UK tax, but also taxes levied by other European Union states or other countries with which the UK has tax agreements.

The Revenue must send you a written notice requesting the information and/or documents (called an 'information notice'), giving a reasonable time limit for their production. You can provide copies, unless the notice specifies that you must supply originals. You and the Revenue may agree a place where the information and documents can be inspected. Alternatively, the Revenue can select a venue but this cannot be somewhere used solely as a private home. The Revenue may copy or retain documents (giving you a receipt for them).

The Revenue also has wide powers to request information from third parties to help in checking your tax position. The tax officer should normally ask for your agreement before contacting a third party, unless he or she has obtained permission in any case from the First-Tier Tribunal (see p. 54).

You will not normally be expected to produce documents that are more than six years old and you can appeal again to the First-Tier Tribunal against the requirements in an information notice. Apart from that safeguard, if you fail to comply, you can be fined £300 and, for persistent failure, up to £60 a day. Deliberately concealing documents will be a criminal offence punishable by a fine or up to two years in prison. In addition, if the Revenue believes that you have paid less tax than you would have done had the information or documents been produced, it can apply to the Upper Tribunal (see p. 56) to impose a tax-related penalty.

If the Revenue loses or damages any of your documents, you can claim compensation for replacing or repairing them, but the legislation has no provisions for compensating you for any consequential loss.

Inspecting business premises

Since 1 April 2009, the Revenue can enter business premises to inspect the premises themselves, together with business assets and business documents kept there. The Revenue may remove any documents, record information (electronically or otherwise) and put marks on assets to show they have been inspected.

There are three ways that the Revenue may legally enter the premises:

- with the permission of the occupier. The Revenue does not have to give any notice and agreement does not have to be sought in writing – it could just be oral. For example, a tax officer could phone you or knock on the door and, if you agree to the inspection, it can take place there and then

- at any reasonable time if the Revenue gives you seven days' notice. This does not have to be written notice

- at any reasonable time if the inspection has been authorised by an appropriate Revenue officer or approved by the First-Tier Tribunal. In this case, you must be given written notice but the amount of notice could be more or less than seven days.

You have the right of appeal against the inspection to the First-Tier Tribunal but only if you have been given written notice. If the inspection has been approved by the First-Tier Tribunal (which will be stated on the written notice), obstructing the inspection can result in a fine of £300 and, if the obstruction persists, up to £60 a day. These penalties do not apply if the inspection was not approved by the First-Tier Tribunal, but the Revenue will then undoubtedly seek approval and return, so you may just be delaying the inevitable. If the Revenue believes tax is being lost, it can apply to the Upper Tribunal (see p. 54) to impose a tax-related penalty as well.

If you work from home, the Revenue can inspect those parts of your home used for business, but not the purely private parts of your dwelling.

Tax-saving idea 28

The Revenue's powers to specify which records must be kept (see p. 28) and to require information and to inspect documents at any time (see p. 50) put pressure on you to keep your records up to date, especially if you are running a small business. Stuffing documents in an old carrier bag to be sorted out after the end of the tax year is likely to be interpreted by the Revenue as, at best, careless. It could trigger enquiries and discovery assessments with possible back-tax, interest and penalties to pay. Try to get into the habit of organising your book-keeping and relevant tax records on at least a weekly basis.

Penalties, appeals and complaints

Penalties

The self assessment system is underpinned by a range of penalties, the most important of which are summarised in the table on p. 55. In addition, interest is added to overdue tax and also to penalties that remain unpaid. Your tax office has discretion to reduce some penalties based, for example, on the gravity of your case and the extent of your co-operation.

The penalty system is being reviewed and updated in stages. For returns submitted from April 2009 onwards (in other words covering tax periods from 2008–09 onwards), a new range of penalties applies if your tax return or any related documents, such as business accounts, are incorrect. Penalties are chargeable if the error is either deliberate or due to carelessness. You are expected to take reasonable care both when you prepare your return and when you check documents sent to you by someone acting for you. This means you can be penalised for an error made by a tax adviser or even by the Revenue itself.

The penalties are set by reference to the amount of tax you owe and there are three levels as shown in the table below. The maximum penalty may be reduced if you co-operate in disclosing and correcting the error. The Revenue can also suspend a penalty for up to two years if you agree to make changes aimed at avoiding a repeat of the error. If you keep to the conditions, the penalty is cancelled at the end of the suspension period. But, if you do not keep to the conditions (or you incur a penalty for another error during the suspension period), the penalty has to be paid.

Also since April 2009, an almost identical range of penalties applies if you fail to notify the Revenue of a new source of income or gains – see footnote 2 to the table below.

Incorrect return or failure to notify: size of penalty as a percentage of tax owed

	Type of error		
	Careless or Revenue error	*Deliberate not concealed*	*Deliberate with steps taken to conceal it*
Maximum penalty	30%	70%	100%
Minimum penalty if unprompted you disclose the error[1]	0%[2]	20%	30%
Minimum penalty if prompted you disclose the error[1]	15%[2]	35%	50%

(1) The size of the reduction depends on the extent to which you co-operate with the Revenue, for example, by providing information.
(2) Amounts shown in the table apply to incorrect return. In the case of failure to notify a new source of income or gain, the minimum penalties are: unprompted disclosure, 10 per cent (or 0 per cent if disclosure is within 12 months of tax becoming due); prompted disclosure, 20 per cent (or 10 per cent if disclosure is within 12 months of tax becoming due).

Tax-saving idea 29

Don't be late sending in your tax return. The 2010 paper return must be sent back by 31 October 2010 and online returns by 31 January 2011 to avoid an automatic £100 penalty. However, provided you have paid all the tax you owe by 31 January 2011, the penalty is reduced to nil – this limit on the penalty is due to be abolished from a date yet to be announced.

In 2001, a criminal offence was introduced of being *'knowingly concerned in the fraudulent evasion of income tax'*. This is aimed at catching people who deliberately dodge tax, for example, employers and employees colluding to pay less through PAYE, or householders and tradespeople deliberately negotiating a cash price so they benefit from tax saved. The maximum penalty for serious cases is an unlimited fine and/or seven years in prison.

Appeals and complaints

You can appeal against the following: an assessment that is not a self assessment, an amendment to your self assessment by the Revenue after an enquiry, an amendment of a partnership statement where a loss of tax is discovered, a disallowance in whole or in part of a claim or election included in a tax return, penalty determinations, or a formal notice requesting documents or entry to business premises.

Tax-saving idea 30

You can appeal against the £100 penalty for missing the deadline for sending in your tax return, by writing to your tax office. You would need a reasonable excuse, for example, an unexpected postal strike, serious illness, the death of a close relative, or loss of records due to fire, flood or theft. Pressure of work, a failure by your tax adviser or lack of information would not be regarded as a reasonable excuse. If you have tried to file online but the software has rejected your return, this may qualify as a reasonable excuse provided you send your tax office the error message or error code produced by the software.

You have to give written notice of appeal within 30 days after the issue of the notice of assessment, amendment or disallowance. But you may not appeal against an amendment as a result of an enquiry until you've had notice that the enquiry is complete, although certain questions may be referred for decision to a tribunal or the courts while an enquiry is in process.

If you disagree about the amount of the tax bill, you should first of all exhaust the avenues within the Revenue by asking for an internal review – your tax office may take the first step and offer you this option. In general, the Revenue must then set out its initial view of the matter within 30 days and then have to complete the review within a further 45 days. Where possible, the review should be carried out by different tax officials from those involved in the original decision. If you do not agree with the outcome of the internal review, you have 30 days within which to appeal to the tribunal (see below). You do not have to go through the Revenue internal review process, but can go straight to the tribunal if you prefer.

A new tribunal system (www.tribunals.gov.uk) for handling all sorts of disputes with government departments, not just tax, went live in November 2008. Tax affairs were transferred to its jurisdiction from April 2009 onwards (replacing the previous system of general and special commissioners). There are two types of tribunal, each divided into chambers for different types of

Action/omission triggering penalty	Penalty	Deadline for 2009–10 tax year
Failure to tell your tax office (if you have had no tax return) within six months of the end of the tax yera about income or gains on which tax is due	Based on the amount of tax due and unpaid by 31 January following end of tax year (see p. 53)	5 October 2010
Failure to send in tax return by the due date	£100 or, if less, penalty equal to amount of tax due[1]	31 January 2011
Tax return still not sent in six months after due date	Further £100 or, if less, penalty equal to amount of tax due[1]	31 July 2011
Tax return still not sent in one year after due date	Equal to amount of tax due (may be reduced at Revenue discretion)[1]	31 January 2012
Continued failure to submit return	Up to £60 a day[1]	
Sending incorrect return	Based on amount of tax due (see p. 53)	
Failure to keep records for a tax or accounting year and to preserve them for required period	£3,000	
Failure to produce documents on reques	£300	
Continuing failure to produce documents	Up to £60 a day and, if suspected tax unpaid, a tax-related penalty	
Tax unpaid more than 30 days after the due date	Equal to 5% of the unpaid tax	
Tax unpaid more than six months after due date	Further 5% of unpaid tax	
Tax unpaid more than 12 months after due date	Further 5% of unpaid tax	

[1] These penalties are due to change from a date yet to be announced (see p. 53).

dispute. Normally, appeals will go first to the tax chamber of the First-Tier Tribunal. If either you or the Revenue is unhappy with the decision of the First-Tier Tribunal, you may have the right to appeal to the finance and tax chamber of the Upper Tribunal but only on a question of law. Complex disputes or cases relevant to large numbers of taxpayers may go straight to the Upper Tribunal. The aim of the tribunals is to provide a low-cost, accessible way for resolving disputes. Hearings are described as 'informal' and you choose whether or not to use a lawyer. The tribunal service itself is free to use, but you will have to pay the costs of preparing your case and hiring a legal representative, if you use one.

If (rather than disputing a tax bill) you are dissatisfied with the way the Revenue handles your tax affairs, you should first complain to your tax officer. If you get no satisfaction, you should direct your complaints to the regional controller responsible for your tax office (ask the tax office for the name and address). If this doesn't work, you should channel your next communication to the independent Adjudicator's Office (www.adjudicatorsoffice.gov.uk). The Adjudicator's remit covers matters such as excessive delay, errors, discourtesy or the way your tax officer has exercised his or her discretion.

Getting help

Although you can handle disputes with the Revenue yourself, this can be difficult and daunting, especially if you are faced with a Revenue enquiry or need to take a case to a tribunal. You may need the help of a tax adviser – contact the Chartered Institute of Taxation (www.tax.org.uk) for a list of its members.

If your income is low and you cannot afford to pay a tax adviser, you may be eligible for free professional tax advice through TaxAid (www.taxaid.org.uk). Older people on low incomes can get free tax advice through TaxHelp for Older People (www.taxvol.org.uk). These organisations focus their help on households with an income of £15,000 and £17,000, respectively, or less. See Appendix E for full contact details.

5

Tax and your household

In general, the tax system treats you as an independent person. But there are special rules designed to help (or sometimes to prevent tax avoidance) where particular circumstances relate to you or your household. This applies, for example, if you are married, in a civil partnership, have children or you are on a low income.

Marriage and civil partnerships

Married couples and civil partners are treated as two independent entities for the purpose of paying tax (though not when it comes to claiming tax credits – p. 66). Each person is taxed on their own income and gains and has their own allowances. Each is responsible for filling in their own tax return and paying their own tax bills. There is no longer a tax allowance for married couples unless either or both husband and wife were born before 6 April 1935 – this allowance is also available to older civil partners.

However, there are some aspects of the tax system which recognise that husband and wife, or civil partners, are more than just two individuals living together. One is that they can transfer some allowances between them in certain circumstances. Gifts between them don't normally trigger a capital gains tax or inheritance tax bill. And by sharing their wealth, a couple can each use their tax-free allowances to reduce the amounts paid in tax.

Tax-saving ideas 31 and 32

If one of you pays tax at a higher rate than the other, or one of you is losing personal allowance and the other has income under £100,000 (see p. 24), consider giving investments which produce a taxable income to the spouse or civil partner who would pay least tax on the income.

Gifts between married couples or civil partners must be genuine with no strings attached. If you are reluctant to give away the investments completely, consider putting them into joint names so the income is shared equally (see below).

Example

Janet Lardon is on a salary of £60,000 a year and has interest from savings accounts of £5,000 a year before tax. She pays tax at the higher rate of 40 per cent on her earnings and her savings interest.

She decides to share the savings accounts with her husband Ted, who pays tax at the basic rate only. She puts them in their joint names, so £2,500 of the interest is taxed as his. He has to pay tax on interest at 20 per cent, so they save higher rate tax of 20 per cent of £2,500, that is £500 a year.

This section explains the opportunities to save tax in marriage or civil partnership. For how marriage or civil partnership affects home ownership, see p. 74; information about capital gains tax is on p. 153, and on inheritance tax on p. 165.

Civil partnership

Since 5 December 2005, same-sex couples who register their relationship as a civil partnership are treated for tax in the same way as married couples.

Jointly owned assets

If you have investments which are jointly owned, your tax officer will assume the income from them is split equally between you. If the investments are not owned in equal proportions, you can have the income divided between you to reflect your actual shares of it. You do this by both signing a declaration of beneficial interests on form 17 (available from tax offices) and sending it to your tax officer.

The new split of joint income applies from when the declaration is signed – it can't be backdated. If you acquire new assets on which the 50:50 split is not to apply, you must make a further declaration. Note the split for income will also be used to allocate any gain on selling an asset between you when you dispose of it (p. 130).

The exception to the above rules is where you jointly own shares in a close company. (A close company is basically one controlled by five or fewer people. Typically this could be a company that you or your spouse or civil partner owns and manages.) Since 6 April 2004, you will automatically be taxed on dividends from these shares according to the actual proportion in which you own them or have rights to income from them.

In recent years, the Revenue has attacked arrangements where husbands and wives share the income from a family business (for example, by drawing dividends) and one of the couple seems to generate the majority of the company's revenue. Following the settlement of a case known as Arctic Systems (*Jones* v *Garnett*) in the taxpayer's favour, new legislation was proposed to remove any tax advantages from what the Revenue calls 'income shifting' (transferring income on a non-commercial basis between people involved in a company or partnership). The legislation was criticised by tax experts as complex and unworkable. In November 2008, the Revenue announced that the legislation had been deferred indefinitely although the area would be kept under review.

Personal allowances

A husband, wife and civil partner are each entitled to a personal tax allowance in the same way as single people – usually £6,475 in 2009–10 and 2010–11 but more if aged 65 or over (p. 25).

Married couple's allowance

Married couple's allowance is given only where one (or both) of a couple was born before 6 April 1935.

The allowance gives tax relief at 10 per cent as a reduction in the tax bill.

The table overleaf shows the amounts of married couple's allowance in 2009–10 and 2010–11. Usually, allowances are increased each year in line with price inflation as measured by changes in the Retail Prices Index up to the September preceding the start of the tax year. In September 2009, inflation was negative and the government decided to freeze allowances for 2010–11 at their 2009–10 level. The allowance is made up of two parts: a basic element and an age-related addition.

For couples who were married before 5 December 2005, the whole allowance is initially awarded to the husband, but half or all of the basic amount may be transferred to the wife. But the age-related addition stays with the husband (unless his income is too low to use it – see opposite).

For couples who marry, and for same-sex couples who form a civil partnership on or after 5 December 2005, the whole allowance is initially awarded to whichever of the couple has the highest income. Once again, half or all of the basic amount (but not normally any of the age-related addition) can be transferred to the other spouse or partner.

You must normally make an election to transfer half or all of the basic amount before the start of the tax year – for example, an election for 2010–11 must have been made before 6 April 2010.

Married couple's allowance

	2009–10 and 2010–11	
Age of older partner during tax year	*Maximum allowance (1)*	*Which would save this much tax:*
75 and over	£6,965	£696.50
Of which, basic amount:	£2,670	£267.00

(1) Total income limit at which allowance reduced: £22,900 in 2009–10 and 2010–11.

The married couple's allowance is reduced if the adjusted net income (see p. 15) of the person who gets the age-related addition is above a certain level. But the allowance is never reduced below the basic amount (£2,670 in 2009–10 and 2010–11). The allowance is reduced by £1 for each £2 of income over £22,900 in 2009–10 and 2010–11. But any age-related personal allowance (p. 24) is reduced first.

For example, suppose a husband aged 75 (married before 5 December 2005) has an income of £30,900. This is £8,000 above the income limit for 2009–10 of £22,900, which means he stands to lose ½ × £8,000 = £4,000 of age-related allowances. He initially has a personal allowance of £9,640 but this is reduced by £3,165 to the standard £6,475 because of his excess income. That leaves a further reduction of £835, which is set against his married couple's allowance of £6,965 reducing it to £6,130.

The table opposite shows the income level in 2010–11 at which all the age-related married couple's allowance would be lost (and so only the basic amount would be given).

Income level at which all age-related married couple's allowance lost in 2010–11

Age that recipient of the age-related addition reaches during tax year	Age partner reaches during tax year	Income level at which allowance reduced to basic amount (£2,670)
Under 65	75 and over	£31,490
65–74	75 and over	£37,520
75 and over	Any age	£37,820

Tax-saving idea 33

Is one of you 75 or over in 2010–11? And does whichever of you gets the age-related part of the married couple's allowance have adjusted net income high enough to be losing part of the allowance? You may be able to save tax by transferring investments that produce income to the other spouse or partner.

Transfer of allowances because of low income

If either spouse or civil partner has a tax bill that is too low to use up all their married couple's allowance, they can ask to have the unused part deducted from the tax bill of their spouse or partner. Even the age-related addition can be transferred in these circumstances. You can do this after the end of the tax year in which you got the allowance – see p. 252 for how to claim this. You can go back four years if, in the past, you had not realised you could transfer the allowance in this way – so, provided you claim by 5 April 2011, you can go back as far as the 2006–07 tax year.

Example

Jasper Duffy, 75, has a total income of £33,000 – of which £8,000 a year is from savings and investments. Because his total income is well over the £22,900 limit, it reduces the amount of personal allowance he gets to the amount for under-65s (£6,475). It also reduces the married couple's allowance the Duffys get from £6,965 to £5,080.

He decides to share his savings and investments equally with his wife Ellen, whose total income is well below the £22,900 limit. He puts them all into their joint names, which means only half the income they produce is his. This reduces his total income by half of £8,000 = £4,000 to £29,000.

This is still above £22,900 but the reduction in his personal allowance is less (he gets £6,590) and the couple now get the full married couple's allowance of £6,965.

Tax-saving ideas 34 and 35

> If your income is too low to use all the married couple's allowance, even the age-related part can be transferred to your spouse or civil partner.
>
> Married couples and civil partners of any age can transfer blind person's allowance between them if the recipient has too little income to be able to use the allowance fully. The unused part can be transferred to the spouse or partner even if they themselves are not blind.

Just married or registered?

If you newly marry or register a civil partnership and either of you was born before 6 April 1935, you qualify for the married couple's allowance.

In the tax year of your marriage or registration, you get one-twelfth of the allowance for each month or part-month of the union. In the 2010–11 tax year, you could get an allowance of up to £581 a month if either of you is aged 75 or over. A month runs from the sixth day to the fifth day of the next calendar month.

As described on p. 60, you can elect to transfer half or all of the basic amount of the allowance to your spouse or partner. In the year of marriage or registration only, you have until the end of the year to make this election – in other words until 5 April 2011 for the 2010–11 tax year.

Separation and divorce/dissolving a partnership

Separation, divorce or dissolving a civil partnership may affect:

- tax relief on maintenance you pay, but only if you or your spouse or partner were born before 6 April 1935
- national insurance contributions you pay if you are a married woman who has been paying contributions at the married women's reduced rate
- your entitlement to tax credits (p. 66)
- the tax allowances you get in the year it happens, but only if you or your spouse or partner were born before 6 April 1935.

If any of the above apply to you, you should tell your tax officer when you separate (and within one month for tax credits), even if you have not yet made a formal deed of separation or sought a court order. The Revenue will then treat you as no longer living with your spouse or partner, provided your circumstances suggest that the separation will be permanent.

Maintenance payments

Maintenance can take several forms, including direct payments of cash or the provision of support such as a home to live in. The person receiving maintenance does not pay any tax on the amount they get.

Where the maintenance is provided voluntarily – that is, the payment cannot be enforced – the person paying it gets no tax relief. This is also true for enforceable maintenance payments, except where you or your spouse or partner were born before 6 April 1935.

Provided you or your former (or separated) spouse or partner were born before 6 April 1935, you can claim relief for payments made under a legally binding agreement, such as a court order, a Child Support Agency assessment or a written agreement. Only payments up to a set limit qualify for relief. The limit is £2,670 in 2010–11. Relief is given at a fixed rate of 10 per cent through your PAYE code (see Chapter 3) or through an adjustment to your tax bill.

National insurance contributions

Paying certain types of national insurance contributions entitles you to some state benefits, such as state retirement pension. If you are a woman and you married before May 1977, you may have opted to pay contributions at the 'married women's reduced rate'. In return for paying less national insurance, you gave up the right to those state benefits and instead relied on your husband. Although, from May 1977 onwards, wives could not newly opt to pay the reduced rate, anyone who had already made the option could continue.

Your right to pay national insurance at the reduced rate ends at the time your marriage ends – generally, on the date of the decree absolute. If you are an employee, tell your employer so that he can arrange for you to pay full rate contributions. If you are self-employed, notify your tax office. For more information, see the Revenue website at www.hmrc.gov.uk/ni/reducedrate/marriedwomen.htm. See p. 97 for steps you might be able to take to boost your state pension.

Capital gains tax and inheritance tax on separation

You can carry on making gifts to your ex-spouse or ex-partner in the year of separation without falling into the net for capital gains tax. After this, gifts may lead to a capital gains tax bill in the same way as for any other gifts (p. 153).

However, if you move out of the family home and later dispose of the property or your share in it as part of the divorce settlement, there is no capital gains tax to pay, provided: your former spouse or partner continues to live there as their only or main home; and you have not elected for any other property to be your only or main home. For example, you might consider renting until the sale or transfer of the home is sorted out.

Gifts between separated spouses or separated civil partners are normally free of inheritance tax (p. 162). Once you are divorced or the partnership is dissolved, gifts may fall into the inheritance tax net unless they are for the maintenance of the ex-spouse, ex-partner or any children.

Married couple's allowance

Each of you retains your personal allowances. And each of you will retain any married couple's allowance you were getting before the separation – but only for the rest of the tax year.

Bereavement

If your husband, wife or civil partner dies, you carry on getting your own personal allowance as usual. If you have been claiming tax credits, within one month of becoming bereaved you need to make a new claim as a single person (p. 66).

If you or your spouse or partner were born before 6 April 1935, you keep any married couple's allowance you were getting for the rest of the tax year in which death occurs. Any married couple's allowance unused in the year of death by the person who has died can be transferred to the surviving spouse or partner. Married couple's allowance ceases from the following year.

Living together

If you live with someone without being married or registered as a civil partnership, you are treated for tax purposes as single people. However, the same is not true for tax credits (p. 66). The amount of any tax credits you can claim depends on your household income and couples are treated as being part of the same household whether or not they are married.

Children and young people

In general, the tax system does not treat people differently on the grounds of age. Therefore a child, just like an adult, has their own income tax allowance, tax bands and capital gains tax allowance. However, there are some rules specific to children and young people, in particular:

- to counter tax avoidance, where a parent gives money or investments to a child and these produce an income, that income is taxed as the income of the parent not the child unless it comes to no more than £100 a year. The £100 limit applies per parent per child

- individual savings accounts (ISAs) – see Chapter 7 – are generally not available to people under age 18 except that young people may hold cash ISAs from age 16 onwards

- child trust funds – see Chapter 7 – are tax-efficient investments available to children born on or after 1 September 2002 up to their 18th birthday

- some payments commonly received by young people and students are tax-free – these include: educational maintenance allowance; student loans, grants and bursaries; and most youth training scheme allowances

- although children can be taxpayers, until they reach age 16 they have no liability for national insurance on any earnings or profits

- if you are a student working only during your holidays and earning too little to pay tax, you may be able to arrange to receive your wages without any tax deducted using form P38S (p. 46)

- since 6 April 2006, if a parent puts assets into a trust that can benefit their child, the trust counts as 'settlor-interested'. Both income and gains made by the trust are taxed as those of the parent

- transfers to most types of trust on or after 22 March 2006 count as taxable gifts for inheritance tax and the trust may periodically have to pay inheritance tax (see Chapter 10). These rules do not apply where a trust is set up in a parent's will to benefit their dependent child (called a 'bereaved minor's trust')

■ accumulation and maintenance (A&M) trusts have in the past been a popular way to make gifts to children and grandchildren because of favourable inheritance tax treatment. This treatment no longer applies for A&M trusts set up on or after 22 March 2006. Existing A&M trusts are now also subject to harsher tax treatment, unless their terms were amended before 6 April 2008 so that beneficiaries become entitled outright to the trust assets by age 18. If they become entitled by age 25, inheritance tax will be due only in the years from age 18 to 25 and only at a maximum rate of 4.2 per cent of the value of the trust assets.

Tax-saving ideas 36–38

> If you give capital to your children and it produces over £100 income a year, that income will normally be taxed as yours. Choose investments that produce a tax-free income instead (see Chapter 7).
>
> If you are a student with an income of no more than £6,475 in 2010–11, you should not be paying tax. Claim back any tax deducted from earnings (p. 46) and claim back any tax deducted from savings using form R40 (p. 45). Arrange to have savings interest paid without tax deducted by giving the bank or building society form R85 (p. 81). If you work only in the holidays, arrange to get your wages paid gross by filling in form P38S. All forms are available from tax offices and the Revenue website, www.hmrc.gov.uk.
>
> As a school or college student, you are likely to be a non-taxpayer, so you may think there is no point using the individual savings account (ISA) allowance you get from age 16 onwards – see p. 97. But, once you have invested in an ISA, those savings are sheltered indefinitely from tax. So the protection from tax will continue even after you start work and become a taxpayer.

Households with children or on a low income

If you are working and have a low income or if you have children (in which case you do not need to be working and can have a fairly substantial income), you may be eligible for tax credits.

Tax-saving ideas 39 and 40

> Households with children and an income up to £58,175 (£66,350 for the year a new child is born) are eligible for child tax credit. This is not given automatically – make sure you claim (p. 70).
>
> Even with an income just over £50,000, you can qualify for working tax credit if you pay for childcare. In 2010–11, the maximum childcare element is worth up to £12,480. However, you may instead be able to get help with childcare costs from your employer (see Chapter 8).

Working tax credit (WTC) and child tax credit (CTC) are – despite their names – state benefits, not tax allowances. However, the amount you can get depends broadly on your gross income for tax purposes (or joint income if you are married, in a civil partnership or living with someone). This means that measures which save you tax might increase your tax credits too. And don't assume these are benefits just for the poor. If you have children, you might qualify even with an income well over £60,000 a year.

Tax credits if you have no children

You may be able to claim WTC if you or your partner are in work but on a low income. You must either be: aged 25 or more and working at least 30 hours a week; 16 or more, working at least 16 hours and disabled; or aged 50 or more and have recently started work after a period claiming certain state benefits. You are unlikely to be eligible in 2010–11 if your income comes to more than £13,369 a year (single) or £18,215 (couple) – unless you are entitled to the extra credits available to people with a disability or some over-50s.

Tax-saving idea 41

Your tax credit claim is initially based on your income for the previous year and is adjusted only if your income for the current year is higher by more than £25,000 (see p. 68). This means, if your income was low last year – for example, due to a period of unemployment – you may still be eligible for tax credits this tax year even if you are now back in work.

Tax credits if you have children

You may be eligible for both the credits or just the CTC. For 2010–11, you can get at least some CTC provided your household income does not exceed £58,175 (or £66,350 if you have a child under one).

How the credits work

WTC is made up of eight elements – see the table overleaf. Your claim is based on as many of these elements as apply to you and you add on the relevant individual element of CTC for each child you look after. However, for every £1 by which your income exceeds the first threshold (£6,420 in 2010–11), the credits are reduced by 39p. WTC is reduced first with the childcare element being the last to go, then the CTC.

If you qualify only for CTC and no WTC, the first threshold at which you start to lose the individual elements of CTC is higher (£16,190 in 2010–11).

Every household with children also qualifies for the family element of CTC. This is not reduced at all until the household income reaches the second threshold (£50,000 in 2010–11). You then lose £1 of credit for every £15 of income over the threshold.

Rate of tax credits in 2010–11

Element	Who qualifies[1]	Amount
Working Tax Credit (WTC)		
Basic	Everyone eligible for WTC	£1,920
Lone parent	Single, caring for a child	£1,890
Second adult	Most couples	£1,890
30-hour	Working at least 30 hours a week	£790
Disabled worker	Satisfy range of disability conditions	£2,570
Severe disability	Eligible for highest rate of disability benefit	£1,095
50-plus	Aged 50 or more and returning to work.	£1,320
	Higher rate applies if work at least 30 hours a week	or £1,965
Childcare	Incurring eligible childcare costs	80% of eligible costs[2]
Child Tax Credit (CTC)		
Individual element	For each child in your care	£2,300[3]
Family element	First year following new birth	£1,090
Family element	Families without a newborn child	£545

(1) The rules are complicated and just a brief indication is given here.
(2) Eligible costs are up to £175 a week for one child and £300 a week for two or more.
(3) Increased to £5,015 or £6,110 for a disabled child depending on severity of disability.

Income on which your tax credits are based

The amount of tax credits you get for any year is based on your income for that same year. However, because there is a delay before you know your income for the year, your claim is initially based on your income for the previous tax year. So, for the 2010–11 tax year, your credits are based initially on your income for 2009–10 and then revised after 5 April 2011 when your actual income for 2010–11 is known.

If it turns out that your income was lower than initially estimated, you will have received too little in tax credits and should receive an extra sum after the end of the year. Conversely, if it turns out that your actual income was higher than the estimate, you will have received too much in tax credits and the excess may be clawed back. But increases in income up to £25,000 are disregarded. You are required to report some changes in your circumstances during the year instead of waiting for the end-of-year review. Where a change would increase the tax credits you can claim (for example, a fall in income or rise in childcare costs), it makes sense to report the change and get an adjustment straight away rather than waiting for the year-end.

Example

Julie Brown is a single parent, working full-time and earning £13,000 a year. She has two children both at primary school and spends £225 a week (£11,700 a year) on childcare. She qualifies for both WTC and CTC in 2010–11 as follows:

Income in excess of first threshold	
(£13,000 − £6,420)	£6,580
Taper (39p for each £1 of excess)	£2,566
WTC	
Basic element	£1,920
Lone parent element	£1,890
30-hour element	£790
Childcare element (80% × £11,700)	£9,360
WTC before taper	£13,960
WTC after deducting taper (£2,566)	£11,394
CTC	
Individual elements (2 × £2,300)	£4,600
Family element	£545
Total CTC	£5,145
Total credits after taper	£16,539

Julie receives £16,539 in tax credits, taking her income (before tax and national insurance) to £29,539 a year.

Tax-saving ideas 42–44

If your income for 2009–10 was over the limit for tax credits but you do not know what your income for 2010–11 will be and so do not know whether you will be eligible for credits this year, you should nevertheless put in a claim by 5 July 2010. Otherwise, if you do turn out to be eligible, it will be too late to backdate your claim to the start of the tax year. This can apply if, for example, you are self-employed with income that varies from year to year, or an employee fearing redundancy.

Any payment that qualifies for tax relief can be super tax-efficient if it also reduces your income and so increases the amount of CTC or WTC you can claim. This applies to, for example, pension contributions, Gift Aid donations, purchases through your business if you are self-employed, and claims against income for loss relief. See Example overleaf.

Because increases in income up to £25,000 are disregarded when finalising your tax credit claim, making large pension contributions in alternate tax years can maximise the tax credits you claim year after year – see Example overleaf.

Example

> Douglas and Angela have two children, income of £42,000 a year and spend £100 a week on childcare. Because their income is fairly high, all they can claim in tax credits is the family element of £545 a year. But, if Douglas pays a gross pension contribution of £10,000 in 2010–11, this reduces his income for tax credit purposes to £32,000 and at that level the family is able to claim around £3,900 in tax credits. After tax relief of £2,000 and taking into account the increase in tax credits for 2010–11, the pension contribution has cost Douglas only £4,616.
>
> If Douglas does not make any pension contribution next year, the 2011–12 tax credit claim will be based on his 2010–11 income of £32,000. The actual increase in his income back to £42,000 in 2011–12 is ignored because it is less than the £25,000 disregard. To carry on qualifying for tax credits, in 2012–13, Douglas should make another large pension contribution so that tax credits for 2012–13 and 2013–14 are based on his reduced income for 2012–13.

Between April and July 2009, you will receive an annual review form (TC603R) to finalise your award for 2009–10. You are asked either to confirm the details on the form or to notify any changes by 31 July 2010. If you still do not know your income for last year, give a provisional figure and then supply the exact figure once known but no later than 31 January 2011.

Broadly, credits are based on your income for tax purposes, but there are differences. For example, some fringe benefits, such as cheap loans, are ignored, as is the first £300 of income from savings and pensions. Deduct any amounts paid to a pension arrangement or under Gift Aid but ignore the Gift Aid carry back rules (p. 234) and deduct only what you actually paid during the year. Business losses are taken into account in the year in which they arise and, unlike the tax rules, are set against the income of the couple in a joint tax credit claim. Losses not used in this way may be carried forward for tax credit purposes, regardless of the way they have been claimed for tax.

How to claim

Tax credits are not paid automatically – you must claim them. You make a single claim for both credits by phoning the Tax Credits Helpline (0845 300 3900). Claims can be backdated no more than three months, so you need to send in a new claim by 5 July to get credits for the full tax year.

6

Tax and your home

Buying a home is probably the biggest purchase you will make. This chapter explains the limited situations in which you can still get tax relief on mortgage interest and how to make sure you don't pay a hefty capital gains tax bill if you sell your home for a lot more than you paid for it.

Mortgage interest tax relief

Home income schemes

People aged 65 or over can still get tax relief on the interest paid on a mortgage loan taken out as part of a home income scheme before 9 March 1999. Provided 90 per cent or more of the loan was used to buy an annuity, tax relief is given on the interest payments on up to £30,000 of the loan at a rate of 23 per cent. You go on getting tax relief even if you move house or switch mortgage. Usually relief is automatically deducted from the interest by the lender through a system called Mortgage Interest Relief At Source (MIRAS).

Running a business or letting your home

If you use your home for business purposes, you may be able to set off some of the interest against business income (p. 322).

If you take out or extend a mortgage against your home and use the money raised in your business or to finance property you rent out, you can claim part of the interest as an allowable expense (pp. 324 and 355).

If you let part or all of your home, you may be able to deduct mortgage interest when working out your profit or loss (see Chapter 19).

Whether or not you can claim tax relief on mortgage interest depends on the purpose or use of the loan. It does not depend on the value of the property against which the mortgage is secured, even if the property value falls below the level of the mortgage (negative equity).

Capital gains tax on homes

If you sell most types of investments (including property) for more than you paid for them, there may be capital gains tax to pay (see Chapter 9). But if you sell your only or main home, there is normally no capital gains tax. This exemption is known as private residence relief.

If you own more than one home, only one of them qualifies for private residence relief. And you may lose the relief if you use the home for business, leave it for prolonged periods or let it out. If you do have to pay capital gains tax on selling a home, it can mean a hefty tax bill – the gain, after deducting allowable expenses and your annual allowance, is taxed at 18 per cent. Major changes to capital gains tax since 6 April 2008 (see Chapter 9) mean there is no longer any relief for gains due to inflation.

Which homes?

Private residence relief is given for your only or main home, whether it is a house or flat, freehold or leasehold, and wherever in the world it is.

You must occupy the home exclusively as your residence if it is to be free of capital gains tax. If part of the home is used exclusively for business, you may have to pay tax on part of the gain (p. 75). And letting out some or all of your home can also mean a capital gains tax bill (p. 77).

If you live in a caravan or houseboat, there's normally no capital gains tax to pay on it, even if it is not your only or main home. Caravans and boats count as wasting assets with a useful life of 50 years or less – and are thus outside the net for capital gains tax (p. 128). But if you own the land on which a caravan stands, you might have to pay capital gains tax if you sell it, unless the caravan was your only or main home.

Gains on a former home that continues to be occupied by your ex-spouse are tax-free if you sell within three years of your leaving. A longer exemption period applies if this is your ex-spouse's only or main home and you have not nominated any other property as your own only or main home.

A home in which a dependent relative lives rent-free is also free of capital gains tax provided it fell into this category on or before 5 April 1988. This exemption lasts only as long as the relative continues to live in the home. Dependent relatives are: your mother or the mother of your spouse or civil partner if she is widowed, separated or divorced; any relative of yours or your spouse or civil partner who is unable to look after themselves because of permanent illness, disablement or old age (usually 65 or over).

Gardens

Private residence relief extends to the garden that goes with your home provided either the area of your home and garden come to no more than half a hectare (about 1¼ acres) or, if larger, a garden of that size is required for the reasonable enjoyment of the home. Gains related to any extra land will usually be taxable.

If your plot is no more than half a hectare, you can sell part of it without having to pay any capital gains tax even if you have obtained planning permission to build on the land. But the relief is lost if you fence off or start to develop the land and then sell it.

If your plot exceeds half a hectare and you sell part of it, the Revenue will usually argue this is strong evidence that the garden was larger than required for reasonable enjoyment, so a gain will be taxable. Exceptions may be where you sell to a family member or where the sale was forced on you by financial necessity.

Private residence relief does not apply to a garden if you have already sold (or given away) the home that went with it.

If you have more than one home

If you have more than one home, you can choose which is your main one and so free of capital gains tax. It doesn't have to be the home where you spend most time.

Tax-saving ideas 45 and 46

If you have more than one home, you can nominate which one is to be treated as your main home for tax purposes. Normally, choose the one on which you expect to make the largest gain.

Married couples and registered civil partners must nominate just one home between them as their main home. But unmarried and unregistered partners can each elect a different residence as their main home even if, say, one is used only for weekends.

Tax-saving ideas 47 and 48

> Every time the number of homes you have – whether or not you own them – changes you have a new opportunity to elect your main home. You could create a new opportunity by, for example, renting a flat for a few weeks. This could be worth doing if you previously missed the two-year time limit for electing which of two homes should count as your main home.
>
> Electing a second home as your main home even for just a week can save you capital gains tax if it means you can claim other reliefs such as the last three years of ownership (p. 76) or lettings relief (p. 77).

Example

> Mahmoud Sherani has a flat in London and a weekend home in Dorset. Years ago he elected the London flat as his main home. He now plans to sell the house in Dorset on which he will make a large gain. On 1 May 2010 he changes his election so that the Dorset house is treated as his main home. A week later, he changes the election back to the London flat. Because the Dorset house has now been his main home albeit for a very short time, gains relating to the last three years of ownership are tax-free. When he sells the London flat, gains attributable to one week will be taxable but should fall comfortably within his capital gains tax-free allowance (see Chapter 9).

You must make the election in writing and within two years of acquiring a second or further home. Once made, you can vary the election whenever you like and as often as you like and any variation can be backdated up to two years.

The Revenue takes the view that, if you miss the two-year deadline, you have lost the opportunity to make any election at all. Your main home will then be determined by the facts, such as your postal address and where you are registered to vote and you can be required to provide evidence to support this.

Married couples and civil partners can have only one main home even if in reality they spend a lot of time living in separate homes (for example, because one works away during the week). Unmarried and unregistered couples can each have a different main home.

Tax-saving idea 49

If you live most of the time in rented accommodation but also own a home and did not realise you needed to nominate the one you own as your main home in order to ensure there is no tax when you sell it, the Revenue will, by concession, waive the two-year limit. You must make the nomination within a reasonable time of becoming aware of your need to do so and it can be backdated to the time when you first started to have two homes.

Working from home

If any part of your home is used exclusively for business, there may be a capital gains tax bill (see Chapter 9) when you sell the home. This will not usually apply if you are an employee working from home, but could do if a substantial part of your home is set aside exclusively for the work.

If you use one or more rooms entirely for business (as an office or work-shop, for example), there will be tax on part of the gain when you sell the home. You will have to agree the proportion with the tax officer, who may base it on the number of rooms you use or market value if the business part could be sold separately. If you claim part of the mortgage interest as a business expense (p. 322), the same proportion of the gain is likely to be taxable.

Tax-saving idea 50

If you work from home, you can avoid capital gains tax on the home when you come to sell if you ensure that you do not use part of your home exclusively for business – for example, you use a home-office also for domestic purposes. But, in that case, you will have to scale back the home-related business expenses you claim each year in line with the non-business use (p. 324). You need to weigh up the likely amount of capital gains tax when you sell against the amount of business expenses involved.

Away from home

If you don't live in your home for all the time you own it, you may lose some of the private residence relief – even though it is the only home you own or you have nominated it as your main home. Normally you will have to pay capital gains tax on the following proportion of the taxable gain:

$$\frac{\text{Number of complete months of absence}}{\text{Number of complete months of ownership}}$$

Only months of ownership or absence since 31 March 1982 count in working out the proportion – earlier gains are outside the scope of the tax (p. 133).

In practice, you can be away from the home for considerable spells of absence without losing any private residence relief. You can retain it during absence for the following periods:

- the first year of ownership while you are building, rebuilding or modernising the home. This can be extended for another year if you can convince the tax officer it is necessary. To retain the exemption, you must move in within the one-year (or two-year) period

- the last three years of ownership – even if you have already moved out

- any other absences totalling up to three years, provided you live in the home both before the first absence and after the last.

You may also be able to retain private residence relief if work takes you or your spouse away from home. If your employer requires you to live away from home in the UK, you can go on getting private residence relief for up to four years of absence. If your employer requires you to work abroad, you can get relief indefinitely. But you must live in the home before the first absence and normally also after the final absence.

Provided you intend to live in your home in the future, private residence relief continues if you or your spouse are required to live in job-related accommodation. Self-employed people who have to live in work-related accommodation (for example, over the shop or at the club) can go on getting relief on their own homes as long as they intend to live there eventually.

Tax-saving idea 51

If you are away from home for quite long periods, keep an eye on the capital gains tax position so that you don't lose private residence relief.

Example

Linda March bought a house on 24 June 1999. On 6 July 2002 her employer sent her on an overseas posting lasting until 10 November 2004. On Linda's return to the UK, her employer sent her to work away from home until 15 August 2008. She lived in the home until 22 October 2008, when she bought a new home, eventually selling her old home on 27 February 2010.

During the ten years and eight months Linda owned the home, she was absent for three periods totalling seven years and three months. But she will get private residence relief for the entire time she owned the house.

The two years and four months from July 2002 to November 2004 count for private residence relief because they are a period of employment spent entirely abroad.

The three years and nine months from November 2004 to August 2008 are less than the four years of employment elsewhere in the UK possible without losing private residence relief.

The year and four months from October 2008 to February 2010 are part of the last three years of ownership.

Capital gains tax on lettings

There is no capital gains tax to pay if you take in one lodger who is treated as a member of the family – sharing your living rooms and eating with you. But in other circumstances, there may be capital gains tax to pay when you sell a home that has been let out wholly or in part.

If you let out the whole house for a period, the gain attributable to that period is taxable.

If you let part of your home, you may have to pay capital gains tax on the part that is not occupied by you. If you let two of your six rooms, for example, one-third of the gain on selling the home is taxable (less if you haven't let the two rooms for all the time that you've owned the home).

However, there may still be no capital gains tax to pay if you can claim lettings relief for homes that have been wholly or partly eligible for private residence relief. Lettings relief reduces the taxable gain by £40,000, or the amount of private residence relief, or the amount of the gain, whichever is lower – see the Example overleaf.

Tax-saving idea 52

You can claim letting relief only in respect of a residence that has been your main home at some time. So, if you buy a property mainly to let out, it could be worth moving in and making it your home for a while. There is no minimum time period but you must be able to prove that it was genuinely your permanent home while you were there.

Example

> Jane Mortimer lived in her home for four years and then let it out for six. She sold it making a taxable gain of £50,000.
>
> Jane qualifies for private residence relief for the four years she lived in it, plus the last three years of ownership – seven years in all. The gain attributable to the remaining three years is 3/10 of the £50,000. This £15,000 is taxable.
>
> Jane next works out how much lettings relief she is entitled to. The amount is the lower of £40,000 or the value of private residence relief on the house, which is £50,000 – £15,000 = £35,000 or the amount of the gain, in other words £15,000. The lowest is £15,000 and this reduces her gain to zero, so there is no tax to pay.

Property dealings

If you regularly buy and sell houses for profit, there may be a capital gains tax bill when you sell one – even if you have been living in it as your only or main home. This is meant to catch people who are making a business out of doing up unmodernised homes for sale. If your property dealings are substantial, you could be classified as a dealer in land. You would then have to pay income tax on the profits as a self-employed person (see Chapter 17).

Inheritance

If you inherit a property – for example, a family home on the death of your parents – you are deemed to have acquired it at its market value on the date of death. If you do not take up residence, there could be capital gains tax to pay if you sell the property and its value has risen since the date of death.

7

Savings, investments and pensions

To encourage savings, the government offers various tax incentives to investors, including tax relief on pension contributions and special tax rules to persuade you to build up savings for yourself (individual savings accounts – ISAs) or your children (child trust fund) and invest in new businesses (for example venture capital trusts).

This chapter guides you through the various types of savings and investments and how they are taxed. It explains the rules and tells you how to cash in on the tax breaks offered by the government.

Income tax on investments

Income from some investments is tax-free (that is, there is no income tax to pay). For a list of these, see pp. 192–193.

All other investment income is taxable. With more and more investments, tax is deducted from the income before it is paid to you. There is no more tax to pay on such income unless you pay tax at the higher rate. If you should have paid less tax than was deducted, you may be able to get a refund.

Interest paid after deduction of tax

Interest on most kinds of savings is now normally paid after tax has been deducted from it. This applies to building society accounts, bank accounts, annuities (other than pension annuities), local authority loans and bonds and National Savings & Investments (NS&I) guaranteed income and guaranteed growth bonds.

On these types of interest, tax is deducted at 20 per cent from the gross income before handing it over to you. There is no further tax bill if you pay tax at the basic rate on your income – which is the case for the vast majority of taxpayers. If you pay tax at the higher rate, there will be extra tax to pay on this income (see below). If your income is too low to pay tax or the highest rate of tax you pay is the starting rate of 10 per cent only, you can reclaim all or some of the tax which has been deducted.

The savings income is treated as an upper slice of your income. This means the starting rate band is set first against your earnings and other non-savings income (and taxed at 20 per cent). As a result, most people will have no starting rate band left to attract the 10 per cent rate – see p. 17.

Example

Sonny Dasgupta pays tax at 40 per cent on his income. NS&I certificates offer him an average return of 1.25 per cent a year tax-free over two years. To beat this, he would need a return from a taxable investment of more than 2.08 per cent, since (100% – 40%) × 2.08 = 1.25 per cent.

Sonny's friend, Ash, pays tax at a top rate of 50 per cent. He would need a return of 2.5 per cent from taxed investments to beat the 1.25 per cent tax-free from the NS&I certificates.

Higher or additional rate tax on income paid after deduction of tax

If you get interest after tax has been deducted and pay tax at the higher rate of 40 per cent or additional rate of 50 per cent, there will be a further tax bill to pay – as the first example on p. 82 shows. The higher rate tax will be collected by the Revenue in one of two ways:

■ by increasing the amount of tax you pay on your earnings through PAYE (see Chapter 3)

■ through the payments you have to make in January and July under the self-assessment system (see Chapter 3).

Grossing-up

If you receive investment income after some tax has been deducted from it, what you receive is known as the net income. But you may need to work out how much the income was before tax was deducted from it (the gross income).

You can find the gross income by grossing-up the net income using the ready reckoners in Appendix B, or by using the following formula:

$$\text{Amount paid to you} \times \left(\frac{100}{100 - \text{rate of tax}}\right)$$

> For example, if you receive £50 of income after tax has been deducted at 20 per cent, the grossed-up amount of the income is: £50 × 100/(100 − 20) = £50 × 100/80 = £62.50.

Too much tax deducted?

If too much tax has been deducted from your interest, the excess can be claimed back. This would happen if the rest of your income was below the level at which you pay tax or you pay tax at the lower rate of 10 per cent only on the rest of your income – as the second example overleaf shows. For how to claim back tax, see p. 45.

Tax-saving ideas 53 and 54

> If you pay tax at a top rate of 40 or 50 per cent, tax-free investments can be very attractive. Even if you could get a higher advertised rate of return on a taxable investment, the after-tax return could be considerably lower.
>
> If you have been over-taxed on your savings, claim a refund using form R40 (p. 45). You can go back four years to claim tax back – for example, if you claim by 5 April 2011, you can claim back tax paid as long ago as the 2006–07 tax year. Non-taxpayers can arrange to receive gross interest in future by completing form R85.

Not a taxpayer?

If your income is too low to pay tax, you can arrange with the bank or building society to be paid interest without deduction of tax. Fill in form R85 which is available from banks, building societies and post offices, as well as from tax offices and www.hmrc.gov.uk. Also see Revenue leaflet IR111 *Bank and Building Society Interest – Are You Paying Tax When You Don't Need To?* or www.hmrc.gov.uk/tdsi/key-info.htm. Once made, the declaration runs indefinitely, so remember to review it if your circumstances change (for example, on the death of a spouse). There are penalties for making a false declaration.

Arranging for interest to be paid without deduction of tax not only saves you claiming back the tax which has been deducted, you also get the money much earlier. But not all banks and building societies can manage to pay half the interest without tax deducted where only one joint holder is a non-taxpayer.

Example

Niamh Fagan gets £80 interest on her building society account in 2010–11. Tax has already been deducted from the interest at 20 per cent before it is credited to her account, so this £80 is the net (that is, after deduction of tax) amount.

To work out the gross (before deduction of tax) amount of interest, Niamh must add the tax back to the net amount. The grossed-up amount of interest is: £80 × 100/(100 − 20) = £80 × 100/80 = £100.

In other words, Niamh has paid £100 − £80 = £20 in tax and this covers her basic rate tax on the interest.

If Niamh should pay tax at 40 per cent on this interest, her overall tax liability is 40 per cent of £100 = £40. Since she has already paid £20 in tax, she has to pay only £40 − £20 = £20 in higher rate tax. This leaves her with £80 − £20 = £60 of interest after higher rate tax has been paid.

Example

Niall O'Halloran has earnings of £6,500 in 2010–11 and received interest from his savings of £400. The correct tax has already been paid on his earnings. Tax has been deducted from this interest at 20 per cent but Niall reckons he should be paying tax on it at the lower rate of 10 per cent only. He checks to see if he is due a rebate.

First he works out the gross amount of interest he received – the amount before deduction of tax at 20 per cent: £400 × 100/(100 − 20) = £400 × 100/80 = £500.

This means he has been paid a gross amount of £500 from which £100 of tax has been deducted.

He adds the £500 to the £6,500 of earnings to find his total income of £7,000. Like all taxpayers, he is entitled to a personal allowance of £6,475 for the tax year, so his taxable income is £7,000 − £6,475 = £525.

He has a starting rate band of £2,440. £25 of his earnings fall into this band and are taxed at 20 per cent (see p. 17). The remainder of the band more than covers his savings income, so the whole £500 should be taxed at 10 per cent. 10 per cent of £500 is £50, so he is due a rebate on the interest of £100 − £50 = £50.

Offshore bank accounts

Interest from UK banks and building societies is usually paid with tax deducted. But, if you have an account based in, say, the Channel Islands, Isle of Man or elsewhere offshore, the interest is generally paid gross. If you are a UK resident, you must nevertheless declare this interest and pay any tax due.

Tax-saving idea 55

The Revenue is pursuing a campaign to track down taxpayers who have failed to declare interest from offshore accounts. The Revenue has the power to force banks and other institutions to disclose details of customers with offshore accounts or credit card transactions linked to such accounts. Although it is now too late to take advantage of any special disclosure opportunities offered by the Revenue (except where you wish to disclose offshore holdings in Liechtenstein), you will still pay less in penalties if you voluntarily tell the Revenue about your foreign income than if you are found out later (see Chapter 4).

Sharia-compliant products

Alternative financial products, where the return is in the form of a share of profits or a mark-up paid at a future date, have been developed to comply with Sharia law. The return on these is treated in the same way for tax as interest.

Gilt-edged stock

Interest on all British government stocks (gilts) is usually paid gross – i.e. without any tax already deducted. But you can opt to be paid with tax at 20 per cent already deducted. To change the way your interest is taxed complete the appropriate form from Computershare (Tel: 0870 703 0143 www.computershare.com).

Corporate bonds

Interest from bonds listed on a stock exchange is paid gross (without any tax deducted).

Bond-based unit trusts

Unit trusts and open-ended investment companies (OEICS) that invest wholly or mainly in gilts and/or corporate bonds pay 'income distributions'. They are taxed like other savings income and paid with 20 per cent tax deducted. Distributions from share-based unit trusts are taxed differently (see below).

Shares and unit trusts

Dividends from UK companies and distributions from share-based unit trusts are paid with a tax credit – the amount is given on the tax voucher that comes with the dividend or distribution. The tax credit is 10 per cent of the gross amount. So if you receive a dividend of £80, the grossed-up amount of this dividend is:

$$£80 \times \left(\frac{100}{100 - 10}\right)$$

$$= £80 \times \frac{100}{90}$$

$$= £88.89$$

The tax credit is £88.89 − £80 = £8.89.

The tax on the grossed up amount of dividends and distributions is 10 per cent for starting rate and basic rate taxpayers. Since this is the same amount as the tax credit, they need pay nothing extra. Note that the 10 per cent tax credit does not eat up any of your starting rate band: you can still have up to £2,440 of savings income taxed at the 10 per cent starting rate in 2010–11.

If you pay tax at the higher or additional rate, there is extra tax to pay. Higher rate taxpayers pay tax on the grossed-up amount of dividends and distributions at 32.5 per cent. So on a net dividend of £80, your total tax bill is 32.5 per cent of the grossed-up amount of £88.89 = £28.89. Since you have a tax credit of £8.89, the higher rate tax due is £28.89 − £8.89 = £20. That leaves you with £80 − £20 = £60 after paying the higher rate tax.

As an additional rate taxpayer, you pay tax of 42.5 per cent on the grossed-up dividend. So, if you received £80, your total bill is 42.5% × £88.89 = £37.78. You have a tax credit of £8.89, so the additional rate tax due is £37.78 − £8.89 = £28.89. That leaves you with £80 − £28.89 = £51.11 after paying the additional rate tax.

The tax credit cannot be claimed back if the income is not taxable in your hands. So if your income is too low to pay tax you cannot claim it back. This means that if most or all of your income is dividends and distributions, you would not get the full value of your tax allowance.

Since 2008–09, dividends you receive from foreign companies are taxed in broadly the same way as UK dividends. You are treated as having a 10 per cent tax credit along with the dividend. For this purpose the dividend treated as received includes any foreign tax on it. You can set the tax credit against your UK tax bill (but cannot reclaim the credit if you are a non-taxpayer). In 2008–09 to qualify for the credit, you had to be a minority shareholder, meaning that you owned less than 10 per cent of the shares of the company concerned. Since 2009–10, this condition has been removed.

Property funds (REITs and PAIFs)

Investment trusts are companies, quoted on a stock exchange, whose business is running an investment fund. You invest by buying shares in the fund and, in general, your investment is taxed in the same way as any other shares would be.

However, on 1 January 2007, a new type of investment trust called a real estate investment trust (REIT) became available. A REIT is a company that invests mainly in a portfolio of rented commercial and/or residential properties. Provided various rules are met, including that at least 90 per cent of all the profits received by the REIT are distributed to shareholders, the REIT pays no tax on the profits.

As an investor, you pay tax on your REIT income at the same rate that you would if you invested direct in rental property. The REIT pays out dividends – called property income distributions – with tax at the basic rate (20 per cent in 2010–11) deducted. (From mid-2010, these can be stock, rather than cash, dividends.) If you are a non-taxpayer, you can claim this back. If you are a starting-rate taxpayer you can claim back part of the tax. Higher-rate taxpayers have extra tax to pay.

Since 2008–09, the same tax treatment is extended to open-ended investment companies that invest in property and meet the required conditions, called property authorised investment funds (PAIFs).

Tax-saving idea 56

You can hold REITs and PAIFs through an individual savings account (p. 97), self-invested personal pension plan (p. 95) or a child trust fund (p. 100), in which case distributions, as well as any gains from selling the shares, are tax-free.

Investing for capital gains

One way of reducing your income tax bill is to invest for capital gains rather than income. Capital gains tax is paid on increases in the value of investments – for example if the value of shares rises and then the shares are sold. Chargeable gains are taxed at a flat rate of 18 per cent.

But there's no tax to pay if your total net capital gains in 2010–11 are no more than £10,100. A husband and wife and civil partners can each make total net capital gains of this amount before paying capital gains tax.

Tax-saving idea 57

> Many people are careful to make the most of their income tax-free allowances each year, but overlook the tax-free capital gains limit. To make regular use of the limit, you could consider selling assets each year and buying them back later or immediately buying similar assets (p. 148).

For more about capital gains tax and how to minimise it, see Chapter 9.

Life insurance policies

Many types of life insurance build up a cash-in value that makes it possible to use them as a form of investment. With most, the insurance company has paid tax on the investment income and gains before paying out the return to you. In 2010–11 this is deemed to be equivalent to tax at the basic rate (the savings rate before 2008–09) but you cannot reclaim any of it even if you pay tax at less than this rate. However, provided certain rules are met, higher rate taxpayers do not have any further tax to pay on the return. There may be higher tax to pay if you cash in a savings-type life insurance policy after less than ten years or three-quarters of the term, if this is shorter (p. 217).

Many policies let you withdraw up to 5 per cent a year of the premium(s) you have paid without this counting towards your income for tax purposes at the time. The withdrawals are added to any other gain you make when the policy comes to an end and any tax due is payable in that year. If you are not a higher rate or additional rate taxpayer, there will be no more tax for you to pay on the gain itself, but it will count towards your adjusted net income and so could cause you to lose age allowance (pp. 24, 60 and 247). For more about the taxation of life insurance gains, see p. 217.

Tax-saving ideas 58 and 59

> Although there is often no tax for you to pay when you cash in a life insurance policy, the insurance company has already paid tax, which you can't reclaim. Other investments will usually be more tax-efficient. For example, consider unit trusts, investment trusts or open-ended investment companies as alternatives to unit-linked life insurance policies.
>
> If you get age allowance (pp. 24 and 60), bear in mind that an investment-type life insurance policy lets you withdraw money during the policy term without affecting your age allowance at the time, but you may lose age allowance in the year the policy comes to an end. Similarly, whatever your age, you may lose personal allowance if your adjusted net income exceeds £100,000 (see p. 24).

Tax-saving ideas 60 and 61

Everyone should try to make sure that they are saving for retirement through a pension – and the earlier you start, the better the pension you should get at the end. You can usually get tax relief at your highest rate of tax (but see below and p. 226). This means a contribution of £1,000 usually costs you just £600 if you are a higher rate taxpayer, and just £800 if you are a basic rate taxpayer in 2010–11. If your income level means you are losing tax credits, a £1,000 pension contribution could increase your credits by up to £390, or £67 if you just get the child tax credit family element. The effective cost of a £1,000 contribution after tax relief and credits could be reduced to £210 for a higher rate taxpayer and £410 for a basic rate taxpayer.

From 2010–11 onwards, if your income is the region of £100,000 to £112,950 you will be losing personal allowance. Making pension contributions can prevent some of this loss and means that every £1,000 you pay in contributions effectively costs you just £400.

60% tax relief

Pensions

The government offers tax incentives to encourage you to provide for your retirement by saving with an employer's occupational pension scheme or through your own personal pension or stakeholder scheme. These mean that saving for the future through a pension often provides a better return than any other type of investment:

■ there is tax relief on your contributions to the scheme (within limits)

■ any employer's contributions made for you are not taxable as your income or as a fringe benefit

■ the fund the money goes into pays no capital gains tax and some of the income builds up tax-free

■ you can trade in some pension to get a tax-free lump sum when you retire.

Restriction of relief from 2011-12

From 2011–12 onwards, some of the tax relief you get may be clawed back through an extra tax charge if:

■ your income before deducting your own pension contributions and any charitable donations you make comes to more than £130,000, and

■ your income as defined above plus any pension contributions made by your employer and any third party comes to £150,000 or more.

Pension contributions are broadly defined and include any increase in the benefits you are promised from a defined benefit scheme. (A defined benefit pension scheme is one where you are promised a level of pension at retirement calculated according to some formula – often based on your pre-retirement pay. Final salary schemes are the most common example.) The benefits will be multiplied by a factor to arrive at a deemed equivalent contribution value. In early 2010, the government had not published the factors, but they will be age-related and might, for example, be as high as 22 or 23 for someone close to the normal pension age for their scheme. The example below shows how this might work.

The main aim of the clawback will be to restrict relief on pension savings for high earners to just the basic rate. See p. 8 for an outline of how this will work. Mostly, the clawback targets additional rate taxpayers but some higher rate taxpayers will be caught as well.

To prevent anyone pre-empting the new clawback rules by making large pension contributions ahead of 6 April 2011, the government has also introduced anti-forestalling rules which affect contributions made in 2009–10 and 2010–11, and are explained in Chapter 13.

Example

Andy earns £180,000 a year and belongs to a defined benefit pension scheme through work. The scheme promises him a pension of 1/60th of his final salary for each year he has been in the scheme. Last year, he earned £170,000 and had been in the scheme ten years, so he was promised a pension of 1/60 × £170,000 × 10 = £28,333. This year, with a higher salary and one more year of membership, his promised pension is 1/60 × £180,000 × 11 = £33,000. This is an increase in his promised pension of £4,667 a year. Assuming he is close to retirement, under the proposed new rules, this may be deemed equivalent to a pension contribution of 22 × £4,667 = £102,674.

How much you can save

A single, unified regime for all types of pension scheme was introduced from 6 April 2006, replacing the previous patchwork of eight sets of rules. The new regime gives most people great flexibility over the pension schemes they use and the amount they can save.

There is no limit on the amount you can pay into registered pension schemes (which means virtually all occupational and personal schemes).

But you can get tax relief only on contributions you pay under age 75 and up to the greater of:

■ £3,600 a year, or

■ 100 per cent of your relevant UK earnings for the year. (Relevant earnings means earnings chargeable to tax, including, for example, salary, bonuses, taxable fringe benefits and profits if you are self-employed.)

This annual limit for relief applies to contributions paid by you and by most people on your behalf, but excludes, for example, contributions paid by your employer and amounts paid in by the government because you are 'contracted out' of part of the state pension scheme. It applies to the total of your contributions to all your pension schemes.

If you are a high earner, the amount you pay in may also be restricted because of the annual allowance (p. 91) and, from 2011–12, the claw-back rules described opposite with transitional rules in the meantime as described on p. 226.

Tax-saving ideas 62–64

Everyone – even a child – can put at least £3,600 a year into a pension scheme. You can make contributions on behalf of someone else – for example, your child or a non-working partner.

In any one year, you can get tax relief on payments into pension schemes up to 100 per cent of your UK earnings for the year. This may give you scope, for example, if you inherit a lump sum to invest the whole amount tax efficiently for retirement.

Usually your contributions have to be in money but if you get shares from an employee savings-related share option scheme or share incentive plan (see Chapter 16) you can transfer these tax-free to a pension scheme within 90 days of acquiring them. Future capital growth will then be tax-free and higher rate taxpayers will also pay less tax on any dividends they produce.

How you get tax relief: occupational schemes

If you pay into an occupational scheme, the contributions are deducted from your pay before income tax is worked out ensuring that you get tax relief on the contributions up to your top rate of tax.

How you get tax relief: other schemes

You get relief on contributions to a personal pension by making payments from which you have deducted tax relief at the basic rate (20 per cent in

2010–11). For example, if you want to pay in £3,600, you first deduct 20% × £3,600 = £720 and hand over just the remaining £2,880. The pension provider then claims the £720 from the Revenue and adds it to your scheme. In this way, £3,600 is paid in at a cost to you of £2,880. This system applies to everyone, even if they pay tax at less than the basic rate.

If you are a higher rate taxpayer, you can get extra relief through PAYE or self-assessment. Either claim through your tax return or tax review form P810. Extra relief is given by raising the threshold at which higher rate tax starts. In the example above, up to £3,600 would be taxed at the basic instead of higher rate giving maximum extra relief of (40 − 20)% × £3,600 = £720.

Tax relief on contributions to retirement annuity contracts can be given as described above. But normally you pay gross contributions and need to claim all the tax relief due through your tax return or form P810.

Tax-saving idea 65

If you are a starting rate taxpayer or non-taxpayer, you still hand over contributions to a personal pension after deducting tax relief at the basic rate. The relief is claimed by the provider from the Revenue and added to your scheme. In this way, you are getting a bonus added to your pension savings. As a non-taxpayer, for every £10 you contribute, the bonus increases your savings by £2.50 in 2010–11.

Examples

Marion Mould is an employee. Her monthly contributions of £50 to her employer's occupational pension scheme are deducted from her salary before tax is worked out under PAYE.

Margaret May is an employee. She saves for retirement through a stakeholder scheme. She saves £50 a month but hands over only £40 to the pension provider because she has deducted £10 basic rate relief (at 20 per cent in 2010–11). The provider claims £10 from the Revenue and adds it to her scheme.

Marcia Mumps is self-employed, saving £50 a month through a retirement annuity contract. She hands over £50 to the provider each month and claims tax relief through her tax return.

Example

In 2010–11, Arif Gupta has earnings of £60,000 on which he pays tax of £13,930. He inherits £48,000 and decides to pay the whole lot into a personal pension. The

£48,000 is treated as a net contribution from which tax relief at 20 per cent has already been deducted. The relief comes to £12,000 which is 20% × (£48,000 + £12,000). He also gets some higher-rate tax relief given by raising the threshold at which he starts to pay higher rate tax by the amount of the gross pension contribution (£60,000). This reduces his tax bill to £10,705, giving higher-rate relief of £13,930 − £10,705 = £3,225. In total, the tax relief on the contribution comes to £12,000 + £3,225 = £15,225. This exceeds the tax he would actually have paid due to the way relief is given on personal pensions.

Annual allowance

Each year you have an allowance to cover the increase in your pension savings and/or the value of your pension rights. If your savings/rights increase by more than the annual allowance, you have to pay tax on the excess at a rate of 40 per cent. The annual allowance for 2010–11 is £255,000 – see the table below for the level in future years. How the increase in your savings/rights from each scheme is measured depends on the type of scheme – your scheme can advise. The annual allowance does not apply in the year that you start to draw benefits. This clears the way, for example, for your employer to pay a large contribution to your scheme if you are retiring early. From 22 April 2009, the special allowance to claw back additional relief also applies (see p. 226).

Annual and lifetime allowances

Tax year	Annual allowance	Lifetime allowance (see p. 93)
2006–7	£215,000	£1.5 million
2007–8	£225,000	£1.6 million
2008–9	£235,000	£1.65 million
2009–10	£245,000	£1.75 million
2010–11	£255,000	£1.8 million
2011–12 to 2015–16	£255,000	£1.8 million

Tax-saving idea 66

Your employer can pay up to £255,000 into a pension scheme for you in the 2010–11 tax year. This can be particularly useful if you run your own company and so can control how much the employer (the company) pays in. The company gets tax relief on the contributions provided they are 'wholly and exclusively' for the purpose of the business. In practice, this means the contributions must be proportionate to the value of your work. Check the rules described on p. 226 to see if any of the tax relief on such contributions will be clawed back through a special tax charge.

Topping up your pension

The tax rules no longer put any restriction on the combination of pension schemes you have. For example, there is nothing to stop a member of an occupational scheme also paying into a personal pension, regardless of how much they earn. However, individual schemes may impose restrictions on who can join, so check the rules.

Options at retirement

Under the tax rules, you can start to draw your pension at any age from 55 (50 before 6 April 2010), though individual schemes may set their own age limits.

You do not have to stop work in order to start your pension. So, provided your employer and the pension scheme rules allow it, you could, perhaps, switch to part-time work while drawing part of your pension to top up your earnings.

Depending on the scheme, you may have various pension options:

- **scheme pension.** This is a pension determined by your occupational scheme

- **lifetime annuity.** All money purchase schemes (occupational or personal) must let you shop around with your pension fund to buy a lifetime annuity. This is an investment where you swap your fund for an income payable for the rest of your life

- **short-term annuity.** You use part of your fund to buy an annuity which pays an income for up to five years. You can then buy another short-term annuity or take up another option. But any short-term annuity must end before you reach age 75

- **income withdrawal.** You leave your pension fund invested and draw a pension direct from the fund. If you are under age 75, this is called an 'unsecured pension' and must be broadly between nil and 120 per cent of the lifetime annuity you could otherwise have had. From age 75 onwards it is called an 'alternatively secured pension', and, since 6 April 2007, a pension must be drawn and must be between 55 and 90 per cent of the comparable annuity for a person aged 75.

When you become entitled to start a pension, the tax rules let you take part of your benefits as a tax-free lump sum. The maximum tax-free lump sum is normally 25 per cent of the pension fund or, in the case of a defined benefit scheme, 25 per cent of the capital value of the pension plus the lump sum. The capital value of the pension is usually the yearly pension multiplied by 20.

Tax-saving ideas 67–69

Provided the individual scheme rules allow it, you can take a tax-free lump sum from any type of pension scheme – this includes additional voluntary contribution schemes and all contracted-out schemes.

If you opt for income withdrawal before age 75, you do not have to draw any pension at all. You could just take a quarter of your fund as tax-free cash and leave the rest of the fund invested for later. But income withdrawal involves extra costs and investment risks so is not suitable for everyone.

If you are at least age 55 and want to make a sizeable contribution to your pension fund, consider borrowing part of the outlay, immediately opting for income withdrawal and using the tax-free lump sum to repay the loan – see Example.

Example

Mark Fisher, aged 60, has relevant earnings of around £120,000 in 2010–11 and has £21,000 to pay into his personal pension. First he borrows £27,000, boosting the amount he can pay in to £48,000. This is treated as a contribution net of basic rate tax relief making a gross contribution of £60,000. He immediately starts income drawdown, opting for a nil pension but drawing 25% × £60,000 = £15,000 cash. As a higher-rate taxpayer, Mark also gets £12,000 higher-rate tax relief. He uses the lump sum and extra tax relief, £15,000 + £12,000 = £27,000 to repay the loan. Borrowing has enabled Mark's £21,000 investment to produce a pension fund of £45,000 (but less after charges). Note that anti-avoidance rules generally prevent this and other methods of 'recycling' the tax-free lump sum, but the anti-avoidance rules do not apply where the lump sum involved is no more than 1 per cent of the standard lifetime allowance – in other words £18,000 in 2010–11.

Lifetime allowance

There is no limit on the value of pension and other benefits that your pension schemes can provide. Instead, you have a lifetime allowance and anything above that is taxed at a rate of 25 per cent of the excess if drawn as (taxable) pension and 55 per cent if it is drawn as a lump sum. The lifetime allowance for 2010–11 is £1.8 million and is frozen at this level until 5 April 2016.

The total of any lump sums you take must not come to more than 25 per cent of your available lifetime allowance.

You have to compare the benefits you are drawing against the allowance each time there is a 'benefit crystallisation event'. These events are:

becoming entitled to a scheme pension or lifetime annuity, starting income withdrawal, reaching age 75 without having already started a scheme pension or lifetime annuity, becoming entitled to a lump sum, a lump sum being paid out on your death (see below), a larger-than-inflation increase in your pension after it starts, and transferring to an overseas pension scheme. Each benefit crystallisation event uses up part of the lifetime allowance leaving less to be set against the next event.

Example

In 2010–11, Bina Zengeza retires at 65. She qualifies for a pension of £40,000 from her final salary scheme plus a lump sum of £120,000. She also has £20,000 in an additional voluntary contribution scheme. Her schemes advise that the value of her pension savings and rights is £940,000. This is within the lifetime allowance of £1.8 million so there is no lifetime tax charge.

Small pensions

Provided you have reached age 60, if the total of your pension savings in all the schemes you have comes to no more than 1 per cent of the standard lifetime allowance (£18,000 in 2010–11), you can draw the whole amount as a lump sum rather than as pension. As usual, up to 25 per cent can be tax-free but the rest of the lump sum is added to your income for the year and is taxable. The standard lifetime limit is being frozen at £1.8 million from 2010–11 until 2015–16 and the government has stated that this means the limit for converting small pensions to lump sums is also frozen (at £18,000) unless special announcements are made otherwise.

Using pension schemes to provide life cover

On death at any age, a pension scheme can pay out pension(s) to your dependants. A dependant is your spouse or civil partner, children under age 23 and anyone else who was fully or partly financially dependent on you (which could include, for example, an unmarried partner with whom you shared household expenses).

If you die before age 75 and without having started to draw any benefits, a scheme can pay out a tax-free lump sum to your heirs (who do not have to be dependants). The lump sum may be provided by life cover and/or through paying out any pension fund.

If you die before age 75, having already started your pension or income withdrawal, a lump sum can still be passed to your heirs but only after deduction of income tax at 35 per cent. The lump sum may be provided by, say, an option available with an annuity or the remainder of your pension fund. Normally there will be no inheritance tax on this lump sum. The exception is where you had made choices to deliberately leave a bigger inheritance to heirs other than genuine dependants at a time when you knew you did not have long to live.

On death from age 75 onwards, a lump sum can be paid out only if it goes to a charity you have nominated. Otherwise any remaining pension fund must be used to provide dependants' pensions.

Originally, it was also possible to transfer any remaining pension fund to other pension funds of members of the same scheme but, from 6 April 2007 onwards, generally this would trigger such punitive tax charges (up to 82 per cent) that it is no longer worth considering.

It has long been possible to use pension contributions to buy life cover, which means that you get tax relief on the premiums you pay. The new April 2006 regime initially removed restrictions on the amount you could pay towards such cover. However, in a government U-turn, it is no longer possible to newly take out life cover through a personal pension. Where you applied for your policy before 14 December 2006, the policy can carry on and you continue to get tax relief on the premiums. For policies taken out since, tax relief ceased from 6 April 2007 onwards. Employers can still provide life cover through occupational schemes.

Tax-saving idea 70

If you are getting tax relief on premiums for life cover applied for before 14 December 2006 through a personal pension, be wary of switching to another policy or provider. Premiums for your new policy will not qualify for tax relief and so are likely to cost more overall.

Pension scheme investments

If you save through a self-invested personal pension (SIPP), you can choose how your pension fund is invested. However, the government puts some restrictions on your choice (by imposing hefty tax penalties). In particular, you may not invest either directly or indirectly in:

▧ tangible moveable property – for example, art, wine, cars, boats, jewellery, stamps, books and so on

▧ residential property (including beach huts). But you may invest in hotels provided you do not have any rights to stay there, prisons, care homes, student halls of residence, and similar. You may also invest indirectly through a real estate investment trust (p. 85) or through an investment vehicle that meets certain conditions. The conditions include: the vehicle holds at least £1 million of property or at least three separate properties and no single property accounts for more than 40 per cent of the total; and there are several unconnected investors, none of whom holds more than 10 per cent of the vehicle.

Protecting pre-April 2006 pension rights

If by 6 April 2006, your pension savings/rights already exceeded the standard lifetime allowance, you could have registered for 'primary protection' by 5 April 2009. This gives you a personalised lifetime limit equal to the value of your savings/rights on 5 April 2006. This limit is increased in line with increases in the standard limit. Any increase in your savings/rights above that – for example, because of exceptional investment growth – will be taxable. You can continue to build up more pension savings and rights if you want to, but they will be in excess of your lifetime limit and so taxed when you start to draw benefits from them.

Whether or not your pension savings/rights exceeded the lifetime limit by 6 April 2006, you might have asked for 'enhanced protection' by 5 April 2009. This ensures that all the savings/rights you had built up by 5 April 2006 will not be taxed however much they increase up to the time you start to draw benefits. But, in this case, you may not build up any further savings or rights – if you do, the enhanced protection is lost, though if applicable you can revert to primary protection instead.

Under the pre-April 2006 rules, it was possible to build up tax-free lump sums equal to more than 25 per cent of your pension fund. Provided the scheme has a record of your entitlement, you keep your right to draw this extra-large tax-free sum later on. But you normally lose this right if you transfer to another scheme. There was no need to register with the Revenue for this protection.

Tax-saving idea 71

There was no need to register to protect the right to a tax-free lump sum that by 6 April 2006 exceeded the 25 per cent rule. But, to escape an eventual tax charge, the scheme must have records of your entitlement. Write to the scheme asking it to confirm your entitlement and store its response in a safe place.

Increasing your state pension

For anyone reaching state pension age on or after 6 April 2010, you can qualify for the full state basic pension (£97.65 a week in 2010–11) provided you have paid or been credited with a full year's worth of national insurance contributions (called a 'qualifying year') for 30 years of your working life. Your working life is deemed to run from the tax year in which you reach age 16 to the last full tax year before you reach state pension age. A year will be qualifying if you were working throughout and earning more than a minimum amount (£97 a week in 2010–11) or had paid class 2 contributions for the self-employed every week. You may have credits for any week when you were, for example, unemployed, unable to work because of pregnancy, illness or caring for a child.

It has long been possible to fill gaps in your national insurance record during the most recent six years by paying voluntary class 3 contributions. As a temporary measure, in particular to help people who have gaps in their record because of family responsibilities, the opportunity to make class 3 contributions has been extended. If you reach state pension age between 6 April 2008 and 5 April 2015 and you already have at least 20 qualifying years on your record, you can buy up to an additional six years by paying voluntary contributions to fill gaps anywhere in your working life.

Tax-saving idea 72

If you have fewer than 30 qualifying years in your national insurance record, paying voluntary class 3 national insurance contributions could be a good deal. Each contribution costs £12.05 a week in 2010–11 or £626.60 for a full year. A year's worth of contributions would buy you £169 a year extra state pension, index-linked, and payable from state pension age for the rest of your life.

Individual savings accounts

Individual savings accounts (ISAs) let you invest tax-efficiently in two ways:

▨ **Cash ISAs**. These are savings accounts with banks, building societies or National Savings & Investments

▨ **Stocks and shares ISAs**. These are based on stock market investments, such as shares, gilts and corporate bonds or funds investing in these investments (for example, via unit trusts and insurance policies).

Originally, the government had promised that ISAs would be available only until 2010. But now the government has said that they will continue to be available indefinitely. See the table below for the amount you can invest each year.

How much you can invest in ISAs each tax year

Type of ISA	From 2010–11 you can invest[1]
Stocks and shares ISA	£10,200 less any amount invested in a cash ISA
Cash ISA	£5,100

(1) The March 2010 Budget included a proposal to increase these limits each year in line with inflation from 2011–12.

The lower age limit for investing in a cash ISA is 16. The limit for stocks and shares ISAs is 18. The accounts are provided by ISA managers – banks, building societies, insurance companies, investment managers and other financial institutions.

You can take your money out of an ISA at any time and there will be no capital gains tax to pay when you cash in part or all of an ISA. Interest and interest distributions from accounts and investments in an ISA are tax-free. Dividends and similar income are taxed at 10 per cent (because ISA managers cannot reclaim the tax credit – see p. 83). However, income from real estate investment trusts (REITs) and property authorised investment funds (PAIFs) (p. 85) held in an ISA is tax-free.

Tax-saving ideas 73–75

Saving through a cash ISA means no tax to pay on your interest. If you would, in any case, save with a bank or building society make sure you use your ISA allowance each year.

Higher rate and additional rate taxpayers pay less tax on dividends and similar income earned by investments held in a stocks and shares ISA. This does not apply to other taxpayers – their income is taxed the same whether these investments are held in or outside the ISA. But stocks and shares ISAs investing in gilts and/or corporate bonds produce tax-free income for everyone.

Stocks and shares ISAs can still be a tax-efficient growth investment if you normally use up your capital gains tax allowance each year or if you use them to invest in REITs or PAIFs, because these provide tax-free income when held within an ISA.

You declare neither income nor gains from ISAs on your tax return. This can give a big admin saving over holding investments outside an ISA.

Note that you have to be resident in the UK (unless you are a Crown servant working abroad, or their spouse or civil partner) to put money into an ISA, but if you go abroad after starting one, you don't have to cash it in – it still goes on getting tax relief.

Investing in ISAs

Normally you must pay cash into an ISA, so if you want to transfer in shares or other investments that you already own, you must sell them first and buy them back within the ISA. However, if you receive shares from a savings-related share option scheme or share incentive plan (see Chapter 16) you can transfer these directly into an ISA up to the maximum you are allowed to invest. So in 2010–11, you can transfer £10,200 of such shares into an ISA provided you made no other ISA investments in the tax year. There will be no capital gains tax to pay on the transfer and no capital gains tax on any profits on selling the shares later. You must make the transfer within 90 days of the shares being issued.

Each year, you can take out just one ISA of each type. (So you can't, for example, start two or more cash ISAs with different managers.) A cash ISA and a stocks and shares ISA can each be with a different manager. They do not have to be the same managers that you chose in earlier years.

You can transfer your existing ISAs from one manager to another. In the year the ISA was taken out, however, you can do this only by closing the old ISA and switching everything in it to a new one. Once the tax year in which you took out the ISA has ended, you can switch just part without closing the old one. Ask the ISA managers to organise the switch – if you withdraw cash yourself from one ISA to pay into another, your savings lose their ISA status and do not qualify for any more tax relief. Note that there may be charges for switching.

Since 6 April 2008, you can transfer your savings from a cash ISA to another cash ISA or a stocks and shares ISA. Savings in a stocks and shares ISA can be transferred only to another stocks and shares ISA.

Tax-saving idea 76

Try to use your ISA allowance each year. Unused allowance can't be carried forward. Once your savings and investments are in an ISA they carry on being sheltered from tax indefinitely and can give you good tax savings. For example, if you had used your full cash ISA allowance every year since ISAs started, you could have built up a fund of over £46,000 by the end of 2010, including tax savings of over £2,000 for a basic rate taxpayer and over £4,000 for a higher rate taxpayer.

Child trust fund

To encourage the savings habit and help young adults take advantage of opportunities that require some capital, the government has introduced the child trust fund (CTF). The scheme covers every child born on or after 1 September 2002.

A CTF is awarded automatically to your child if you are receiving child benefit and the child lives in the UK. You receive a voucher from the government for £250 with which to open the account. If your household income is low, the government adds another £250 to the fund. (Children in Wales get an extra £50, or £100 if household income is low.) If you haven't opened the CTF within a year, the Revenue will open it instead opting for a stakeholder account (see below). The government will pay a further amount (£250 or £500 depending on household income) into the account when the child reaches age seven. From 2010–11 onwards, the government contributes an extra £100 each year for a child with a disability (or £200 if severely disabled).

You, other family members and friends can also pay into your child's CTF. The maximum you can contribute between you is £1,200 a year. From April 2010, the government contributes £100 a year to the CTF of a child with a disability (£200 in the case of severe disability). This does not count towards the £1,200 a year limit.

Your child can't take money out of the CTF until he or she reaches age 18 but then there are no restrictions on the amount withdrawn or what it can be used for. The government has proposed that, on maturity a CTF should be able to roll over automatically into an ISA to encourage the young person to carry on saving.

Money in the CTF may be invested in a choice of ways – for example, cash, unit trusts or investment-type life insurance. Every provider must offer a stakeholder account that is invested at least partly in shares and is 'lifestyled' so that it automatically shifts towards safer investments as your child approaches age 18.

CTF managers are not able to reclaim the tax credit on dividends and similar income from share-based investments in the CTF, so such income is effectively taxed at 10 per cent. But other income and gains from investments in the CTF will be tax-free. CTFs can invest in real estate investment trusts (REITs) and property authorised investment funds (PAIFs) – see p. 85 – and the income, as well as gains, from these is tax-free within a CTF.

Tax-saving idea 77

If you give capital to your children and it produces over £100 income a year, that income will normally be taxed as yours. You can avoid this trap by investing in a child trust fund, friendly society tax-efficient plan ('baby bond'), NS&I children's bonus bonds or a stakeholder pension scheme.

Saving gateway

This is a new scheme to encourage saving that is open to low-income households from July 2010. Broadly it works like this:

■ the scheme is open to individuals on a low income and receiving working tax credit, child tax credit (CTC) at the maximum rate (in other words, household income no more than the CTC threshold of £16,190 in 2010–11), income support, incapacity benefit or the new employment and support allowance, severe disablement allowance, jobseeker's allowance or carer's allowance

■ you receive a letter from the government telling you if you are eligible. The letter is valid for a fixed period during which you can open an account if you want to. If your circumstances change after you have opened the account (for example, you stop claiming the relevant benefit), you can still carry on the account to maturity

■ accounts are run by banks, building societies and credit unions

■ accounts will run for two years

■ you pay up to £25 into the account each month

■ the government adds a bonus to the account that depends on the amount you have saved. The bonus is 50p for each £1 you save up to a maximum bonus of £300

■ your money also earns interest tax-free

■ you can withdraw your money (but not the government matching) at any time provided you leave at least £1 in the account. But government matching will restart only once you have built your savings back up to the level they were at before the withdrawal.

Investing in growing businesses

The government offers a variety of incentives to encourage you to invest in small and growing companies or to support social regeneration. The tax breaks are welcome, but bear in mind these are, by their nature, high-risk investments, so losses could outweigh any up-front tax relief and returns might not materialise to become tax-free. However, if a company does take off, your handsome profits will be sheltered from tax and at least losses can be set off against other capital or income. The main incentives are:

■ loss relief

■ enterprise investment scheme

■ venture capital trusts

■ community investment tax relief (unlikely to produce a gain – p. 106).

The table below broadly summarises the tax incentives you can get.

Tax reliefs for investment in unquoted trading companies

Type of investment	Income tax relief on amount you invest	Capital gains deferral relief	Tax-free income	Tax-free gains	Can set losses against taxable gains on other assets	Income tax relief on losses
Investing directly in unquoted trading company shares	No	No	No	No	Yes	Yes
Enterprise investment scheme	Yes at 20%	Yes	No	Yes	Yes	Yes
Venture capital trusts	Yes at 30%	No	Yes	Yes	No	No

Income tax loss relief

If you buy newly issued shares in an unquoted trading company and subsequently sell them at a loss, you can under the normal capital gains tax rules set the loss against capital gains you make on other assets (p. 137). Otherwise, you can deduct the loss from:

■ your income for the tax year in which you make the loss, and/or

■ your income for the tax year before the one in which you make the loss.

To be eligible for this relief, the shares must match the definition of shares that can qualify for the EIS (see below) and meet certain other conditions, but you do not have to have invested in the shares through an EIS.

You must claim loss relief in writing within one year of 31 January following the year in which you make the loss. For example, if you make a loss in 2010–11, you must make your claim by 31 January 2013.

See p. 347 for information about loss relief if you provide financial backing by being a non-active partner in a venture.

Enterprise investment scheme (EIS)

If you invest £500 or more in new shares issued by certain unquoted trading companies, you can get tax relief on the investment – provided you hold the shares for a minimum period of three years from the issue of the shares (or when the company starts trading if this is later). The period is not broken if the company floats on a stock exchange, provided the flotation had not been arranged at the time you invested in the shares.

Investments in EIS-approved investment funds that invest in such companies also qualify – even if less than £500.

If you dispose of the investments after the minimum period, there will be no capital gains tax to pay when you sell your investment.

You get income tax relief at 20 per cent on up to £500,000 from 6 April 2008 onwards (previously £400,000) of EIS investments in any tax year. From 2010–11 onwards you can elect to have part or all of the amount you invest treated as if it had been paid in the previous tax year. For 2009–10 and previous years, you could carry back only half your investment made by 5 October and subject to a maximum of £50,000 (£25,000 before 6 April 2006). With a married couple or civil partnership, each of you can invest up to these limits.

Making EIS investments can also allow you to put off paying capital gains tax made on other assets if you are able to claim capital gains deferral relief (p. 155). To get the relief, you must reinvest at least part of the proceeds within one year before and three years after receiving them.

The companies you can invest in must be unquoted; this includes those with shares traded on the Alternative Investment Market (AIM). They have to be trading companies, which excludes those engaged in banking, insurance, share-dealing, dealing in land or property, farming, market gardening, forestry, managing hotels, leasing and legal or accountancy services. From 2008–09, businesses involved in shipbuilding and coal and steel production are also excluded. From mid-2010 the company must have a permanent establishment in the UK, but can carry on its trade wholly or mainly elsewhere. Investments in schemes where a substantial part of the return is guaranteed or backed by property are also excluded.

Warning

The EIS rules limit your investment to smaller and possibly riskier companies:

■ from 6 April 2006, to be eligible for EIS, a company can have assets only up to £8 million (previously £16 million) including money raised from investors through the scheme

■ from 6 April 2007 onwards, a company must have fewer than 50 employees and the total venture capital the company can raise through EIS, VCT and similar schemes is restricted to £2 million over the previous 12 months.

You won't get tax relief on investments if you are connected with the companies – broadly this means being an employee or director or owning over 30 per cent of the shares. In deciding how much of a company you own, you must include the holdings of connected persons – your spouse, civil partner and your or their children, parents and grandparents (but not brothers or sisters) – and associates such as business partners. Once you have made your EIS investment, however, you can take part in the active management of the company as a paid director (or 'business angel') pro-vided you had not been connected with the company before you made the EIS investment.

You can't claim the tax relief until the company has carried out its quali-fying trade for at least four months, and you lose it if it ceases to do so within three years. If you sell the shares within the minimum period, you lose tax relief on the amount you sell them for (that is, if you sell them for more than they cost you, you have to pay back all the relief). If you sell the shares after the minimum period and the company still qualifies under the scheme there will be no capital gains tax to pay on any gain you make. If you make a loss, this can be set off against other income or capital gains (see loss relief on p. 102) – reducing your overall tax bill for the year.

Tax-saving ideas 78 and 79

If you want to put off a large capital gains tax bill (say, to a future year when you may have more allowances and reliefs available), consider reinvesting your money in an EIS and claiming capital gains tax deferral relief – but only if you are comfortable with this type of high-risk investment.

If you sold your business before 6 April 2008 and deferred tax on part or all of any gain by reinvesting it in EIS or VCT shares, you may still be able to claim entrepre-neurs' relief (p. 156) againsts the deferred gain when you sell the EIS or VCT shares on or after 6 April 2008.

Venture capital trusts (VCTs)

VCTs are a type of investment trust listed on a stock exchange whose business is investing in the shares of unquoted trading companies. By buying VCT shares, you are investing in a spread of small, growing companies. This should help to spread your risks, and the fact that the VCT is itself quoted may make it easier to find buyers if you want to sell your investment later on.

Warning

As with EIS, the rules mean your money is likely to be invested in smaller and possibly riskier companies:

■ from 6 April 2006, a VCT can have assets only up to £8 million (previously £16 million) including money raised from investors through the scheme

■ from 6 April 2007 onwards, a VCT can invest only in companies that have fewer than 50 employees and have raised no more than £2 million over the previous 12 months through EIS, VCT and similar schemes.

You must be aged at least 18 to invest in a VCT and you must buy the VCT shares when they are newly issued. There must be no promise or guarantee that you'll get your money back. But, from mid-2010, VCT shares can be preference shares.

The unquoted trading shares in which the VCT invests must meet basically the same definition as shares eligible for EIS (p. 103).

Provided you hold the shares for at least five years for investments on or after 6 April 2006 (previously three years), you get income tax relief on up to £200,000 invested in VCT shares each tax year. For shares issued during the two-year period 6 April 2004 to 5 April 2006, tax relief was increased to a rate of 40 per cent but is now reduced to 30 per cent.

You get tax relief on any dividends paid by the VCT provided certain conditions are met.

Provided you've held the shares for five (previously three) years, there is no tax on any gain you make when you sell VCT shares. But any loss you make is also ignored – so it can't be used to reduce capital gains tax on other assets or set off against your income.

Community investment tax relief

This scheme offers tax relief on money you invest or lend that is used to set up small businesses or community projects in socially deprived areas. (The scheme may also be extended to loans to individuals.) You cannot invest directly in these ventures – only via an accredited community development finance institution (CDFI).

You invest by subscribing for shares or securities in the CDFI or by making it a loan. Alternatively, some CDFIs are structured as banks with which you can open an account to make your investment. You can earn some return on your investment, which you can keep or donate to the CDFI's work.

You get tax relief equal to 5 per cent of the amount you invest in the year you make the investment and in each of the following four years, provided your money is still invested. This gives you a maximum of 25 per cent tax relief overall. Tax relief is given as a reduction in your tax bill. If the relief comes to more than your tax bill for the year, the excess is lost.

Claim the tax relief each year through your tax return (p. 238) or by contacting your tax office. For more details, see the Revenue leaflet CITM9900 CITR: *A brief guide for investors* from www.hmrc.gov.uk/manuals/citmanual/ CITM9900.htm. For details of CDFI schemes open to private investors, see the Community Development Finance Association website at www.cdfa. org.uk.

Example

In 2010–11, Sam lends £10,000 to a community development finance initiative. He can claim 5% × £10,000 = £500 tax relief to set against his tax bill for 2010–11. Provided the loan is not repaid, he can claim a further £500 relief in the tax years 2011–12 to 2014–15.

8

Making the most of fringe benefits

Many employers give their employees non-cash fringe benefits as part of their pay package. Typical examples are employer's contributions to a pension scheme, company cars, luncheon vouchers or interest-free loans to buy a season ticket for the railway.

Salary sacrifice

Increasingly, employers are offering flexible benefits where you choose which fringe benefits you want either within an overall allowance or in exchange for giving up some pay, called salary sacrifice. The benefits most commonly offered through salary sacrifice schemes are extra pension contributions, childcare costs and bicycles.

Salary sacrifice involves 'permanently' giving up part of your cash earnings in exchange for non-cash benefits. The arrangement may be altered again later and, in practice 'permanently' generally means for at least a year. (If benefits can easily be converted back to cash, the Revenue will tax them as cash earnings.)

Salary sacrifice can mean tax savings for both you and your employer (see Example overleaf). However, a reduction in your pay can have a knock-on effect on pay-related arrangements such as pension contributions, sick pay, maternity pay and tax credits (p. 66), so think through the arrangement carefully before going ahead.

Example

In 2010–11, Jan gives up £2,860 of her basic pay through a salary sacrifice scheme and gets £55 a week (£2,860 a year) in childcare vouchers. Before the salary sacrifice, Jan had gross pay of £28,000 which was reduced to £21,244 after tax and national insurance. After the sacrifice, her basic pay is £25,140 and her take-home pay plus vouchers comes to £22,131. The reduction in her pay is more than offset by the value of the vouchers and tax and national insurance savings of £886.60. Her employer also saves over £366 in national insurance.

Tax-free for all

Many fringe benefits are tax-free for all employees regardless of what you are paid – see the list below. Some other benefits are tax-free for some employees, but not all. There are more details of these on p. 117.

Your employer's goods and services

Where these are provided to you free or at a lower price than the public would pay, they are tax-free as long as they cost your employer nothing to provide. The courts have decided the cost to your employer is nothing if the extra (marginal) cost is nil regardless of the average cost. Tax-free items could include, for example, goods sold to you at the wholesale price, cheap conveyancing for solicitors where the firm does not have to take on extra staff, and free bus travel for bus company employees that does not displace fare-paying customers.

Tax-free mileage allowances

- If you use your own car for work, mileage allowance up the Revenue's authorised scale is tax-free. The scale is 40p per mile for the first 10,000 business miles and 25p for each additional business mile. See p. 116 for mileage allowance in excess of the authorised scale.
- Up to 20p per mile if you use your own bicycle for business.
- Up to 24p per mile if you use your own motorbike on business.
- Up to 5p per passenger per mile if colleagues travel on business in your car.

Tax-saving ideas 80–82

Many fringe benefits are tax-free, and even those which are not can remain good value for employees because the taxable value put on them may be less than it would cost you to pay for the benefit yourself. Try to take advantage of fringe benefits in negotiations with your boss. You do not normally pay national insurance contributions on fringe benefits unless they can be readily converted to cash.

With some fringe benefits, such as pension contributions and childcare vouchers, your employer saves national insurance too and so might be particularly willing to consider a salary sacrifice arrangement. Your contract is amended so you receive less salary but get extra benefits instead. This can be worth doing if you will be better off overall, taking into account the value of the benefits, the tax and national insurance you save and any savings your employer is willing to share with you. But check whether you'll lose out on other pay-related items, such as sick pay.

The government has announced that, from 6 April 2011 onwards, tax relief on childcare vouchers for new recipients will be restricted to the basic rate. Under the proposals, parents already getting vouchers at that date will continue to qualify for relief at their existing rate. Therefore to maximise your tax relief, if you are a higher rate or additional rate taxpayer using childcare, it makes sense to start a voucher arrangement before 6 April 2011.

Tax-saving ideas 83 and 84

If your employer pays mileage allowance at less than the tax-free authorised rates or doesn't pay any allowance at all, you can claim the shortfall up to the amount of the authorised rate as an allowable expense (p. 273).

The tax-free authorised mileage rates will not cover all your costs if you drive a gas-guzzler car. You can save most tax by using a small, fuel-efficient car.

Other tax-free travel benefits

- Travel to and from work in a company van you have to take home (including cost of the fuel used) provided your employer prohibits any other substantial private use of the van.

- For members of the police, fire and ambulance services, having an emergency vehicle available for private use if you have to take it home because you are on call.

- A car parking or bicycle space at or near work.

- The loan of bicycles and safety equipment for employees for cycling between home and work.

- Work buses that can transport nine or more employees; discounted or free travel on public bus services subsidised by your employer.

■ The cost of transport home if you are occasionally required to work after public transport has shut down or cannot reasonably be used.

■ Reasonable extra travel or overnight subsistence expenses paid to you because of disruption to public transport by industrial action.

■ Financial help with the cost of travelling to and from work if you are severely and permanently disabled and cannot use public transport. This could be the loan of a car provided it is adapted for your use and you are not allowed to make private journeys other than travel between home and work.

■ Travel expenses paid for your spouse if they accompany you when you go to work abroad subject to certain conditions.

■ Incidental overnight expenses (for example, newspapers and phone calls home) paid or reimbursed by your employer if you are away overnight on business. The maximum is £5 per night (£10 outside the UK). If more is paid, the whole amount not just the excess is taxable.

Tax-free financial benefits

■ Your employer's contributions to a pension, life insurance or sick pay insurance policy for you. (But premiums to a private medical insurance policy are a taxable benefit unless related to overseas business travel.)

■ Loans on preferential terms (including Sharia-compliant loans) where the total loan(s) outstanding does not exceed £5,000.

■ Pensions advice arranged by your employer up to a cost of £150 per employee per year. (If it costs more, the whole amount is taxable not just the excess.)

Tax-free meals, subsistence and entertainment benefits

■ Free or subsidised meals at work provided they are available to all employees and not in a public restaurant. However, from 6 April 2011 onwards, you will be taxed on this benefit, if it is provided to you through a salary sacrifice arrangement (or similar arrangements), since the salary sacrifice deal already gives you a tax and national insurance saving (see p. 107). Taxable value will be worked out according to the normal rules (see p. 114 onwards).

■ Luncheon vouchers (or equivalent) up to a maximum 15p per day.

■ Free meal on arrival if you participate in cycle-to-work days.

▦ Annual parties or similar functions, such as a Christmas dinner, which are open to staff generally and together cost your employer no more than £150 per head per year.

▦ Entertainment for you and your family provided by someone other than your employer purely as a gesture of goodwill – but not if there are strings attached or if the gift counts as payment for your services.

▦ Sports facilities generally available to all staff and their families (and not available to the general public).

Tax-free accommodation benefits

▦ Living accommodation provided it is either necessary for you to do your job, or beneficial and customary for someone in your line of work (for example, a caretaker). Not tax-free if you are a director unless you have no material interest in the company and you are either a full-time working director or director of a not-for-profit company or charity.

▦ Living accommodation (and other security precautions) provided as part of special security arrangements if there is a security threat to you because of your job.

▦ Council tax paid by your employer if either of the two living accommodation benefits above applies to you.

▦ Relocation expenses if you move home for your job, such as the costs of buying and selling property, some travel and subsistence costs, and bridging loan expenses. The maximum is £8,000 per move. Any excess is taxable.

Tax-saving ideas 85 and 86

Check carefully whether employer-provided childcare is a good idea for you. Anything your employer pays is balanced by a reduction in any working tax credit childcare element for which you qualify (p. 66). Bear in mind that if accepting childcare benefits ultimately means you are paid less, any pay-related benefits such as pension savings and life cover would be reduced.

Childcare vouchers from your employer can be used only to pay for approved childcare. This could include, say, a grandparent who gets approval, provided they also look after at least one other unrelated child and the care is not in your own home.

Other tax-free benefits

▦ Up to £55 (£50 before 6 April 2006) a week of employer-contracted approved childcare or vouchers to pay for such care. Approved childcare can include, say, a nursery, childminders or after-school club. The £55 limit applies per employee regardless of number of children. (See p. 109 for proposed restriction of tax relief on this benefit from 6 April 2011.)

■ Childcare (up to any value) in a nursery or play scheme run by your employer or at least partly financed and managed by your employer (often referred to as a 'workplace nursery').

■ Up to £3 (£2 before 2008–09) a week towards extra household expenses if you work from home under an arrangement agreed with your employer. (More if your employer has evidence to show you incur higher extra costs.)

■ Private use of a mobile phone provided by your employer. This includes more sophisticated handheld devices that include a mobile. For phones provided from 6 April 2006 limited to one per employee.

■ The continuing loan of computer equipment worth up to £2,500 even if for private use where the loan started before 6 April 2006. For loans after that date, the normal rules for use of an asset apply – see p. 126.

■ Changing room or shower facilities at work, provided they are available to all employees.

■ Routine medical check-ups or medical screening for you or your family.

■ Cost of medical treatment while working abroad (or insurance for it).

■ Equipment, for example, a hearing aid or wheelchair, provided if you are disabled and which is primarily to enable you to do your job even if you also use it privately.

■ Retraining and counselling costs paid by your employer when you leave a job, provided you have worked for your employer for at least two years.

■ The cost of fees and books for further education or training courses paid for by your employer if the course is either necessary or directly beneficial for your work, or if you are under 21 when starting a general education course. If you have to be away from your normal workplace for no more than 12 months and will return after training, some travel and subsistence too.

■ Payments from your employer up to £15,000 a year to cover lodging, subsistence and travelling if you are released to attend a full-time course lasting at least a year at a university or a technical college.

▨ Truly personal gifts from your employer of an appropriate size and nature (not cash), including gifts on marriage, and long-service awards of things or shares in the company. However, long-service awards are tax-free only if they are to mark service of 20 years or more, they do not cost more than £50 for each year of service and you have received no similar award in the previous ten years.

▨ Small non-cash gifts from someone other than your employer. To qualify, the total cost of all gifts you received from the same donor must be no more than £250 in any tax year and they must not be provided on any sort of conditions, for example, that you will provide a particular service.

▨ Suggestion scheme (incentive) awards (p. 263).

Tax-saving ideas 87 and 88

You can receive up to £156 a year tax-free from your employer towards additional household expenses without having to keep records if you have to work from home. Higher amounts can be tax-free but you'll then need records to back up the claim. Additional expenses might include, say, heating, lighting, metered water and business phone calls.

If you can arrange your work so that you count as self-employed rather than an employee, you will be able to claim a much wider range of expenses (see Chapter 17). But remember there may be disadvantages in not having the protection of employment law. For more about the distinction between employees and the self-employed, see p. 304.

Taxable for all

Four types of benefits are always taxable. These are:

▨ assets transferred to you or payments made for you

▨ vouchers (with a few exceptions – see p. 269) and any goods or services paid for by credit card

▨ living accommodation provided by your employer (apart from the few exceptions listed on p. 111)

▨ mileage allowances in excess of the authorised rate if you use your own transport for work.

Assets transferred to you or payments made for you

Your employer may give you as a present, or allow you to buy cheaply, an item such as a television set, furniture, groceries or your employer's own product. These payments in kind may be taxed in a number of ways depending on how much you earn and whether you have the alternative of cash instead.

If you earn less than £8,500 (p. 117)

The taxable value is the second-hand value of the payment in kind (whether or not you actually sell it). Since many assets have a much lower second-hand value than the cost of buying them new this can be advantageous to you.

If you earn at the rate of £8,500 or more (p. 117)

The tax rules are tougher for those who earn at a rate of £8,500 or more, or directors. They pay tax on the larger of:

- the second-hand value, or

- the cost to the employer of providing the asset, including ancillary costs such as installation or servicing. Remember, though, that if it is the employer's own product, you pay only the extra cost to the employer. So if it does not cost the employer anything (after taking into account anything you have paid for it) it should be tax-free.

If you are being given something you have already had the use of (apart from a car), the taxable value is the larger of the following, less any amount you have paid:

- the market value when you are given it (this basis always applies to a bicycle or up to £2,500-worth of computer equipment provided as a tax-free benefit), or

- the market value of the asset when it was first loaned out (either to you or to anyone else), less the total amount on which tax has already been charged. This is because assets which have been on loan will already have had some tax paid on them.

If you are given a car, for example on leaving a job, you are taxed on its second-hand value when you are given it, less anything you pay for it. If you buy your company car for a low price, you may have to pay tax on the difference between the price you paid and what your tax office reckons it would fetch on the open market.

Cash or perks?

You may be given the alternative of either a particular payment in kind, such as free board and lodging, or cash. If you have a perk you can convert into money either immediately or at short notice, you have to pay tax on the value of the cash alternative, even if you opt for the perk. However, note that there is a concession for some workers, including farm workers, and for cash alternatives to cars. And you usually will not be taxed on a reduction in salary in exchange for your employer paying for work-related training or lending you up to £2,500-worth of computer equipment under a pre-6 April 2006 arrangement.

Payments made for you

However much you earn, you pay tax on the full amount of any bill paid directly by your employer on your behalf, such as:

■ your phone bill

■ your personal credit card bill

■ your council tax (unless it is tax-free because you live in tax-free accommodation, see p. 111)

■ rent paid direct to your landlord

■ a tax bill.

Note, though, that this normally applies only to payments settled directly by your employer, for example to the telephone company, the credit card company or your landlord. If you were given cash to settle the bill yourself, it should already have been added to your other pay on your payslip and taxed through PAYE.

Vouchers and credit cards

You may be given a voucher for a particular service (for example, a season ticket), a credit token or a company credit or charge card. If so, you are taxed on their cash equivalent unless they appear in the list of tax-free fringe benefits on p. 269 (for example, childcare vouchers, gift vouchers which count as a small gift), or the voucher gives you access to benefits that are in the tax-free list, such as a pass for an employer-subsidised bus service. Cash vouchers worth a specified amount of cash will usually be taxed under PAYE.

For vouchers and cards which do count as a taxable fringe benefit, broadly speaking you pay tax on the expense incurred by the person who provided them, less any amount that you have paid yourself. You will not have to pay tax on any annual card fee or interest paid by your employer.

Company credit cards and charge cards are often provided as a convenient way of paying business expenses. But you will have to pay tax on anything which is not an allowable business expense.

Living accommodation

In some cases living accommodation may count as a tax-free fringe benefit – see the list on p. 111. But if it does not, it counts as a taxable perk however much you earn. It includes houses, flats, houseboats and holiday homes but not board and lodging or hotel-type accommodation where typically you get food and other services.

The taxable value of the accommodation is based on the higher of:

■ the rateable value of the property, or

■ if the property is let, the rent paid for it.

From the taxable value, you can deduct anything you pay for the accommodation, and also, if part of the property is used exclusively for your work, a proportion for that.

Rateable values are still used, although rates are no longer payable. However, for properties in Scotland, where rateable values were revalued more recently than elsewhere, only a percentage of the rateable value is used (found by multiplying the rateable value by 100 and dividing by 270). If there is no rateable value your employer will have to agree a value with your tax office.

If the tax is based on the rateable value, there may be an extra charge if the property cost more than £75,000, including the cost of any improvements made before the current tax year, but deducting anything you paid towards the cost. Broadly, you pay interest at the Revenue's official rate at the start of the tax year (4.75 per cent from 1 March 2009 – see p. 125) on the excess over £75,000, reduced in line with the number of days you do not have the property if it is provided for only part of the year. You can deduct any rent you pay not already deducted when working out the basic taxable value, and an amount for business use.

Mileage allowances

If, when you use your own transport for work, your employer pays you a mileage allowance that is more than the Revenue authorised rates (p. 108), the excess is taxable. This is the case even if your actual costs are so high that you do not make any profit from your mileage allowance.

Taxable for some, tax-free for others

The following benefits are tax-free if, for the particular employment, you earn at a rate of less than £8,500 and are not a director:

▓ a company car or van

▓ private medical or dental insurance

▓ services without a second-hand value, such as hairdressing at work

▓ loans of things or money.

However, these benefits are taxable for employees who earn at the rate of £8,500 or more. You cannot get around this by asking to be paid under £8,500 and getting substantial perks instead. To work out whether you earn at a rate of £8,500 a year, you need to take into account two rules:

Rule 1

Your earnings for this purpose are any kind of pay you receive for the job – that is, including your expenses and the taxable value of any perks worked out as if you earned £8,500 or more. However, you can exclude any contributions you make to an employer's pension scheme, and payroll giving donations.

Rule 2

The earnings are worked out assuming you work full-time for a whole year. So if you leave a job half-way through the year, having earned £5,000, you will still count as earning more than £8,500 – because in the second part of the year you would have earned another £5,000, that is, £10,000 in total.

If you are a director you are automatically counted as earning £8,500 or more unless all of the following three conditions apply:

▓ you are either a full-time working director or a director of a charity or non-profit-making concern

▓ you do not own or control more than 5 per cent of the share capital

▓ you earn under £8,500.

Your employer should take account of your rate of earnings when filling in your taxable benefits and their cash equivalent: you can tell what category you fall into depending on whether you get a form P11D (which is the form for people who earn at a rate of £8,500 or more) or P9D (the alternative form if you earn under £8,500).

Company cars

Some employers provide a company car that is also available for your private use (including travel between home and work). Since 6 April 2002, the way of taxing this benefit aims to cut polluting emissions and you'll pay a lot of tax if you drive a gas-guzzler. Some employers offer employees cash instead of a car and require you to use your own car for business – but the structure of the mileage allowance (p. 108) aims to stop you or your employer profiting from this move. If you only need a car for work occasionally, note that a 'pool car' is tax-free. To qualify it must not normally be kept overnight near your home, it must be used by more than one employee, and any private use must be a consequence of business use. But before you can work out which option is better for you, you need to be able to work out the taxable value of a company car and any free fuel you get.

Working out the tax on a company car

Here we explain how the rules work and the data you need, but rather than crunching the numbers yourself, you can use a calculator on the Revenue website at http://cccfcalculator.hmrc.gov.uk/CCF0.aspx.

The taxable value of your company car is usually its price when new multiplied by a percentage based on the carbon dioxide (CO_2) emissions figure for your type of car. There are five steps to arrive at the taxable value:

- take the list price of your car when new
- find out the CO_2 emissions figure for your car
- use Revenue tables to find out the percentage corresponding to that CO_2 emissions figure
- increase or reduce the percentage by any supplement or discount (but only if the car was registered on or after 1 January 1998)
- multiply the list price by the percentage.

If you had the car for only part of the year, you can scale down the taxable value in proportion to the number of days in the tax year it was not available. And, you can deduct anything you pay yourself for use of the car.

The car's list price when new

This is the list price of the car at registration (not the dealer's price), including delivery charges, VAT and car tax. Any contribution you make towards the cost of the car is deducted from its price, up to a limit of

£5,000, and the maximum price for tax purposes is currently capped at £80,000 (though this cap will be abolished from 2011–12). For cars without a list price, your employer will have to reach agreement with the Revenue, usually on the basis of published car price guides. The market value is used for classic cars worth at least £15,000 and aged 15 years or more at the end of the tax year.

Tax-saving ideas 89–92

If you use a car infrequently on business, a pool car from work may be a better option than a company car, since use of a pool care is tax-free. However, the Revenue carefully checks claims to ensure these truly are pool cars. In particular, you should avoid taking a car home overnight.

From 6 April 2010 to 5 April 2015, a zero-emission company car is a tax-free benefit.

The taxation of an inefficient company car is onerous. With the tightening of the car scales each year, increasingly this applies to medium-sized as well as large cars. If you are about to get a new car, consider a smaller, more fuel-efficient model.

Typically both the list price and CO_2 emissions of an automatic are higher than for an equivalent manual car. If your employer provides you with a company car that is an automatic because disability prevents you driving a manual car, the taxable value can already be based on the lower emissions for the equivalent manual. From 2009–10 onwards, you can also use the lower list price.

You cannot create an artificially low price by getting a basic model and adding accessories. The price includes any accessories fitted before the car was made available to you, and any accessories or set of accessories worth more than £100 which are fitted after that. Accessories needed because you are disabled are excluded.

The CO2 emissions figure

Cars registered in the UK from 1 March 2001 onwards have an official CO_2 emissions figure that is shown on the vehicle registration document. You can also get the figure for your car from the Vehicle Certification Agency website or a free booklet, *Car Fuel Consumption & Emissions Figures*. Contact: VCA (FCB requests), 1 The Eastgate Office Centre, Eastgate Road, Bristol BS5 6XX, Tel: 0117 951 5151 www.vcacarfueldata.org.uk.

Cars registered between 1 January 1998 and 28 February 2001 also usually have an emissions figure but this is not shown on the registration document. You can get the figure either free from the Society for Motor Manufacturers and Traders website (www.smmt.co.uk/co2/co2intro.cfm) or from the car manufacturer or importer (there may be a small charge).

Cars registered before 1998 – and a few other more recent but unusual models – do not have a CO_2 emissions figure. Instead, the taxable value is the list price multiplied by a percentage based on the car's engine size (see table overleaf).

The percentage charge

The CO_2 emissions figure is given in grams per kilometre. The minimum percentage of list price that you will normally be taxed on is 15 per cent. Over the years, this lowest 15 per cent rate is being progressively assigned to cars with lower and lower emissions. In 2010–11, it applies to cars with emissions of 130 g/km but this will be reduced to 125 g/km in 2011–12. The percentage increases in steps of 1 per cent for every extra 5 g/km up to a normal maximum percentage of 35 per cent – see table below. If the emissions figure for your car does not end in '0' or '5' you normally round it down to the nearest amount that does.

CO_2-related car benefit percentage charges for 2009–10 to 2011–12

% of car's price to be taxed	CO₂ emission figure (g/km)			% of car's price to be taxed	CO₂ emission figure (g/km)		
	2009–10	2010–11	2011–12		2009–10	2010–11	2011–12
10	120	120	110	25	185	180	175
15	135	130	125	26	190	185	180
16	140	135	130	27	195	190	185
17	145	140	135	28	200	195	190
18	150	145	140	29	205	200	195
19	155	150	145	30	210	205	200
20	160	155	150	31	215	210	205
21	165	160	155	32	220	215	210
22	170	165	160	33	225	220	215
23	175	170	165	34	230	225	220
24	180	175	170	35	235	230	225
					or more	or more	or more

Car benefit percentage charges for cars without a CO_2 emissions figure

Engine size	Percentage of car's price to be taxed	
	Cars registered before January 1998	Cars registered on or after 1 January 1998
Up to 1,400 cc	15	15
1,401–2,000 cc	22	25
Over 2,000 cc	32	35
Cars without a cylinder capacity	32	35

From 2012–13, the normal minimum percentage of 15 per cent is to be reduced to 11 per cent and this will apply to cars with emissions of 100 g/km. Currently, there are special reduced percentage rates for cars that have low CO_2 emissions, as follows:

■ zero-emission cars (in other words, cars that cannot emit any CO_2 when being driven). From 2010–11 to 2014–15, 0 per cent; from 2015–16, 9 per cent

■ cars emitting 75 g/km or less. From 2010–11 to 2014–15, 5 per cent

■ cars emitting less than the amount shown in the first line of the table opposite, 10 per cent.

For the purpose of these rules, you do not round your car's emission figure – it must be exactly at the threshold or lower.

Supplements and discounts for cars registered on or after 1 January 1998

If your company car is a diesel, you must add an extra 3 per cent to the percentage charge, but the overall percentage is still capped at 35 per cent. The diesel supplement is waived for some cars meeting EU standards for cleaner diesels, but the waiver was cancelled from 6 April 2006 for cars registered from 1 January 2006 onwards.

Tax-saving idea 93

If you drive a company car or van in central London, the taxable value of your vehicle already includes any congestion charges (or related penalty charges) that are reimbursed by your employer. There is no need to declare these amounts separately and no further tax to pay on them.

Example

Sanjay O'Rourke chose a new company car in March 2010. He could have any make or model up to a cost of £20,000. He was thinking about an Alfa Romeo 159. He checked its CO_2 emissions figure which was 218 g/km. The table on p. 120 told him that in 2010–11 he would be taxed on 32 per cent of the car's list price: 32% × £20,000 = £6,400. As Sanjay is a higher rate taxpayer, the car would cost him 40% × £6,400 = £2,560 in tax. Instead Sanjay opted for a Toyota Prius hybrid fuel (petrol-electric) car. It cost the same, but with an emissions figure of just 104 g/km, he is taxed on just 10 per cent of the list price, giving a taxable value of 10% × £20,000 = £2,000 and a tax bill of 40% × £2,000 = £800. Going green has saved Sanjay £1,760 tax this year.

Fuel for company cars

If you get a company car, you may get free fuel for private use as well. The taxable value of fuel is a percentage of a set figure, which is £18,000 from 2010–11 onwards (£16,900 in 2009–10). The percentage is the same as that used to find the taxable value of the company car (see table on p. 120). Therefore in 2010–11, the taxable value of fuel will lie between 10% × £18,000 = £1,800 and 35% × £18,000 = £6,300. The fuel charge is proportionately reduced if you stop receiving free fuel for part of the tax year or your company car is not available for the full year. There is no fuel charge for a zero-emission company car.

You can avoid the fuel charge if you are required by your employer to reimburse the full cost of fuel used for private purposes and you actually do so. Bear in mind that commuting between home and work normally counts as private use. But fuel provided for travel between home and work for disabled employees is tax-free.

Vans

A van available for your private use was very lightly taxed compared with a company car, but this changed from 6 April 2007 onwards. From 2007–08 onwards, the yearly taxable value is £3,000 a year. The taxable value is reduced if:

- the van is unavailable for part of the tax year in line with the number of days it is unavailable
- the van is shared with other employees. The taxable value is split between the employees concerned on a just and reasonable basis
- you have to pay your employer for your private use. The amount you pay is deducted from the taxable value.

From 6 April 2010 to 5 April 2015, the taxable value of a zero-emission van is nil.

The taxable value of fuel provided by your employer for private use of the van is £550 in 2010–11 (£500 in 2009–10), reduced by any amount you have to pay. The taxable value of fuel for a zero-emission van is nil.

Since 6 April 2006, a van you take home each night is a tax-free benefit provided the only private use you (and your family and household) are allowed to make is commuting to and from work. In practice, incidental private use – such as an occasional trip to the rubbish dump or stopping to buy a newspaper en route to work – is overlooked. But using the van to, say, do your weekly shop would breach the rules and bring the van into the taxable benefit rules above.

Tax-saving ideas 94 and 95

If your employer provides you with a van you take home at night, consider asking your employer to put in writing that you are not allowed to use the van privately. Then, provided any private use is only incidental, the van will be a tax-free benefit. Otherwise, the taxable value of the van and fuel will be £3,500 a year which would mean a yearly tax bill of 20% × £3,500 = £700 if you are a basic rate taxpayer.

Consider asking your employer to provide you with a zero-emission van. For five years from 6 April 2010, there is no tax on this benefit, even if the van is available for your private use.

Cheap or free loans

The basic rule is that if your employer provides a cheap or interest-free loan, you have to pay tax on the difference between the interest you pay and the interest worked out at an official rate – 4.75 per cent during 2009–10 and 4 per cent from 6 April 2010 (see table on p. 125). Where the rate changes during the tax year, you normally use an average rate published by the Revenue. You do not need to worry about any of this, however, if:

■ your employer lends money as part of its normal business, comparable loans were available to members of the general public (a substantial proportion actually being sold to them), and the loan was made to you on the same terms as those comparable loans. Such loans are tax-free

■ the total loans you have outstanding are no more than £5,000 throughout the tax year. If you have several loans, one of which qualifies for tax relief, then the qualifying loan is ignored when deciding whether the other loans fall within the limit.

Example

Lene Mikkelsen has a £10,000 loan from her employer to help buy a flat, at a special low interest rate of 2 per cent (compared with the average official interest rate of 4.75 per cent). She paid off £1,000 of the loan halfway through the year. The taxable value of the perk is £199 in 2009–10, worked out as follows:

Amount outstanding:

At start of tax year	£10,000
At end of tax year	£9,000
Average:	£19,000 ÷ 2 = £9,500

Interest payable at official rate	£9,500 × 4.75% = £451
Actual interest payable	£190
Difference (taxable value)	£261

Lene is a basic rate taxpayer, so the loan costs her 20% × £261 = £52.20 in tax in 2009–10.

To work out the tax on a loan, you take the average amount owing during the year (the whole amount, not just the amount above £5,000), adjusted if the loan was only outstanding for part of the year. You then multiply the average loan by the average official rate of interest for the period in the year during which the loan was outstanding – see the table opposite or, for earlier years, the Revenue website, www.hmrc.gov.uk/rates/interest -beneficial.htm for actual and average rates. Lastly, you deduct the interest you were actually liable to pay during the tax year, to find the amount on which you will be taxed.

If you think that you will lose out under this averaging method, you can choose to calculate the figures using the daily amounts of the loan and official rates of interest. However, you have to use the same method for all your taxable loans, and the calculations can get quite complex. If you want to make this choice, you have to tell your tax office within 12 months of 31 January falling after the end of the relevant tax year.

Note that under either method, if the loan qualifies for tax relief, you get tax relief on both the interest you actually paid and the difference between that and the official rate of interest. Effectively, the tax relief is worked out assuming you paid the official rate of interest.

HM Revenue & Customs official interest rate

Tax year	Average rate for year	Date rate changed	Rate
2006–07	5.00%	6 April 2006	5.00%
2007–08	6.25%	6 April 2007	6.25%
2008–09	6.10%	1 March 2009	4.75%
2009–10	4.75%	6 April 2010	4.00%

Private medical or dental insurance

If your employer pays premiums for a private medical expenses policy for you (for example, through a group scheme for all employees), the amount is a taxable benefit. The same applies to dental insurance schemes. You pay tax on the cost to your employer, less any amount you pay for the benefit. However, private medical insurance is a tax-free benefit if related to overseas business travel.

Other benefits

There is a variety of other perks taxable only if you earn at the rate of £8,500 a year or more. These include:

■ relocation expenses that would normally be tax-free but which are above the £8,000 tax-free limit for each move

■ approved childcare paid for by your employer in excess of the £55 limit (p. 111). This does not apply to 'workplace nurseries', which are not subject to the £55 limit

■ services supplied, such as free hairdressing, holidays, gardening or a free chauffeur – but remember that you pay tax only on the extra cost to your employer, so services that your employer provides as part of their normal business may be tax-free

■ share schemes or share options that are not tax-free – see Chapter 16

■ subscriptions and fees paid for by your employer for you to join professional bodies, societies, leisure or sports clubs, etc. Note that if you had paid a professional subscription yourself and could have claimed the cost against your tax because it was necessary for your work (p. 276), there would be no tax charge

- any income tax paid for you by your employer, other than through PAYE. This may sometimes apply if PAYE was not deducted from your pay at the proper time, and the tax was later paid for you or if there was insufficient pay from which to deduct the tax under PAYE

- the value of anything provided for your use, except for cars, vans, mobile phones and living accommodation (for example, a television, furniture, a yacht or aircraft). The value is 20 per cent of the market value when it was first provided (to you or to anyone else), plus any expense of providing it met by your employer. If you are later given whatever it is, you will be taxed as explained on p. 113

- help with educating your children (unless this is nothing to do with your job, for example it is pure coincidence that your child gets one of the generally available scholarships your employer's firm provides).

9

Minimising capital gains tax

From 2008–09, there were major changes to the capital gains tax rules. This chapter describes the new rules that you will need when completing your 2009–10 tax return and the old simpler rules that you will need if you are revising your tax return for a year earlier than 2008–09.

If you own items that increase in value, you may find yourself paying capital gains tax. For example, shares, unit trusts, land, property and antiques can increase in price, giving you a capital gain. If you sell them – or even give them away – you may be faced with a tax bill at a flat rate of 18 per cent of the chargeable gain in 2009–10 and up to 40 per cent in earlier years. In April 2010, the rate was still 18 per cent, but it was expected that this might be increased after the General Election.

The average taxpayer is unlikely to pay capital gains tax, however. There is a long list of assets on which gains are tax-free (pp. 128–129). And you have an annual tax-free allowance (£10,100 in 2009–10 and 2010–11). If you are selling a business, from 2008–09 onwards you may be able to claim entrepreneurs' relief (p. 156).

When might tax be due?

You may have to pay this tax whenever you dispose of an asset. What is meant by dispose is not defined by law. But if you sell an asset, swap one asset for another or give something away, this will normally count as a disposal. So will the loss or destruction of an asset (although not if you replace or restore it by claiming on an insurance policy, or by using compensation received).

There are some occasions when there is no capital gains tax to pay, regardless of what is being disposed of or how much it is worth:

- assets passed on when someone dies
- gifts to a husband or wife or between civil partners, unless separated
- gifts to charity and community amateur sports clubs.

Although there are no taxable gains in these circumstances, there are also no losses if the asset is worth less than when you acquired it.

Tax-saving idea 96

If you are thinking of making a gift to charity of an asset which is showing a loss, think again. You won't be able to claim the loss to reduce other taxable gains (though with gifts of quoted shares or property, you may be able to claim income tax relief – see p. 234). Ideally, find something which is showing a taxable gain to give – there will be no tax to pay on the disposal. Alternatively, sell the asset which is showing a loss and give the proceeds to the charity. That would create an allowable loss which could reduce your tax bill on other disposals.

Example

Leonie Dale is trying to decide whether to give some shares worth £12,000 to a charity or whether to make a cash donation. If she sells the shares on the stock market, they would produce an allowable loss of £10,000. But she sold her share of a rental property earlier in 2009–10, making a chargeable gain of £10,000. Because she has already used up her tax-free allowance, her best course of action would be to sell the shares and give the resulting proceeds to charity. She can then deduct the loss on the shares from the gain on the property sale, saving herself £1,800 capital gains tax.

Tax-free gains

There is no capital gains tax to pay on any gain you make on the following assets:

- your home (though not a second home in most cases – see Chapter 6)
- private cars
- wasting assets with a useful life of 50 years or less (for example, a boat or caravan), so long as you could not have claimed a capital allowance on it

- personal belongings – known as chattels – sold for less than £6,000 (p. 134)

- British money, including sovereigns dated after 1837

- foreign currency for your personal spending abroad (including what you spend on maintaining a home abroad), but not foreign currency accounts

- gains on insurance policies, unless you bought them and were not the original holder, or your wife did so and gave them to you (though you may have to pay part of the insurance company's capital gains tax bill – see p. 217)

- betting, pools or lottery winnings

- National Savings & Investments such as NS&I Certificates and Capital Bonds

- Individual savings accounts (ISAs) – see p. 97

- Enterprise Investment Scheme (EIS) shares, provided you have owned them for a minimum period and they carried on their qualifying activity for at least three years – see p. 103

- shares in venture capital trusts (VCTs) – see p. 105

- terminal bonuses on Save-As-You-Earn (SAYE) contracts

- British government stock and any options to buy and sell such stock

- certain corporate bonds such as company loan stock and debentures issued after 13 March 1984 and options to buy and sell such bonds

- interests in trusts or settlements, unless you bought them

- decorations for bravery, unless you bought them

- gifts to certain bodies (such as museums) and gifts of certain heritage property in line with the inheritance tax exemptions (p. 162)

- gifts to charity and to community amateur sports clubs

- damages or compensation for a personal injury or wrong to yourself or in your personal capacity (for example, libel)

- compensation for being given bad investment advice that left you worse off after being persuaded to buy a personal pension between 29 April 1988 and 30 June 1994

- from 6 April 2008 onwards, sale of a business or business assets if you can claim entrepreneurs' relief – see p. 156.

Tax-saving idea 97

If your spouse or partner is terminally ill, consider giving them any assets you own that are showing large taxable gains, assuming your spouse or partner plans to leave you their estate in their will. There is capital gains tax neither on the transfer to them nor on death. Moreover, you inherit the assets at their market value at the time of death, wiping out the previous gains. Bear in mind that the initial gift will not be accepted as genuine and will not save the intended tax, if leaving the assets back to you in the will is a condition of the gift.

Disposals of land to housing associations may also be free of capital gains tax.

If an asset is one where there is no capital gains tax to pay on disposal, any loss you make on it cannot normally be used to reduce your overall tax bill. Exceptions are enterprise investment scheme shares (p. 103) and chattels worth £6,000 or less (p. 134).

Who has to pay?

Capital gains tax applies to you as an individual in your private life or in your business whether self-employed or in partnership. Trustees may also have to pay capital gains tax on the assets that are held in trust (see below).

Executors of the estate of someone who has died may have to pay capital gains tax on any increase in value of estate assets between the death and distributing them to beneficiaries.

Any capital gains tax for 2010–11 will have to be paid by 31 January 2012, along with the final payment for any income tax still unpaid from the same tax year. Capital gains tax for 2009–10 will have to be paid by 31 January 2011.

Married couples and civil partners

A husband and wife are treated as two single people for capital gains tax purposes, and each is responsible for paying their own capital gains tax bills. With assets jointly owned by husband and wife – second homes, shares, valuables and so on – the gain or loss should be split 50:50 between you unless you own them in different shares.

You may have filled in form 17 (p. 58) to allocate income from the asset in unequal shares. If so, the same shares are presumed to apply for capital gains tax. Otherwise, the gain or loss is split in whatever proportions the evidence supports. If you have no evidence, the split is assumed to be 50:50.

Since 5 December 2005, same sex couples who register their relationship as a civil partnership are treated for tax in the same way as married couples.

Trusts

Where assets are held in trust, the trustees are liable for capital gains tax on disposals of the assets in the trust, in much the same way as individuals. The rate of capital gains tax paid by trustees is 18 per cent in 2009–10 and 2010–11 (at the time of writing, although this may be reviewed following the General Election).

Trusts are entitled to a tax-free capital gains tax allowance in the same way as individual taxpayers. For most trusts, the allowance is half the figure that applies to individuals. So for 2009–10 and 2010–11, the first £5,050 of net chargeable gains is free of tax for a trust. Trusts for certain disabled people get the same tax-exemption as individuals: £10,100 for 2009–10 and 2010–11.

Estates

There is no capital gains tax on assets you leave when you die. But any increase in their value between your death and their being distributed may be taxed at the same rate that applies to trusts: 18 per cent in 2009–10 and 2010–11 (at the time of writing). The executors (or administrators if there is no will) are responsible for paying the tax.

In the tax year of death and the following two tax years, the executors are entitled to the same tax-free capital gains tax that individuals get (£10,100 in 2009–10 and 2010–11). After that, there is no tax-free allowance at all. Therefore, executors may wish to ensure that before the start of the third year assets, even if still unsold, are transferred to beneficiaries, who can then set their own tax-free allowances against any gains.

How to work out the gain or loss

The starting point for working out your tax bill is to calculate the net gain or loss you have made. This is simply:

Final value − Initial value − Allowable expenses.

But in some situations special rules apply – see opposite and, for shares and similar investments, p. 145.

Initial and final value

The final value is normally what you get for selling an asset or its market value when you give it away. The initial value is usually what you paid for it or its market value when you first acquired it. If you acquired something by inheritance, its initial value is its probate value.

With a gift, the value is its market value: what anyone selling it at the time of the gift would get for it on the open market. However, in certain circumstances, the initial value of a gift may be what the giver acquired it for if you agreed at the time of the gift to take over the giver's capital gain (p. 153).

The market value is also the final value if you dispose of an asset to a connected person, however much you sell it for. For capital gains tax, a connected person includes your husband or wife, your business partner and their spouse, a relative of yours or these others (brother, sister, parents, child, grandchild) and the spouse of one of these relatives.

When a person (the settlor) puts money or assets into trust, the trustees become connected with the settlor (and any people connected to the settlor).

If you have owned something since before 31 March 1982 and you dispose of it on or after 6 April 2008, the initial value is set at the market value on 31 March 1982. The actual price or value you acquired it at is not relevant and you cannot claim any otherwise allowable expenses incurred on or before that date. If you disposed of it before 6 April 2008, special rules apply – see opposite.

Allowable expenses

Deducting the initial value of an asset from its final value gives you the gross capital gain or gross capital loss. However, you can then deduct certain allowable expenses in computing the gain on an asset for capital gains tax. These include:

■ acquisition costs, such as payments to a professional adviser (for example, surveyor, accountant, solicitor), conveyancing costs and stamp duty, and advertising to find a seller

■ what you spend improving the asset (though not your own time)

provided the improvement is still reflected in the asset when you dispose of it

■ what you spend establishing or defending your rights or title to the asset

■ disposal costs, similar to acquisition costs, but including the cost of valuing it for capital gains tax.

Deducting these expenses gives you the net capital gain or net allowable loss. If the asset was a gift to you and the giver got hold-over relief (see p. 153), you can also claim any allowable expenses incurred while the giver owned it.

Tax-saving idea 98

If you own a second home, investment property, antiques, collectables or other valuables, keep careful records of what they cost you to buy and maintain. You could face a capital gains tax bill when you dispose of them but allowable expenses can reduce the bill.

Special rules

Assets owned on or before 31 March 1982

If you owned an asset on or before 31 March 1982, only the gain since that date is liable to capital gains tax. Any gain made before 1 April 1982 is effectively tax-free.

With such assets, if you dispose of them on or after 6 April 2008, the initial value is always the market value on 31 March 1982 and you do not deduct expenses incurred on or before that date.

If you disposed of such assets before 6 April 2008, the initial value is *normally* the market value on 31 March 1982 with no account for expenses on or before that date. And indexation allowance (p. 140) runs from March 1982.

However, another approach, which does take into account earlier expenses, could be adopted in some cases. But only for pre-6 April 2008 disposals and not if you had made a 'rebasing election', which meant that you had chosen for all your gains and losses on assets owned on or before 31 March 1982 to be based on their market value at that date. The rebasing election had to be made within two years of the first disposal of such an asset and was irrevocable.

Personal belongings – chattels

Personal belongings with a useful life of less than 50 years count as wasting assets and any gains on their disposal are tax-free (p. 128). When more enduring personal belongings – often referred to as chattels or tangible moveable property – are sold for less than £6,000, the gain is also tax-free. Chattels include, for example, furniture, silver, paintings and so on. A set (for example, a silver tea-set) counts as one chattel for this exemption.

Example

> William Baxter bought a piece of furniture for £4,000 and sold it for £7,500 in 2010–11. This produces a gain of £7,500 − £4,000 = £3,500. The sale price is over the £6,000 chattels limit so the gain is not tax-free. But for capital gains tax purposes, the gain cannot be more than 5/3 of £7,500 − £6,000. This is 5/3 of £1,500 = £2,500, thus reducing William's taxable gain by £1,000.

If a chattel is sold for more than the tax-free limit, the taxable gain is restricted to 5/3 of the amount of the disposal value over the limit. So the maximum gain on a chattel sold for £7,200 would be 5/3 of £7,200 − £6,000 = 5/3 of £1,200 = £2,000.

In most cases, disposing of an asset that would produce a tax-free gain means that you cannot claim any allowable loss made on such an asset. With a chattel, you can claim a loss even if it is sold for less than £6,000 – but the loss is calculated as if it had fetched £6,000.

Example

> William Baxter sold a painting for £4,500 which he had bought for £9,500. His gross loss is calculated as if he had sold it for £6,000: it is therefore £9,500 − £6,000 = £3,500 – rather than the £5,000 loss William actually made.

For more about chattels, ask for Help Sheet HS293 *Chattels and capital gains tax.*

Tax-saving idea 99

> The generous treatment of chattels means that collecting can be a very tax-efficient activity. This is especially true if the items in the collection can be sold individually and so taxed separately instead of being treated as a set. This might apply to, say, rare books or unrelated bits of silver.

Gifts

With some things you are given, you may have agreed to take over the giver's capital gains tax bill by agreeing to a claim for hold-over relief (p. 153). Since 14 March 1989, this can be done for only a limited range of gifts, but before that date it could be done with almost anything.

When you come to dispose of an asset on which hold-over relief has been claimed when you got it, its initial value is what the giver acquired it for, not its market value when you were given it.

Part disposals

If you dispose of part of an asset, you will need to allocate expenses between the part you are getting rid of and the part you have kept.

Any expense connected only with the part being disposed of can be fully deducted from the proceeds in working out the gain. Anything connected only with the part you are keeping cannot be deducted. But some of the expenditure will be impossible to allocate in this way, and will thus have to be divided between the two parts, in proportion to their value. The proportion of such a cost that you can deduct from the gain is as follows:

$$\frac{\text{Disposal proceeds}}{\text{Disposal proceeds} + \text{Value of the part retained}}$$

Example

When Melanie Hill sold her holiday cottage in September 2010 for £138,000, she feared an enormous capital gains tax bill – she had bought it in August 1996 for £72,000. But she soon realised there were a lot of expenses she could claim to reduce the capital gain:

▒ acquisition costs of £1,935 – the £790 legal bill incurred in buying it, the £720 stamp duty and the £425 surveyor's fee for inspecting and valuing it

▒ improvement costs of £18,750 – the cost of installing modern plumbing and central heating, rewiring and building an extension which were all paid for in May 1995

▒ disposal costs of £4,140 – legal bills for the sale of £1,725 and £2,415 commission paid to the estate agent.

▶

The net capital gain is worked out as follows:

Final value		£138,000
minus allowable expenses:		
original cost	£72,000	
acquisition costs	£1,935	
improvement costs	£18,750	
disposal costs	£4,140	
Total allowable expenses		£96,825
Net capital gain		**£41,175**

Melanie will not pay tax on the full net gain because she can also deduct her tax-free allowance (p. 139).

There are special rules for allocating costs to shares and unit trusts where holdings are divided or added to (p. 145).

Example

Martin Thompson buys a house which he converts into a pair of flats. He spends £5,000 converting one into a weekend retreat for himself and £3,000 on doing up the other one to sell off.

Each of the flats is given identical valuations at the time of the sale. So any money spent on the whole house can be divided equally between the two flats. He can therefore claim the following expenses to reduce the gain on the flat he sells off:

■ the £3,000 spent improving the flat he sells off

■ the expenses of selling the flat

■ half the expenses of buying the house including the purchase price.

Working out the bill – 2008–9 onwards

For disposals you make on or after 6 April 2008, capital gains tax is greatly simplified:

■ *Step 1*: Work out each net gain as described above.

■ *Step 2*: Deduct any special reliefs – for example, when you sell your only or main home (see Chapter 6) or your business (p. 156).

■ *Step 3*: Add together all your gains for the tax year and deduct any capital losses (see opposite).

■ *Step 4*: Subtract your annual allowance (p. 139).

■ *Step 5*: Multiply the result by the tax rate (p. 139).

Capital losses

Current year losses

If the initial cost of an asset and its expenses add up to more than its final value, you have made a net capital loss on that asset. Net capital losses are deducted from your chargeable gains for the same tax year to find the total chargeable gain on which your capital gains tax bill is based. If your net capital losses are bigger than your total chargeable gains, the difference – your net allowable loss – can be carried over to reduce your chargeable gains in later tax years.

Note that a loss made when you dispose of an asset to a connected person (p. 132) can be set off only against a gain made on a disposal to the same connected person. This is called a 'clogged loss' and applies even if the loss was made when you disposed of the asset for a genuine commercial value.

Warning

For disposals made on or after 6 December 2006, you cannot claim as an allowable loss, any loss you make as a result of an arrangement if a main purpose of the arrangement was to save tax. The legislation is very widely drawn and could potentially catch any type of transaction. The Revenue have specifically said that it does not apply, for example, to timing your disposals so that losses can be set against gains for the same tax year, or giving an asset to your spouse or civil partner so they can sell it to realise a loss to set against other capital gains they have. Provided there is either a permanent change in who owns the assets or you are exposed to a genuine commercial risk (for example, you sell shares and buy them back more than 30 days later), you probably will not be caught by the anti-avoidance rule. But it is unclear whether, say, selling shares to crystallise a loss and immediately buying them back within an individual savings account (p. 148) would be attacked.

Tax-saving idea 100

You usually have to deduct losses made in the same tax year as a gain even if this takes your chargeable gains below the level of your tax-free allowance. This means some allowance is wasted. You may be able to avoid this if you can dispose of the item bearing the loss to a connected person. The loss is then clogged and can only be set against gains on disposals to the same person.

Example

> Gus Henry made chargeable gains of £10,000 in 2010–11 and allowable losses of £4,000 in the same year. All the losses have to be set off against the gains for this tax year, even though this brings the net chargeable gain below the tax-free allowance of £10,100 for the tax year.
>
> So his net chargeable gain is £10,000 − £4,000 = £6,000 – on which no tax is payable.

Losses from previous years

If your net chargeable gain for the tax year is bigger than the tax-free allowance, you must use any losses from previous tax years to reduce your tax bill. If you have enough such losses, you must reduce your total chargeable gain to the level of the tax-free allowance and pay no capital gains tax at all. Note that – unlike with losses from the same tax year – you don't have to deduct more than is necessary to get down to the tax-free amount.

If your losses from previous tax years are not sufficient to reduce your total chargeable gain below the level of the tax-free allowance, then they can still be used to reduce your capital gains tax bill.

In general, losses can never be carried back to an earlier tax year. An exception is when you die. On death, your executors can carry back losses to set against gains you made in the three previous tax years – starting with the gains in the most recent year. There is further information in Help Sheet HS282 *Death, personal representatives and legatees*.

Claiming losses

You must claim losses within four years of the end of the tax year in which they were made. So losses made in 2010–11 must be claimed by 5 April 2015.

You can claim the losses by giving details on the capital gains pages of the tax return (see Chapter 22). If you haven't been sent these pages, write and tell your tax inspector about your losses.

Tax-saving idea 101

> Do not forget to claim losses you make when you dispose of, say, shares or valuables. Make sure you claim them within the time limit and keep careful records so that you don't forget them later on.

Example

Elizabeth Ong has a total chargeable gain in 2010–11 of £12,000. The tax-free amount for that tax year is £10,100, which would mean paying capital gains tax on £12,000 − £10,100 = £1,900. But she has losses of £3,500 carried over from previous years and she can use £1,900 of this amount to reduce her total chargeable gain to nil – with no capital gains tax to pay.

This still leaves her with £3,500 − £1,900 = £1,600 of unused losses to be carried forward to 2011–12 and beyond.

The tax-free allowance

The first slice of total chargeable gain in any tax year is free of capital gains tax. For 2009–10 and 2010–11, the allowance is £10,100.

Tax-saving ideas 102 and 103

Try to use your tax-free allowance every year – you can't carry any unused part over to another year.

Spouses and civil partners each have a tax-free allowance, so in 2010–11 can have tax-free gains of £20,200 between them. Consider reorganising your possessions and investments (for example, holding them jointly) so that each of you uses up your full allowance before the other starts to pay tax.

Your tax bill

If after subtracting losses, your tax-free allowance and any special reliefs that you qualify for (p. 152 onwards), you still have some net chargeable gains, tax is charged at a flat rate of 18 per cent in 2009–10 and 2010–11 (unless the rate is changed following the General Election).

Example

In June 2010, Mick sold a house he inherited from his mother several years ago. The house was valued at £190,000 on her death and he has now sold it for £245,000. He works out the capital gains tax bill as follows:

■ *Step 1*: The final value is £245,000 and the initial value is £190,000. He claims the £5,500 he spent in estate agents' and legal fees as allowable expenses, leaving him with a net gain of £245,000 − £190,000 − £5,500 = £49,500.

■ *Step 2*: There are no special reliefs he can claim.

■ *Step 3*: Mick has no other gains this year but he sold some shares at a loss of £4,000 and has carried-forward losses of £6,500. Deducting these, leaves Mick with a net chargeable gain of £39,000.

▶

> ▩ *Step 4*: He subtracts his tax-free allowance for the year of £10,100. This leaves a taxable gain of £28,900.
>
> ▩ *Step 5*: Tax on the gain is 18% × £28,900 = £5,202.

Working out the tax bill – before 2008–09

For disposals you made in 2007–08 and earlier tax years, you can claim additional reliefs when working out your tax bill but tax is generally charged at higher rates. There is a more complex set of steps to follow:

▩ *Step 1*: Work out each capital gain as described on pp. 131–3.

▩ *Step 2*: Deduct any indexation allowance (see below).

▩ *Step 3*: Deduct any special reliefs (for example, see Chapter 6 if you are selling your home or p. 155 for a business).

▩ *Step 4*: Subtract any losses made in the current tax year and any carried forward losses (p. 142) from your indexed gains. Take care to subtract losses first from gains that qualify for the lowest rate of taper relief (Step 5).

▩ *Step 5*: If any gains remain, subtract the appropriate amount of taper relief from each gain (see p. 142).

▩ *Step 6*: Add together all the tapered gains. Deduct you annual allowance (p. 145).

▩ *Step 7*: If any gain remains, work out the tax due. The tax rate(s) will depend on your income as well as the gain (p. 145).

Indexation allowance and taper relief cannot be claimed for disposals made on or after 6 April 2008.

Indexation allowance

If, before 6 April 2008, you dispose of an asset you started to own before 1 April 1998 and, having subtracted the initial value and allowable expenses from the final value, you have a net capital gain, you can claim indexation allowance. This removes some or all of the gain created by inflation during the period 1 April 1982 (or, if later, the date you started to own the asset) and 31 March 1998. But you can't use indexation allowance to create or increase a loss.

To work out the indexation allowance for an asset you sell or give away after 1 April 1998, multiply the initial value and each allowable expense by the indexation factor for the month in which the money was spent as shown in the table.

Indexation factors

Year	Jan	Feb	Mar	Apr	May	Month Jun	Jul	Aug	Sep	Oct	Nov	Dec
1982			1.047	1.006	0.992	0.987	0.986	0.985	0.987	0.977	0.967	0.971
1983	0.968	0.960	0.956	0.929	0.921	0.917	0.906	0.898	0.889	0.883	0.876	0.871
1984	0.872	0.865	0.859	0.834	0.828	0.823	0.825	0.808	0.804	0.793	0.788	0.789
1985	0.783	0.769	0.752	0.716	0.708	0.704	0.707	0.703	0.704	0.701	0.695	0.693
1986	0.689	0.683	0.681	0.665	0.662	0.663	0.667	0.662	0.654	0.652	0.638	0.632
1987	0.626	0.620	0.616	0.597	0.596	0.596	0.597	0.593	0.588	0.580	0.573	0.574
1988	0.574	0.568	0.562	0.537	0.531	0.525	0.524	0.507	0.500	0.485	0.478	0.474
1989	0.465	0.454	0.448	0.423	0.414	0.409	0.408	0.404	0.395	0.384	0.372	0.369
1990	0.361	0.353	0.339	0.300	0.288	0.283	0.282	0.269	0.258	0.248	0.251	0.252
1991	0.249	0.242	0.237	0.222	0.218	0.213	0.215	0.213	0.208	0.204	0.199	0.198
1992	0.199	0.193	0.189	0.171	0.167	0.167	0.171	0.171	0.166	0.162	0.164	0.168
1993	0.179	0.171	0.167	0.156	0.152	0.153	0.156	0.151	0.146	0.147	0.148	0.146
1994	0.151	0.144	0.141	0.128	0.124	0.124	0.129	0.124	0.121	0.120	0.119	0.114
1995	0.114	0.107	0.102	0.091	0.087	0.085	0.091	0.085	0.080	0.085	0.085	0.079
1996	0.083	0.078	0.073	0.066	0.063	0.063	0.067	0.062	0.057	0.057	0.057	0.053
1997	0.053	0.049	0.046	0.040	0.036	0.032	0.032	0.026	0.021	0.019	0.019	0.016
1998	0.019	0.014	0.011									

Example

Ben Barber bought a small paddock for £7,000 in April 1987, paying a valuation fee of £100. In August 1989, he spent £1,500 laying on a water supply to the field. The paddock was sold in May 2007 for £35,000 with an estate agent's fee of £400. Ben works out the indexed gain as follows:

▦ *Step 1*: The final value is £35,000. From this, Ben can deduct the initial value of £7,000 and allowable expenses of £100 + £1,500 + £400 = £2,000. This leaves Ben with a net gain of £26,000.

▦ *Step 2*: Using the table above, Ben works out the indexation allowance on each eligible expense as follows:

Month of expense	Amount	Indexation factor		Indexation allowance
April 1987	£7,100	× 0.597	=	£4,239
August 1989	£1,500	× 0.404	=	£606
TOTAL				£4,845

Therefore, the indexed gain is £26,000 − £4,845 = £21,155.

Capital losses

You subtract losses for the current and earlier years as described on pp. 137–138. In particular, note that:

- you subtract the full amount of current year losses even if this reduces the remaining gain to less that your tax-free allowance, but

- you subtract only as much of your brought forward losses as are needed to reduce your gains to the amount of the tax-free allowance.

However, when you are working out your tax bill for 2007–08 or an earlier tax year, you need to take into account the interaction of losses with taper relief (see below). This means you deduct the losses in the way that ensures the largest possible reduction in your tax bill, by subtracting them first from the gains that qualify for the lowest rate of taper relief.

Taper relief

Taper relief was designed to encourage you to invest for the longer term. For assets disposed of before 6 April 2008, it reduces the amount of the gain according to the number of complete years the asset has been owned after 5 April 1998. The reduction is bigger for business assets.

For a non-business asset owned for three full years, taper relief reduces the gain by 5 per cent – so 95 per cent of the gain on it is chargeable. After ten years, taper relief rises to the maximum 40 per cent, leaving 60 per cent of the gain chargeable.

For business assets, the rate of taper relief is higher – a maximum of 75 per cent that leaves just 25 per cent of the gain chargeable. For disposals between 6 April 2000 and 5 April 2002, the maximum is reached after four years; and, for disposals from 6 April 2002 onwards, the maximum is reached after just two years.

If you owned a non-business asset before 17 March 1998, you are given one bonus year of ownership if you sell it after 5 April 1998. So if you bought the asset on 1 January 1998 and sold it on 1 July 2007, you would be treated as having owned it for ten years after 5 April 1998 – the nine complete years after that date plus the one bonus year. Business assets disposed of on or after 6 April 2000 no longer qualify for a bonus year because taper relief was enhanced for such assets.

Number of complete years asset owned after 5 April 1998	Non-business assets		Business assets			
			Disposal on or after 6 April 2000 and before 6 April 2002		Disposal on or after 6 April 2002	
	Taper relief	% of gain chargeable	Taper relief	% of gain chargeable	Taper relief	% of gain chargeable
0	0	100	0	100	0	100
1	0	100	12.5	87.5	50	50
2	0	100	25	75	75	25
3	5	95	50	50	75	25
4	10	90	75	25	75	25
5	15	85	75	25	75	25
6	20	80	75	25	75	25
7	25	75	75	25	75	25
8	30	70	75	25	75	25
9	35	65	75	25	75	25
10	40	60	75	25	75	25

Taper relief is calculated on the chargeable gain after deducting any losses for the tax year and previous tax years. To maximise the amount of taper relief you can claim, losses are deducted first from the gains that qualify for least taper relief, then the next least and so on. So, for example, if you have a non-business asset that qualifies for 10 per cent taper relief and one that qualifies for 20 per cent, the losses are deducted from the first gain – if it is too small to use up all the losses, they are then deducted from the second gain. Note that a business asset owned for just a few years qualifies for a higher rate of taper relief than a non-business asset owned rather longer, so may come behind the non-business asset in the queue for losses.

Business assets

The definition of 'business asset' was changed from 6 April 2000 onwards and again from 6 April 2004 (see overleaf).

If you had an asset that was a business asset for only part of the time you owned it (perhaps because of the changes to the definition), you must apportion any gain into two parts: a business part and a non-business part. Different rates of taper relief will apply to each part.

What counts as a qualifying company for business asset taper relief

Period to which definition applies	———— Definition of qualifying company ————		
	Your relationship with the company (apart from holding shares)	Type of company	Nature of your shareholding
6 April 1998 to 5 April 2000	None required	Trading company[1]	Shares giving you at least 25% of the voting rights
	Full-time working officer or employee	Trading company[1]	Shares giving you at least 5% of the voting rights
6 April 2000 onwards	None required	Unquoted trading company[1] [2]	Any
	None required	Quoted trading company[2]	Shares giving you at least 5% of the voting rights
	Officer or employee (full- or part-time)	Quoted trading company[2]	Any
	Officer or employee (full- or part-time)	Non-trading company	No more than 10% of any class of shares or 10% of the voting rights or rights to no more than 10% of distributable income or assets

(1) Or holding company of trading group.
(2) Quoted means listed on the London Stock Exchange or a recognised overseas exchange. Other companies are unquoted. 'Unquoted' includes shares listed on the Alternative Investment Market (AIM).

A business asset was:

- any item you used in your trade or profession

- from 6 April 2004 onwards, any item used in a trade or profession carried on by someone else

- until 5 April 2000, any item you held for the purpose of your employment (including as a director) by a trading company, provided you were required to devote at least 75 per cent of your working hours to that job

- from 6 April 2000 onwards, any item you held for the purpose of your employment (including as a director) by a trading company

▓ shares or securities in a qualifying company – see table opposite for what counts as a qualifying company.

Tax-saving ideas 104 and 105

The abolition of taper relief for disposals from 6 April 2008 onwards has generally increased the tax on business assets. If you have employee shares (see Chapter 16) or AIM-listed shares that would previously have qualified for business asset taper relief, try to spread your sales so that you keep the gains you make each tax year within your tax-free allowance (£10,100 in 2010–11).

If you are selling your busines on or after 6 April 2008, although you can no longer claim business asset taper relief, you may instead be able to claim entrepreneurs' relief (p. 156) which effectively reduces the tax rate on the first £2 million of business gains over your lifetime to just 10 per cent (the same as the minimum rate you would have paid with taper relief – assuming the main rate of CGT is 18 per cent).

Calculating your capital gains tax bill

If there is anything left after deducting expenses, indexation allowance, losses, taper relief and the tax-free allowance for the relevant year, there is capital gains tax to pay.

For 2007–08 and earlier years, your total net tapered gains minus the tax-free allowance is added to your taxable income for the year and taxed as if it was savings income. So if the combined total comes to less than the starting rate band, the tax rate on the gains is 10 per cent. Any amount over the upper limit for the basic rate of income tax, is taxed at the top rate of 40 per cent. Between the upper and lower limit for the basic rate, gains are taxed at 20 per cent.

Shares and unit trusts

Shares and unit trusts are treated in the same way as other assets for capital gains tax purposes. But if you buy and sell identical shares in a particular company or units in a particular unit trust at different times, how do you decide which you have bought or sold when working out the gain? And there are further complications when companies merge, are taken over or otherwise reorganise their capital. This section explains the special rules for working out the gains and losses on share transactions. Help Sheet HS284 *Shares and capital gains tax* has more details.

Valuing shares

The market value of shares bought and sold on a stock exchange is normally the amount you paid for them or got for selling them.

But you should use the market value when valuing gifts or disposals to a connected person (p. 132). If they are traded on the London Stock Exchange use the prices recorded in the Stock Exchange Daily Official List (which can be obtained from a stockbroker, bank or the Historic Price Service London Stock Exchange, 10 Paternoster Square, London EC4M 7LS or www.london stockexchange.com). The market value is the lower of the following two figures, calculated using prices on the date of the gift or disposal:

- the selling price, plus a quarter of the difference between the selling price and the (higher) buying price – the quarter-up rule
- the half-way point between the highest and lowest prices of recorded bargains for the day.

With any disposal of unquoted shares, the market value must be agreed with Shares Valuation, part of the Revenue (Tel: 0115 974 2222). This cannot be negotiated in advance and reaching agreement can be a lengthy business.

Unit trusts and investment trusts

The gain on disposing of unit trusts and investment trusts is worked out in the same way as for shares. If you receive an equalisation payment with your first distribution from a unit trust, this is a return of part of your original investment and should be deducted from the acquisition price in working out your gain or loss.

Which shares or unit trusts have you sold?

If you buy one batch of shares in a company and later sell it without any other dealings in the shares, it is quite simple to calculate the gain or loss. But if you buy shares in the same company on different occasions and then sell some of them, how can you tell which of the shares you have sold? The tax rules solve this problem by requiring you to match your sales to your purchases in a set order. The rules have changed with the simplification of capital gains tax from 6 April 2008 onwards, so the order you use depends on when you dispose of your shares.

Disposals on or after 6 April 2008

Disposals are matched to acquisitions in the following order:

■ first, shares acquired on the same day

■ second, shares acquired at any time in the next 30 days

■ all the rest of the shares are pooled (called a 'section 104 holding') and treated as if they are a single asset. When you dispose of some of the shares, this is treated as a part disposal of an asset (p. 135).

Example

Diane has a holding of shares in United Enterprises plc that she has built up over a number of years as follows:

Purchase date	Number of shares	Price per share	Total paid	Allowable expenses
June 1991	2,000	£3.50	£7,000	£119
December 1998	1,500	£2.00	£3,000	£51
March 2005	3,000	£4.00	£12,000	£15
Totals	6,500		£22,000	£185

In May 2010, she sells 2,500 of the shares, when their price is standing at £5 each, for a total of £12,000. She works out the capital gain as follows:

■ The value of the shares she is selling is 2,500 × £5 = £12,500

■ The value of the shares she is keeping is 4,000 × £5 = £20,000

■ Therefore her initial value and allowable expenses are £12,500/£32,500 = 38.46 per cent of the relevant totals for the pool

■ The initial value is 38.46% × £22,000 = £8,461

■ She claims allowable expenses of 38.46% × £185 = £72 plus the dealing costs of the disposal which come to £12

■ Her net gain is £12,500 − £8,461 − £72 − £12 = £3,955

■ She has no other gains or losses and £3,955 falls comfortably within her tax-free allowance, so there is no tax to pay.

Disposals before 6 April 2008

Disposals are matched to acquisitions in the following order:

■ first, shares acquired the same day

■ second, shares acquired at any time in the next 30 days (see overleaf)

■ third, shares acquired before the day of sale and after 5 April 1998 – with the most recent acquisitions first (last in, first out, or LIFO)

■ fourth, shares acquired between 6 April 1982 and 5 April 1998.

These are pooled to form the section 104 holding and are treated as a single asset. Selling some of the shares is treated as a part disposal and indexation allowance is worked out in a similar way to the initial value and allowable expenses (as shown in the Example on p. 147)

■ fifth, shares acquired between 6 April 1965 and 5 April 1982. These form a second pool (called the '1982 holding') and are treated as a single asset. The shares are treated as acquired at their value of 31 March 1982 unless you had opted to use their actual cost (p. 133)

■ finally, shares acquired on or before 5 April 1965 (matching to the most recent acquisitions first using the LIFO basis).

Tax-saving idea 106

It could still pay you to sell some shares towards the end of the tax year to use up the tax-free allowance. In 2010–11, you can have chargeable gains of up to £10,100 tax-free – saving up to £1,818 in capital gains tax. You could buy the same shares back after the 30 days – taking the risk that the shares shoot up in price during the 30-day period. Or you could buy different shares – perhaps in a similar company. Another option is to sell shares you own directly and buy them back within a stocks and shares ISA or SIPP or get your spouse or civil partner to buy the shares back – these are effective for tax purposes without waiting 30 days. Remember to take the costs of buying and selling shares (including stamp duty on purchase) into account. Be wary if you intend to sell shares and buy them back within an ISA in order to realise a capital loss to set against gains you have made on other assets – you could be caught by the capital losses anti-avoidance rule (p. 137).

Anti-tax-avoidance rule

Shares bought in the 30 days after a sale are treated as those sold before those bought earlier to stop a practice that was known as 'bed and break-fasting'. This involved selling some shares towards the end of the tax year and buying them back the next day to realise a gain which could help use up the tax-free allowance or realise a loss for offsetting gains made on other assets.

This can no longer be done. If you sell shares and buy them back within 30 days of the sale, the shares you sell are matched to those you buy back, not shares bought earlier. So if you sell some shares for £5 each which you originally bought for £3 and then buy them back for £5 the next day, the initial value of the shares you sold will be £5 each not £3 – and there would be no gain realised.

Employee share schemes

Employee share schemes allow employees to acquire shares in their companies free or cheaply – and if they are certain types approved by the Revenue, without an income tax bill. There could be a capital gains tax bill when the shares are sold. For disposals from 6 April 2000 to 5 April 2008, you could claim taper relief at the higher rates that applied to business assets (p. 142). For disposals from 6 April 2008 onwards, there are no special reliefs to reduce any gain you make on employee shares.

The initial cost of the shares and when you are deemed to have received them depends on the type of scheme:

▪ approved savings-related share option schemes – you acquire the shares at the price you paid on the day that you opted to buy them

▪ approved profit-sharing schemes – you acquire the shares at the market value on the day they are allocated to you, even though you can't sell them for three years

▪ approved discretionary share option schemes – you acquire the shares at the price you pay for them on the day you exercise the option. If you paid anything for the option, this an allowable expense

▪ share incentive plan – when the shares are first awarded to you or, in the case of partnership shares, first acquired on your behalf, even though you have to hold them for a minimum period (see Chapter 16).

You can transfer shares from a savings-related share option scheme or share incentive plan direct to an ISA (p. 97) or pension scheme (p. 95). Shares transferred in this way are free of capital gains tax on transfer and when they are subsequently sold.

Identical shares acquired on the same day are normally pooled together. But, if you acquire shares from two employee schemes on the same day (or from one employee scheme and buy a second batch on the open market on the same day), you can opt to match a disposal with the shares that have the higher initial value (i.e. produce the lowest gain).

Help Sheet HS287 *Employee share and security schemes and capital gains tax* has more details.

Other rules for shares

Rights issues

If you get extra shares through a rights issue or a bonus issue, they are allocated to the relevant shares or pool. Whatever you pay for the rights issue is added to the initial costs of the original shares. For pre-6-April-2008 disposals, indexation allowance runs from the time you paid for the rights issue and taper relief runs from the date the original shares were acquired (since a rights issue counts as a share reorganisation).

Stock dividends and accumulation unit trusts

If you get extra shares instead of dividends, this is known as a stock dividend (or scrip dividend). The value of the new shares is the amount of dividend foregone excluding the value of the tax credit – the cash equivalent. Any indexation allowance or taper relief runs from the date of the dividend. Accumulation unit trusts work in a similar way, with extra units allocated to the appropriate pool.

Takeovers and mergers

If you own shares in a company which is taken over, you may get shares in the new parent company in exchange for your old shares. This exchange does not count as a disposal. The new shares are assumed to have been acquired at the cost of the old ones and on the same dates.

If part of the price for the old shares is cash, this is a disposal. For example, if you get half cash, half shares, you have disposed of half the old shares.

Sometimes you are offered loan notes as an alternative to taking cash. Usually, these are treated as the same asset as the shares you have given up, so no disposal takes place until you cash in the loan notes.

Tax-saving idea 107

If you accept cash for shares in a takeover, this counts as a disposal for capital gains tax. Sometimes you can opt for loan notes instead. If so, the disposal is deferred until you cash in the loan notes. This is useful if putting off the disposal would reduce the tax you pay (for example, by using a new tax year's allowance).

When mutuals become PLCs

Some building societies and mutual insurance companies convert to public limited companies or are involved in other organisational changes that may produce benefits for members. If you receive shares or cash – or both – in such circumstances, there may be a bill for income tax or capital gains tax. Ask the building society or insurance company for guidance.

Payment by instalments

If you have bought newly issued shares, you may have paid for them in instalments.

For pre-6-April-2008 disposals, indexation allowance and taper relief on the full purchase price runs from when the shares were acquired only if all the instalments were paid within 12 months of acquisition. If instalments are paid more than 12 months after the shares were acquired, indexation allowance and taper relief on those instalments runs from when the payments were made. However, if you paid in instalments when buying newly issued shares in a privatised state enterprise, indexation allowance and taper relief run from the date you acquired the shares (even though you hand over some of the money months or even years later).

Monthly savings schemes

Many unit trusts, open-ended investment companies and investment trusts run monthly savings schemes. If you invest this way, normally each monthly payment is treated as a separate investment. Where you disposed of some or all of these shares before 6 April 2008, basing your calculations on separate monthly acquisitions involved a large number of calculations to work out the correct amount of indexation allowance and taper relief.

To reduce the number of calculations, you could request that the monthly payments for a year were grouped together and treated as a single payment made on a single date during the year (either the end of the year or the seventh month, depending on the year in question). You could request this treatment for payments made during investment fund years ending on or before 5 April 1999 but not any later years.

With the simplification of the tax rules for disposals from 6 April 2008 onwards, there is no longer any advantage to be gained from this option.

Tax treatment of Northern Rock shares

> Northern Rock Bank was transferred into government ownership on 22 February 2008 without, to date, providing any payment or compensation to the then shareholders. If you were a Northern Rock shareholder, the transfer in February 2008 counts as a disposal for CGT at a final value of zero. If you had previously bought the shares, you have made a loss which you can use as described on pp. 137–138. If you acquired the shares free when Northern Rock demutalised, you have made neither a gain nor a loss. CGT will be due on any compensation (unless it is covered by your tax-free allowance). If you were an employee of Northern Rock and had acquired shares or options to buy shares through an employee share scheme, see p. 286.

How to reduce or delay a capital gains tax bill

There are several ways to reduce or delay a CGT bill. For a start, it is important to claim all the allowable expenses you can (p. 132) and not to overlook any losses that you can set off against gains (p. 137). Be aware of your annual tax-free allowance (p. 139) and try to use it each year, if you can.

These are all ways to minimise your tax bill once you have made a disposal. But there are several steps you can take before reaching a disposal to keep your tax bill down:

- take advantage of the allowances of your spouse or civil partner (see opposite)
- make the best use of losses (see opposite)
- pass the tax bill for gifts of business assets and certain other gifts on to the recipient if possible, or pay it in instalments if not (see opposite)
- invest the gains from any disposals in growing businesses if you don't need the proceeds immediately – you may be able to defer the tax bill by claiming capital gains deferral relief on buying shares through the EIS (pp. 155 and 103)
- claim the special reliefs which can reduce your tax bill if you are disposing of a business or farm, including entrepreneurs' relief (p. 156).

To minimise your capital gains tax bill, it is essential to keep a record of the assets you have acquired which may fall into the tax net, together with relevant receipts (for example, for allowable expenses).

Husbands, wives and civil partners

Spouses and civil partners are treated as separate individuals for capital gains tax. They pay tax on their own gains and can deduct their losses only from their own gains. They have their own tax-free allowances to deduct from their own net chargeable gains.

But if a married or registered couple living together dispose of assets to each other, this is ignored for the purposes of capital gains tax. For example, if a husband buys shares worth £10,000 in June 2006 and gives them to his wife at a later date, her gain or loss when she sells them will be calculated as if she had bought them for £10,000 in June 2006. Anything they pay each other on such transfers is ignored.

A married or registered couple is treated as living together unless legally separated or where the separation appears to be permanent. Gifts between spouses or civil partners in the year of separation are free of capital gains tax, but after this, tax may be payable. For more about marriage and capital gains tax, see Help Sheet HS281 *Husband and wife, civil partners, divorce, dissolution and separation*. The information in this Help Sheet also applies to civil partners.

Tax-saving idea 108

Since there is no capital gains tax on gifts between spouses or civil partners, you can effectively double your tax-free band if you are married by giving assets to your spouse to dispose of. So in 2010–11 a married couple can effectively make £20,200 of disposals.

Making the best use of losses

If your allowable losses in a tax year look likely to mean you will not be able to use the whole tax-free allowance for the year, there are two options:

■ make more disposals to increase your chargeable gains – by selling some shares that have done well, for example

■ hold back on loss-making disposals to a later year when there are no gains or they can be used to reduce future gains.

Gifts

If you give away certain assets or sell them for less than their market value, you can avoid paying capital gains tax by claiming hold-over relief. This means the recipient is treated as having acquired the assets when you did and having paid the costs you paid (less anything paid to you). The recipient's agreement is necessary, since he or she is taking over the tax bill for your period of ownership.

Hold-over relief is available only for the following gifts, however:

■ business assets

■ heritage property

■ gifts to political parties

■ gifts which result in an immediate inheritance tax bill. Since 22 March 2006, this includes lifetime gifts to most types of trust.

Hold-over relief cannot normally apply to a gift to a settlor-interested trust, in other words, a trust in which you have an interest (or later acquire an interest) by, for example, being one of a class of beneficiaries who can receive benefits from the trust. There are also restrictions if a trust (in which you do not have an interest) makes a gain on property which has been the subject of both a hold-over relief claim and a claim for private residence relief (see Chapter 6).

If the person you have made the gift to becomes non-resident without having sold or given it away, you might have to pay a capital gains tax bill.

There is no point in claiming hold-over relief if your net taxable gains for the year, including the gift, will be covered by the tax-free allowance (£10,100 in 2009–10 and 2010–11). There would be no capital gains tax for you to pay, but you might add to the tax the person you are making the gift to has to pay eventually.

Example

In August 2009, Suzy Richmond gave a second home to a discretionary trust under which the home could be used for the benefit of any of her grandchildren. (Suzy herself cannot benefit at all under the terms of the trust.) She had owned the home since April 1992 when she bought it for £60,000.

By August 2009, there was a chargeable gain of £100,000 on the property but, instead of paying tax on this, Suzy and the trust jointly claimed hold-over relief. This means when the trust eventually sells or gives away the property, the trust will be treated as if it had owned the home since April 1992 and the initial value will be £60,000.

However, under anti-avoidance rules introduced from 10 December 2003, the trust may not claim private residence relief if the grandchildren use the home as their main residence, having had hold-over relief. To be eligible for private residence relief, Suzy and the trust would have to forgo the claim for hold-over relief, in which case Suzy would have to pay tax on the £100,000 gain. The trust's initial value would then be the market value of the property at the time of the gift.

Business assets include land or buildings used by the business, goodwill, fixed plant and machinery, and shares or securities of a trading company, where the company is unlisted (but including those quoted on AIM – the Alternative Investment Market) or is the transferer's personal company.

If you make a gift of land or certain types of shareholdings that do not qualify for hold-over relief, you may be able to pay the capital gains tax in ten annual instalments. The shareholdings in question are a controlling shareholding in a company or minority holdings in unquoted companies. Interest is charged on the unpaid tax in the usual way. For more about hold-over relief, see Help Sheet HS295 *Relief for gifts and similar transactions*.

Tax-saving idea 109

If you give, say, a second home to a discretionary trust and one of the beneficiaries uses the property as their main home, you have to choose between hold-over relief on the gift or private residence relief (see Example opposite). Choose whichever is likely to produce the lowest CGT bill.

Capital gains deferral relief

If you're facing a capital gains tax bill that you can't reduce by claiming losses or other reliefs, consider investing the gain in the shares of certain types of small companies through the Enterprise Investment Scheme (EIS) (p. 103). You can claim deferral relief, which allows you to put off the tax bill.

You must make the investment any time between one year before and three years after the disposal that produces the gain. The amount of the gain that you reinvest will generally be taxed only when you eventually sell the shares.

Businesses and farms

If you are disposing of a business or farm, you could face an enormous tax bill on the gain. There are two reliefs to reduce the impact on entrepreneurs and others who create small businesses:

■ entrepreneurs' relief (see overleaf)

■ roll-over relief if you replace business assets (p. 157). With large sums at stake, it would pay to seek professional advice on this relief to ensure you meet the complex requirements.

Entrepreneurs' relief

If you sell a business or you cease trading and sell off the assets used in the business, you may be able to claim entrepreneurs' relief to reduce CGT on any gain. This relief was introduced for disposals from 2008–09 onwards to fill the gap left by the abolition of business asset taper relief (see p. 143).

The effect of entrepreneurs' relief is that the first £2 million of business gains (£1 million before 6 April 2010) that you make over your lifetime are effectively taxed at 10 per cent, assuming a standard CGT rate of 18 per cent. Relief is given by reducing the gain by 4/9ths – in other words multiply the gain by 5/9ths. Since 5/9ths × 18% = 10% this has the effect of reducing the effective tax rate to 10 per cent.

There is no minimum age limit for qualifying for the relief. It is available to businesses of any size and where you sell part or all of:

- a trading business that you have run as a sole trader
- your share in a trading business of which you were a partner
- assets used in a trading business that is ceasing
- shares or securities in a trading company (or the holding company of a trading group) where you were a director, company secretary or employee, owned at least 5 per cent of the shares and controlled at least 5 per cent of the voting rights.

You must have been in the business for at least a year before you sell up. If you sell assets that have been used in the business, the sale must be within three years of the date the business ceased.

You must claim the relief within one year of 31 January following the end of the tax year in which you make the disposal. For example, if you sell your business in 2010–11, you must claim the relief by 31 January 2013.

For more information, see Revenue Help Sheet HS275 *Entreprenuers' relief.*

Example

John runs an organic fruit and vegetable business from a leasehold shop. In September 2010, he sells the business as a going concern, making a gain of £90,000. If he claims entrepreneurs' relief, the gain is reduced to 5/9 × £90,000 = £50,000. After deducting his tax-free allowance of £10,100, he pays capital gains tax of 18% × £39,900 = £7,182. He has used up £90,000 of his lifetime allowance so can carry forward £1,910,000 to use against future business gains.

Tax-saving ideas 110–114

Entrepreneurs' relief is available only in respect of trading businesses. For example, it does not normally include property rental businesses. But furnished holiday lettings (p. 352) do qualify – though this treatment was due to end from April 2010.

If you sold your business before 6 April 2008, you can't normally claim entrepreneurs' relief (but could usually have claimed taper relief instead). However, if the gain would have qualified for entrepreneurs' relief had it been available and you deferred tax on the gain by reinvesting in enterprise investment scheme (EIS) or venture capital trusts (VCT) shares (pp. 103 and 105), you should be able to claim entrepreneurs' relief when you sell your EIS or VCT shares on or after 6 April 2008.

If you sold shares in your trading company before 6 April 2008 and received loan notes (so that you could defer tax on the gain), you should be able to claim entrepreneurs' relief when you redeem the loan notes on or after 6 April 2008.

You cannot claim entrepreneurs' relief for any gain on selling assets used in the business if you are not closing down. However, you may be able to claim roll-over relief instead (see below).

Business disposals of up to £40 million (£20 million before 6 April 2010) can be covered by entrepreneurs' relief if a company has 20 shareholders who each have 5 per cent of the company and all work as directors or employees. However, there is no 5 per cent holding requirement for people working together as partners, so a limited liability partnership (see Chapter 18) could be a more tax-efficient structure if you are setting up a larger business.

Roll-over relief

Roll-over relief allows you to defer the capital gains tax bill when you sell or otherwise dispose of assets from your business, providing you replace them in the three years after the sale or the one year before it. You can claim relief even if you do not buy an identical replacement as long as you use the proceeds to buy another qualifying business asset. Assets which qualify include land or buildings used by the business, goodwill, fixed plant and machinery.

You usually get the relief by deducting the gain for the old asset from the acquisition cost of the new one. So when you come to sell the new asset, the gain on it has been increased by the gain on the old asset. However, if you replace again, you can claim further roll-over relief, and currently capital gains tax will not have to be paid until you fail to replace the business asset.

You can make a claim for roll-over relief up to four years following the end of the tax year in which you dispose of the asset or the year in which you replace it if this is later. You must reinvest all of the sale proceeds from the disposal of the first asset to get full relief.

For more information see Revenue Help Sheet HS290 *Business asset rollover relief.*

Warning

The lifetime limit for entrepreneurs' relief was doubled from £1 million to £2 million from 2010–11. The higher limit applies only to disposals made on or after 6 April 2010, so any excess over £1 million realised before 6 April 2010 is not relievable.

10

Gifts and passing your money on

There is no space on the 2010 tax return for inheritance tax. This is because it is largely a tax on what you leave when you die (including gifts made in the seven years before). The number of estates which are taxed is expected to be around one in 25 by 2014–15.

The tax rate is a hefty 40 per cent of anything over £325,000 in 2010–11. There is plenty that can be done to reduce the amount paid – as long as you plan carefully.

This chapter tells you how inheritance tax works and how to reduce the amount that goes to the Revenue. It also explains the pre-owned assets tax that came into effect from 6 April 2005 and which does have to be reported on your tax return.

How inheritance tax works

Your chargeable estate

When you die, everything you own – your home, possessions, investments and savings – goes into your estate. So does money paid out by life insurance policies unless they are written in trust (p. 169), and the value of things you have given away but reserved the right to use for yourself (gifts with reservation – p. 171). Debts such as outstanding mortgages and funeral expenses are deducted from the total to find the value of your estate.

Inheritance tax is worked out on a rolling total of gifts you have made over the last seven years. What you leave on death is in effect your final gift.

So to the estate you leave are added any gifts you made in the seven years before death unless they were tax-free gifts (p. 162).

Some or all of your estate may be free of inheritance tax: anything left to your spouse or civil partner, or to a UK charity, for example (for a full list of what is tax-free, see p. 162). These tax-free bequests and legacies are deducted from the value of your estate before the tax bill is worked out.

Your tax-free allowance

If the resulting total exceeds a certain limit – see table opposite – –inheritance tax is payable on the excess at 40 per cent. So in 2010–11 if the total is £350,000, tax is payable on £350,000 − £325,000 = £25,000 and the bill would be 40% × £25,000 = £10,000.

Each person has their own tax-free allowance (called the 'nil-rate band'). But, under special rules, the allowance of a person dying on or after 9 October 2007 may be increased by any unused allowance from a husband, wife or civil partner who predeceased them (whatever the date of their death). For example, if when a husband died, his estate used up only 30 per cent of his allowance, the allowance available at the wife's death could be increased by up to 70 per cent. This means that a widow, widower or bereaved civil partner who dies in 2010–11 may have a tax-free allowance up to 2 × £325,000 = £650,000.

To transfer unused allowance, no action is required when the first of a married couple or civil partnership dies. On the second death, the personal representatives need to fill in form IHT216 and submit it within two years of the month in which the second death occurred, together with documents to support the claim. These documents which relate to the first death include, for example, a copy of the inheritance tax form submitted (IHT 200, C5 or IHT205), the death certificate, will or details of how the estate was passed on if there was no will, any deed of variation (p. 171), any valuations. Note that there is unlikely to be any unused allowance to carry forward if your spouse died before March 1975 because the exemption for gifts between husbands and wives was then very small and non-existent before March 1972.

Example

Kamil died in October 2003, leaving an estate worth £153,000. This used up 60 per cent of the tax-free allowance for 2003–04, which was £255,000. His wife Ayesha dies in July 2010. Her estate is worth £410,000 which exceeds the tax-free allowance for 2010–11 of £325,000. But her personal representatives can claim the unused part of Kamil's allowance to boost Ayesha's allowance up to 140% × £325,000 = £455,000. This would more than cover her estate, so no inheritance tax would be due.

Tax-saving ideas 115–117

When the first of a married couple or civil partners dies it may not be clear whether their survivor will need any of their unused tax-free allowance later on. To keep your options open, make sure you keep all the documents relating to the first death.

You can inherit the unused tax-free allowance from more than one spouse or civil partner who dies before you. But the maximum tax-free allowance you can have is capped at twice the normal personal limit.

If you will leave assets whose value is likely to grow by more than the increase in the tax-free allowance (usually broadly in line with price inflation), it will generally be more tax-efficient to include a discretionary trust in your will (p. 167) rather than rely on leaving your spouse or civil partner some unused tax-free allowance.

Inheritance tax-free limits

Tax year	2008–09	2009–10	2010–11	2011–12 to 2014–15
Tax-free limit	£312,000	£325,000	£325,000[1]	£325,000

(1) Previously the government had announced that this limit would increase to £350,000, but has subsequently frozen the limit at the 2009–10 level.

Tax on gifts within seven years before death

Quite separately from tax on your estate, potentially exempt transfers (p. 164) and taxable gifts you made in the last seven years are reassessed on death and tax (or extra tax) may be due on them. Initially, the person you made the gift to will be asked to pay. If they can't or won't, tax is paid from your estate. But taper relief can be claimed to reduce the tax bill if the gift was made more than three years before death (see below). Note that taper relief does not reduce the tax bill on the estate, and will only be useful if the life-time gifts exceed the nil band of £325,000.

Years between gift and death	% of inheritance tax payable
Up to 3	100%
More than 3 and up to 4	80%
More than 4 and up to 5	60%
More than 5 and up to 6	40%
More than 6 and up to 7	20%

Example

> Angela Framing died in May 2010, leaving an estate worth £316,000 (largely the value of her home). In December 1999, she had made a taxable gift of £15,000 to help a grandchild with the cost of studying. Subsequently, in August 2002, she gave another grandchild a taxable gift of £5,000 to start a business.
>
> In calculating the tax due on Angela's estate, the £20,000 of taxable lifetime gifts is added to the £316,000 left on death to produce a total of £336,000. The first £325,000 of that is free of tax, leaving £336,000 − £325,000 = £11,000 on which tax is due.
>
> Tax at 40 per cent on £11,000 is £4,400 – tax that will be entirely paid out of Angela's estate, since the life-time gifts are deemed to use up part of the £325,000 before the balance is used to calculate the tax on the estate.

Gifts free of inheritance tax

Gifts that are always tax-free:

- gifts between husband and wife or civil partners – even if the two are legally separated. But only the first £55,000 is tax-free if the gifts are to someone who is not domiciled in the UK (domicile reflects the individual's natural home, see Chapter 23)

- gifts to UK charities and community amateur sports clubs

- gifts to certain national institutions such as the National Trust, National Gallery, British Museum (and their Scottish, Welsh and Northern Ireland equivalents)

- gifts of certain types of heritage property such as paintings, archives, land or historic buildings to non-profit-making concerns like local museums

- gifts of land in the UK to registered housing associations

- gifts of shares in a company into a trust for the benefit of most or all of the employees which will control the company

- gifts to established political parties.

Gifts that are tax-free on death only:

- lump sums paid out on your death by a pension scheme provided the trustees of the scheme have discretion about who gets the money

- refunds of personal pension contributions (and interest) paid directly to someone else or a trust – in other words, not paid into your estate

- the estate of anyone killed on active military service in war or whose death was hastened by such service

■ £10,000 *ex gratia* payments received by survivors (and their spouses) held as Japanese prisoners of war during World War Two and amounts from other specified schemes that also provide compensation for wrongs suffered during the war.

Gifts that are tax-free in lifetime only:

■ anything given to an individual more than seven years before your death – unless there are strings attached (p. 171)

■ small gifts worth up to £250 to any number of people in any tax year. But you can't give anyone more than this limit and claim exemption on the first £250 – if you give someone £500, the whole £500 will be taxable unless it is tax-free for one of the other reasons below

■ regular gifts that are treated as normal expenditure out of income. The gifts must come out of your after-tax income and not from your capital. After paying for the gifts, you should have enough income to maintain your normal standard of living

■ gifts on marriage to a bride or groom or on registration to civil partners: each parent of the bride, groom or partner can give £5,000, grandparents or remoter relatives and the bride, groom or partners themselves can give £2,500 and anyone else £1,000. The gifts must be made before the big day – and if the marriage or registration is called off, the gift becomes taxable

■ gifts for the maintenance of your family – your current or a former husband, wife or civil partner, certain dependent relatives and children under 18 or still in full-time education. The children can be yours, stepchildren, adopted children or any other children in your care

■ up to £3,000 in total a year of other gifts. If you don't use the whole £3,000 annual exemption in one year, you can carry forward the unused part to the next tax year only. You can't use the annual exemption to top up the small gifts exemption. If you give someone more than £250 in a year, all of it must come off the annual exemption if it is to be free of inheritance tax.

Planning for inheritance tax

If your estate is likely to be well below the threshold for paying inheritance tax, there is no need to worry about it. But if it looks as if you are above it, there is much you can do to reduce the tax bill. An important first step is to draw up a will. This will make you think about what you own and how you want it to be disposed of after you die.

Many of the ways of minimising inheritance tax involve making gifts which are free of tax or making potentially taxable gifts more than seven years before your death. But remember your heirs will still gain from what you leave them even if tax is due on your estate. Don't give away so much that you or your spouse are left impoverished in old age, merely to starve the Revenue of every last penny of tax.

Tax-saving ideas 118–120

Draw up a will. There are simple steps you can take to minimise the tax payable on your estate when you die and to reduce the complications for those you leave behind.

Make as full use as possible of the lifetime gifts you can make which do not fall into the inheritance tax net, such as those which count as normal expenditure from income or fall within the £3,000 annual allowance.

Share your wealth with your spouse or civil partner so that you can each make tax-free lifetime gifts and efficient wills. There is no inheritance tax or capital gains tax (see Chapter 9) on gifts between spouses or civil partners.

Tax-free gifts and PETs

If you do have some resources to spare, make as full use as possible of the annual £3,000 exemption, regular gifts out of income and such like. And make sure your spouse has enough to make similar gifts tax-free.

If you want to make larger gifts, the earlier you make them the better – because inheritance tax may have to be paid on a gift if you die within seven years of making it. For this reason, most lifetime gifts are called potentially exempt transfers (PETs). They are potentially free of inheritance tax but you must survive for seven years after they are made for the tax to be avoided.

Even if you die within seven years of making the gift, there will be no inheritance tax if the gift is fully covered by your nil-rate band. If tax is payable, it will be reduced by taper relief (p. 161) if the gift was made more than three years before your death. Tax is initially due from the person to whom you made the gift but, if they can't or won't pay, your estate has to pick up the bill.

Note that gifts in your lifetime, other than cash, may mean a capital gains tax bill – see Chapter 9.

Share your wealth

A married couple or civil partners can share their wealth – what they give to each other is free of inheritance tax. But this strategy – called estate splitting – has become less important now that they can leave each other their unused tax-free allowance (p. 160). Being able to inherit unused allowance means the couple's joint wealth up to twice the allowance (£650,000 in 2010–11) can be tax-free regardless of which of them owns the assets. However, splitting your wealth means you can each make lifetime tax-free gifts.

In practice, it may not be easy to split your worldly goods and give them away during your lifetime. It may make more sense to pass all or most of them on to the survivor so he or she has enough to live on.

Where you split a single asset between you, such as the family home, note that there are two ways to own it. If you own it as joint tenants, you each have equal shares in the asset and, when the first of you dies, their share automatically passes to the survivor. If you own an asset as tenants in common, you each have distinct shares which can be different – for example, one person can own 40 per cent and the other 60 per cent. Moreover, you can specify in your will who should inherit your share when you die – it does not have to pass to your co-owner.

Example

Veronica McGough wants to give away as much as possible free of inheritance tax before she dies.

First, she gives £1,000 a year to each of her three children – taking advantage of the £3,000 a year annual exemption. Then she makes £250 gifts every year to each of her ten grandchildren – a total of £2,500 a year free of inheritance tax as small gifts. She also gives the maximum £2,500 to any of her grandchildren who get married.

She can afford to pay the premiums on insurance policies on her own life out of her income. So she takes out policies written in trust (p. 169) for each of her three children. The premiums come to £60 a month each and will be tax-free as normal expenditure out of income. (When she dies, the money from the insurance policies will be paid straight to the children without being taxable.)

Overall, Veronica manages to give away £7,660 every year free of inheritance tax. Even if she dies within seven years of making the gifts, there will be no inheritance tax to pay on them because they are all exempt gifts.

Your home

Your home is almost certainly your most valuable possession – and may be the main reason why your estate ends up over the threshold for paying inheritance tax. But it is one of the hardest assets to remove from the tax net – assuming you intend to go on living in it until you die.

For example, you can't make a lifetime gift of it to your children on condition you can continue to live in it. That would count as a gift with reservation (p. 171), and the home would still be treated as yours. More complex planning can trigger a charge to the pre-owned asset tax (p. 174).

The problem of inheritance tax on the family home has been removed for many married couples and civil partners by the effective doubling of the tax-free allowance through the ability to inherit each other's unused tax allowance (p. 160). There is no inheritance tax to pay if the first to die leaves their share of the home to their spouse or civil partner. When the second dies, there is no tax to pay on the home if it is worth less than £650,000 in 2010–11.

Inheritance tax on the home remains a major problem for unmarried couples and other people who live together (for example, siblings, parents and adult children, and infirm people living with carers). If you are in any of these situations and would want your cohabitee to remain in the home if you die first, if possible you should from the outset buy your home jointly rather than in the name of just one of you. This increases the chance that your tax-free allowance will fully cover the share of the home you leave. If you are the sole owner of your home, you can put it into your joint names by giving or selling a share to your cohabitee, but to avoid the gift with reservation rules (p. 171) or pre-owned assets tax (p. 174), you must not benefit from the part of the home you transfer to them. This means taking care to pay your full share of the household bills. Provided you escape these traps, a gift of part of the home will count as a PET and so become tax-free provided you survive seven years.

Note that, if you sell a share of your home to someone you live with, they will have to pay stamp duty land tax on the price they pay. If you give them part of your home, normally there will be no stamp duty. But, if there is a mortgage on the property that they become jointly responsible for paying, this will count as if it is a price they have paid and stamp duty will be charged on the value of this commitment.

Example

> Geoff, 67 and divorced, has owned his own home for many years and it's worth around £450,000. Recently his older sister, Pat, now widowed, has moved in with him. He wants to be sure she could stay in the home if he dies before her. But, if he died in 2010–11, there would be tax on the home of 40% × (£450,000 – £325,000) = £50,000. Neither of them have much in savings or other assets, so she would have to sell the home to pay the tax. A possible solution would be for Geoff to give Pat a half share in the house. Provided he does not benefit from the half he gives away and he survives seven years, then this would remove £225,000 from his estate. His remaining share of the home would be covered by his tax-free allowance on death, so there would be no tax to pay.

Consider will trusts

Before spouses and civil partners could inherit each other's unused tax-free allowance (p. 160), one way you could make sure your tax-free allowance was not wasted was to set up a discretionary trust in your will. Using 2010–11 figures, the will would leave £325,000 to the trust – which could be a share in the family home – and the trustees would have the right to allow anyone from the specified beneficiaries to live in the home. The surviving spouse would be included amongst the beneficiaries. The bequest to the trust would use the £325,000 tax-free allowance and would not become part of the surviving spouse's estate. A variant on the scheme has the spouse inheriting the home outright but issuing an IOU to the trust for the £325,000 left to it under the will. Another option may be to set up an interest-in-possession will trust giving your surviving spouse the right to remain in the home during their lifetime, provided the trust did not comply with the rules for an immediate post-death-interest trust (see box overleaf).

Some experts have suggested that being able to inherit your spouse or civil partner's allowance means that will trusts are now redundant, but that depends on your view about possible future increases in the tax-free allowance and the assets you expect to leave – see the Example overleaf. This is a complex area, so seek advice from a tax expert (see Appendix E).

Example

Scott died in August 2008 and his wife Kay dies in May 2010. For simplicity, assume their only asset is the family home in which they owned half each as tenants in common. In 2008, the home was worth £700,000. The table shows some possible inheritance tax positions depending on how Scott left his share of the home and what happened to house prices.

	Scott leaves:			
	Everything to Kay		Some to will trust, rest to Kay	
House price inflation	0%	10%	0%	10%
Value of Scott's estate 2008–09	£350,000	£350,000	£350,000	£350,000
Tax-free allowance used	£0	£0	£312,000	£312,000
Inheritance tax on Scott's death	£0	£0	£0	£0
Value of Kay's estate 2010–11	£700,000	£847,000	£388,000	£469,480
Tax-free allowance used	£700,000	£700,000	£350,000	£350,000
Inheritance tax on Kay's death	£0	£58,800	£15,200	£47,792

If house prices rise by less than the tax-free allowance, the couple pay less tax if Scott left everything to Kay and she inherited his tax-free allowance. If house prices rise by more than the tax-free allowance, they save tax if Scott used his allowance to leave most of his share of the home to a will trust.

Inheritance tax and trusts

A trust is a legal arrangement where one or more people (the trustees) hold assets (the trust property) to be used for the benefit of one or more people (the beneficiaries) in accordance with the rules of the trust. The person who gives the trust property is called the settlor. There are two main types of trust:

- **interest in possession trust**. The beneficiary/ies has the right to use the trust property or receive income from it during their lifetime or for some other specified period. They are said to have the life interest. Other beneficiaries, or sometimes the same people, have the right to become the outright owners of the trust property when the life interest ends – this is called the reversionary interest

- **discretionary trust**. The trustees decide who among the beneficiaries will receive payments of income and/or capital from the trust and when this will be, subject to whatever the trust rules say.

Under the discretionary trust regime, gifts to the trust are taxable, so there is inheritance tax to pay at the time of the gift unless it falls within the £325,000 tax-free allowance. In addition, there is an inheritance tax charge every ten years on the value of the trust property and an exit charges when assets leave the trust. Before 22 March 2006, interest in possession trusts and certain discretionary trusts, called accumulation and maintenance (A&M) trusts, were subject to a more lenient regime under which gifts to the trust counted as potentially exempt transfers, there were no 10-yearly or exit charges and, where someone had a life interest, they were treated as if they owned the trust assets for inheritance tax purposes.

From 22 March 2006 onwards, the discretionary trust regime applies to nearly all types of trust, including interest in possession trusts and A&M trusts. The few exceptions are:

■ immediate-post-death-interest (IPDI) trusts set up in a will to give a life interest to a survivor

■ bereaved minor trusts set up in a will to benefit a dependent child of the person who has died

■ disabled person's trusts set up either in life or on death to benefit a person with a physical or mental disability.

Life insurance

If you want to make sure there is enough money to pay an inheritance tax bill on a home or business, you can take out a term life insurance policy which pays out if you die within seven years of giving it away. And if you plan to leave a large asset on death, whole life insurance policies pay out whenever you die, again providing cash to pay the inheritance tax.

Tax-saving ideas 121–123

Holding assets as tenants in common (p. 165) rather than joint tenants gives you flexibility over how you leave your share of those assets and so can save tax. You can sever a joint tenancy by writing to the co-owner(s).

If you expect the value of assets that you leave to rise faster in future than the tax-free allowance (which usually increases broadly in line with inflation) using a will trust may save you and your spouse or civil partner tax.

Use life insurance to blunt the impact of inheritance tax. Policies written in trust go straight to the beneficiary and don't form part of your estate. Premiums you pay are tax-free gifts if they count as normal expenditure out of income or fall within the £3,000 a year exemption.

Make sure you have any such policies written in trust to the person you want to have the money. The proceeds will then be paid directly to that person on your death and be free of inheritance tax. The premiums for a policy written in trust count as gifts, but will be free of inheritance tax if the policy is for your spouse or civil partner. And if you pay the premiums as normal spending out of income or the £3,000 annual allowance applies, they will be tax-free whoever benefits.

Shares

The market value of any shares left on death must normally be included in your estate in working out the inheritance tax bill. But some sorts of shares qualify for business relief (also available on lifetime gifts). This reduces the value for inheritance tax purposes – or even removes them from the calculation altogether:

- shares in a listed company which form a controlling interest, the value of the shares is halved

- unquoted shares in most companies – including those listed on the Alternative Investment Market (AIM) – qualify for full relief

- unquoted securities which either alone or with other securities and unquoted shares give you a controlling interest qualify for full relief.

To prevent 'death-bed' purchases of business property, all these shares and securities must have been owned for at least two years.

Your own business or farm

If you own or have an interest in a small business or a farm, seek professional advice on inheritance tax, since there are substantial concessions which can reduce or eliminate the tax:

- business property relief means there will be no inheritance tax to pay on business assets such as goodwill, land, buildings, plant, stock, patents and so on (reduced by debts incurred in the business)

- agricultural property relief can mean no inheritance tax on the agricultural value of owner-occupied farmlands and farm tenancies (including cottages and farm buildings). There are also reliefs for landowners who let farmland. Agricultural property relief has been extended to land anywhere in the European Economic Area (see p. 424) back dated to 23 April 2003.

Estate freezing

Estate freezing is a way of freezing some of the value of your wealth now so the increase in value in future years benefits someone else.

A simple way of doing this is by investing in an endowment or unit-linked life insurance policy written in trust for your children or grandchildren (p. 169). Any growth in its value accumulates in the policy free of inheritance tax. Some unit trust managers can do something similar with investments in unit trusts.

Changing inheritances after a death

Whether or not there is a will, those who are entitled to a share of a dead person's estate can agree to vary the way the estate is divided up and this may save tax. For example, the variation could direct some of the estate towards tax-free bequests – from the children to the dead person's husband or wife, for example. The variation must be made within two years of the date of death. Get advice from a solicitor who can draw up a suitably worded deed.

Tax-saving ideas 124–126

Consider estate freezing by, for example, paying premiums to an investment-type life insurance policy written in trust for the person to whom you wish to make the gift. They get any growth in the value of the investment instead of it counting as part of your estate.

A deed of variation can be used to alter the way an estate is shared out. This could save tax on a subsequent death where, say, part of a tax-free bequest to a spouse or civil partner was diverted instead to a child or grandchild and the new gift fell within the deceased's £325,000 tax-free limit.

If a subsequent death occurs within two years, it may be more tax-efficient to use a deed of variation rather than claim successive charges relief (p. 173).

Inheritance tax planning pitfalls

You may think there are some rather obvious wheezes that will help you avoid inheritance tax. It is unlikely that the Revenue will not have thought of them and blocked their use.

Gifts with strings attached

If you give something away but reserve the right to use it, it counts as a gift with reservation – and is treated as remaining your property. The gift would not be recognised for inheritance tax purposes and its value would be added to your estate when you died. This applies to any such gifts made on or after 18 March 1986.

For example, if you give your home to a child on condition that you can go on living in it until your death, this would count as a gift with reservation. This could apply even if there was no formal agreement that you go on living in the home.

Accountants, insurance companies and others have been fairly successful in devising schemes – often using trusts and generally complicated – that let you continue to enjoy the income or use of an asset that you have given away without falling foul of the gift with reservation rules. The Revenue has now pulled the plug on most of these schemes by introducing the pre-owned assets tax (p. 174).

Associated operations

If you try to get round the inheritance tax rules by making a series of gifts, the Revenue is allowed to treat them as associated operations which form a single direct gift. For example, you might think you could give an extra £2,500 to an adult child by making ten tax-free gifts of £250 to friends which they pass on. The taxman will treat this as a single £2,500 gift, however – and potentially subject to tax.

Related property

In working out the value of a bequest or gift, the Revenue may treat as yours property which it reckons is related to yours – in particular, anything owned by your husband, wife or civil partner. This means you can't reduce its value by splitting it with your spouse or partner.

Suppose, for example, you own 30 per cent of the shares in a company and your spouse owns another 30 per cent. The Revenue will value your 30 per cent as worth half the value of a 60 per cent controlling interest, which is generally higher than the value of a 30 per cent minority interest.

Retroactive/retrospective legislation

The government has made clear that it is prepared to introduce new tax charges (like the pre-owned assets tax – p. 174) to ensure that successful tax-avoidance schemes do not after all save tax.

Payment of inheritance tax

Inheritance tax is due six months after the end of the month in which death occurred. If tax is due, you need to make a return to the Revenue on form IHT400. In other cases, you can normally use the much simpler form IHT205. In general, the property in the estate cannot be distributed until probate has been granted, but probate will not be granted until the tax has been paid. Therefore, the personal representatives may have to borrow to pay the tax bill. However, certain National Savings & Investments products can be used before probate solely for paying tax and, since 2003, the balances in the deceased's bank and building society accounts can usually also be used in this way.

Interest is charged if the tax is paid after the six-month deadline, running from the time the tax was due. Likewise, if you pay too much inheritance tax, you will get interest on the over-payment from the Revenue.

If you take out a loan to pay inheritance tax before probate is granted, you can get tax relief on the interest on it for up to 12 months by setting it against taxable income accruing to the estate after death and before distribution.

You can spread inheritance tax on land, property and business assets over ten equal yearly instalments.

If you inherit investments or land and buildings that fall in value after the death of the person who bequeathed them, you might be able to reduce the inheritance tax bill.

Where you make a lifetime gift that is neither tax-free nor a PET, you must report the gift to the Revenue on form IHT100 if the total of such gifts during the tax year comes to more than £10,000 or your running total of such gifts over the last ten years comes to more than £40,000. Report the gift within 12 months of the end of the month in which you made it.

Facing a second inheritance tax bill within five years?

If you inherit something that has only recently been subject to inheritance tax, the tax due on this second change of ownership is reduced by what is known as successive charges relief (formerly quick succession relief). Provided the death which led to the first payment was within five years of the death that has led to a second tax bill, the second bill can be reduced by a fraction of the first bill.

If the first death was within one year of the second death, the second bill is reduced by the following fraction of the first bill:

$$\frac{\text{Value of inheritance at the time of first transfer}}{\text{Value of inheritance at transfer} + \text{tax paid on first transfer}}$$

If the first death was more than one year before the second death, the fraction is reduced by 20 per cent for each complete year – see Example overleaf.

Example

Maurice Thornton inherits a share of his mother's estate, worth £160,000. Inheritance tax of £7,000 is due on this share.

However, Maurice's mother had inherited £80,000 from her father only two-and-a-half years earlier – an inheritance on which tax of £20,000 had been paid. Because Maurice's legacy is within five years of his mother's own legacy, he is entitled to reduce the inheritance tax on his legacy by a fraction of what was paid on hers.

The fraction of the tax bill on his mother's legacy which can be taken into account is worked out as follows:

$$\frac{£80,000}{£80,000 + £20,000}$$

$$= \frac{£80,000}{£100,000}$$

$$= 4/5$$

This means if the second death had occurred within one year of the first, the tax bill would be reduced to 4/5 × £20,000 = £16,000. However, the period between the two deaths is two-and-a-half years, so the fraction is reduced to just 60 per cent (100 per cent less 20 per cent for each complete year) of 4/5. This means the tax bill is 60% × £16,000 = £9,600. This means Maurice's bill is reduced to zero.

Pre-owned assets tax

If you still use something you have given away or sold for less than its full value at any time since 18 March 1986 and the gift is not caught by the gift with reservation rules (p. 171) it may from 6 April 2005 be caught instead by the pre-owned assets tax (POAT). The tax may also apply to something you use which belongs to someone to whom you made a cash gift in the last seven years.

POAT is an extra charge to income tax that aims to tax the yearly benefit you are deemed to get from your continued use of the gift. You can be liable for POAT even if you have no income with which to pay it. You will need to report any POAT liability on your tax return (p. 213).

With land and property, the benefit you are deemed to get is the market rent you would otherwise pay. For chattels (for example, paintings and antiques) and other assets, the benefit is a percentage of the asset's market value. The percentage is the official rate of interest (p. 125) which was 4.00 per cent in April 2010. The taxable value is reduced by anything you actually pay for using the asset under a legally binding agreement. Land, property and chattels need to be valued every five years.

There are some exceptions. For example, there will be no POAT charge if:

- the value of all the items otherwise subject to POAT is £5,000 or less (before deducting anything you pay)

- you sold the whole of the asset you still use for its full market value

- the gift was covered by the £3,000 yearly inheritance tax exemption or the £250 small gift exemption (p. 163)

- you gave away your home to your children, say, but now have to live with them because of old age or illness

- you gave away a part-share of the asset – for example, your home – which you share with the co-owner(s) and you pay your full share of the expenses (or more) so you derive no benefit from the arrangement

- this is an equity release scheme with a commercial company. Non-commercial equity release schemes (for example, where a family member buys a share of your home) are exempt if the transaction was completed before 7 March 2005 or the payment is not in money or readily convertible assets (for example, in return for personal care when you have become infirm). But the transaction is not exempt if you have sold only part of your home to someone connected to you. 'Connected' is defined very widely to mean any ancestor (parent, grandparent and so on), any descendant (child, grandchild and so on), brother, sister, uncle, aunt, nephew, niece, your spouse or civil partner and any of their relatives, and any husbands and wives of any of your, your spouse's or civil partner's relatives.

Tax-saving ideas 127–129

If a relative – say, a son or daughter – offers to buy part of your home as a way of giving you cash while you still live in the home, the arrangement will be caught by POAT and you may have to pay tax each year on the benefit you are deemed to receive. But POAT will not apply if you sell them the whole of your home at its full market value. And, even where you sell only part of the property, POAT does not apply if the buyer is not treated as connected to you – for example, an unmarried partner.

To provide you with financial help, instead of a relative buying a share of your home, they could lend you money to be repaid eventually out of your estate. This would not be caught by POAT.

You will be caught by POAT if assets you use that are owned by someone else can be matched to any cash you gave them within the previous seven years. But there are no forward matching rules. So you may escape POAT if, say, your children pay for your home by building a granny annexe onto their home and later on you are able to give them some financial help.

What to do about POAT

Make the most of the exemptions on p. 175. But if POAT seems likely to apply, you have three choices:

- stay within the POAT regime. You can reduce or eliminate the bill if under a legally binding agreement you pay the owner of the asset for using it

- unravel the arrangement so that it is instead caught by the gift with reservation rules

- elect to be treated as if the gift with reservation rules apply. This means the asset will be treated as if it is part of your estate on your death so inheritance tax may become due. But there is no elimination of capital gains on your death (p. 131) and the current owner's acquisition value for CGT is still the value at the time of the gift.

In general, you must make the election by 31 January following the end of the tax year in which you first become liable for POAT. For example, if you first start to use the asset in the 2010–11 tax year, you must make the election by 31 January 2012. However, all is not necessarily lost if you miss the deadline because the Revenue has powers to accept a late election. The election is made by you alone but you might wish to discuss it with the owner of the asset who could become liable for inheritance tax on your death. Make the election on form IHT500 and send it to the Revenue Capital Taxes Office (see Appendix E).

Tax-saving ideas 130 and 131

If a transaction is caught by POAT but you want to make future gifts to the person to whom you sold or gave the asset, consider paying them a full market rent under a legally binding agreement. POAT is then reduced to zero and the rent stands in place of the gifts you want to make. But the recipient will be taxed on the rental income.

If you use an asset you gave away and are caught by POAT, consider electing for the gift with reservation rules to apply instead if the value of your estate will in any case be below the inheritance tax-free limit (£325,000 in 2010–11).

Filling in your tax return

11

Getting started

The Revenue has been trying to reduce the number of people who have to fill in the full tax return. If you get most of your income through the PAYE system, you may just be sent a PAYE review form (see Chapter 3). If your affairs are fairly straightforward, you may be sent a short tax return of four pages and no supplements – see Appendix C for guidance on completing this form.

If your affairs are more complex, you will be sent the full tax return. It is also up to you to request the full return if the review form or short return is not suitable given your circumstances. When you get the full return for 2009–10, this is what you should have:

■ a six-page booklet entitled *Tax Return 2009*. We show you how to complete these pages in this chapter and Chapters 12 to 14

■ supplementary pages to cater for your individual circumstances. There are eight sets of supplementary pages. If your tax office knows that a supplement is relevant to you, it may be bound into the front of your Main tax return booklet. We explain how to fill in these pages in Chapters 16 to 23

■ a 30-page guide called *How to fill in your Tax Return* that explains how to fill in the main form. It will include extra guidance for any supplementary pages that are bound into your tax return

■ a four-page booklet headed *Additional information*. You are not automatically sent any guidance on filling in this form and have to order separately the 28-page guide (see overleaf). Chapters 12 to 16 will help you decide whether you need to fill in these pages as well as helping you to complete them

■ a two-page guide and form for giving a tax repayment to charity.

What you should do next

Step 1

If you will be filing the paper return, check you have the correct supplementary pages. If you will be filing online using the Revenue software (see Chapter 3), an early screen invites you to tailor the software by selecting the supplements that are relevant to you. You can go back to this screen at any time to add further supplements if necessary. Although this part of the book shows you how to complete the paper return, the guidance and tax-saving ideas apply equally if you are filing online.

Step 2

If you have not been sent all the supplementary pages you need or you want the Tax calculation summary or notes for the additional pages, contact the Revenue Orderline – see box below.

Contacting the Revenue

The Revenue Orderline is a one-stop shop for all the tax forms, notes and help-sheets. The Orderline is open every day from 8am to 8pm, except Christmas Day, Boxing Day and New Year's Day. The phone number is 0845 900 0404, fax number 0845 900 0604 or you can download all the forms and guidance, except the short tax return, from the Revenue website www.hmrc.gov.uk/sa/forms/content.htm.

The Revenue Helpline gives advice on all aspects of filling in your tax return and general advice on the self assessment process. It is open 8am to 8pm every day, except Christmas Day, Boxing Day and New Year's Day. Call 0845 900 0444.

Step 3

Gather together all your records and supporting documentation, which you need to fill in the tax return.

Step 4

Fill in your supplementary pages FIRST, using the guidance in Chapters 16 to 23 of this Guide. Next, check whether any of the entries in the Additional information form apply to you, using Chapters 12 to 16 of this book. If you need further help, contact your tax office (see your return or correspondence) or, if that is closed, the Revenue Helpline.

Step 5

After filling in the supplementary and additional pages, complete the tax return.

Step 6

Provided you meet the Revenue deadlines for sending back your return, either the Revenue or the online filing software will automatically work out your tax bill based on the figures you supply. If you are filing a paper return, you can if you prefer send in your own tax calculation. In that case, ask the Revenue Orderline (see box opposite) to send you the Tax calculation summary and accompanying notes.

Step 7

If you are not going to work out your tax bill yourself, send in your tax return and supplementary pages by 31 October 2010, or by 31 January 2011 if you file by internet (see Chapter 3).

Step 8

If you are an employee and the tax you owe is less than £2,000, choose to send in your tax return and supplementary pages by 31 October, or, if you use the internet, by 31 December. Then you can pay your tax bill through the PAYE system monthly starting in April 2011.

Step 9

Send your final tax payment for the 2009–10 tax year by 31 January 2011, together with your first payment on account for 2010–11 if that applies to you – see Chapter 3. If you intend to file a paper tax return but miss the 31 October deadline, you will normally have to pay an automatic penalty of £100, but you can avoid this if instead you file online by 31 January 2011, or you file a paper return but also pay all the tax due by 31 January 2011 – see Chapter 4.

Starting your tax return

The first page, TR1, of the return asks you to check or supply your name, contact details and national insurance number. Also give your date of birth – this should ensure you are given the correct allowances (see Chapter 14 for details).

The first eight questions on page TR2 of the Main tax return check whether you need to fill in any supplementary pages. If you answer yes to a question and the supplement is not already bound into your tax return, get a copy either from the Orderline or the Revenue website (p. 180).

Employment

> **1 | Employment**
>
> If you were an employee, director, office holder or agency worker in the year to 5 April 2010, do you need to complete *Employment* pages? Please read pages TRG 2 and TRG 3 of the guide before answering.
>
> Fill in a separate *Employment* page for each employment, directorship etc., for which you need to complete an *Employment* page and say how many pages you are completing.
>
> Yes ☐ No ☐ Number ☐

You are required to fill in the Employment supplementary pages if you answer YES to this question. If you have more than one job, you will need a set of Employment pages for each job. The supplement has space for two jobs – order an extra supplement if you have more jobs. The Revenue will regard you as an employee even if you work on a part-time or casual basis. There are more guidelines on who counts as an employee in Chapter 15.

Self-employment

> **2 | Self-employment**
>
> Did you work for yourself (on your 'own account' or in self-employment) in the year to 5 April 2010? (Answer 'Yes' if you were a 'Name' at Lloyd's.) Fill in a separate *Self-employment* page for each business and say how many pages you are completing.
>
> Yes ☐ No ☐ Number ☐

If you carried on a trade, profession or vocation as a self-employed person during 2009–10 you need to complete this supplementary section. Chapter 17 has guidelines on who counts as self-employed. If your turnover was under £68,000, you can probably complete the short supplement, otherwise you need the full supplement. If you have more than one business, you need more than one supplement.

If you are in partnership you need to complete a different set of supplementary pages (see below).

Partnership

3	Partnership

Were you in partnership? Fill in a separate *Partnership* page for each partnership you were a partner in and say how many pages you are completing.

Yes ☐   No ☐   Number ☐

If you are in business with one or more partners, you should answer YES to this question and complete a set of supplementary pages. There is a short version and a long version. You will find guidance on which version you should complete in Chapter 18.

UK property

4	**UK property**

Did you receive any income from UK property (including rents and other income from land you own or lease out)?

Yes ☐   No ☐

You need to complete this supplement if you had rental income from a buy-to-let property, a holiday home, lodgers in your own home or any other UK land or property during 2009–10. However, if you provide additional services, such as meals, you will need to complete the Self-employment supplementary pages instead, as you are considered to be carrying on a trade. You can get more guidance from Chapter 19.

If you have a property abroad that you rent out, you need the Foreign supplement (see overleaf) not this one.

Do not include dividends from real estate investment trusts (REITs) or property authorised investment funds (PAIFs) in this supplement – they go on page TR3 of the Main tax return (p. 211).

Foreign

> **5** **Foreign**
>
> If you:
> - were entitled to any foreign income, or income gains
> - have, or could have, received (directly or indirectly) income, or a capital payment or benefit from a person abroad as a result of any transfer of assets
> - want to claim relief for foreign tax paid
>
> please read the notes on page TRG 4 to decide if you have to fill in the *Foreign* pages.
>
> Do you need to complete the *Foreign* pages?
>
> Yes ☐   No ☐

There are six supplementary pages which have space to give details about your foreign savings, pensions and benefits, income from offshore trusts, gains on foreign life policies, property income, other investment income from abroad and tax deducted from foreign earnings that you want to reclaim. Turn to Chapter 20 for more information on what is foreign income and how it is taxed.

Trusts

> **6** **Trusts etc.**
>
> Did you receive, or are you treated as having received, income from a trust, settlement or the residue of a deceased person's estate?
>
> Yes ☐   No ☐

You need to complete this supplement if you were a beneficiary or settlor of a trust, or had income from the estate of someone who has died. You can find more information and guidance on filling in this supplementary page in Chapter 21. A beneficiary of a bare trust enters the income in the Main tax return, p. 193.

Capital gains summary

7 Capital gains summary

If you disposed of any chargeable assets (including, for example, stocks, shares, units in a unit trust, land and property, goodwill in a business), or had any chargeable gains, or you wish to claim an allowable loss or make any other claim or election, read pages TRG 5 of the guide to decide if you have to fill in the *Capital gains summary* page.

Do you need to complete the *Capital gains summary* page?

Yes ☐   No ☐

You must complete these supplementary pages if you have made a capital gain (with some exceptions – see below) or you wish to claim an allowable capital loss for 2009–10.

You normally won't need to return the supplementary pages if your gains for the year totalled £10,100 or less (the tax-free slice for the year) and the value of the assets you disposed of totalled no more than £40,400 (four times the tax-free slice). Do not include tax-free gains or assets in these calculations (such as the sale of your main home if the gain was tax-free).

For more information on which gains are tax-free and guidance on whether the gain on selling your home will be taxable or not, see Chapter 9. See Chapter 22 for guidance on filling in the supplement and the supporting calculations that you'll need to send in.

Non-resident

8 Residence, remittance basis etc.

Were you, for all or part of the year to 5 April 2010, one or more of the following - not resident, not ordinarily resident or not domiciled in the UK and claiming the remittance basis; or dual resident in the UK and another country?

Yes ☐   No ☐

If at any time during 2009–10, you consider yourself to be non-resident, not ordinarily resident or not domiciled in the UK, or resident in the UK at the same time as being resident in a country with which the UK has a double-taxation agreement, then you will need to complete this supplement. Chapter 23 will give you guidance.

Student loan repayments

1	If you have received notification from the Student Loans Company that repayment of an Income Contingent Student Loan began before 6 April 2010, put 'X' in the box	2	If your employer has deducted Student Loan repayments enter the amount deducted
	[ ]		£ [ ] [ ] [ ] [ ] [ ] [ ] [ ] . [0] [0]

The final section on page TR2 asks you for information about any student loan repayments.

Student loans taken out from August 1998 onwards are 'income contingent'. This means under the current rules that you start to repay them once you're earning and your income exceeds a set threshold – £15,000 a year from 6 April 2005 (£10,000 in earlier years). This is equivalent to £1,250 a month or £288 a week. If your income for 2009–10 exceeds £15,000, you are required to make a loan repayment equal to 9 per cent of the income in excess of £15,000. Some income is ignored, for example, unearned income (from savings, pensions, benefits, and so on) unless it comes to more than £2,000, and benefits in kind. In calculating your income, relief is given for pension contributions and some types of losses that qualify for tax relief.

If the Student Loan Company has notified you that repayment of your loan started before 6 April 2010 (and you had not fully repaid the loan before the start of the tax year on 6 April 2009), put a cross in box 1. Provided you send in your tax return on time, the Revenue or the online filing software will work out the repayment due. Any amount entered in box 2 will be deducted to arrive at the amount due. If you have repaid too much (which may happen in the year you finish paying off the loan), you will get a refund.

Normally, the Revenue will have instructed your employer to deduct the loan repayments through PAYE. Enter the amount deducted in box 2 of this section. If you have more than one employer, add together the repayments deducted by them all and put the total in box 2 of this section.

In some circumstances, the amount deducted might not be the full repayment due for the year. This will be the case if, for example:

- you have more than one job. Each employer will ignore the first £15,000 of your earnings from the job concerned
- you have unearned income of more than £2,000.

The Revenue will collect any extra repayments due through the self-assessment system. A person who does not receive a tax return is not required to pay any more than has already been deducted through PAYE but can voluntarily pay extra.

Finishing your tax return

You can fill in pages TR3 and TR4 of the Main return and the first page of the Additional information form, if you need it, using Chapters 12 to 14 of this book. Chapter 12 completes the income pages, Chapter 13 explains the reliefs sections, Chapter 14 deals with allowances.

On page TR5 of the main tax return, you are asked for information about tax collection and refunds.

| 1 | If you have had any 2009-10 Income Tax refunded or set off by us or Jobcentre Plus, enter the amount |

£ ⬚⬚⬚⬚⬚⬚⬚⬚ . 0 0

If this does not apply to you, go straight to question 2. Otherwise, enter the amount you were refunded, either directly from your tax office (including repayments of tax deducted from savings and investments) or from Jobcentre Plus (such as refunds of tax deducted from jobseeker's allowance). You should also include similar amounts which, rather than being paid directly to you, have been set off against payments of tax that you owe.

| 2 | If you owe tax for 2009-10 and have a PAYE tax code, we will try to collect the tax due (if less than £2,000) through your tax code for 2011-12, unless you put 'X' in the box - *read page TRG 21 of the guide* | 3 | If you are likely to owe tax for **2010-11** on income other than employed earnings or pensions, and you do **not** want us to use your 2010-11 PAYE tax code to collect that tax during the year, put 'X' in the box - *read page TRG 21 of the guide* |

If you are on PAYE and owe tax of less than £2,000, it will normally be collected through the PAYE system. You are asked to put a cross in box 2 if you do not want this to happen, but do not do so without some thought. PAYE spreads out and delays the payment of your tax.

You may have non-PAYE income for 2009–10 which is expected to continue in 2010–11 and on which tax or extra tax is expected to be due. This might include, say, interest from savings, rents from property or earnings from freelance work. Where this income is £10,000 or less, the Revenue will usually adjust your PAYE code for 2010–11 to collect the estimated tax due.

But, if you would prefer to wait and sort out the tax bill after the end of the tax year, put a cross in box 3.

If you have paid too much tax (for example, your payments on account for 2009–10 exceed the amount of tax now calculated as due), you get the excess back. If you will soon be getting a tax bill – for example, your first payment on account for 2010–11 – the Revenue will normally deduct the refund from the tax due. In other cases, the refund will be paid out to you.

Fill in boxes 4 to 8 as appropriate to say where the refund should be sent. Also fill in boxes 10 to 14 if you have directed that someone else should receive the refund on your behalf.

| 9 | If you do not have a bank or building society account, or if you want a cheque to be sent to you or to your nominee, put 'X' in the box |

The Revenue assumes you will accept repayment direct to a bank or building society account unless you don't have one. While direct payment is more secure, you can't be forced to accept payment this way. If you have an account but would prefer a cheque, put a cross in box 9.

If you want to donate your tax refund to charity, fill in the separate charity form (see opposite).

On page TR6 give details of your tax adviser (if applicable) in boxes 15 to 18.

Box 19 is for any extra information you want to tell the Revenue. A lot of the questions on the Main tax return ask you just for totals but supported by detailed breakdowns in box 19. The box is small and, if you do not have enough space, continue on the blank pages at the back of the Main tax return with a note in box 19 directing the Revenue to those pages.

And finally

| 20 | If this Tax Return contains provisional or estimated figures, put 'X' in the box | 21 | If you are enclosing separate supplementary pages, put 'X' in the box |

Put a cross in box 20 if any of the figures on the Main tax return, Additional information form or any of the supplements are provisional. In box 19

(*Any other information*), explain which figures are provisional (including the form, page and box number), why they are provisional and when they will be finalised. If you know you are not going to be able to give reliable figures, because you have lost information or have had to estimate a valuation, for example, explain what they are and how you have arrived at the estimates.

If you negligently submit a provisional figure that is inaccurate or unnecessary, you may be liable to a penalty.

Do not put a cross in box 20 if your tax return includes estimated figures (such as valuations) which you reckon to be final. Give details of how such figures have been estimated either in the appropriate supplements or in box 19.

Tax-saving idea 132

Avoid simple mistakes that could cause your tax return to be rejected and possibly cause a £100 late-filing penalty. Common errors include: ticking yes to any of Qs 1 to 8 on page TR2 but failing to send the supplementary pages, sending information on a separate sheet instead of on the tax return itself, writing notes such as 'per accounts' or 'information to follow' instead of putting in figures (albeit provisional ones), and failing to sign and date the return.

Giving a tax refund to charity

You can use your tax return to instruct that part or all of any tax refund is paid direct to a charity of your choice by filling in the separate Charity form.

3 | If you would like all of your repayment to go to a charity, put 'X' in the box

4 | If you only want some of your repayment to go to charity, enter the maximum amount we can send

£ [   ] · [0][0]

If you are not sure how much your refund will be, you can limit your donation to a maximum amount by writing a sum in box 4 (instead of donating the whole amount by putting a cross in box 3). If your refund comes to less than the amount in box 4, the whole refund will go to charity. If it comes to more, the excess will be paid back to you.

> **5** Please enter the charity code – *you can get this from*
> *www.hmrc.gov.uk/charities/charities-search.htm*
> *or phone us*
>
> ☐☐ ☐☐ ☐☐ G
>
> **6** If you want Gift Aid to apply to the payment, put 'X' in the box. The charity will receive basic rate Income Tax on your gift
>
> ☐

You can choose only from participating charities and you need to get the charity's code from the Revenue Helpline (p. 180) or the website address given on the form. Put a cross in box 6 if you want this to be a Gift Aid donation (p. 231). You will then be able to claim higher-rate tax relief on the donation if you are a higher-rate taxpayer in 2010–11 by entering details in box 5 on page TR4 of next year's Main tax return (not this one).

Tax-saving idea 133

If you use your tax return to donate a tax refund to charity (by completing the separate charity form), do not opt for Gift Aid if you are a non-taxpayer or pay too little tax to cover the tax relief due on the donation. In that event, you will get a tax bill to cover the relief given (p. 232).

12

Income

The first stage in working out your income tax bill for 2009–10 is to find your taxable income. Page TR3 of the Main tax return asks about the most common types of income, such as interest from savings accounts, pensions and some state benefits. If you have any more unusual types of income, such as interest from gilts or gains from life insurance policies, you will need to complete the Additional information form. This chapter will help you decide what income you need to declare and on which form. We start with the Main tax return. Guidance on completing the first page of the Additional information form starts on p. 214.

This is not the only way in which your tax inspector will find out about your income. There are also supplementary pages, for example, Employment, Self-employment and UK property, where you must give details of other sorts of income. And these should be filled in before you tackle the Main tax return or Additional information pages.

You don't need to enter in the tax return any income which is tax-free. A comprehensive list is given in Appendix A.

When entering your income in the tax return, you should enter the amount you received in 2009–10 (although in a few cases there are special rules for what counts as received). If you receive income of the same type from more than one source – for example, you have several savings accounts – enter the overall total for each type, but keep records for each separate account in case your tax office asks to see them.

When you enter amounts of income, round any odd pence down to the nearest £. When you enter amounts of tax already deducted, round any odd pence up to the nearest £. If you are entering the total of income or tax from several sources (several savings accounts, say), add up each amount including the pence and round just the total.

Savings and investment income

You can get an income from your investments or savings in the form of interest, dividends or distributions; for example, interest on a building society account, dividends from shares or distributions from unit trusts. Although the income from these sources can be paid out to you, this is not always the case. For example, interest can be added to your account rather than paid out, and with distributions from unit trusts it can be reinvested if you choose. It counts as income whether it is paid out to you or not. However, you do not enter anywhere in your tax return any saving and investment income that is tax-free – see the box below.

Tax-free investment income

Some investment income is free of income tax. This income does not have to be entered in the tax return. Income from the following investments count as tax-free:

- prizes from premium bonds, National Lottery and gambling

- an ISA (individual savings account). (Since 6 April 2004, dividends and similar income from investments within a stocks and shares ISA do have some tax deducted which you cannot reclaim. But these still count as tax-free investments.) Note that, since 6 April 2008, PEPs have been reclassified as ISAs

- SAYE schemes

- NS&I Certificates, including the index-linked ones

- NS&I Children's Bonus Bonds

- Ulster Savings Certificates, if you normally live in Northern Ireland and you bought the certificates or they were repaid while you were living there

- dividends on shares in venture capital trusts (up to £200,000 of shares a year from 6 April 2004 or £100,000 in earlier years)

- Saving Gateway interest and Maturity payment.

There are other less obvious forms of investment income that are tax-free and don't need to be entered in the tax return:

- interest awarded by a UK court as part of a claim for damages for personal injury or death. There is an extra-statutory concession which means that this can also apply to awards from a foreign court

- interest awarded as part of compensation for being mis-sold a personal pension or free-standing AVC scheme. However, interest that is part of a compensation award for being mis-sold an endowment policy (typically as part of a mortgage) is not tax-free and should be entered in boxes 15 to 17 on page TR3.

■ lump sum compensation made in accordance with Financial Services Authority policies relating to being mis-sold a free-standing AVC scheme

■ compensation (which would normally count as interest for tax purposes) paid by UK and foreign banks and building societies on dormant accounts opened by Holocaust victims and frozen during World War Two.

Tax-saving idea 134

Take advantage of the ways you can save which are free of tax: pension schemes, some ISAs and some National Savings & Investment (NS&I) products. These are especially helpful if you are a higher rate taxpayer. If you are a basic rate taxpayer, check to see that any expenses, for example for managing an ISA, are not more than the tax saved.

There are many opportunities for tax saving and tax planning with investments. Chapter 7 should help you maximise your tax-efficient investing.

Jointly owned savings and investments

Only enter details of investments you own. If you own an investment jointly, you need to enter only the amount in the tax return which is your share. If you are married or in a civil partnership, the income from a jointly owned investment normally will be split equally. But if you own an investment in a different proportion, the income can be split to reflect ownership (p. 58).

Income treated as yours

If you are the beneficiary of a bare trust, that is one in which you have an immediate absolute title to the capital and income, you should enter the amount of (or your share of) the income on this page of the return. Your trustee will be able to give you the details of your share. Which boxes you complete on this page depends on the type of income concerned. Income from other types of trust goes in the Trust supplement (see Chapter 21).

Your income from investments includes income from investments which you have given to your children aged 18 or less and unmarried. You need to enter details if the amount of such income per child for the tax year is more than £100 before tax. This tax treatment applies even to a bare trust you have set up for your child, if the trust was set up on or after 9 March 1999. If you make additional gifts on or after that date to an existing trust, income

from the extra gifts is also treated in the same way. This tax treatment also
applies to money you have given your child to invest in a cash ISA, even
though interest from the ISA would otherwise be tax-free. However, income
produced by sums you pay into your son's or daughter's child trust fund
and some other investments (p. 101) will not be treated as your income.

Example

Sidney Barrow has the following investments and accounts: NS&I Certificates, a
stocks and shares ISA, a cash ISA and a bank current account which pays interest
on credit balances. If he didn't have the bank current account boxes 1 and 2 on page
TR3 would not apply to him. But the interest payable on his bank current account
means that he has to complete this section.

Quick guide to where to enter saving and investment income

Type of income	Position on tax return
Annuity income – from pension scheme	Main return, page TR3, boxes 10 and 11
Annuity income – not from a pension scheme	Main return, page TR3, box 1
Authorised unit trusts and open-ended investment companies – interest distributions	Main return, page TR3, box 1
Authorised unit trusts and open-ended investment companies – dividend distributions	Main return, page TR3, box 4
Bank and building society interest – taxed when you get it	Main return, page TR3, box 1
Bank and building society interest – untaxed	Main return, page TR3, box 2
Certificates of tax deposit interest	Main return, page TR3, box 2
Credit union interest	Main return, page TR3, box 2
Enterprise zone property trust – interest	Main return, page TR3, box 1 if taxed or box 2 if received without tax deducted
Enterprise zone property trust – rents	Property supplementary pages
Foreign share dividends – up to £300	Main return, page TR3, box 5
Foreign share dividends – if more than £300	Foreign supplementary pages

Quick guide to where to enter saving and investment income (continued)

Type of income	Position on tax return
Gilts and most other bonds – interest	Additional information, page Ai1, boxes 1 to 3
Life insurance policies gains boxes 4 to 11	Additional information, page Ai1,
Loans to individuals and organisations	Main return, page TR3, box 2
National Savings & Investments – fixed rate savings bonds, guaranteed growth bonds, guaranteed income bonds	Main return, page TR3, box 1
National Savings & Investments – capital bonds, pensioners bonds, income bonds, investment account, easy access account	Main return, page TR3, box 2
National Savings & Investments – guaranteed equity bonds	Additional information, page Ai1, boxes 1 to 3
Partnership investment income – your share	Partnership supplementary pages
Property income dividends – from real-estate investment trusts and property authorised investment funds	Main return, page TR3, box 16
Share dividends	Main return, page TR3, box 3
Unauthorised unit trusts	Main return, page TR3, box 16

Tax-saving idea 135

Couples, where one person pays tax at a higher rate than the other, can adjust their investments between them, so that more investments are in the name of the lower taxpayer. Thus less of the return will be taxed at the higher rates. Couples, where one pays tax at the starting rate or pays no tax at all and the other pays at the basic rate, can save tax in the same way by shifting interest-earning investments (but not shares or unit trusts) to the lower taxpayer.

Tax-saving idea 136

Compensation paid by UK banks to Holocaust victims or their heirs has been tax-free since 8 May 2000. This exemption has been backdated to 1996–97 and applies to similar compensation paid by foreign banks. If you have paid tax on such a payment in the past, you should send an amended tax return to your tax office in order to claim the tax back – the normal time limit for amending returns does not apply.

The documents you need

Get together all your interest statements, tax deduction certificates, dividend and distribution tax vouchers and trust vouchers. Keep them safe; don't send them with your tax return.

Main tax return: interest and dividends from UK banks, building societies, etc.

UK bank, building society, unit trust, etc., interest

> 1 Taxed UK interest etc. - *the net amount after tax has been taken off (see notes)*
>
> £ ▢▢▢▢▢▢▢ · 0 0

Most savings income is paid with tax deducted and the rate of tax for 2009–10 is 20 per cent. This applies to:

- interest from most accounts with UK banks, building societies, finance houses, organisations offering high-interest cheque accounts and other licensed deposit takers
- equivalent income from Sharia-compliant products (often called 'alternative finance receipts')
- interest from National Savings & Investments (NS&I) fixed rate savings bonds, guaranteed growth bonds and guaranteed income bonds
- distributions from unit trusts that invest in gilts and other fixed-interest investments
- income from most annuities that are not linked to a pension scheme.

Add together the income you get from all these sources after the tax has been deducted (the net amounts) and put the total in box 1 on page TR3. You do not enter the gross amount or the amount of tax taken off.

Income from all these sources is usually paid with tax at 20 per cent already taken off. If you paid tax at the higher rate in 2009–10, there will be a further 20 per cent tax to pay (see Chapter 7). If your top rate of tax was the starting rate (or higher but most of the income on which you pay tax is savings income), all (or part) of your interest is taxable at 10 per cent and you can reclaim the excess tax already deducted. If you were a non-taxpayer, you can reclaim all the tax – see page 45 for how to make your claim.

Bank and building society interest

Instead of claiming tax back, if your income is too low to pay tax and you expect to carry on being a non-taxpayer, you should register to receive your interest without any tax deducted – see Chapter 7.

You may have a term account where the interest is paid to you only when the account matures or you cash it in early. The whole of the interest is taxed in the year you receive it (not spread out over the term). Interest from NS&I guaranteed growth bonds is also taxed in this way.

If you are self-employed, put interest from your business bank account in box 9 on page SES1 of the Self employment short supplement or box 15 on page SEF1 of the full supplement.

Unit trusts

You get a tax voucher for the 20 per cent tax as proof of the tax already deducted. Don't enter here any dividend distributions from unit trusts (which come with a 10 per cent tax voucher); they go in box 4.

The interest distributions may not be paid out to you but automatically reinvested in accumulation or other units. Even so, you still have to enter them on your tax return.

When you buy units in a unit trust, part of the purchase price includes an amount for income which the trust has received but has not yet paid out to its investors. The first payment you get will include an 'equalisation payment', which is not income but a refund of part of the original purchase price you paid. It is not taxable, so do not include it in box 1. (The equalisation payment is deducted for capital gains tax purposes – p. 146.)

Annuities

An annuity is an investment made with a life insurance company. You invest a lump sum and in return the insurance company pays you an income. This could be for a set period, say, ten years or for the rest of your life, depending on the type of annuity you buy. The income you get is considered to be in two parts: some of it is your original investment being returned to you bit by bit; the rest is interest. Only the interest part is taxed and this is the only part you include in box 1 after deducting the tax paid.

The certificate you get with each payment will tell you how much counts as taxable interest and how much tax has been taken off.

Untaxed UK interest etc.

2	Untaxed UK interest etc. - *amounts which have not been taxed (see notes)*
	£ ⬚⬚⬚⬚⬚⬚⬚⬚ · 0 0

You may have received interest from your bank or building society paid gross, that is without tax deducted. The most common circumstance where this might apply is if you have registered to receive interest gross because you are a non-taxpayer (p. 81). If you had gross interest from an offshore bank account up to £2,000 and that is the only foreign income you received, you can include the interest in box 2. Otherwise, the interest should go on the Foreign supplement. If the amount you enter in box 2 includes foreign interest, give details in the *Any other information* box on page TR6.

Include here interest from credit unions, certificates of tax deposit and the following NS&I products: capital bonds, pensioners bonds, income bonds, investment account and easy access savings account. Do not include the return from NS&I guaranteed equity bonds – these count as 'deeply discounted securities' and are entered on the Additional information form (p. 216).

Also include in box 2 income from securities where you have sold or transferred the right to the income but not the security itself, even though you have not received the income.

If you are a beneficiary of a trust and you are entitled to income as it arises, you should include in box 2 any untaxed interest paid direct to you because the trustee has authorised the payer to do so.

Add up the interest you received from all these sources (which will all be gross amounts) and put the total in box 2. Do not include in box 2 the gross amount of any income that you have already put in box 1: if you do, the income will be taxed twice.

Dividends

You will receive share dividends from UK companies and distributions from authorised unit trusts with no more basic rate tax to pay because you also receive a tax credit. The payments are accompanied by a tax voucher which sets out the amount of the tax credit (10 per cent). You just enter the net amount of dividends and distributions on your tax return. Do not enter details about the tax deducted or add it back to the sum you received.

Non-taxpayers cannot claim back the tax credit. Basic rate taxpayers have no further tax to pay, but higher rate taxpayers pay extra bringing the rate they pay up to 32.5 per cent in 2009–10 (see p. 83).

If you are a beneficiary of a trust and you are entitled to income as it arises, include in these boxes any dividends or distributions shown on your trust voucher.

Dividends from UK companies

Add together all the dividends you receive from UK companies during 2009–10. These are the amounts actually paid to you, which you can get from the dividend vouchers. Do not include the tax credits. Put the total in box 3 on page TR3.

Note that scrip dividends go in box 12 on page Ai1 of the Additional information form. If you received property income dividends from a real estate investment trust (or a property authorised investment fund), do not enter them here – they go in box 16 of page TR3 of the Main tax return.

Include dividends you get from shares acquired through employee share schemes, unless the dividends were used to buy more shares through a share incentive plan (see Chapter 15). However, if during the year you've sold shares bought with dividends before holding the shares three years, include them here after all – enter the amount of the dividend originally reinvested.

A company can make other distributions as well as dividends – for example, if it sells you an asset at less than the open-market price. Some distributions are defined as non-qualifying and are entered in box 13 on page Ai1 of the Additional information form (p. 221). All other distributions are qualifying and entered here in box 3. Explain how you got the distribution in the *Any other information* box on page TR6.

In the past, you may have had a bonus issue of redeemable shares. If they are now redeemed, the amount you receive counts as a qualifying distribution and should be entered in box 3. If, when you originally got the shares, you paid higher rate tax on them, you can now claim some tax relief in box 10 on page Ai2 of the Additional information form (p. 243).

IR35 companies

Do not include dividends you have received from your own personal service company if the company's tax office has agreed that the dividends are not taxable in your hands. This may be the case if, under the 'IR35 rules', you are treated as if you were an employee of your client(s) and your company has been deemed to pay you a salary (whether or not it actually did) on which income tax and national insurance contributions have been charged. If, in fact, you take money out of the company in the form of dividends rather than salary, you would be taxed twice on the same income if the dividends were taxed as well. Your company rather than you must claim relief for the dividends. Once the Revenue has agreed the claim, you do not include the dividends on your tax return at all.

If you have received any income (earnings or dividends) in 2009–10 from an IR35 company, you must complete the *Service companies* section on page TR4 of the Main tax return (p. 214).

Managed service companies

Similarly, do not include payments you have received from a managed service company if the company's tax office has agreed that these payments should not be taxed as dividends. This situation may arise where you provide services to end-customers through a company, set up and run by someone else, of which you are a shareholder. The aim was to pay you tax efficiently through dividends but all payments are now treated as earnings for income tax purposes (since 6 April 2007) and for national insurance (since 6 August 2007). If you have received any income (earnings or dividends) in 2009–10 from a managed service company, you must complete the *Service companies* section on page TR4 of the Main tax return (p. 214).

Tax-saving idea 137

If you are an owner/manager of your own company and your spouse or civil partner owns shares in it but you do substantially all of the work, your tax office may have argued that any of the company's dividends paid to your spouse or partner were, in effect, gifts from you and should be taxed as your income. This treatment was the subject of lengthy litigation (in a case known as *Jones* v *Garnett* or 'Arctic Systems') and, in December 2005, the Court of Appeal decided the Revenue view was wrong and that such dividends should correctly be treated as income of the spouse or partner. In July 2007, the House of Lords upheld this judgment. Your tax returns for 2005–06 and 2006–07 should have been completed in line with these judgments, so you should not have included your spouse's or partner's dividends on your tax return. If you did, ask to have your 2005–06 and 2006–07 tax returns corrected (p. 47). Do not include your spouse's or partner's dividends in your 2009–10 tax return.

Dividends from authorised unit trusts and open-ended investment companies

4 Other dividends - *do not include the tax credit (see notes)*

£ ⬛⬛⬛⬛⬛⬛⬛⬛ • 0 0

Distributions from most authorised unit trusts and open-ended investment companies (OEICs) are treated in the same way as dividends and come with a tax credit for 10 per cent tax already deducted (p. 83). They are entered in box 4 on page TR3 of the Main tax return. Do not include any distributions that are treated as interest – they go in box 1 (p. 196).

If you have invested in accumulation units, you don't receive the distributions but they are automatically reinvested for you by the unit trust or OEIC manager. However, for tax purposes, you are treated in exactly the same way as if the distributions had been paid out, so you must include them in box 4. Do not include any property income distributions from property authorised investment funds – they go in box 16 on page TR3 of the Main return.

Add together all the distributions you received during 2009–10. These are the amounts actually paid or credited to you, which you can get from the dividend vouchers. Do not include the tax credits or any equalisation payments (p. 146). Put the total in box 4.

Foreign dividends

5 Foreign dividends (up to £300) - *the amount in sterling after foreign tax was taken off. Do not include this amount in the Foreign pages*

£ ☐☐☐ . 0 0

6 Tax taken off foreign dividends - *the sterling equivalent*

£ ☐☐☐ . 0 0

Normally any dividends you get from shareholdings in overseas companies go on the foreign supplementary pages (see Chapter 20). You can instead put foreign dividends here if this is the only foreign income you had in 2009–10 and all the foreign dividends net of any foreign tax already deducted come to no more than £300.

Find the equivalent value in £s of each foreign dividend before deducting any foreign tax (the gross dividends). Use the exchange rate for the date of the dividend. Add together all the sterling amounts and put the answer in box 5. Convert any foreign tax that was deducted from each dividend into sterling using the exchange rate for each relevant dividend date. Add the sterling amounts together and put the total in box 6.

Tax-saving idea 138

If your only foreign income is up to £300 of dividends from shares in foreign companies, such as Banco Santander, you can report these on page TR3 of the Main tax return instead of completing the Foreign supplement. However, you will be treated as having paid tax only at 10 per cent (the standard tax credit for UK dividends). This means you will pay slightly too much tax if you are a higher-rate taxpayer and, in fact, have paid foreign tax on the dividends at more than 10 per cent. To pay the correct tax, report the dividends on the Foreign supplement not page TR3.

Main tax return: UK pensions, annuities and other state benefits

Complete boxes 7 to 15 on page TR3 of the Main tax return if you received any taxable pensions or state benefits in 2009–10. Some pensions and benefits are not taxable and are not entered on your tax return at all. Use the lists opposite and overleaf to check whether you need to enter anything in this section.

Pensions and benefits that should not be included in your tax return

If you received any of the following, you do not need to give details here in the tax return because they are tax-free:

■ attendance allowance, disability living allowance, severe disablement allowance, including age-related addition

■ bereavement payment

■ council tax benefit, housing benefit (rent rebates and allowances), home renovation and repair grants

■ educational maintenance allowance

■ Employment Zone payments

■ guardian's allowance

■ income-related employment and support allowance (and incapacity benefit if it replaced invalidity benefit that you were receiving before 13 April 1995 and there has been no break in your claim; otherwise incapacity benefit is taxable)

■ income support (if you're not required to be available for work)

■ industrial injuries benefit (except death benefit)

■ jobfinder's grant, employment training and employment rehabilitation allowances, back-to-work bonus and New Deal training allowances

■ maternity allowance, child benefit, child tax credit, additions to benefits or state pensions because you have a dependent child, school unform grants and fares to school

■ pension credit, pensioners' Christmas bonus including the extra £60 paid in spring 2009

■ pensions and benefits for wounds or disability in military service or for other war injuries, war widow's pension and some similar pensions for dependants. See Helpsheet HS310 *War widow's and dependant's pensions* from the Orderline (p. 180)

■ social fund payments

■ student grants, bursaries, scholarships and loans

■ vaccine damage payments

■ winter fuel payments and cold weather payments

- working tax credit
- similar benefits to those above paid by foreign governments.

Pensions and benefits that should be entered in your tax return

Details of the following should be entered here:

- additions to benefits or state pensions for an adult dependant
- carer's allowance
- contribution-based employment and support allowance, incapacity benefit
- income withdrawals from a personal pension plan where the purchase of an annuity has been deferred
- industrial death benefit pension (but not child allowance), pension for injuries at work or for work-related illnesses
- jobseeker's allowance (up to the taxable amount)
- pension from a former employer or a pension from your late husband or wife's employer, pension from a free-standing additional voluntary contribution, pension from service in the armed forces
- pension from a personal pension scheme or retirement annuity contract or trust scheme
- state retirement pension, including the basic pension, state additional pension and graduated pension and lump sum from deferring state pension
- statutory sick pay, statutory maternity pay, statutory paternity pay and statutory adoption pay paid by the Revenue
- widowed mother's allowance and widowed parent's allowance, widow's pension and bereavement pension.

If you receive any of the above pensions or benefits, you need to give details on page TR3.

Overseas pensions and taxable benefits paid under the rules of another country should be entered in the foreign supplementary pages (covered in Chapter 20).

The documents you need

Gather details of any state retirement pension and bereavement benefits – you can ask for form BR735 showing how much you have received during the tax year by phoning the National Pension Centre on 0845 3013 011 or from your local Pensions Centre. The Department for Work and Pensions (DWP) should send you details of the taxable amount of other social security benefits that you have had, for example on form P60(U) or P45(U) for jobseeker's allowance. For non-state pensions, you need the P60 the pension payer gives you or any other certificate of pension paid and tax deducted.

In the case of state pensions and benefits, enter the amount of pension or benefit you were entitled to for 2009–10, whether or not you actually received that amount in the year. You should enter the total of all the weekly amounts that you were entitled to in the year, even if you chose to receive your pension or benefit monthly or quarterly.

State pension

7 State Pension - *the amount due for the year (see notes)*

£ ⬜⬜⬜⬜⬜ · 0 0

The state retirement pension is taxable but paid without tax deducted. So if you have other income you will find that tax on your state retirement pension is usually collected from your other income.

In box 7 on page TR3, you should enter the amount you were entitled to receive in 2009–10, but excluding any amount for a dependent child, the Christmas bonus and winter fuel payment. Also subtract any part of the pension you did not in fact receive because of periods you spent in hospital (this would affect only extra amounts you were claiming in respect of a dependant).

A married woman might receive a pension which is based on her husband's contributions and not her own. This pension (but not any dependency allowance which he receives for her before her 60th birthday) should be entered in her tax return, not her husband's.

If you have chosen to defer your state pension (to earn extra pension or a lump sum), while your pension is deferred you do not have any income to enter in box 7. Once your pension restarts, the amount in box 7 should include any extra pension you have earned.

State pension lump sum

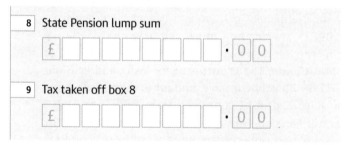

| 8 | State Pension lump sum |
| 9 | Tax taken off box 8 |

If you had previously deferred your state pension and chose to take a lump sum that was paid to you in 2009–10, enter the gross amount of the lump sum (in other words before taking off any tax paid) in box 8. The DWP deducts tax from this before handing over the payment to you. Enter the tax deducted in box 9.

Tax-saving ideas 139 and 140

Taking a lump sum as a result of deferring your state pension will not push you into a higher tax bracket. The whole lump sum is taxed at the highest rate you were paying without the lump sum (ignoring the special rate that applies to savings income and dividends). For example, a basic rate taxpayer pays tax on the whole lump sum at the basic rate (20 per cent in 2009–10). The lump sum does not affect age allowance (see Chapter 2).

You usually get the state pension lump sum when your state pension starts to be paid and the lump sum is taxed at your top rate for that year. But you can opt to delay receiving the lump sum until the following year. This will normally be worth doing if you expect your top rate of tax to be lower in the following year.

Pensions (other than state pensions)

| 10 | Pensions (other than State Pension), retirement annuities and taxable triviality payments - *give details of the payers, amounts paid and tax deducted in box 19 on page TR 6* |

| 11 | Tax taken off box 10 |

Apart from the state pension, you may get a pension from your current or a previous employer or from savings you have made through a personal pension scheme or retirement annuity contract. You may also have received taxable lump sums from these schemes. See Chapter 6 for details about the taxation of pension schemes.

In box 10 on page TR3, enter the total of all such pensions and lump sums before any tax has been taken off (the gross amounts). These pensions are usually paid through PAYE with tax already deducted. Put the total amount of tax in box 11. You will find the information you need on the P60 or similar statement sent to you by the pension provider after the end of the tax year.

Give full details of each pension and the amount of tax deducted in the *Any other information* box on page TR6.

To work out the total for box 10, add together pensions and lump sums from all these sources:

▨ pension from a previous employer's occupational pension scheme (but excluding any tax-free amount – see below)

▨ annuity payments from personal pension schemes and retirement annuity contracts. (Do not include payments from annuities that are not related to a pension scheme. They go in box 1 on page TR3 – see p. 196)

▨ payments from a personal pension scheme under an income withdrawal arrangement

▨ pension from any additional voluntary contribution (AVC) scheme

▨ pension you get because of an injury at work or a work-related illness (but excluding any tax-free part – see below)

▨ pension for service in the armed forces

▨ taxable part of any lump sum you get because you have opted for a lump sum in place of a small (trivial) pension (see below)

▨ pension from any of the above sorts of schemes that you get because you are the widow, widower or survivor of the pension scheme member who has died.

In some cases, part of the pension or lump sum you get may be tax-free. Do not include any tax-free parts in the amounts you report on your tax return. This may apply in the following cases:

▨ pension for service to some overseas governments (for example, of a Commonwealth country). If you get a pension from the overseas government or its agencies for employment you had in the service of the Crown or the government concerned, 10 per cent may be tax-free. If this applies, deduct the 10 per cent and just include 90 per cent of the pension in the total in box 10

■ pension for injury at work or work-related illness. If the pension is more than the amount you would have received had you retired at the same time on the grounds of ordinary ill-health, the extra amount is tax-free. Do not include the tax-free part in box 10

■ tax-free lump sum. In general, you can take a quarter of any pension fund as a tax-free lump sum. This will usually apply even when you are converting a trivial pension into a lump sum. Just include in box 10 the taxable part.

Taxable employment and support allowance and incapacity benefit

12   Taxable Incapacity Benefit and contribution-based
Employment and Support Allowance - *see notes*

£ [   ] · [0][0]

13   Tax taken off Incapacity Benefit in box 12

£ [   ] · [0][0]

From October 2008, employment and support allowance (ESA) was introduced for people unable to work because of illness and replaced incapacity benefit for new claimants. Income-based ESA is not taxable and should not be included on your tax return. Contribution-based ESA is taxable but paid without tax deducted. Include any contribution-based ESA in box 12.

If your claim started before October 2008, you will usually be getting incapacity benefit. In most cases, this is taxable. But you will not pay tax on it if you are receiving it for a period of incapacity which began before 13 April 1995, and for which invalidity benefit used to be payable.

The DWP will give you a form showing you whether your ESA or incapacity benefit is taxable or not. If it is taxable, enter the gross amount of the benefit (in other words, before deducting tax) in box 12 and any tax that has been deducted from incapacity benefit in box 13.

Jobseeker's allowance

14 Jobseeker's Allowance

£ ☐☐☐☐☐ . 0 0

There are two types of jobseeker's allowance (JSA): income-based is not taxable and should not be included on your tax return. Contribution-based JSA is taxable, though only up to a limit, and is paid without tax deducted. Enter the taxable amount of contribution-based JSA you get in box 14. This is shown on your P60(U) from the Department for Work and Pensions or P45(U) if you went back to work before 5 April 2010. If you do not have a P60(U) or P45(U), contact Jobcentre Plus.

Other taxable state pensions and benefits

15 Total of any other taxable State Pensions and benefits

£ ☐☐☐☐☐ . 0 0

Box 15 on page TR3 is the place to enter any other taxable state benefits that you get. Although taxable, they are paid without any tax deducted. Add up the before-tax amounts you received and put the total in box 15. Include:

■ bereavement allowance (or widow's pension if your claim started before 6 April 2001)

■ widowed parent's allowance (or widowed mother's allowance if your claim started before 6 April 2001)

■ industrial death benefit pension. Enter the yearly amount you are entitled to receive but exclude any industrial death benefit child allowance which is tax free

■ carer's allowance. Include any addition you get for a dependent adult but not any amount for a child (which is tax free)

■ statutory payment paid by the Revenue. Normally any statutory sick, maternity, paternity or adoption pay is paid by your employer and taxed through PAYE. Details will be on your P60 or P45 and should be entered in the Employment supplement, not here. But, occasionally, these payments are made to you direct by the Revenue and, in that case, you should include the amount you received in box 15. If you were paid statutory sick pay by the Revenue and also have made an entry in the student loan repayment boxes on page TR2 (p. 186), also put the amount of the statutory sick pay you received in the *Any other information* box on page TR6.

Main tax return: Other UK income

Other taxable income

16 Other taxable income – *before expenses and tax taken off*

£ ⬜⬜⬜⬜⬜⬜⬜⬜ · 0 0

17 Total amount of allowable expenses – *read page TRG 14 of the guide*

£ ⬜⬜⬜⬜⬜⬜⬜⬜ · 0 0

18 Any tax taken off box 16

£ ⬜⬜⬜⬜⬜⬜⬜⬜ · 0 0

Boxes 16 to 18 on page TR3 are a catch-all section for income that you have not included anywhere else on your tax return. Before putting anything in this section, you should have completed:

◼ all the relevant supplementary pages (see Chapters 15 to 23). For example, income from employment should go in the Employment supplement, business income should go on the Self-employment or Partnership pages, foreign income in the Foreign supplement, and so on, and

◼ the Additional information form if you have any of the types of income covered there. Check pp. 210–213 below to see if the Additional information form applies to any income you get.

The income that you need to report in boxes 16 to 18 on page TR3 of the Main tax return can be divided into two sorts which we have called A and B in the lists below.

A: Income against which you can set expenses and losses

◼ freelance or casual income

■ profits from the odd literary or artistic activity

■ income received after you close a business (post-cessation receipts). This could include money which you have recovered from a bad debt or royalties arising after the business ceased from contracts made before it ceased. You can claim to have this treated as income for the year in which the business ceased (boxes 14 and 15 on page Ai1 of the Additional information form, p. 221). Or you can enter the total here

■ any recovery of expenses or debts for which you claimed relief as post-cessation expenses

■ sale of patent rights if you received a capital sum

■ rental from leasing equipment you own

■ income from guaranteeing loans, dealing in futures and some income from underwriting

■ other miscellaneous sources.

B: Income you can't set expenses and losses against

■ receipts from covenants entered into for genuine commercial reasons in connection with the payer's trade, profession or vocation

■ annual payments received in the year, including those from UK unauthorised unit trusts and annual payments paid by a former employer that do not count as a pension

■ benefits of certain insurance policies relating to sickness or disability

■ a taxable lump sum from an employer-financed retirement benefits scheme

■ distributions from UK real estate investment trusts (REITs) and property authorised investment funds (PAIFs).

If you have more than one source of other income, you should ask for Help Sheet HS325 *Other taxable income*, which contains a Worksheet to help you keep track of your different income sources and the losses you can claim.

From any type of income in list A above (but not list B), you can deduct expenses that you had to incur wholly in order to earn the income. You can't deduct expenses incurred partly or wholly for private reasons. And, if you had to buy capital items, instead deduct the annual investment allowance or other capital allowances (p. 327).

If your expenses come to more than the income from a particular source, you have made a loss. You can set the loss against any of the types of income in list A above, but not against any of the income in list B. If you can't use up all your losses in 2009–10, you can carry them forward to set against any of the list-A types of income in future years. Similarly, if you have made losses in previous years and elected to carry them forward, you can now set part or all of them against any list-A income you have in 2009–10.

Add together all the gross income you have from the sources above (both A and B) before deducting any expenses or tax. Put the total in box 16. Add together all the expenses incurred in 2009–10 that you are claiming and put the total in box 17. If you have already paid any tax on the income included in box 16, put the total tax paid in box 18.

You must also provide a breakdown of each income source, the expenses set against it and any tax already paid. Give these details in box 20 on page TR3 or, if there is not enough room, in the *Any other information* box on page TR6.

If you are now claiming any losses brought forward from earlier years, do not enter them in boxes 16 to 18. Instead, they go in box 1 of the *Income tax losses* section of page Ai3 of the Additional information form (p. 244).

Cashbacks and incentives

Enter as other income any cashbacks or other incentives you received to take out a mortgage or purchase something (such as a car) if there is tax to pay. Ask the person who gave you the incentive or check with your tax office to find out if it is taxable. Include it in box 16. If you are not sure whether there is any tax to pay, include the amount in box 16 on page TR3 but also put a cross in box 20 on page TR6 to show that this is a provisional figure and give details in the *Any other information* box on that page.

Insurance policies relating to sickness and disability

Some part of income received under an income protection (also called 'permanent health') insurance policy may be taxable and should be entered as other income. This does not include income from a policy which you paid for yourself, as that is tax-free. Income from your employer for sickness and disability should go on the Employment pages. But if you have left your employer and you are still receiving benefits because you are covered by your former employer's scheme, you should enter that amount here (part might be tax-free if you contributed to the cost of the scheme). Check with your tax office if you are not sure how much is taxable.

Employer-financed retirement benefits schemes

Most, but not all, pension schemes set up by employers are registered schemes and so qualify for special tax treatment. If you belong to an unregistered scheme, any lump sum you receive from it is treated as taxable income unless you can show that the lump sum had built up from contributions you paid yourself or contributions paid by your employer but on which you paid tax, or the payment was made because of accidental death or disablement. If the lump sum is the only retirement benefit you get from that employment and you do not also belong to a registered pension scheme, the lump sum might be tax-free – contact your tax office. If you have filled in the Employment supplement, you should have entered this income in box 1 of that supplement and do not need to give details again here.

Benefit from pre-owned assets

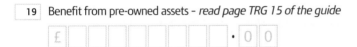

19 Benefit from pre-owned assets - *read page TRG 15 of the guide*

£ ⬚⬚⬚⬚⬚⬚⬚⬚ • 0 0

A pre-owned asset is anything you have owned at any time on or after 18 March 1986 that you have given away or, in some cases, sold but can still use. It can also be an asset owned by someone else that you can use, if you helped them to acquire it. In either case, you may have to pay income tax (called pre-owned asset tax) each year on the benefit you are deemed to get from your use of the asset. For more details and exceptions, see Chapter 10.

In box 19, enter the taxable value of the benefit you are deemed to get. This is usually:

■ land or buildings: the open market rent

■ other assets: a percentage of the value of the asset. The percentage was 4.75 per cent for the whole of 2009–10. See p. 125 for rates for earlier years.

In either case, deduct anything you are legally obliged to pay for the use.

Give details of how you have worked out the figure in box 20 or in the *Any further information* box on page TR6.

Tax-saving idea 141

> It is easy to overlook pre-owned assets tax and think it cannot apply to you. But actions you took many years ago might now give rise to a bill and you could incur interest and penalties if you fail to pay. If you still use or benefit from something you gave away or sold on or after 18 March 1986, check whether you should be paying tax on the benefit you are deemed to be getting. If so, there may be steps you can take to remove yourself from the scope of the tax – see Chapter 10 for details.

Main tax return: service companies

> 1 If you provided your services through a service company (a company which provides your personal services to third parties), enter the total of the dividends (including the tax credit) and salary (before tax was taken off) you withdrew from the company in the tax year - *read page TRG 20 of the guide*
>
> £ ⬚⬚⬚⬚⬚⬚⬚ · 0 0

If you have received any earnings or dividends in 2009–10 from an IR35 company or managed service company (p. 200), you must complete the *Service companies* section on page TR4 of the Main tax return. Add together your before-tax earnings from such companies (as entered in box 1 in the Employment supplement) and the amount you received in dividends excluding the tax credit (as entered in box 3 on page TR3 of the Main tax return). Put the total in box 1 in the *Service companies* section on page TR4.

Additional information form: other UK income

Before turning to this Additional information form, you should have completed all the relevant supplementary pages (see Chapters 15 to 23). Now check whether you have any of the more unusual types of income that are listed on page Ai1 of this form. Any remaining income goes on page TR3 of the Main tax return as described earlier in this chapter.

Interest from gilts and other UK securities

1 Gilt etc. interest after tax taken off	3 Gross amount before tax
£ ⬚⬚⬚⬚⬚ · 0 0	£ ⬚⬚⬚⬚⬚ · 0 0

2 Tax taken off	
£ ⬚⬚⬚⬚⬚ · 0 0	

In boxes 1 to 3 of page Ai1 include income from the following investments:

- gilts (also called British government stocks or gilt-edged securities)
- other loan stocks, such as corporate bonds and local authority bonds and stocks
- permanent interest-bearing shares (PIBs) of building societies and the equivalent perpetual sub-bonds (PSBs) of demutualised building societies
- discounts on deeply discounted securities.

Whether you receive the income net (with tax at the savings rate already deducted) or gross (without any tax deducted) depends on the type of investment and, in some cases, the choices you have made. The notes below will help you decide what to put in each box.

Gilts

Interest from gilts is usually paid without any tax deducted but you can choose to receive it with tax at 20 per cent already deducted. To switch from one basis to another, contact your stockbroker or Computershare Investor Services (tel: 0870 703 0143; www-uk.computershare.com).

If you receive the interest gross, include the amount in box 3 but leave boxes 1 and 2 blank. If you receive interest with tax deducted, include the net amount in box 1, the tax paid in box 2 and the grossed-up amount (in other words the net interest plus the tax) in box 3. You will find the relevant amounts on the tax voucher that comes with the payment. See Appendix B for guidance on grossing up.

Tax-saving idea 142

If you are a basic-rate taxpayer and your only untaxed income each year is interest from gilts, it could be worth opting to receive interest from gilts with tax already deducted. That way, you may not need to fill in a tax return in future.

Corporate bonds and other loan stocks

Since 1 April 2001, corporate bonds and other stocks listed on a recognised stock exchange pay interest gross (without any tax deducted). Put the amount in box 3 but leave boxes 1 and 2 blank.

Accrued income scheme

If the nominal value of all the fixed-interest securities you own comes to more than £5,000, special rules apply that were designed to stop tax avoidance. Fixed-interest securities mean gilts, corporate bonds, local authority stocks, PIBs and similar securities, but you do not include securities that you hold through an individual savings account or investment fund (such as a unit trust or open-ended investment company).

The rules prevent you turning income (which is often heavily taxed) into capital gain (which may be tax-free or lightly taxed) by recognising that part of the sale or purchase price of the securities is really a payment for interest that has built up but not yet been paid out. Revenue Help Sheet HS343 *Accrued income scheme* explains the rules and what adjustments you need to make.

Deeply discounted securities

Some corporate and other bonds do not pay interest. Instead you get a return by selling or redeeming the bond at a higher price than you paid – the difference is called the 'discount'. (In the past, these investments were often called 'deep discount bonds'.) Usually, you are taxed on the proceeds only when you sell the bond or it is redeemed (but see below for different rules applying to gilt strips). In box 3, enter the sale or redemption proceeds less the price you originally paid. Note that NS&I guaranteed equity bonds count as deeply discounted securities.

You used to be able to claim tax relief for any loss provided you had other taxable income for the same tax year. But this now applies only where you started to own the securities before 27 March 2003 and the security was listed on a recognised stock exchange, in which case you enter a loss not here but in box 6 in the section called *Other tax reliefs* on page Ai2 of the Additional information form (see p. 239). There is no tax relief for losses made on securities acquired on or after 27 March 2003.

Gilt strips

A traditional gilt provides regular interest payments (usually twice a year) and possibly a capital sum at the end of its lifespan. Each of these payments can be stripped out and sold as a separate investment, called a gilt strip. A gilt strip entitles you to one payment on a specified future date. Strips can be bought and sold before the payment falls due at a market price which is at a discount to the payment. Strips are taxed in a special way. At the end of each tax year, you are treated as if you had sold each strip and bought it back the following day. You are then taxed on any increase in value over the tax year. So, in 2009–10, income tax is due on any increase in the market value of the strip between 6 April 2009 (or, if later, the date you bought the strip) and 5 April 2010. The relevant market values are available from your tax office. Enter the change in value in box 3. Enter any loss on actual disposal or redemption in box 6 in the *Other tax reliefs* section on page Ai2 of the Additional information form (p. 239). Since 15 January 2004, rules prevent claims for tax relief through the artificial creation of losses on strips.

For securities owned from 27 March 2003 onwards, the above rules also apply to strips of securities issued by non-UK governments.

Life insurance gains

Gains on life insurance policies, contracts for life annuities and capital redemption policies are treated as investment income and may be taxable.

With most policies, the life insurance company will have paid tax on the income and gains which its life fund makes as they arise. This is deemed to be equivalent to income tax at the basic rate of 20 per cent in 2009–10 (the savings rate for years before 2008–09). So if you pay tax at the basic rate or less, there is no tax for you personally to pay. But you cannot reclaim any of the tax already paid even if you personally would not be liable for tax on income or gains or would be liable only at a lower rate.

The further tax treatment of a life insurance gain depends on whether the policy is qualifying or non-qualifying. Most policies where you pay regular premiums are qualifying. If you pay just a single premium, the policy will be non-qualifying and have less favourable tax treatment.

Taxation of qualifying policies

Tax at the basic rate is treated as already paid. There is usually no higher rate tax when the policy matures – that is, comes to the end of its term or the person insured by the policy dies. You do not enter details in your tax return.

The exception is if you cash in the policy or make it paid up before it has run for ten years, or three-quarters of its term if this is less. The policy is then treated as a non-qualifying policy (see overleaf).

Taxation of non-qualifying policies

---

4 UK life insurance policy etc. gains on which tax was
treated as paid - *the amount of the gain*

£ ☐☐☐☐☐☐☐☐ . 0 0

5 Number of years the policy has been held or since the
last gain - *whichever is less*

☐☐

Higher rate income tax may be due when you receive proceeds from a non-qualifying policy. A gain from this type of policy can cause you to lose age allowance (pp. 24 and 60), personal allowance (p. 24) or tax credits (p. 66).

A chargeable event may occur when a policy matures, the holder dies, the policy is assigned or surrendered, or a partial withdrawal is made. Each time there is an event, the gain (if any) is calculated. The gain is usually the total you have received from the policy since it started less any earlier gains that have already been taxed and less whatever you have paid into the policy. Where the person insured dies, the calculation uses the cash-in value just before death, which may be less than the death benefit actually paid out.

Where a life insurance policy is transferred from one spouse to another as part of a divorce settlement, this was often in the past treated as giving rise to a chargeable gain and a possible tax bill. The Revenue's view has now changed and such transfers, provided they are ordered or ratified by a court, do not now create a gain or tax bill.

Many non-qualifying policies let you draw an income by regularly cashing in part of the policy. There is no tax to pay at the time you make such withdrawals provided they come to no more than 5 per cent a year of the amount you have paid into the policy. If you don't cash in the full 5 per cent each year, you can carry forward the unused amount, meaning you may be able to cash in more than 5 per cent in a later year. You can make 5 per cent withdrawals for up to 20 years. When the policy comes to an end, the amounts you have withdrawn are added to your final gain or loss to work out the tax due.

If, in any year, you withdraw more than the cumulative 5 per cent a year limit, there may be an immediate tax bill on the excess. If, on maturity, you make a loss, you can claim deficiency relief in box 11 (see p. 220) up to the amount of the earlier withdrawals on which tax was paid.

Whenever there is a chargeable event producing a gain, the insurance company must send you a 'chargeable event certificate'. This tells you the amount of the gain, whether basic rate tax is treated as already paid and, if so, the amount. There will be higher rate tax to pay if your taxable income plus the gain come to more than the threshold at which higher rate tax starts to be paid. For 2009–10, this is usually £37,400 but will be higher if you have paid pension contributions or made Gift Aid donations.

Tax is due at the difference between the higher and basic rates: $40 - 20 = 20$ per cent. But if it is to your advantage, you automatically get top-slicing relief: divide the gain by the number of full years you held the policy to find the average gain. (But, if you have previously made a taxable gain, instead divide by the number of full years since the last gain.) Work out the tax due if the average gain was added to your income and multiply this by the number of years the policy was held (or since the last gain).

From 2010–11 onwards, part or all of a gain may fall into the additional rate tax band of 50 per cent. The threshold for this band is normally £150,000 but will be higher if you have made pension contributions or Gift Aid donations. Tax on the gain, or the part of it that falls within the 50 per cent band is due at $50 - 20 = 30$ per cent. Top-slicing relief, as described above, may reduce the tax due.

Although most UK life insurance gains are treated as having had basic rate tax deducted, some are not. The chargeable event certificate should make clear where this is the case. If the gain has not been taxed, instead of using boxes 4 and 5, give details in boxes 6 and 7.

Sometimes an insurance policy will be set up as a cluster of identical policies. If you have more than one policy in a cluster, you can add all the gains together and put the total and relevant number of years in boxes 4 and 5 or 6 and 7.

If, during 2009–10, you have gains on more than one life insurance policy and they are not identical, you can still add the gains and put the total in box 4 or box 6, but leave boxes 5 and 7 blank. Give details of each policy, gain, years held and whether tax has been treated as paid in box 19 (*Additional information*) on page Ai4 of the Additional information form.

Details of offshore insurance policies should be entered on the Foreign supplementary pages, not here.

If there is anything complicated or unusual about your life insurance policy (for example, you own it jointly with people other than your husband, wife or civil partner or this is a traded endowment policy that you bought in an auction or from someone else), get Help Sheet HS320 *Gains on UK life insurance policies* from the Revenue Orderline (p. 180).

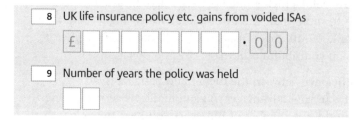

Normally, gains on life insurance policies held within an ISA are tax-free and you do not include them in your tax return. But there are strict rules on the types of policy which qualify to be held through an ISA. If it's found that the life policy you hold does not qualify or has ceased to qualify, the policy may come to an end and there may be tax to pay on any gain. Tax is worked out as for a non-qualifying policy – see opposite. Your ISA manager will give you the information you need. Enter the amount of gain in box 8, the number of complete years the policy ran in box 9 and tax already paid by the ISA manager in box 10.

Deficiency relief

If you had a life insurance policy on which you made a loss on final sur-render, you may be able to claim a relief to ensure that the amount treated as income is not more than the total gain made under the policy (p. 218). Ask for Help Sheet HS320 *Gains on UK life insurance policies*.

Stock dividends

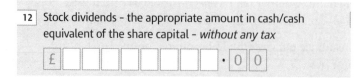

If you received new shares instead of cash as a dividend, this is known as a scrip dividend or stock dividend. The value of the scrip dividend is its cash equivalent and is the amount of cash dividend forgone. It should be shown on your dividend statement as 'the appropriate amount in cash'. This is what you enter in the dividend box. For 2009–10, you are treated as having received the cash equivalent plus tax already paid at 10 per cent, but you do not include the tax in box 12.

Do not confuse scrip dividends with shares you get through a dividend reinvestment plan (DRIP). Under a DRIP, your cash dividend is automatically used to buy additional shares in the company. But you still need to declare the cash dividend as usual in box 3 on page TR3 of the Main tax return.

Non-qualifying distributions

13 | Non-qualifying distributions and close company loans written off or released

£ ⬚⬚⬚⬚⬚⬚⬚⬚ · 0 0

A non-qualifying distribution is broadly one which gives a future rather than a current claim on the company's assets, such as a bonus issue of redeemable shares. The amount of the distribution is the nominal value of the securities you received less any consideration (for example, cash) you paid. Enter the amount of the distribution in box 13.

For loans written off, contact your tax adviser or tax office.

Business receipts taxed as income of an earlier year

14 | The amount of post-cessation or other business receipts

£ ⬚⬚⬚⬚⬚⬚ · 0 0

15 | Tax year income to be taxed, for example 2008-09 *YYYY YY*

⬚⬚⬚⬚ – ⬚⬚

You may receive income after you have closed down a business (post-cessation receipts). This could include, for example, money you have recovered from bad debts or royalties from contracts made before the business ceased. You can choose whether to have this taxed as:

■ income for 2009–10, in which case you should include it in box 16 on page TR3 of the Main tax return (p. 210)

■ income of an earlier tax year. In this case, enter the amount in box 14 on page Ai1 of the Additional information form and put the year to which you are carrying the income back in box 15.

13

Reliefs

You can pay less tax by spending more money on things the government wants to encourage – and thus gives tax relief on – such as pensions and gifts to charity. In some instances you can get tax relief at your highest rate of tax, which from 2010–11 could be 50 per cent or in some cases effectively more – see the Tax-saving ideas overleaf. Assuming that you want to spend the money, buying any of these things could be highly advantageous, although for higher earners, from 2011–12 onwards the tax relief for pension con-trbutions is heavily restricted and transitional rules apply before then – see Chapter 7 for details. You claim reliefs on page TR4 of the Main tax return and pages Ai2 to Ai4 of the Additional information form. We start by looking at the more common reliefs that you claim through the Main tax return. Guidance on completing the Additional information form starts on p. 236.

You get your tax relief in different ways. Frequently you get basic rate tax relief by deducting it from what you spend. Any higher rate tax relief that is due you will claim here in the tax return and give yourself the relief when you are working out your tax bill. Or you could get higher rate relief through your PAYE code. Non-taxpayers will not have to repay the tax deducted, except in the case of Gift Aid.

If you don't get basic rate relief by deducting it from what you pay, you will claim the relief here in the tax return and get it through your tax bill or your PAYE code.

The documents you need

You must gather together all the supporting documents you need to be able to prove to your tax inspector that you are entitled to the relief you are claiming (but keep the documents safe, don't send them with your tax return). These could include:

- certificates of premiums paid from your pension provider
- details of donations to charity by Gift Aid
- certificates from charities accepting gifts of land or buildings
- certificates of interest paid on loans
- share certificate in a venture capital trust
- Forms EIS3 or EIS5 for Enterprise Investment Scheme
- certificates from community development finance institutions.

Tax-saving ideas 143–145

If, in 2009–10 or 2010–11, you are a higher rate (40 per cent) taxpayer or, from 2010–11, an additional rate (50 per cent) taxpayer, you get higher or additional rate relief on Gift Aid donations by adding the grossed-up amount paid to your basic rate band (p. 21). This takes some or all of your income that would have been taxed at the higher or additional rate out of that tax band. If your top slice of income is earnings or savings taxed at 40 per cent, the effect of making the donation is to save you tax at 40 per cent (20 per cent relief at source and 20 per cent higher rate relief). If your top slice of income is dividends, you save tax at 42.5 per cent (20 per cent at source plus 22.5 per cent at the higher rate). Similarly, if your top slice of income is earnings or savings taxed at 50 per cent, the donation saves you tax at 50 per cent (20 per cent at source and 30 per cent additional rate relief) but, if your top slice of income is dividends, the tax saving is 52.5 per cent (20 per cent at source plus 32.5 per cent additional rate relief).

If you are a higher rate taxpayer, making pension contributions can also save you tax in the same way as described above for Gift Aid. However, from 2010–11, some of this relief may be clawed back if your income is £130,000 or more. See p. 226 and Chapter 7 for details.

Making pension contributions or Gift Aid donations reduces the income used to calculate whether you lose age allowance (over 65s) or personal allowance (anyone with income over £100,000 from 2010–11 onwards) and so increases the effective tax relief to as much as 60 per cent for a higher rate taxpayer – see the Example below. Pension contributions and Gift Aid donations can also increase the amount of tax credits you can claim – see p. 66.

Example

In 2010–11, Angela earns £110,000. This is £10,000 more than the threshold at which personal allowance starts to be lost (see p. 24), so her personal allowance is reduced to £6,475 – (1/2 × £10,000) = £1,475. Her tax bill is worked out as shown in the table below.

Adam also earns £110,000 in 2010–11 but he pays £8,000 into a personal pension scheme. Including tax relief at source, the gross pension contribution is £10,000. This means his income for working out the personal allowance is reduced to £110,000 − £10,000 = £100,000, so that he gets the full allowance of £6,475. He also gets higher rate tax relief on his contribution by extending his basic rate tax band. The table shows how Adam pays £4,000 less tax than Angela – this is on top of the £2,000 tax relief at source on the pension contribution.

The effective tax relief on Adam's gross pension contribution of £10,000 is £6,000 or 60 per cent made up of: £2,000 tax relief at source; 40% × £5,000 = £2,000 through eliminating the reduction in his personal allowance; and (40% − 20%) × £10,000 = £2,000 through the extension of his basic rate tax band.

	Angela's tax position in 2010–11	Adam's tax position in 2010–11
Income	£110,000	£110,000
Personal allowance	£1,475	£6,475
Taxable income	£108,525	£103,525
Taxed at basic rate (20%)	£37,400	£47,400
Taxed at higher rate (40%)	£71,125	£56,125
Basic rate tax	£37,400 × 20% = £7,480	£47,400 × 20% = £9,480
Higher rate tax	£71,125 × 40% = £28,450	£56,125 × 40% = £22,450
Total tax bill	£35,930	£31,930

What deductions can you claim?

You can claim for:

■ pension contributions

■ additional voluntary contributions to a pension scheme

■ certain contributions to a compulsory employer's scheme to provide benefits for your husband, wife or children in the event of your death

■ payments to charities (through Gift Aid)

■ gifts of shares, unit trusts or property to charities

■ interest paid on qualifying loans

■ investments in growing business (venture capital trusts or enterprise investment scheme)

■ investments in certain community development schemes

■ post-cessation expenses for a business and losses on relevant discounted securities

■ payments under annuities made in connection with your business

■ certain payments to a trade union or friendly society

■ relief for higher rate tax paid on the issue of bonus shares where they are subsequently redeemed

■ maintenance payments but only if you or your former partner were born before 6 April 1935.

Tax-saving idea 146

You can go back four years to claim deductions which you forgot to claim at the time or didn't know you were able to. You will get tax relief at the rate you should have got it had you claimed the deduction at the right time. Provided you claim by 5 April 2011, you can go back as far as the 2006–07 tax year.

Example

Tony Jabot is saving for his retirement through a stakeholder pension scheme. He paid in £1,000 in 2009–10, but this costs him just £800 because he is a basic rate taxpayer and received 20 per cent tax relief.

Main tax return: pensions

The first four boxes on page TR4 of the Main tax return ask about any payments you made to pension schemes in 2009–10. You get income tax relief up to your highest rate of tax on these contributions. If you are an employee, your employer can also pay contributions to a registered pension scheme on your behalf and these do not count as taxable fringe benefits (see Chapter 8 for details). Note that pension contributions do not get relief from national insurance.

Restrictions on relief for 'high-income individuals'

From 2011–12 onwards, if your income comes to £130,000 or more, tax relief on your pension contributions will be restricted to less than your highest rate of tax. But, with effect from April 2009 onwards, there are transitional rules to prevent you lessening the impact of the 2011–12 change by bringing forward large contributions. The transitional rules are complicated. If you think they may apply, you are strongly advised to get help from a tax adviser (see Appendix E).

The transitional rules apply if you are what the Revenue calls a 'high-income individual' with income above the limits described opposite.

Do the transitional rules apply to you for 2009–10?

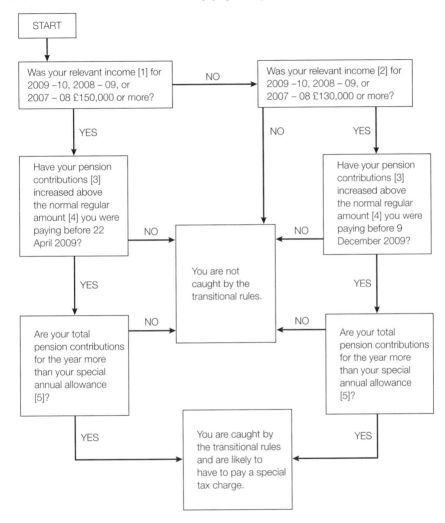

[1] Broadly, income before tax less Gift Aid donations and less pension contributions up to your special allowance. Add back any reduction in salary through a salary sacrifice deal arranged on or after 22 April 2009 that increases your pension contributions or benefits. Also include contributions made on your behalf by your employer on or after 9 December 2009.

[2] Broadly, income before tax less Gift Aid donations and less pension contributions up to your special allowance. Add back any reduction in salary through a salary sacrifice deal arranged on or after 9 December 2009 that increases your pension contributions or benefits. But do not include contributions made on your behalf by your employer.

[3] Including contributions paid for you by your employer or a third party. In a final salary or similar scheme, multiply the increase in your benefits over the year by 10 to find the deemed contribution.

[4] Regular means quarterly or more frequently.

[5] Usually £20,000, but may be up to £30,000 if you pay some or all of your contributions less frequently than quarterly.

Broadly, the rules work by giving you a 'special annual allowance'. If your pension contributions (including any paid for you by your employer or a third party) exceed the allowance, you must pay a special tax charge (20 per cent in 2009–10) on the excess. In 2010–11, when there will be an additional (50 per cent) as well as higher rate of tax, the special tax charge is the rate that reduces your relief to the basic rate.

The special allowance is normally £20,000 but may be increased if you make infrequent (less than quarterly) pension contributions to a non-work-related pension scheme. For example, if you are self-employed, you might pay into a personal pension just once a year after you have worked out your profits for the year. If your infrequent contributions for 2006–07, 2007–08 and 2008–09 average more than £20,000, your special allowance is increased to either the average or £30,000, whichever is lower.

Enter your total contributions on page TR4 of the Main return and the amount of any contributions that are subject to the special tax charge in box 9 on page Ai4 of the Additional information form. For more information, see Help Sheet HS345 *Pensions – tax charges on any excess over the lifetime allowance, annual allowance and special annual allowance, and on unauthorised payments* available from the Revenue Orderline (see p. 180).

How tax relief is given

Tax relief is given in one of three ways, depending on the type of pension scheme:

- occupational pension scheme. You normally get full tax relief at source through the PAYE system, because your employer deducts the contributions from your pay before working out how much tax is due. If this is the only way you are saving for a pension, or if you are not saving for a pension at all, you will not need to fill in this section of the Main tax return. Occasionally, tax relief is not given through PAYE and you will then need to fill in box 3 or 4

- personal pensions. You automatically get tax relief at the basic rate. You may also be eligible for higher-rate relief, so you need to give details about these contributions on page TR4

- retirement annuity contracts (an old type of personal pension started before July 1988). If the provider chooses, tax relief can be given in the same way as for personal pensions. If not, you pay the full contribution and have to claim all the tax relief by completing this section on page TR4.

In addition to the transitional rules already described, there are some other unusual situations where tax relief on your pension savings may be clawed back, but these are unlikely to apply to most people. If you are affected, you need to give details on page Ai4 of the Additional information form – see p. 245 for details.

Contributions you paid with basic rate deducted

1 Payments to registered pension schemes where basic rate tax relief will be claimed by your pension provider (called 'relief at source'). Enter the payments and basic rate tax

£ [   ] · [0][0]

Basic rate tax relief on contributions you pay to most types of pension scheme that you arrange for yourself – such as personal pensions, stake-holder schemes and free-standing additional voluntary contribution schemes – is given at source. This means the amount you pay in is treated as if tax relief at the basic rate (20 per cent in 2009–10) has been deducted. The scheme provider then claims this relief from the Revenue and adds it to your plan. For example, if you paid £1,000 in 2009–10, the provider will have claimed £250 from the Revenue, which is 20 per cent of the total £1,250 that went into your plan.

You get the full amount of this basic rate relief even if you are a non-tax-payer or pay tax only at the starting rate. If you are a higher rate taxpayer, you qualify for extra relief. (This extra relief is given by adding the gross value of the contributions to your basic rate band when working out your tax bill for the year.)

Add together the amount you actually paid in 2009–10 and the basic rate tax relief. The amounts should be shown on your certificate of premiums paid. (Alternatively you can gross-up the amount you paid using the tables in Appendix B.) Enter the total in box 1.

Contributions you paid in full

2 Payments to a retirement annuity contract where basic rate
tax relief will not be claimed by your provider

£ [   ] . [0] [0]

3 Payments to your employer's scheme which were not
deducted from your pay before tax

£ [   ] . [0] [0]

4 Payments to an overseas pension scheme which is not
UK-registered which are eligible for tax relief and were not
deducted from your pay before tax

£ [   ] . [0] [0]

Contributions to most retirement annuity contracts (old types of personal
pension started before July 1988) are usually paid without any tax relief
deducted. You get tax relief on them up to your top rate by deducting the
contributions from your income before working out your tax bill for the
year. Enter the amount you paid in box 2.

Contributions to overseas pension schemes are usually also paid in this
way. So too are contributions to a UK employer's scheme where, unusually,
tax relief was not given through PAYE.

Retirement annuity contract providers can opt to accept contributions
using the tax-relief-at-source system. If this applies to any contributions
you paid during 2009–10, enter them in box 1, not here.

Tax-saving ideas 147 and 148

Nearly everyone can pay up to £3,600 a year into a pension scheme (see Chapter 7).
In 2009–10 and 2010–11 this works out at £2,880 a year after deducting the basic
rate tax relief. You get the relief even if you are a non-taxpayer or pay tax only at the
starting rate.

You cannot ask for pension contributions paid in one tax year to be treated as if they
were paid in the previous year. Therefore, you may need to plan carefully to maximise
tax relief on your pension contributions. Be prepared to vary them from year-to-year
so that you pay more in years when your taxable income is higher. Varying the
amount you contribute each year can also maximise the amount of personal allowance (p. 24) and tax credits you can claim (p. 66).

Main tax return: charitable giving

As well as making donations in the street, you can make more formal donations and use the tax system to reduce what it costs you to make the donation. You can get tax relief up to your highest rate on donations made using the Gift Aid scheme, which also includes any charitable donations you make by deed of covenant. You can also claim income tax relief on shares, similar investments and property that you give to charity or sell to a charity for less than their market value.

Gift Aid

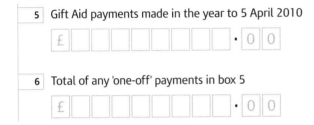

5 | Gift Aid payments made in the year to 5 April 2010

£ ⬚⬚⬚⬚⬚⬚⬚⬚⬚ · 0 0

6 | Total of any 'one-off' payments in box 5

£ ⬚⬚⬚⬚⬚⬚⬚⬚⬚ · 0 0

In 2009–10, you get tax relief at your highest rate on any cash gifts made to charity under the Gift Aid scheme. There is no minimum or maximum on the amount of donations that can qualify. You can also use Gift Aid to make cash gifts to community amateur sports clubs registered with the Revenue. (Membership fees do not count as gifts.) For a list of registered clubs, see www.hmrc.gov.uk/casc/clubs.htm.

The amount you give is treated as a payment from which tax relief at the basic rate has already been deducted. The charity claims back the relief, so increasing the amount of your gift. If you are a higher rate taxpayer, you get extra relief deducted from your self-assessment tax bill or through PAYE. From 2008–09 onwards, the basic rate of tax – and so tax relief – was reduced from 22 per cent to 20 per cent. Although you personally now get basic rate relief at 20 per cent, for a transitional period of three years, the charity can claim back extra bringing its total to 22 per cent.

Tax-saving ideas 149–152

Provided you are a taxpayer, try to arrange gifts to charity through the Gift Aid scheme. The charity you support can receive more by reclaiming basic rate tax relief on what you give.

If you are a couple, make sure the donation is made by whichever one of you has the highest rate of tax.

If you're aged 65 or over and losing age allowance (pp. 24 and 60) or, from 2010–11, you are losing personal allowance (see p. 24), gifts to charity can be especially tax-efficient. This is because the grossed-up value of donations made under the Gift Aid scheme are deducted from your total income when working out how much age allowance or personal allowance you qualify for.

From 2010–11, if your income is over £150,000, your top rate of tax is 50 per cent and this is the rate of relief you will get on Gift Aid donations, making your gifts to charity particularly tax-efficient.

Example

In 2009–10, an envelope was pushed through Julia West's door requesting a donation to charity. Julia gave £20 and completed the Gift Aid declaration on the back of the envelope. This is treated as if it is a gift from which basic rate tax relief of £5 has already been deducted. The grossed-up value of Julia's donation for the purpose of her own tax position is £25 (since £5 is 20 per cent of grossed up donation of £25). However, the charity claimed £5.64 from the Revenue, bringing the total value of Julia's gift to £25.64 (£5.64 is 22 per cent of the grossed up gift of £25.64). Because she is a higher rate taxpayer, Julia is entitled to more tax relief and claims it through her tax return. In box 5, she enters the amount she actually gave, £20 (not the grossed up amount of £25). She gets her higher rate tax relief as a deduction from her tax bill due on 31 January 2010.

If you don't pay enough income tax and/or capital gains tax to cover the relief you have deducted from your donation, you will have to hand money back to the Revenue. This may affect you if you pay tax at the starting rate or you are a non-taxpayer. For example, if you make a donation in 2010–11 of £80, you are treated as having made a gross donation of £100. If your tax bill for 2010–11 comes to only £10, you would have to repay £20 − £10 = £10 to the Revenue. Although the Revenue might not actively seek the repayment, it would automatically be taken into account when working out your overall tax bill if you have to fill in a tax return or make a claim for a tax refund on, say, savings income.

To qualify for tax relief, you must give the charity concerned a Gift Aid declaration, stating that you are a UK taxpayer and giving your name and address. If you do this over the phone, the charity no longer has to send you a written record of the declaration but you can request one. Keep a copy of any declarations.

You may be making regular donations to a charity using Gift Aid (for example by direct debit). However, some or all of your gifts might be one-off payments that you will not necessarily repeat in another year. Enter the amount of such one-off payments in box 6 so that your tax office knows not to include them as regular items when working out your PAYE code if you have one.

Some charity shops operate a 'retail Gift Aid scheme' which enables you to make a Gift Aid donation instead of simply giving your unwanted items to the shop. The scheme works as follows: the shop acts as an agent selling your unwanted goods for you through the shop. The goods remain yours throughout the process and you are entitled to keep the proceeds of the sale but may choose to donate them to the charity, in which case you can use the Gift Aid scheme for the donation. Be aware that you could be liable for capital gains tax under the normal rules (see Chapter 9) if you sell a very valuable item this way and, if you use the scheme to sell items regularly – for example, cards or crafts you make – the Revenue may tax you as if you are running a business (see Chapter 18).

Tax-saving ideas 153–155

If a charity you want to give to runs a retail Gift Aid scheme this could be a convenient, as well as tax-efficient, way of donating the proceeds from selling a valuable possession, such s a painting, jewellery, antique furniture or other collectors' item. Provided the exemption for personal belongings – chattels – applies (see p. 134), there will be no capital gains tax and you'll get Gift Aid relief on the donation. You cannot get tax relief on any commission the charity charges for selling the item.

Gift Aid declarations are often indefinite covering any future donations you make to the charity concerned as well as your current gift. Be careful to stop any open-ended declarations if your circumstances change and you are no longer a taxpayer or if you want to make an unusually large gift (out of an inheritance say) which will not be matched by your tax bill. Otherwise you will find the Revenue billing you for tax relief that the charity claims.

It is worth carrying back a Gift Aid donation to the previous year if the tax you would save through higher rate tax relief on the donation or an increase in age allowance (p. 24 and 60) in the earlier year would exceed the tax you could save in the year the donation was made.

7   Gift Aid payments made in the year to 5 April 2010 but treated as if made in the year to 5 April 2009 - *read page TRG 18 of the guide*

£ ⬚⬚⬚⬚⬚⬚⬚⬚⬚ · 0 0

8   Gift Aid payments made after 5 April 2010 but to be treated as if made in the year to 5 April 2010 - *read page TRG 18 of the guide*

£ ⬚⬚⬚⬚⬚⬚⬚⬚⬚ · 0 0

You can elect for a Gift Aid donation made after 5 April 2010 to be carried back and treated as if you had paid it in 2009–10. You must have taxable income or gains in 2009–10 at least equal to the amount carried back plus the basic rate tax relief on it. The election must be in writing and must be made by the earlier of the date you file your tax return or 31 January 2011. Put the amount of any donation you want to carry back in this way in box 8. In box 7 put the amount of any Gift Aid donations made in the period 6 April 2009 to 31 January 2010 that last year you opted to carry back to 2008–09.

Gifts of shares, unit trusts and property to charities

9   Value of any shares or securities gifted to charity

£ ⬚⬚⬚⬚⬚⬚⬚⬚⬚ · 0 0

10   Value of any land and buildings gifted to charity

£ ⬚⬚⬚⬚⬚⬚⬚⬚⬚ · 0 0

You can get income tax relief at your highest rate on gifts to charities of shares, units in unit trusts and shares in open-ended investment companies (OEICS). Shares must be quoted on a recognised stock exchange either in the UK (including the Alternative Investment Market) or in another country. Unit trusts and OEICS must be UK-authorised or equivalent foreign investment schemes.

Tax-saving idea 156

If you're aged 65 or over and losing age allowance (pp. 24 and 60), or from 2010–11 have income over £100,000 and you are losing personal allowance (see p. 24), gifts of shares, unit trusts, OEICS (open-ended investment companies) or property to charity can be especially tax-efficient. This is because the value of such gifts is deducted from your total income when working out how much age allowance or personal allowance you qualify for.

Similarly, since 6 April 2002, you can get income tax relief at your highest rate on a gift to a charity of a freehold or leasehold interest in UK land or buildings. You must have a certificate from the charity showing that it has accepted the gift.

If you own the property jointly, all the owners must agree to give the whole property to the charity and you get relief in proportion to your share.

If you or someone connected to you gets an interest or right in the property within five years of 31 January following the tax year in which you made the gift, the tax relief will be clawed back.

Tax-saving idea 157

Gift Aid donations are especially tax-efficient if your income is above one of the tax-credit thresholds and a reduction in that income would increase your credits (p. 66). For example, in 2010–11, for every £10 of gross donation, you give just £8 net of tax relief. Your tax credits could increase by up to £3.90, reducing the overall cost to you of each £10 donated to just £4.10. For tax credit purposes, donations count only in the year they are paid – there is no carry-back arrangement.

Relief is given by deducting the value of your gift from your total income for 2009–10. (There is also no capital gains tax on gains made on shares or property given to charity – see Chapter 9.)

Enter the value of your gift in box 9 or 10 on page TR4 as appropriate. This is the market value of the shares, units or property at the time of the gift plus any disposal costs less any sum you receive (for example, if you are selling the shares or property to the charity at a knock-down price) and less the value of any benefits you receive from the charity as a result of the gift.

For more information, ask the Orderline (p. 180) for Help Sheet HS342 *Charitable giving.*

Tax-saving idea 158

> If you want to make a substantial gift to charity and you own shares or property which are standing at a substantial profit, it will usually be more tax-efficient to give the shares or property direct to the charity rather than selling them first and making a Gift Aid donation of the cash raised. But the tax relief you get can only be set against your income – not any capital gains.

Additional information form: other reliefs

Investing in growing businesses

There are some schemes which encourage investment into growing businesses which require risk capital. These types of investments can carry a high degree of risk and to compensate for this investors are offered tax incentives. For more details, see Chapter 7.

Venture capital trusts

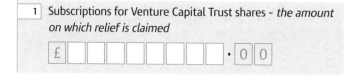

1 Subscriptions for Venture Capital Trust shares - *the amount on which relief is claimed*

£ ⬚⬚⬚⬚⬚⬚⬚⬚ · 0 0

If you invest in a venture capital trust (VCT), you are not investing directly in these companies but in a fund like an investment trust that is quoted on a stock exchange.

When you buy new ordinary shares in a venture capital trust, you can get income tax relief at 30 per cent on an investment up to £200,000 in 2009–10. If 30 per cent tax relief would come to more, relief is restricted to your tax bill for the year in which you make the investment. In working this out, the effect of most other reliefs – such as some allowances, enterprise investment scheme relief, Gift Aid relief, and so on – is ignored.

Any dividends paid out by the venture capital trust and gains you make on the shares in the trust are all free of tax.

In box 1 of the *Other tax reliefs* section on page Ai2, put the amount you have invested in venture capital trusts, up to a maximum of £200,000. Keep in a safe place any certificates you get from venture capital trusts as your tax office may ask to see them.

Enterprise Investment Scheme

2 | Subscriptions for shares under the Enterprise Investment
Scheme - *the amount on which relief is claimed (and
provide more information on page Ai 4)*

£ [ ][ ][ ][ ][ ][ ][ ] . [0][0]

You can get tax relief of 20 per cent on investments (not more than
£500,000 in 2009–10) made in the shares of unquoted trading companies.
If 20 per cent tax relief would come to more, relief is restricted to your tax
bill for the year in which you make the investment. In working this out,
the effect of most other reliefs – such as some allowances, Gift Aid relief,
and so on – is ignored.

You can claim here in this tax return for an investment only if you have
received Form EIS3 from the company in which you invested (Form EIS5
for an investment made through a fund). This form certifies that the
company qualifies for the scheme.

If you have invested in shares eligible for the enterprise investment scheme
after 5 April, but before 6 October 2010, you can ask for half the investment up to a maximum of £50,000 to be deducted from your income for
2009–10. Make this carry-back claim on form EIS3.

Any gain you make on the shares may be free of capital gains tax. You
can also claim capital gains tax deferral relief where the enterprise investment scheme investment was funded out of the proceeds of the disposal of
another asset on which you made a capital gain – see p. 155. (Deferral relief
is available regardless of whether you get any income tax relief.) There are
a lot of detailed rules about which companies are eligible and whether you
yourself are eligible (p. 103).

Enter in box 2 of the *Other tax reliefs* section on page Ai2 the total investments (up to £500,000) for which you are claiming income tax relief in
2009–10, deducting any amount carried back to 2008–09. If you have made
an investment for which you have not yet received Form EIS3, or form EIS5,
don't enter it here. Wait until you receive the EIS3 or EIS5 and then claim
by sending the form that comes with it to your tax office.

Enter details of each investment for which you are claiming relief in box 19
(*Additional information*) on page Ai4 of the Additional information form.

Community investment tax relief

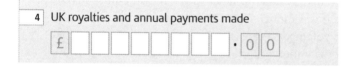

3 | Community Investment Tax Relief - *the amount on which relief is claimed*

You can claim tax relief on loans you make to, or shares you buy in, a community development finance institution. These institutions have been set up to finance small businesses and social enterprise projects in disadvantaged communities. The institutions must be accredited by the Revenue and, to get tax relief, you must have a certificate from the institution.

You get income tax relief of up to 5 per cent a year of the amount you lend or invest for a maximum of five years. If the 5 per cent relief would come to more, relief is restricted to your tax bill for the year. In working this out, the effect of most other reliefs – such as some allowances, Gift Aid relief, and so on – is ignored. For more information, get Help Sheet HS237 *Community Investment Tax Relief – relief for individuals* from the Revenue Orderline (p. 180).

Enter the amount you lent or invested in 2009–10 plus the relevant amounts for earlier years in box 3 of the *Other tax reliefs* section on page Ai2.

UK royalties and annual payments

4 | UK royalties and annual payments made

Annuities and covenants entered into for full value, for genuine commercial reasons, that you pay in connection with your trade or profession and patent royalties are eligible for tax relief at your highest rate. (But covenants paid to individuals in other circumstances do not qualify for any relief.)

Your payments are treated as if basic rate tax relief has already been deducted. If you're a higher rate taxpayer, extra relief is given through your self-assessment tax bill.

In box 4, enter the total you actually paid during 2009–10.

Loan interest

| 5 | Qualifying loan interest payable in the year |

£ ⌐⌐⌐⌐⌐⌐⌐⌐⌐ . 0 0

Claim here for tax relief on the interest for a variety of loans, including loans to buy:

- a share in or putting capital into a co-operative or a partnership (but not if you are a limited partner)

- plant or machinery (but not a car – p. 276) for use in your job if you are an employee or partner (if you are self-employed you claim in the Self-employment supplementary pages)

- shares in or putting capital into a close company (see below). To be eligible you should own more than 5 per cent of the company or be a shareholder and work for most of your time in the business. Broadly, a close company is one which is controlled by five or fewer 'participators', such as shareholders, or any number of shareholder directors.

Provided the loan is for one of the purposes above, if it is a low-interest loan from your employer (p. 123), the loan is a tax-free benefit and you can claim relief for any interest you actually pay by including the amount paid in box 5 of the *Other tax reliefs* section on page Ai2.

Don't enter here to claim tax relief on the interest on a loan for a self-employed business (use box 16 on the short Self-employment supplement or box 24 of the full supplement) or to buy a property you let (use box 7 on the UK Property supplement or box 17 on the Foreign supplement if you rent out a property abroad) or a mortgage that is part of a home income plan (p. 71). Nor should you enter interest on a loan to purchase your home, an overdraft or credit cards – they do not qualify for tax relief.

You claim tax relief in the same way for payments you make for Sharia-compliant products (called 'alternative finance payments' in your tax return) for the purposes listed above.

Closing a business

| 6 | Post-cessation expenses and certain other losses |

£ ⌐⌐⌐⌐⌐⌐⌐⌐⌐ . 0 0

Even after you have closed a business, you may find that there are certain obligations and expenses which you have to meet. For example, you may need to put right some defect in work which you carried out.

You can deduct some expenses from any other income and gains you have in the year in which the business expense arises, if you have no income from your closed business. The relief is available for expenses incurred within seven years after the business closure. You must claim for the relief by 31 January in the second year after the tax year in which you incurred the expense. So for an expense which you met in 2009–10, you must claim by 31 January 2012.

The expenses which qualify for this special relief are:

- costs of putting right defective work you did or faulty goods or services which you supplied and the cost of paying any damages as a result
- premiums for insurance against claims due to defective work or faulty goods and services
- legal and other professional expenses you incur in defending yourself against accusations of defective work or providing faulty goods or services
- debts owed to the business which you included in your accounts but which have subsequently turned out to be bad debts
- cost of collecting debts owed to the business and included in its accounts.

Expenses which don't qualify for post-cessation relief can only be set against future income which comes from the closed business. There are some special rules about unpaid expenses. Ask your tax adviser or tax office for help.

Enter in box 6 of the *Other tax reliefs* section on page Ai2 the amount of expenses which you want to deduct from your income in 2009–10 (and in box 14 of the Capital gains summary pages the amount you want to deduct from your capital gains but giving details in box 19 on page Ai4 of this Additional information form). If you are later reimbursed for any expenses or bad debts entered in this section, remember to enter the amount recovered in box 16 on page TR3 of the Main tax return (p. 210) or box 14 on page Ai1 of this Additional information form if you want to carry the receipts back to an earlier year (p. 221).

Similarly, if you have left a job where you were an employee, you can claim relief here for costs you incur because of actual or alleged wrongful acts in your former employment. If the amount you are claiming exceeds your income for 2009–10 you may be able to set the excess off against any capital gains tax due for the year – put the relevant amount in box 14 on the Capital gains summary pages (p. 400).

If you used to run a business on a self-employed basis but have converted the business to a company, you may be able to claim relief for losses made while you were self-employed against your income from the company. You must previously have opted to carry forward the losses to set against future profits (p. 365), you must have transferred the self-employed business solely or mainly in exchange for shares in the new company and you must meet certain other conditions. Enter the loss you are claiming in box 6.

You also claim in box 6 for losses on gilt strips, strips from other government securities, and the few other deeply discounted securities that still qualify for loss relief (p. 216). A loss incurred in 2009–10 can be deducted only from the income in the same tax year.

Give details of the amounts you are claiming in box 6 in the *Additional information* box on page Ai4.

Maintenance payments

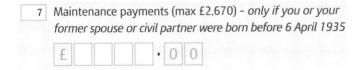

7 Maintenance payments (max £2,670) - *only if you or your former spouse or civil partner were born before 6 April 1935*

£ ⬚⬚⬚⬚ · 0 0

In general, from 6 April 2000 onwards, you can no longer get tax relief on maintenance payments you make to your former (or separated) wife, husband or civil partner. However, if either of you was born before 6 April 1935, you can still qualify for some relief.

Provided you or your former spouse or civil partner were aged 75 or over on 5 April 2010, you can claim relief for payments made under a legally binding agreement, such as a court order, a Child Support Agency assessment, or a written agreement.

No relief is available for voluntary payments. Although maintenance paid to your former spouse or civil partner to maintain your children under the age of 21 is allowed, payments made *to* your children do not qualify for relief.

Payments cease to qualify for relief from the date on which your former spouse or civil partner remarries.

Only payments up to a set limit qualify for relief. The limit is £2,670 in 2009–10. The £2,670 limit applies even if you are making payments to more than one former spouse or partner. You do not get tax relief at the rate of tax you pay. Relief is given at a fixed rate of 10 per cent in 2009–10.

Example

> Peter Smith pays maintenance to his ex-wife, Pat. Since Pat was born before 6 April 1935, Peter's maintenance payments qualify for tax relief. In 2009–10, Peter paid Pat £400 on the first day of each month (£4,800 over the whole year). However, Pat remarried on 20 November 2009, and although Peter carried on paying maintenance, the payments from that date onwards do not qualify for relief. Peter's qualifying payments (May to November) come to £2,800. This is more than the maximum relief of £2,670, so he puts £2,670 in box 7.

In box 7 of the *Other tax reliefs* section on page Ai2, enter the amount of qualifying maintenance you paid during 2009–10 or £2,670, whichever is lower. Give details of the relevant court order or agreement in box 17 (*Additional information*) on page Ai4.

Payments to a trade union, etc.

8	Payments to a trade union etc. for death benefits
	– half the amount paid (max £100)
	£ ⬚⬚⬚ · 0 0

Friendly societies supported their members before the arrival of the welfare state by paying sickness benefit, unemployment benefit and widow's pensions. Although rare, some continue in existence and you can get tax relief on premiums you pay on certain combined sickness and life insurance policies they offer. The tax relief is on one half of the premium. You can also get the same tax relief on part of your trade union subscription if it includes pension, funeral or life insurance benefits. With the friendly society policy, to be eligible for tax relief the premiums must be £25 or less a month and 40 per cent or less of the premium should be for the death benefit.

Ask your friendly society or trade union to tell you how much of the premium was for pension, life insurance, funeral or death benefit. Enter in box 8 half that amount.

Employer's compulsory scheme for dependants' benefits

 Relief claimed for employer's compulsory widow's,
widower's or orphan's benefit scheme - *(max £20)*

£ [ ] . 0 0

Some employers require you to join a scheme (separate from any occupational pension scheme) to provide a pension for your widow, widower or
children in the event of your death. Contributions you make may qualify
for tax relief that is normally given through PAYE, in which case you
should leave box 9 blank.

Exceptionally (for example, where you have to make a lump sum contribution at retirement), you might not get all the relief you are entitled to
through PAYE. You can claim relief at the basic rate on up to £100 of an
otherwise unrelieved payment. In box 9, enter the amount of relief you are
claiming (not the payment on which you are claiming relief). To work out
the relief for 2009–10, take the lower of £100 or the payment on which
you have not received relief through PAYE and multiply by 20 per cent. For
example, if the payment was £50, enter 20% × £50 = £10 in box 9.

Relief on qualifying distributions on the redemption of bonus securities or shares

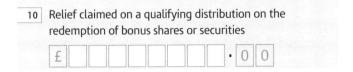

10 Relief claimed on a qualifying distribution on the
redemption of bonus shares or securities

£ [   ] . 0 0

If you receive bonus shares or securities, when they are subsequently
redeemed the amount you receive will count as a distribution for tax
purposes. You will then receive a tax credit and, if you're a higher rate taxpayer, will have extra tax to pay.

This means that you could pay tax twice on the same income, because
higher rate taxpayers are also liable for extra tax when such shares are
issued. To prevent this, you can claim an allowance equal to the extra tax
paid on the issue of the shares. The allowance is given as a reduction in
your tax bill.

If you are liable to higher rate tax on dividends during 2009–10 and have
entered income from a redemption of the shares in box 3 on page TR3 of

the Main tax return (p. 199), enter the amount of relief you are claiming here in box 10 on page Ai2.

The amount of relief is the value of the shares when you first received them (either box 3 on page TR3 of the current style of tax return or box 10.26 on the relevant earlier year's tax return) multiplied by the difference between the higher rate of tax charged on dividends and the rate treated as already paid. This is:

- for the period 6 April 1999 to 5 April 2010, 32.5% − 10% = 22.5%
- for the period 6 April 1993 to 5 April 1999, 40% − 20% = 20%
- for periods before 6 April 1993, 40% − basic rate tax.

Additional information form: income tax losses

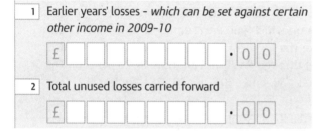

Box 16 of the Main tax return (*Other UK income*) scooped up information about all sorts of miscellaneous income that did not have a place elsewhere in your tax return (p. 210). With the types of income in list A on pp. 210–211, if your expenses exceed the income – in other words, you make a loss – you can set the loss against any other type-A income or carry the loss forward to set against future amounts of type-A income. This section at the bottom of page Ai3 of the Additional information form is where you tell the Revenue what you want to do with these losses.

In box 1, enter the amount of losses brought forward that you are now setting against type A income for 2009–10. In box 2, put the total of losses brought forward that you are not using yet plus the type-A losses that you made during 2009–10 and wish to carry forward.

3 Relief now for 2010-11 trading, or certain capital, losses

£ ⬜⬜⬜⬜⬜⬜⬜⬜ · 0 0

4 Tax year for which you are claiming relief in box 3,
   for example 2008-09 *YYYY YY*

⬜⬜⬜⬜ – ⬜⬜

If you want to carry back a loss made in your business during 2010–11 to set against income made in 2009–10 (or possibly the year before), enter the amount and tax year in boxes 3 and 4. See Chapter 17 for details of relief for business losses.

Additional information form: pension savings tax charges

The government encourages you to plan for retirement by giving a range of tax reliefs when you save through a registered pension scheme – see Chapter 7 for details. There are limits to the amount of relief you can have and rules about how pension savings may be used. If you breach the limits or rules, usually there is a tax charge to claw back the relief that you previously had.

Boxes 5 to 16 on page Ai4 of the Additional information form are the place to report any events in 2009–10 that have triggered a pension saving tax change. For example, you will need to report in box 9 any excess contributions paid by you or by your employer, or someone else on your behalf, if your relevant income for 2009–10 was more than £150,000 or £130,000 and your total contributions exceeded your special annual allowance (see p. 226). Most people do not have to fill in the other boxes in this section of the tax return. Since 6 April 2006, the limits on the amount you can save through registered pension schemes are high and the other circumstances that can trigger a tax charge are unusual.

Your pension scheme provider should tell you if any pension savings tax charge applies. Get Help Sheet HS345 *Pensions – tax charges on any excess over the lifetime allowance, annual allowance and special annual allowance, and on unauthorised payments* from the Revenue Orderline (p. 180). The pension rules are complex, so consider getting help from a tax adviser (see Appendix E).

Additional information form: tax avoidance schemes

17	The scheme reference number	18	The tax year in which the expected advantage arises, for example 2008-09, YYYY YY

Firms or employers that promote schemes designed to reduce or eliminate income tax, capital gains tax or certain other taxes are required to tell the Revenue about each scheme. Examples would be arrangements (often complex, involving for example trusts, loans or derivatives) to reduce capital gains tax or escape national insurance contributions on pay. The Revenue allocates a number to each scheme that must be passed on to each individual using the scheme. If you have entered into such as a scheme, you must declare it in boxes 17 and 18 on page Ai4.

14

Allowances

Another way of reducing the amount of income tax you have to pay is to claim any allowances to which you are entitled. These are deducted from your income, along with reliefs (deductions), to make your taxable income smaller – and so also your tax bill.

Personal allowances

Most people get a personal allowance (which is, however, reduced if your income exceeds £100,000 in 2010–11 and disappears altogether when your income exceeds £112,950 – see p. 24). You get any personal allowance automatically – you don't have to claim it in your tax return.

Tax-saving idea 159

You can go back four years to claim allowances that you forgot to claim at the time or didn't know you were entitled to. You will get tax relief at the rate you should have got it had you claimed the allowance at the right time. Provided you claim by 5 April 2011, you can go back as far as the 2006–07 tax year.

Age-related personal allowances

However, people aged 65 or over during 2009–10, can claim a higher allowance. There is one level of age-related allowance if you were 65 or over during 2009–10 and a still higher rate if you were 75 or over. On page TR1 of the Main tax return, make sure you put your date of birth in box 1 so that the Revenue has the information it needs to get your allowance right. If the Revenue is working out your tax bill for you, when you get a tax calculation form or PAYE coding notice (see Chapter 3), check that you have been given the correct allowance.

Main tax return: blind person's allowance

| 11 | If you are registered blind on a local authority or other register, put 'X' in the box | 13 | If you want your spouse's, or civil partner's, surplus allowance, put 'X' in the box |

| 12 | Enter the name of the local authority or other register | 14 | If you want your spouse, or civil partner, to have your surplus allowance, put 'X' in the box |

Anyone registered as blind with a local authority can claim blind person's allowance. The amount of the allowance for 2009–10 is £1,890.

In England and Wales, local authorities are obliged to enter your name on a register of blind people if you have an ophthalmologist's certificate. Put a cross in box 11 on page TR4 if your name is on a register and write the name of the local authority in box 12.

If you are not registered until after 5 April 2010 but before 6 April 2011, you can still get the allowance for 2009–10 if you can show that you were blind at that date, for example, with an ophthalmologist's certificate.

The authorities for Scotland and Northern Ireland do not have to maintain a register (though some do). So you do not have to be registered blind. You can claim blind person's allowance if your sight is so poor that you cannot do any work for which eyesight is essential. You will normally need a certificate from an eye specialist to prove this is the case. Leave box 11 blank and write 'Scotland' or 'Northern Ireland' in box 12.

If your income is less than your allowances, including blind person's, and you are married and living with your husband or wife, or in a civil partnership and living with your partner, you can transfer the unused part of this allowance to your spouse or partner – put a cross in box 14. Similarly, if your spouse or civil partner is blind and has too little income to use their full blind person's allowance, the unused part can be transferred to you – put a cross in box 13. If both of you are blind, you can claim two allowances between you.

Additional information form: age-related married couple's allowance

1 | Your spouse's or civil partner's full name

[blank field]

[blank field]

2 | Their date of birth if older than you (and at least one of you was born before 6 April 1935) *DD MM YYYY*

[date boxes]

Where husband, wife or civil partner was born before 6 April 1935, a couple can claim the married couple's allowance. For other couples, the allowance was abolished from 6 April 2000 onwards. If you were both born on or after 6 April 1935, do not complete this section.

Where either of you reached 75 or older during 2009–10, the allowance is £6,965. If the total income of the person to whom the allowance is initially awarded exceeds £22,900, the allowance is reduced but never to less than a basic amount of £2,670 (p. 60). The allowance gives tax relief at 10 per cent as a reduction in your tax bill.

A spouse or civil partner can claim married couple's allowance if they were married and living together for at least part of the tax year. A spouse or civil partner can also claim the allowance if they were living apart but neither intended the separation to be permanent.

If you are the husband (where you married before 5 December 2005 and have not elected for the new rules to apply) or the person with the higher income (for later marriages and civil partnerships or marriages before 5 December 2005 where you have elected to be treated under these new rules), complete boxes 1 to 5 in the first section on page Ai3. Put the name of your spouse or civil partner in box 1 and, if they are older than you, their date of birth in box 2. (You do not need to give your own date of birth here – you should already have entered it at box 1 on page TR1 of the Main tax return.)

Sharing the allowance

3 If you have already agreed that **half** the minimum allowance is to go to your spouse or civil partner, put 'X' in the box

☐

4 If you have already agreed that **all** of the minimum allowance is to go to your spouse or civil partner, put 'X' in the box

☐

5 If, in the year to 5 April 2010, you lived with any previous spouse or civil partner, enter their date of birth

☐☐ ☐☐ ☐☐☐☐

6 If you have already agreed that **half** of the minimum allowance is to be given to you, put 'X' in the box

☐

7 If you have already agreed that **all** of the minimum allowance is to be given to you, put 'X' in the box

☐

Married couple's allowance is automatically given to the husband unless:

- either of you has asked for half the basic amount to be given to the wife (in other words, £1,335 is transferred)
- both of you have asked for the whole basic amount of £2,670 to be given to the wife, or
- the first claim was made on or after 5 December 2005 (or earlier but you have elected to be treated under these new rules), in which case the award is made initially to whichever of the couple (in a marriage or civil partnership) has the highest income. In that case, half or all of the basic amount can be transferred to the other spouse or partner.

Any married couple's allowance in excess of £2,670 stays with the person to whom the award was first made.

Normally, you must elect to transfer half or all of the basic allowance before the start of the tax year. This means it is too late to alter the way the allowance is given for 2009–10. In the normal way, it is also too late to alter the way the allowance is given for 2010–11, but you have until 5 April 2011 to make an election for 2011–12.

However, different rules apply in the year of marriage or registration of the civil partnership. In that case, you have until the end of the tax year in which the marriage or civil partnership takes place to make the election. So if you marry on or after 6 April 2010, you have until 5 April 2011 to decide whether to share the allowance for 2010–11.

If you have already made an election for 2009–10 and you are the person who initially claimed the allowance, put a cross in box 3 or 4 to indicate if you are transferring part or all of the basic amount to your spouse or civil partner.

If your spouse or partner initially claimed the allowance and part or all of the basic amount is being transferred to you, leave boxes 1 to 5 blank, but put a cross in box 6 or 7, as appropriate and put your spouse or civil partner's name in box 8.

Marriage or registration in 2009–10

9 | If you were married or formed a civil partnership after 5 April 2009, enter the date of marriage or civil partnership *DD MM YYYY*

If your marriage or registration took place on or after 6 April 2009, put its date in box 9. You can claim one-twelfth of the full allowance for each month of your marriage or partnership (p. 62). If in the same tax year before your marriage or registration you were living with a previous spouse and either of you were born before 6 April 1935, you can instead claim the full married couple's allowance for 2009–10 and you should then put your former spouse's or partner's details in boxes 1 and 5.

Example

> George, 73, was born on 7 June 1935 and would not qualify for married couple's allowance except that his wife, Hannah, who is older than him, was born on 23 February 1935. As a result George qualifies for an allowance of £6,965 in 2009–10. George and Hannah are both taxpayers. Before 6 April 2009, the couple wrote to their tax office electing to have the full basic allowance transferred to Hannah. This means Hannah gets £2,670 of the married couple's allowance, reducing her tax bill by 10% × £2,670 = £267. George keeps the other £4,295, reducing his tax bill by 10% × £4,295 = £429.50.

Transfer of surplus allowance

You can transfer any unused amount of married couple's or blind person's allowance to your spouse or civil partner if you did not have enough income in the year to use up the allowance and you lived with your spouse or partner for at least part of that year.

If you want your spouse or civil partner to have the surplus of married couple's allowance, put a cross in box 11. If you want to claim and use your spouse's or civil partner's unused allowance, put a cross in box 10.

15

Employment

1 **Employment**

If you were an employee, director, office holder or agency worker in the year to 5 April 2010, do you need to complete *Employment* pages? Please read pages TRG 2 and TRG 3 of the guide before answering.

Fill in a separate *Employment* page for each employment, directorship etc., for which you need to complete an *Employment* page and say how many pages you are completing.

Yes ☐   No ☐   Number ☐

Use the Employment supplement to give the most common details about your earnings and deductions if you work for an employer, you are a director of your own company or you receive any expense or benefits from a previous employer. If any of the more unusual circumstances applied to you in 2009–10 – for example, you were made redundant, belonged to an employee share scheme or had earnings from abroad, you may also need to complete page Ai2 of the Additional information form.

The first part of this chapter guides you through completing the Employment supplement. Guidance on filling in page Ai2 starts on page 278 and you should turn to Chapter 16 for detailed information about share schemes.

Employment basics

Are you an employee?

It is usually easy to tell whether or not you are an employee. There are some grey areas, however, where the Revenue will seek to tax you as an employee even if you think of yourself as self-employed:

- if you are a company director (even if you own the company). Note that, from 6 April 2000, if you are a director of your own personal services company, special tax rules may apply and, from 10 April 2003, these were extended to domestic workers (such as nannies) operating through their own company (p. 256). Since 6 April 2007, special rules also apply to managed service companies. This is a company through which you work for other people and are a shareholder without usually being a director of the company. The special rules ensure you are taxed as an employee even if your 'pay' is in the form of dividends

- if you work as a freelance or consultant, but have to work closely under the control of your boss, working a set number of hours at an hourly rate, say, and at a particular location

- if you work on a casual, part-time basis

- if you work as a temp through an agency. This includes, for example, locum doctors; but it does not apply to entertainers or models working through an agency, or to people who work solely from home

- you have more than one job: you may be classed as an employee for one job, even if you are clearly self-employed in another.

The significance of being an employee is that in most cases your employer will have to operate PAYE (see Chapter 3) on your earnings from that job and deduct tax and national insurance before paying you. Exceptionally, the Revenue has agreed that most actors count as employees for national insurance purposes but may be self-employed for income tax.

Special rules apply if you work as a subcontractor in the construction industry or a related trade, for example, a plasterer, decorator, carpenter or electrician. In general, the Revenue will try to treat you as an employee and require the main contractor to withhold tax from your pay. Provided you can convince the Revenue you are genuinely self-employed, you will be able to register to receive your payments gross. This is a complex area. See the Revenue website (http://www.hmrc.gov.uk/cis/index.htm) for details.

For many employees, the advantage of being paid under PAYE is that the right amount of tax on all their income should be deducted from their earnings (but see p. 40) and so they do not have to worry about paying a separate tax bill. If their income from their job is their only income many also do not need to fill in a tax return. But you may still have to fill one in if:

■ you are a higher rate taxpayer and get taxable perks such as a company car

■ you have other income which is paid out before tax is deducted, such as some types of investment income

■ your tax affairs are complex for any other reason.

If you are an employee and are sent a tax return, you need to put a cross in the 'Yes' box at the first question 1 on page TR2 of the Main tax return and fill in a separate Employment page for each job you have. If you are not sure of your status, check with your tax office and try the Revenue's employment status indicator at www.hmrc.gov.uk/calcs/esi.htm.

Tax-saving idea 160

A disadvantage of being an employee is that you cannot deduct as many expenses from your taxable income as you could if you were self-employed. So if you are setting up on your own, check that you will meet the Revenue's conditions for self-employment (p. 304).

What is taxed

Broadly speaking, the Revenue seeks to tax any benefit you get from being employed, even if you get it from someone other than your employer. The tax return organises your remuneration into the following categories:

■ money (including earnings from working abroad)

■ benefits (taxable perks given by your employer) and expenses payments (either flat-rate allowances or reimbursement for expenses you have incurred)

■ lump sums received on retirement, redundancy or death.

Not all of these will actually be taxable. But in general, you have to put it all down first, and the tax return then guides you to enter the various tax reliefs you can deduct, for example, tax relief for expenses incurred in doing your job.

One thing you do not have to enter anywhere on your tax return is details of your national insurance contributions as an employee. These should all be sorted out for you by your employer.

The date income is taxable

As a general rule, you are counted as receiving income from employment from the earlier of:

- the date you get it

- the date you are entitled to it, even if you do not actually get it till later on.

So if, for example, you are entitled to payment on 15 March 2009, but do not actually receive it until 15 April, you must still include it in your tax return for 2009–10. If you receive payment early – on 15 March 2010, for work not completed until 15 April, for example – it is taxable from the date you received it, that is 15 March.

If you are a director, your earnings for a particular period may be decided on one date, credited to you in the company accounts on another date, but not paid out till much later. It is the earliest date that counts, unless the earnings for a particular period were decided before that period ended. In this case, you are treated as receiving them on the last day of the period to which the earnings relate.

IR35: special rules for personal service companies

Special rules may apply if you are a director of a company that hires out your services to clients and:

- you or your family (including an unmarried partner) control more than 5 per cent of the ordinary share capital of the company, or

- you or your family are entitled to more than 5 per cent of any dividends paid out by the company, or

- the company can or does make payments to you other than salary but they are basically payment for the services you provide to clients.

Tax-saving idea 161

You must pay income tax and national insurance on any deemed payment for the tax year in which the money is earned by your personal service company. If that money is paid out to you as salary in a later year, tax and national insurance will again be due – in other words, the same income will be taxed twice. To avoid this, make sure any deemed payment retained within the company is eventually paid out as dividends, not salary. IR35 rules allow dividends up to the amount of any deemed payments to be paid without further tax being due (p. 200) and dividends are not in any case subject to national insurance.

These so-called 'personal service companies' have been popular with people working as contractors or consultants, for example in the information technology and engineering industries. If you were employed direct by a client, you would pay tax and national insurance on your salary and the client would pay employer's national insurance. But if the client contracts with your personal service company to hire your services, the client pays a fee to your company on which there is no employer's national insurance. And if your company pays you dividends instead of salary, you also escape paying national insurance. The Revenue views this as tax avoidance.

For income earned by your company on or after 6 April 2000, the Revenue has closed this loophole. If in the absence of your company your work for a client would essentially be the same as that of an employee (rather than a self-employed person), you may be caught by the IR35 rules (named after the number of the press release which introduced them) and have to pay extra tax and national insurance. The Revenue uses the normal tests for deciding whether you count as an employee or self-employed (p. 304).

Initially, the IR35 rules applied only where your company was contracted for business purposes. But from 10 April 2003, the rules were extended to apply to services performed for any person whether for business purposes or not. This brought domestic workers such as nannies and butlers within the rules.

Example

Bill Brown is a software designer. He is owner-director of a company, BB-IT Ltd, which hires Bill out to clients. For the whole of 2009–10, Bill is contracted to Gigasoft plc, working full-time in their offices for a monthly fee of £6,000. The contract is caught by the IR35 rules. BB-IT Ltd paid Bill a salary of £24,000, £2,500 for an annual season ticket to cover travel to Gigasoft's offices and £4,000 to Bill's pension scheme. At the end of the year, BB-IT Ltd must work out whether there is any deemed payment under the IR35 rules on which income tax and national insurance contributions are due:

Income caught by IR35 (12 × £6,000)	£72,000
Less	
Salary actually paid	£24,000
Employer's national insurance already paid	
([£24,000 − £5,715] × 12.8%)	£2,340
Employee-related expenses (i.e. season ticket) which would be allowed under normal rules	£2,500
Pension scheme contribution	£4,000
Expense allowance to cover costs of running personal service company (5% of £72,000)	£3,600
Deemed payment before deducting employer's national insurance	£35,560
Employer's national insurance on deemed payment	£3,387
Deemed payment	£32,173

Bill is deemed to receive extra salary of £32,173 on 5 April 2009. The company is responsible via PAYE for paying Bill's income tax and employee's national insurance on this amount as well as employer's national insurance of £3,387.

If the IR35 rules do apply, you will be treated for income tax and national insurance purposes as if you had received a salary (called a 'deemed payment') equal to:

- the fees received by your company, less

- any salary paid by the company on which you have paid tax and national insurance in the normal way, less

- a 5 per cent expense allowance designed to cover the costs of running your personal service company.

The deemed payment is treated as paid on the last day of the tax year – in other words, 5 April 2010 in the case of the tax year covered by the current tax return. Tax and national insurance were due to be paid through the PAYE system by 19 April 2010.

The deemed payment, just like salaries that are actually paid out, is deducted from the company's profits when working out corporation tax.

Your company does not actually have to pay you the deemed payment – it could be retained within the company or paid to you as dividends. IR35 includes rules to allow special distributions (dividends) to be made during the tax year or later up to the amount of any deemed payment without further tax being due – see p. 200.

The IR35 rules affect only the income tax and national insurance position. They do not affect the legal status of your company's contract with the client.

The rules apply on a contract-by-contract basis. Some of the work you do through your personal service company may count as equivalent to self-employment and so fall outside the rules; other contracts may be deemed equivalent to employment and so fall within the rules. You can ask your tax office to advise on the status of existing contracts (but not draft contracts).

For more information, see www.hmrc.gov.uk/ir35/index.htm. If you do not have internet access, ask your tax office to send you a copy of these web pages.

Include any deemed payment in box 1 of the Employment page. Income tax on the deemed payment paid through PAYE should be included in box 2.

Managed service companies (MSCs)

Special rules may also apply if your services are hired out to clients via a company of which you are a shareholder and possibly, but not usually, a director but over which you have no control, called a managed service company (MSC). The special rules also apply where the MSC is structured as a partnership rather than a company.

MSCs, typically used by freelancers and contractors, became popular as a way of avoiding the IR35 rules. A scheme provider would promote the use of MSCs and provide you with an off-the-shelf MSC structure that the provider controls and manages. The end-client would contract with the MSC for your services and pay the MSC. The MSC (or its associate) would then pay you in a variety of ways that might include dividends, loans, expenses and benefits without any deduction of PAYE tax or national insurance contributions.

Since 6 April 2007, payments caught by new tax rules are treated as earnings you get from the MSC, which has to hand over the relevant PAYE income tax to the Revenue and, since 6 August 2007, national insurance contributions as well. It makes no difference if the MSC is an offshore company – under the rules it is deemed to have a place of business in the UK whether or not it really does and so is caught by the legislation. The rules work in a similar way to the IR35 rules by treating any payment you get as a result of working through the MSC as giving rise to a 'deemed employment payment'. The deemed payment is worked out as follows:

■ *Step 1*: Start with the payment you actually receive

■ *Step 2*: Deduct any expenses you meet that would qualify as allowable expenses under the usual rules (pp. 272–278). But note that the MSC rules effectively treat working for each end-client as a separate employment with that client. This means, for example, the cost of travelling between your home and the client's premises is not allowable

■ *Step 3*: Assume the answer at step 2 is made up of the deemed employment payment and employer's national insurance contributions at 12.8 per cent on earnings above £110 a week (£476 a month) in 2009–10

■ *Step 4*: Deduct the employer's national insurance contributions to leave the deemed payment. This is the amount on which income tax and employee's national insurance is charged.

The MSC is initially liable to pay the tax and national insurance due but if it cannot or will not make the payments within a reasonable time, the Revenue can transfer the debt to other organisations and people involved in the arrangement, including you.

Where tax and national insurance have been collected on a deemed employment payment, but the payment itself is made as a dividend, there is a risk that you would pay tax twice on the same income. Therefore, the MSC can apply for tax relief to be given for the dividend payment. If the Revenue agrees to this, you do not have to declare the dividend on your tax return, so do not include it in box 3 on page TR3 of the Main tax return (p. 200).

If you have income that seems to be caught by both the IR35 rules (p. 256) and the MSC rules, the IR35 rules cease and just the MSC rules apply.

Example

Clare Charles is an engineer. She works for several big clients, providing her services through a managed service company, Solutions Ltd. The clients pay £6,000 a month to Solutions Ltd, which pays a fee to the MSC provider and then passes £5,400 a month to Clare. The MSC rules catch the payment to Clare and the deemed payment is calculated as follows:

Payment caught by the MSC rules	£5,400
Less	
Allowable expenses	£0
Deemed payment before deducting employer's national insurance	£5,400
Employer's national insurance	£559
Deemed payment [(£5,400 − £476) / 1.128] + £476	£4,841

Apart from paying the £559 employer's national insurance to the Revenue, Solutions Ltd must also collect Clare's income tax and employee's national insurance, which come to £1,459. If Solutions Ltd cannot pay the £2,018 a month due within a reasonable time, the Revenue can seek to recover the debt from, for example, the MSC provider and even Clare herself.

The documents you need

Most of the information you need will be on Forms P60, P11D or P9D.

Your P60 is a form your employer must give you by 31 May after the end of the tax year (that is, by 31 May 2010 for the 2009–10 tax year). The P60 is a summary of how much you have been paid, and how much tax has been deducted. If you haven't got a P60, you should be able to find the information from your pay slips. If you left a job during a tax year, the information will be on your P45.

If you work through your own personal services company, or a managed services company, it must provide you with a P60 in the normal way. The P60 (and any P45) will show any deemed payment under the IR35 or MSC rules and tax on it in the same way as ordinary pay.

Your employer has to declare to the Revenue any taxable benefits or expenses you receive and the cash equivalent on form P11D or form P9D. Which form you get depends on how much you earn. You should get a copy from your employer by 6 July after the end of the tax year, that is by 6 July 2010 for the 2009–10 tax year.

Note that if you leave a job, you will not automatically be given a form P11D or P9D, but your ex-employer must give you one if you ask for it within three years after the end of the tax year in which you left. Your employer has 30 days from receiving your request in which to supply the form (if this is after the normal 6 July deadline).

Your P11D or P9D should be the starting point of all the expenses payments you have received. But you also need to keep receipts or documentation to back up your claim to deduct allowable expenses, particularly if they were not reimbursed by your employer and so did not appear on your P11D or P9D.

If you receive a lump sum from your employer, for example, when you left your job, it may be included on your P60, your P11D, or your P45, or you may just have a letter from your employer. Your employer should be able to help you decide which category a payment falls within. If there is any doubt, employers can get advance decisions from their tax office, so it is worth talking about the tax consequences with your employer before any payment is made.

Employment supplement: money from employment

1 | Pay from this employment - the total from your P45 or P60
- *before tax was taken off*

£ ⬚⬚⬚⬚⬚⬚⬚⬚ · 0 0

You should enter as money:

- ▨ salaries, deemed payments under IR35 or MSC rules, wages, fees, overtime, bonuses, commission and honoraria (after deducting money you have donated to a payroll giving scheme, or contributed to your employer's pension scheme, see below). If you work in the banking sector and received a bonus of more than £25,000 in the period 9 December 2009 to 5 April 2010, this may be caught by a new bank payroll tax of 50 per cent. This is your employer's tax bill, not yours, and the amount you enter in box 1 is the bonus you receive after the bank payroll tax has been deducted

■ amounts voted to you as a director and credited to an account with the company, even if you cannot draw the money straight away

■ voluntary payments and gifts, whether from your employer or anyone else, such as tips and Christmas boxes (excluding some small gifts and personal gifts such as long-service awards, see tax-free fringe benefits on p. 113)

■ incentive awards (but see opposite)

■ the taxable value of shares withdrawn early from an approved profit-sharing scheme

■ sick pay, including statutory sick pay and statutory maternity, paternity and adoption pay (see opposite)

■ holiday pay

■ various payments to do with your employment which are not strictly pay. Examples are golden hellos paid to entice you to join the company; a loan written off because you satisfied or completed an employment condition; payments made to recognise changes in your conditions of service or employment; payments made if you leave a job and agree, in return for a lump sum, not to compete with your employer.

P60 forms vary in design. The figure to look for is your pay 'for tax purposes' or 'this employment pay'. Enter the figure from Form P60 in box 1, but check that it does not include employer's contributions to a pension scheme or what you give under a payroll giving scheme (see opposite). If you were unemployed during the year, your P60 may give details of any jobseeker's allowance you received. Do not enter this in your Employment page – enter it instead in box 14 on page TR3 of the Main tax return.

If the amount you put in box 1 contains any deemed earnings from an IR35 company or MSC, you must also put the amount in box 1 at the bottom of page TR4 of the Main tax return (p. 214).

Contributions to an occupational pension scheme

You can get tax relief on contributions you make to your employer's occupational pension scheme (p. 87). This tax relief is given by deducting your contributions from your pay before tax is worked out on it, so giving you relief up to your top rate of tax. The figure you enter as taxable pay in box 1 should be the figure after deducting pension contributions.

Details of contributions to other types of pension plan or scheme do not go here, even if your employer arranges for them to be paid direct from your salary. Instead they go in boxes 1 to 4 on page TR4 of the Main tax return.

If your income was more than £130,000 in 2009–10, some of the tax relief on your contributions may be clawed back. The rules are explained on p. 226 and, if they apply to you, you will need to complete box 9 on page Ai4 of the Additional information form (see p. 245).

Payroll giving schemes

You can get tax relief on charitable donations of any amount through a payroll giving scheme offered by your employer. The biggest scheme run by the Charities Aid Foundation is called Give As You Earn, or GAYE. The money is deducted from your pay each week or month and passed straight to the charity by your employer. The donations are deducted from your pay before your tax is worked out on it, in the same way as contributions to an occupational pension scheme, so remember to check that what you enter in box 1 is your pay after deduction of payroll giving donations.

Incentive awards

Broadly speaking, these are taxable whether you receive them from your employer or from someone else in connection with your job; for example, a car sales representative may receive prizes from the car manufacturer. However, the person paying the award may pay the tax for you, through a taxed award scheme. In this case, the award still counts as part of your income, but the tax paid on your behalf will reduce your tax bill. Whoever makes the award should give you a Form P443 stating the value of the award and how much tax has been paid on it, unless the figures have been included on your P60. You should include the amount of the award in box 3 and the tax already paid in box 2.

Suggestion scheme awards are tax-free and need not be entered, provided that there is a formal scheme open to all employees, and the suggestion concerned is outside your normal job. If the suggestion is not taken up, the maximum award is £25; if it is implemented, the maximum award is 50 per cent of the first year's expected net benefit, or 10 per cent of the benefit over five years, with an overall maximum of £5,000.

Sick pay, maternity pay, paternity pay and adoption pay

If you are off work through illness or on maternity, paternity or adoption leave, any payment made to you by your employer, including statutory sick pay (SSP), statutory maternity pay (SMP), statutory paternity pay or statutory adoption pay, is taxable. It will be taxed before you get it and shown on your P60 or P45 in the same way as other income, and you enter it with your other taxable pay in box 1. There are two exceptions to this rule:

■ occasionally, these statutory payments may be paid directly to you by the Revenue. In this case, the benefit is still taxable, but tax is not deducted before it is paid to you and rather than enter it under Employment you should enter it in box 15 on page TR3 of the Main tax return (see p. 209)

■ if you pay part or all of the premiums for an insurance policy taken out by your employer to meet the cost of employees' sick pay. In this case, the proportion of the sick pay which arises from your contributions is tax-free and need not be entered on the tax return. Any sick pay arising from your employer's contributions is taxable. Put it in box 1.

Tax deducted

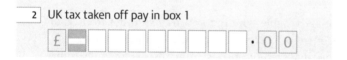

| 2 | UK tax taken off pay in box 1 |

£ ▬ . 0 0

The tax your employer has deducted under PAYE is set against your tax bill. Enter it in box 2, together with any other tax deducted (for example, under a taxed incentive scheme). Occasionally, your employer may have given you more tax back as a refund than was actually deducted. If so, put the refund in box 2 with a minus sign in the shaded box.

If you left a job and later received a tax refund from the Revenue or the Department for Work and Pensions, enter in box 2 the tax shown on your P45. Put the subsequent repayment in box 1 on page TR5 of the Main tax return (p. 187).

Tips and other payments

3 | Tips and other payments not on your P60 - *read page EN 3 of the notes*

£ ▢▢▢▢▢▢▢ . 0 0

Box 3 is there to catch any income that does not appear on your P60 (for example, because it is paid by people other than your employer or it comprises earnings from a foreign source earned in an earlier year but only remitted in 2009–10) and for which there is no other place on the Employment page.

Your employer

4 | PAYE tax reference of your employer (on your P45/P60)

▢▢▢ / ▢▢▢▢▢▢▢▢▢▢

5 | Your employer's name

So that your tax office can tie up the information on your tax return with that provided by your employer, give your employer's PAYE reference (shown on the P60 or P45) in box 4. Give your employer's name and address in box 5.

Put a cross in boxes 6 and 7, as applicable, if you are a director and/or the employer is a close company. (A close company is broadly one that is controlled by five or fewer people or by any number of people who are all directors.) This may affect the way your perks and benefits are taxed.

Student loan repayments

8 | If you are a part-time teacher in England and Wales and are on the Repayment of Teachers' Loans Scheme for this employment, put 'X' in the box

If you have an income-contingent student loan (p. 186), normally the Revenue will have instructed your employer to deduct the loan repayments due through PAYE. You give details of the amount your employer has deducted on page TR2 of the Main tax return not here.

However, if you are a teacher, teaching a shortage subject, you may have been accepted onto the Repayment of Teachers' Loan Scheme, in which case, the government will gradually write off your loan over a period of up to ten years and your employer should not make any loan deductions from your pay. If this applies to you, put a cross in box 8.

Employment supplement: benefits and expenses

Many employers give their employees non-cash fringe benefits, such as a company car or free medical insurance (see Chapter 8). Generally, you are taxed on the cash equivalent of these benefits (and the same applies if the benefit or expense is paid to you by someone other than your employer). Benefits for your family or household are regarded as a payment to you. However, some types of benefits are tax-free for everyone, and others are tax-free if you count as low-paid.

Expense payments you receive are yoked together with benefits in this section and sometimes the dividing line between them can be a fine one; for example, a company car may be a way of covering your travelling costs for work, as well as a perk of the job.

Payments you do not need to enter

There are three sorts of payments which you can ignore when filling out the benefits and expenses section of the Employment supplementary page.

Dispensations

You do not need to enter in your tax return expense payments which are covered by a dispensation. A dispensation is a special permission from the Revenue which means that your employer does not have to include on your P11D or P9D expenses which would be tax-free anyway. Dispensations are usually given for things like travelling and subsistence expenses on an approved scale: they do not generally cover fringe benefits.

PAYE Settlement Agreements

The tax on some of your expenses and benefits may already have been paid by your employer under a PAYE Settlement Agreement (PSA). This is a voluntary agreement between an employer and the Revenue under which the employer undertakes to pay the tax otherwise due from you on some types of benefits and expenses. The advantage for your employer is the saving of paperwork; the advantage for you is that you do not need to enter the payments on your return and they are tax-free in your hands. Only some types of benefits and expenses can be covered by this sort of agreement, for example, minor expenses such as taxi fares and benefits such as parties shared by many employees.

Tax-saving idea 162

Remember – you do not need to enter items covered by a dispensation or PAYE Settlement Agreement.

Tax-free fringe benefits

You do not need to enter the details of any fringe benefits that are tax-free (see Chapter 8 for a list). Note that there are conditions to be met before most of these benefits can be tax-free. Fuller information is given in Help Sheet HS207 *Non-taxable payments or benefits for employees*.

Payments you need to enter

Some benefits are always taxable and need to be entered on the tax return. They are assets which are transferred to you (including payments in kind), vouchers (except, since 6 April 2002, vouchers for minor benefits that are exempt from tax, such as a travel card for free travel on a works bus) and goods paid for by credit cards, living accommodation (with a few exceptions) and mileage allowance in excess of the Revenue authorised mileage allowance payments.

You may receive other benefits. But if you earn at a rate of less than £8,500 a year and are not a director they will be tax-free and you do not need to enter them on the tax return. Chapter 8 gives much more detail. It helps you work out whether you are paid at the rate of £8,500 a year or not and helps you work out the taxable value of benefits which you need to enter here.

Company cars and vans

9	Company cars and vans – *the total 'cash equivalent' amount*

£ ⬜⬜⬜⬜⬜⬜⬜⬜ . 0 0

A company car is taxable only if you earn at the rate of £8,500 a year or more (p. 117). Put in box 9 the cash equivalent of cars made available to you (or to members of your family or household) for private use. Check the figure with your employer or on your form P11D. Chapter 8 and Help Sheet HS203 *Car benefits and car fuel benefits* will be useful.

Also enter in box 9 the taxable value of any company van available for your private use as shown on your P11D. In 2009–10 this is £3,000 but the taxable value is reduced if the van was unavailable for part of the year, you have to share it with others or you pay towards your private use. If you earn at a rate of less than £8,500 and in some other circumstances, a van is a tax-free benefit – see p. 117.

Fuel for company cars and vans

10	Fuel for company cars and vans – *the total 'cash equivalent' amount*

£ ⬜⬜⬜⬜⬜⬜⬜⬜ . 0 0

If you have a company car, you may get free fuel for private use as well. This is taxed in a similar way to company cars with the tax charge based on the car's carbon dioxide emissions (p. 122). Enter the amount in box 10.

The taxable value of fuel provided by your employer for private use of a van is usually £500 a year reduced by any amount you have to pay. The taxable value is also reduced if the van was unavailable for part of the year or you have to share it with others. The value is zero if the only private use you make is driving to and from work – see p. 123. Your P11D will show the amount if any you need to enter in box 9.

Tax-saving idea 163

If you have a choice, consider a zero-emission company van. In that case, the taxable value of fuel for private use of a company van is zero. And, from 6 April 2010 to 5 April 2015, the taxable value of a zero-emission van available for your private use is reduced to zero.

Tax-saving idea 164

The taxable value of a company car is based on its carbon dioxide emissions. This makes larger company cars an expensive fringe benefit. Consider a low-emission car instead. You can find out about different cars' carbon dioxide emissions from www.vcacarfueldata.org.uk.

Private medical or dental insurance

| 11 | Private medical and dental insurance - *the total 'cash equivalent' amount* |

£ ⬚⬚⬚⬚⬚⬚⬚⬚⬚ . 0 0

This is taxable only if you earn at the rate of £8,500 a year or more. Enter the taxable amount, which you should find on Form P11D, in box 11. For more explanation, see p. 125.

Vouchers, credit cards and excess mileage allowance

| 12 | Vouchers, credit cards and excess mileage allowance |

£ ⬚⬚⬚⬚⬚⬚⬚⬚⬚ . 0 0

You may be given a voucher for a particular service (for example, a season ticket), a credit token or a company credit or charge card. If so, you are taxed on their cash equivalent unless they appear in the list of tax-free fringe benefits on pp. 108–112 (for example, luncheon vouchers, gift vouchers which count as a small gift, vouchers for minor benefits that are tax-free). Cash vouchers worth a specified amount of cash should already have been taxed under PAYE, so you will not usually have to enter them here as a benefit. If you used vouchers or your company credit card to settle expenses of your job (such as train fares), include the full value of the vouchers or card bill here, but claim a deduction in box 17 ('Business travel and subsistence expenses') further down the Employment page.

For vouchers and cards that count as a taxable fringe benefit, broadly speaking you pay tax on the expense incurred by the person who provided them, less any amount that you have paid yourself. You will not have to pay tax on any annual card fee or interest paid by your employer.

Company credit cards and charge cards are often provided as a convenient way of paying business expenses. If so, you still have to enter the value of any vouchers or goods or services obtained with a credit card or credit token in box 12. You can claim any allowable business expenses back in boxes 17 to 20. For more information see Help Sheet HS201 *Vouchers, credit cards and tokens*.

If you use your own car, motorbike or bicycle for work, you may be paid a mileage allowance for the business mileage you do. Since 6 April 2002, any allowance up to the Revenue approved mileage allowance payment (p. 108) is tax-free and you do not enter it on your tax return. But anything in excess of the approved payment is taxable and should be entered in box 12. This is the case even if your actual costs are higher than the authorised rate, so that you are not making any profit out of the excess allowance. The amount of any excess should be shown on the P11D.

Similarly, your employer can pay you a tax-free passenger allowance up to the approved payment if you carry a colleague in your vehicle on business trips (p. 108). Any excess over the approved amount is taxable and must be entered in box 12.

If your employer does not pay you any mileage allowance or pays you less than the approved payment, you can claim a deduction up to the approved amount (regardless of your actual costs) in box 17 (p. 273). This does not apply to passenger allowances.

Goods and assets provided

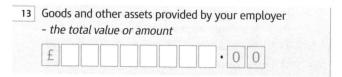

13 | Goods and other assets provided by your employer
   - *the total value or amount*
   £ [   ] . [0][0]

Payments in kind may be taxed in various ways depending on how much you earn and whether you have the option of cash instead (p. 114). If you earn at a rate of less than £8,500 a year (including the value of taxable benefits), the taxable value is the second-hand value of the goods or assets. If you earn more, it is the larger of the second-hand value or the cost to your employer of providing the asset. The amount to enter in box 13 should be shown on your P9D or P11D.

Living accommodation

14 | Accommodation provided by your employer – *the total value or amount*
   £ [   ] . [0][0]

The taxable charge for any living accommodation (unless it counts as a tax-free fringe benefit, see p. 111), and the extra charge if applicable, should be entered in box 14.

If you think all or part of this benefit should be tax-free, contact your tax office before completing box 14.

Help Sheet HS202 *Living accommodation* explains how to work out the taxable value for various types of accommodation.

Other benefits

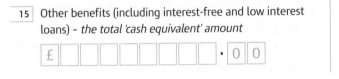

This is a box to sweep up any taxable perks not entered elsewhere. It applies only if you earn at a rate of £8,500 or more and the figures you need should be shown on your P11D. Include in this section cheap or free loans from your employer, any payments your employer makes for you, and other benefits listed on pp. 123–126.

The basic rule for free or cheap loans is that you have to pay tax on the difference between the interest you pay and the interest worked out at an official rate set by the Revenue. But there can be exceptions (p. 123).

In box 15, you should put the cash equivalent (your employer should tell you what this is).

If the loan is for a qualifying purpose (for example, to buy an interest in a partnership) and you are paying interest on the loan, you should claim tax relief in box 5 in the *Other tax reliefs* section on page Ai2 of the Additional information form (p. 239).

If the loan is eventually written off without your having to repay it, you pay tax on the amount written off. Include the amount with the taxable value of any other loans in box 15.

Payments your employer makes for you, such as your phone bill or rent, should be entered in box 15. Also include the taxable benefit you get from assets that remain the property of your employer and which you have the use of, and any services provided by your employer.

Tax-saving idea 165

The loan of a computer from your employer for your private use ceased to be a tax-free benefit for new loans from 6 April 2006 onwards. For loans since then, the value of the benefit is taxed as described on p. 126 and the taxable value should be entered in box 15. Where the computer was first lent to you before that date and qualified as tax-free, this exemption continues to apply and includes replacement of the computer under warranty (but not after the warranty period has expired), and upgrading software and ongoing maintenance contracts if part of the original pre-6-April-2006 agreement with your employer. But the exemption will be lost if, for example, your employer replaces the original computer with a new machine, so think carefully before accepting an upgrade.

Note: If your employer provides you with a computer solely for business use (whether at home or at work), this is not a taxable benefit provided any private use of the equipment is 'not significant'.

Expenses payments and balancing charges

| 16 | Expenses payments received and balancing charges |

£ ☐☐☐☐☐☐☐☐☐ . 0 0

You should enter here the total expenses payments and expense allowances you received. You can deduct tax-free expense payments later on in boxes 17 to 20. The only expenses which you should not enter either here or later on are those for which your employer has a dispensation.

Your expenses payments should be shown in your P11D or P9D. In your P11D they will be broken down into the gross amount received, any contributions you made or amounts on which tax has already been deducted, and the taxable amount. Enter the taxable amount in box 16.

Balancing charges are not something you will see on your P11D or P9D. They apply only if you claimed capital allowances on something that you bought for your work and that you have now disposed of (p. 327). You can find further information in Help Sheet HS206 *Capital allowances for employees and office holders*.

Employment supplement: employment expenses

You should already have entered all the expenses payments and allowances you received in box 16. However, not all these payments will be taxable, and there may be expenses for which you were not reimbursed and on which you can claim tax relief. So you should enter all your tax-allowable expenses, whether or not you were reimbursed, in boxes 17 to 20.

The only exception is expenses for which your employer has a dispensation (p. 266). These should not be entered anywhere on your tax return, unless your allowable expenses came to more than the amount covered by the dispensation (in which case you should enter the extra). Your employer should be able to tell you what dispensations exist.

The overall rule is that only those expenses which are expended wholly, exclusively and necessarily in doing your job are allowable, except for travel and related meal and accommodation expenses, which must be necessarily incurred or incurred as a result of necessary business travel. In all cases, necessarily means that it would be necessary for anybody doing the job, not just necessary for you.

There is no neat list of definitions in tax law, and much depends on previous court judgments. In practice, a lot comes down to agreement with your tax inspector and you should keep all the evidence you have (receipts, mileage details and so on) to back up your claims. However, the main tax-allowable expenses are listed below.

Travel and subsistence expenses

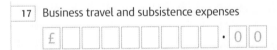

17 Business travel and subsistence expenses

£ ⬜⬜⬜⬜⬜⬜⬜⬜ · 0 0

You can claim tax relief for travel costs, for example fares, you incur making business journeys. If you use your own car, motorcycle or bicycle for work, any tax and tax relief are based on the Revenue approved payments (p. 108) not your actual costs. Mileage allowance you receive up to the Revenue approved payment is tax-free and not entered on your tax return. Any excess is taxable and should already have been entered in box 12 (p. 269), but you cannot claim any tax relief on the excess even if your actual costs exceeded the statutory payment. And you cannot claim capital allowances or interest on a loan to buy a vehicle. If you did not get any mileage allowance, or you received less than the approved payment, use box 17 to claim the shortfall up to the approved payment per mile (regardless of the actual expenses you incurred). You will need to have kept a record of your business mileage during 2009–10 and any allowance you had from your employer.

A business journey is either:

- travel between one place of work and another required in the performance of your duties (travel 'on the job'), or

- travel to and from a workplace, provided it does not count as ordinary commuting or private travel and attendance at the workplace is a requirement of your duties, not just a matter of personal convenience.

You can't claim for journeys that count as ordinary commuting, defined as travel between your home and your *permanent* workplace – even if the journeys take place at abnormal hours. However, the cost of travelling from home to work following an emergency call-out may be allowed in limited circumstances (for example, for NHS employees whose duties of employment commence before starting on the journey).

You can claim for journeys between home and a *temporary* workplace. A workplace counts as temporary if you go there for a limited duration or for a temporary purpose. But it loses its temporary status if you spend at least 40 per cent of your working time there over a period which lasts (or is likely to last) for more than 24 months.

If you have a permanent place of work, you might sometimes travel direct from home to another place where you are required to perform your duties, or travel from that place direct to home. In this situation, you can claim the actual travel expenses you incur unless the journey is not significantly different from the ordinary commuting journey.

If travelling is your job – for example, you are a travelling salesperson or a lorry driver – you might not have any permanent place of work. In that case, journeys from home to the places you visit on business may count as business travel. But if you work in a defined geographical area, any travel from home to the edge of that area, and back again, is ordinary commuting and you cannot claim the costs of that part of your journeys.

If a journey counts as business travel, you can also claim relief for:

- meals and accommodation costs (subsistence) incurred in making the business journey

- other business expenses arising because of the journey, for example telephone costs. You cannot deduct personal expenses, such as phone calls home, daily newspapers and personal laundry – but in practice, you may not have had to include these in box 16 in any case, since small amounts of personal expenses are tax-free (p. 110).

You should ask for and keep receipts for the subsistence and other business expenses you incur to back up your claim.

The rules can be interpreted in a number of ways depending on the facts of the case. If you are unsure what you can claim, the Revenue guide 490: *Employee travel – a tax and NICs guide for employers* (to which your employer should have access and available from the Revenue website www.hmrc.gov.uk/helpsheets/490.htm) gives the full rules and useful examples.

Add together all the allowable travel costs incurred, including accommodation and meal costs on business journeys and any other expenses of business journeys (such as business phone calls, but not personal items like phone calls home). Enter the total in box 17.

Tax-saving idea 166

If your journey counts as business travel, don't forget to include the cost of any meals and accommodation which are attributable to the journey (other than the usual expenses you incur when at your normal place of work).

Fixed deductions for expenses

18 | Fixed deductions for expenses

£ ⬚⬚⬚⬚⬚⬚⬚⬚ · 0 0

The Revenue has agreed flat-rate expenses with various trade unions and other bodies to cover the costs of providing equipment and special clothing which is not provided by employers. For example, carpenters and joiners in the building trade can claim a flat-rate £140 (in 2009–10), uniformed bank employees can claim £60. Ask your union or other staff body if you are covered. You do not have to claim the flat-rate deduction – if you spend more, you can claim more, but if so, you should enter the amount in box 20, under other expenses, not here.

Tax-saving ideas 167 and 168

Revenue-agreed flat-rate expenses were increased from the start of 2008–09 (having been unchanged since 2004–05). Make sure you are claiming the increased amount.

If your actual expenses come to more than the flat-rate, you can claim your actual expenses instead.

Professional fees and subscriptions

You may pay for membership of a particular body or society which is relevant to your work. You can claim it in box 19 as an allowable expense provided that:

- membership of the organisation, or registration with it, is a condition of your job, for example, as a dentist, optician or solicitor, or

- the organisation is approved by the Revenue as being a non-profit body which exists for a worthy purpose such as to maintain professional standards, and membership is relevant to your work.

Any such organisation should be able to tell you whether it is on the Revenue's list of approved bodies. Or you can get the list from www.hmrc. gov.uk/list3/index.htm.

Other expenses and capital allowances

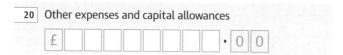

Other expenses must be wholly, exclusively and necessarily incurred in the performance of your duties. This means that you cannot claim expenses which merely put you in a position to do your job – for example, a journalist's expenditure on newspapers, employment agency fees, childcare. There are special rules for business entertaining – check with your employer whether these affect you. The expenses you should be allowed are:

- the costs of providing and maintaining tools and special clothing for which you have not already claimed a fixed deduction in box 18. Special clothing does not cover clothes which you could wear outside work, even if you would never choose to do so

- the cost of special security needed because of your job – you can claim this only if your employer paid for the security or reimbursed you, and you have already entered the appropriate amount as a benefit

- costs and expenses if you are held liable for some wrongful act as an employee, or insurance premiums to cover you against such costs

■ training expenses for which you are not reimbursed, providing that your employer requires or encourages you to attend the course and gives you paid time off to do so, it is full-time (or virtually so) and lasts for at least four weeks. The expenses allowed are fees (unless you have already had tax relief on these), the cost of essential books and the full cost of daily travel to and from the course. You can claim any additional costs incurred if you have to stay away from home, provided you still have to meet the costs of maintaining or renting your own home

■ if you carry out some or all of the central duties of your job from home and the nature of the job itself requires that such work be done from home, a proportion of the heating and lighting costs, and, for a room used exclusively for work, council tax. You're not allowed to claim these expenses if you simply work from home from choice. Moreover, even if your contract of employment requires you to work from home, these expenses are not allowable if the work could in fact be done elsewhere. Do not include home-related expenses which your employer has reimbursed and which count as a tax-free benefit (see Tax-saving idea 169 below)

■ cost of business calls you have to make on your home phone.

Tax-saving ideas 169 and 170

Working from home could mean part being classified as business premises and so trigger a charge for business rates. But, in a case during 2003 (*Tully* v *Jorgensen*) – ironically involving a Revenue employee – a tribunal ruled that, where home-based working used furniture and equipment normally found in a home, there was no breach of residential use and business rates were not due. However, structural alterations, hiring staff, using specialist equipment and customers visiting your home-business could justify business rates.

The rules concerning working from home are less strict where your employer reimburses you for certain costs you incur. Since 6 April 2003, where you regularly work from home with your employer's agreement, you can receive up to £3 a week in 2009–10 tax-free from your employer towards extra day-to-day costs of running part of your home as an office. Neither you nor your employer has to keep any records to back up these payments and there is no requirement to prove that working from home is a necessary feature of the job. Your employer can reimburse larger amounts tax-free but in that case you will need to produce records to back up the claim. The exemption does not apply where you work from home informally and not by arrangement with your employer. (The exemption applies only to expenses reimbursed by your employer or specifically covered by your salary. You cannot simply claim £3 a week as allowable expenses if your employer does not meet these expenses for you.)

You may also be able to claim capital allowances in this section if you buy equipment such as a computer which is necessary (as defined opposite) for your job. You cannot claim an allowance if your employer would have provided the equipment had you not chosen to do so. You used to be able to claim capital allowances on a car or other vehicle you bought to use in your job. But capital allowances and interest on a loan to buy such a vehicle are already taken into account in the Revenue approved mileage payments that can be either paid to you by your employer (p. 108) or claimed by you as an allowable expense (p. 273).

Tax-saving idea 171

> For an employee to claim tax relief on expenses related to working from home, the work must be such that any employee doing the job would of necessity have to carry out some or all of the central duties from home. The Revenue has identified some types of employment where that condition is normally met. They are: insurance agent, university lecturer, councillor, examiner, midwife and minister of religion. If your tax office accepts your home as a workplace, you will also be able to claim the cost of travel to and from home on business.

When you finally dispose of an asset on which you claimed capital allowances there may be a balancing charge to add to your taxable income. (See Chapter 17 for how to work these out.)

Additional information form: share schemes and employment lump sums etc.

The Employment supplement covers only the more common payments and reliefs related to your job. If you have unusual payments, you will also need to fill in the top section on page Ai2 of the Additional information form.

Share schemes

Boxes 1 and 2 concern shares and options you have through a share scheme at work. The boxes look simple, but this is a complex area, so we have devoted Chapter 16 to explaining the rules – turn to page 285.

Lump sums and compensation

You may have something to enter in boxes 3 to 10 if:

- you received a lump sum when you left a job, such as redundancy pay
- you retired and received a lump sum from an unregistered pension scheme (that is, anything other than a Revenue approved, foreign government or other statutory pension scheme)
- your employer (or ex-employer) paid you any other lump sum which you have not already entered as pay (for example, in box 1 or 3 of the Employment page).

Use the working sheet on pages Ain16 to Ain17 of the Additional information notes to work out what to enter in each of the boxes.

It is important to enter the right bit in the right category because each is taxed under different parts of tax legislation. You can get various types of tax relief on some categories, but not on others. One payment might be made up of several different types. They may also affect your overall tax calculation.

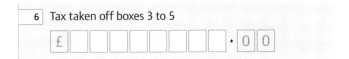

6 Tax taken off boxes 3 to 5

£ ⬚⬚⬚⬚⬚⬚⬚ · 0 0

Your employer may deduct tax from any taxable sums you get before paying you. If so, make sure you enter it in box 6, so that it is taken into account when working out your tax bill. But do not put in this box any tax which you have already included in box 2 on the Employment page and, if this applies, put a cross in box 7.

Payment expected under the terms of your employment

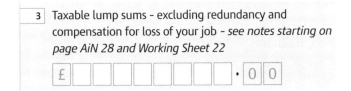

3 Taxable lump sums - excluding redundancy and compensation for loss of your job - *see notes starting on page AiN 28 and Working Sheet 22*

£ ⬚⬚⬚⬚⬚⬚⬚ · 0 0

Lump sums that you should enter in box 3 on page Ai2 include:

- any payment that you receive under the terms and conditions of your contract, or where the expectation that you would get it is firm enough for it to be regarded as part of your contract – for example, a payment based on length of service which it is your employer's established policy to make when a job ends

- payments received in return for your undertaking not to carry out certain actions, sometimes called a restrictive covenant (if not already entered with other pay in box 1 or 3 on the Employment page)

- bonuses on leaving a job (for example, for doing extra work in the period leading up to redundancy). Do not enter redundancy payments themselves in this category – they go in box 5, after deducting various reliefs (boxes 9 and 10).

All these payments are taxable in full. For tax purposes, they are treated just like the rest of your pay.

Payments from unregistered pension schemes

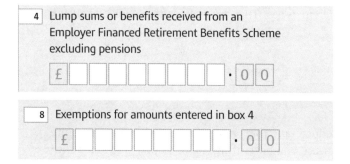

Most pension schemes are registered by the Revenue or statutory schemes, and the lump sums you receive from them are tax-free (within limits). Payments from an unregistered scheme are also tax-free if they:

- arose because of an accident you suffered at work, or

- were funded by a contribution from your employer on which you have already paid tax, or

- arose from your own contributions, or

- came from an overseas scheme, provided further conditions are met. If you think this might apply to you, ask your tax office to explain the rules.

In box 8 enter any amounts that are tax-free. Any remaining taxable amount is included in box 4. The working sheet in the Additional information notes will help you work out the correct figures.

Other payments

9 Compensation and lump sum £30,000 exemption - *see page AiN 28 of the notes*

The first £30,000 of the following payments are tax-free:

■ redundancy pay (either statutory or at the employer's discretion)

■ pay in lieu of notice which is not included in your terms and conditions of employment

■ any other payments on leaving a job which were not part of your terms and conditions, and not 'expected' or received as payment for work done.

Enter the first £30,000 (or total received) in box 9. Anything over £30,000 is taxable and should be entered in box 5. The worksheet in the Additional information notes will help you calculate the correct sum.

10 Disability and foreign service deduction

Some other payments are also tax-free altogether if:

■ you get them as a result of accident or chronic illness which meant that you couldn't do your job

■ 75 per cent of your service in the job was foreign service, or if you worked abroad for least ten out of the last 20 years (and 50 per cent of your time in the job, if longer than 20 years). If you can't meet these conditions, you may still get some relief – see Help Sheet IR204 *Lump sums and compensation payments*.

Enter these payments in box 10.

5 Redundancy and other lump sums and compensation payments

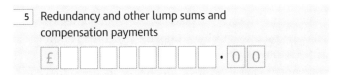

Any remaining sum goes in box 5. The worksheet in the Additional information notes will help you calculate this amount.

Foreign earnings

The broad principle of the UK tax system is that you are taxed on foreign earnings if you are resident or ordinarily resident in this country, even if your permanent home (your domicile) is elsewhere. A full explanation of all these terms is included in Chapter 23. If you think you may be able to claim non-residence you should read that chapter first.

You should include foreign earnings in boxes 1 to 3 of the Employment page (your employer may already have included foreign earnings in your P60). But if you are a UK resident, or a British citizen, a Crown employee or a citizen of some other countries you can claim personal allowances to set against your income. You may also be able to claim deductions in boxes 11 to 14 on page Ai2 of the Additional information form, which make the possibility of tax on foreign earnings a less fearsome prospect.

Seafarers' earnings deduction

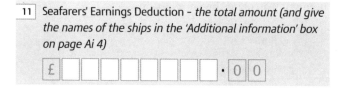

This is a deduction that can be claimed only by seafarers. You can get information on this from Help Sheet HS205 *Foreign Earnings Deduction: Seafarers*. Enter the names of the ships involved in box 19 (*Additional information*) on page Ai4 of the Additional information form.

Foreign earnings not taxable in the UK

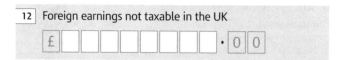

Depending on your residence status and the place where your duties of employment were carried out, you may not have to pay UK income tax on all your foreign earnings for 2009–10. For example, this may apply if you have included in the Employment Pages earnings which you are prevented from bringing back to the UK by law, because of government action or a shortage of foreign currency in the country concerned. The various situations in which your foreign earnings may be tax-free are complex and you should use the worksheet contained in Help Sheet HS211 *Employment – residence and domicile issues*.

Foreign tax

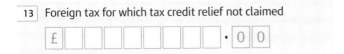

If you work abroad, you may be liable to two lots of tax: tax charged by the country in which you earn the money and UK tax. You have two options for avoiding this double taxation:

■ claiming tax credit relief (if you are a UK resident)

■ deducting the foreign tax from your foreign earnings.

Because tax credit relief can wipe out all or part of the foreign tax, it is usually the best option, but it is not always available. There are various Revenue working sheets that may help you decide which is the best option for you (see Chapter 20 for more details). If you decide to claim tax credit relief, leave box 13 blank and complete the Foreign supplementary page. Otherwise, enter the amount of foreign tax in box 13.

Employers' contributions to overseas pension scheme

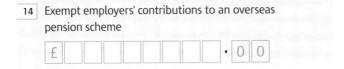

Contributions your employer makes on your behalf to a UK registered pension scheme do not count as taxable pay or taxable benefits. Special rules extend the same treatment to contributions your employer makes to most overseas pension schemes and, if this applies in your case, you should enter the amount your employer pays in box 14. For more information, see Help Sheet HS344 *Exempt employers' contributions to an overseas pension scheme* from the Revenue Orderline (p. 180).

16

Share schemes

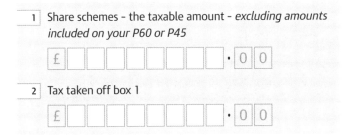

1 Share schemes - the taxable amount - *excluding amounts included on your P60 or P45*

£ [   ] · [0][0]

2 Tax taken off box 1

£ [   ] · [0][0]

Part of your payment from a job may come in the form of shares (or share options – the right to buy shares at a set price at some point in the future) in your employer's company. Generally pay in the form of shares is taxable just as any other form of pay or benefit would be. However, there are special approved schemes under which you can get your shares or options tax-free. You will need to complete boxes 1 and 2 of the upper section on page Ai2 of the Additional Information form only if your shares or share options are not received through an approved scheme, or if you are in a scheme but breach its rules in some respect.

The entries on page Ai2 look deceptively simple, but you will need to use the working sheets on pages Ain8 to Ain14 of the Additional information notes to help you work out what to enter on page Ai2.

In this chapter we explain the rules for the approved schemes and the situations in which you will need to make an entry on page Ai2. Remember, if all your shares and options come from the approved schemes and you have kept to the rules, you do not need to make any entry at all and can ignore this section of the tax return.

Banks transferred into public ownership

Northern Rock Bank was transferred into public ownership on 22 February 2008 and Bradford & Bingley plc on 29 September 2008. If you had rights to acquire shares through a share scheme, this is your position:

- Share incentive plan (SIP) – see p. 289. Given the exceptional circumstances, there was no income tax liability for 2007–08 even if you were technically withdrawing from the plan early. For capital gains tax (CGT) purposes, you are treated as having disposed of the shares on the date of transfer for a zero final value. This means if you paid anything for the shares, you have a capital loss which you can claim in the usual way (see Chapter 9). If, in future, the government pays you any compensation, this will count as a gain for CGT purposes.

- Save-as-you-earn (SAYE) share option scheme – see p. 294. You can continue to make monthly savings and, at the end of the three- or five-year term, you will still receive the tax-free bonus. However, you no longer have the option to use the savings to buy shares and must take the proceeds in cash. If, in future, the government pays you any compensation, this will probably count as employment income for tax purposes.

- Company share option scheme (CSOP) – see p. 292. You no longer have the option to buy any shares. If, in future, the government pays you any compensation, this will probably count as employment income for tax purposes.

- Unapproved share scheme – see p. 297. There was no income tax liability resulting from the transfer. If, in future, the government pays you any compensation, this will probably count as employment income for tax purposes.

Employee shares: the basics

The benefit you get from share schemes may come in the following forms:

- a gift of the shares themselves, or a discount on the purchase price
- an option to buy a set number of shares, at a set price, at a particular time in the future
- dividends from the shares once they become your property
- a capital gain (or loss) arising from movements in the share price once the shares become your property.

Boxes 1 and 2 on page Ai2 are concerned only with the transfer of the shares or options to you as a gift or discounted purchase and the tax advantage this gives you. Very occasionally, with some unapproved schemes, there may also be something to report here when you sell the shares. But, otherwise, information about dividends and selling the shares is not the concern of this section and goes elsewhere on your tax return. The share dividends are taxed like the dividends from any share you own and you enter them at box 3 on page TR3 of the Main tax return (see Chapter 12) or the Foreign supplement (see Chapter 20) if they are paid by an overseas company. Similarly, the shares are generally subject to the normal capital gains tax rules (see Chapter 9) and you give details of capital gains on the Capital gains summary pages (Chapter 22).

In the past, employee shares were particularly attractive because they qualified for favourable capital gains tax treatment. This was abolished from 6 April 2008 onwards, so taxable gains on employee shares are now exposed to the full capital gains tax rate (18 per cent in 2009–10) but you will not necessarily have any tax to pay – see tax-saving ideas 172 and 173. Approved employee share schemes have again started to look attractive as an alternative to straightforward pay if you will have to pay the additional tax rate of 50 per cent on income from 2010–11 onwards. The bank payroll tax (see p. 262) which affects bonuses over £25,000 if you work in the banking industry does not apply to bonuses in the form of shares granted through share incentive plans (see p. 289) or Save-As-You-Earn share option schemes (see p. 294).

The scope of the share scheme tax rules was widened to cover many more types of security from either 16 April 2003 onwards or 1 September 2003 onwards, depending on the type of security involved. For simplicity this chapter uses 'shares' to mean shares and other securities within the scope of the rules.

Many tax-avoidance arrangements have been developed involving paying employees with shares or share options. The government now requires all such arrangements to be declared to the Revenue and has been quick to change the law to close them down. It has also passed legislation enabling avoidance arrangements that emerge in future to be closed with their closure backdated as far as 2 December 2004.

Tax-saving idea 172

The effective maximum rate of tax on gains you make when you sell employee shares is 18 per cent in 2009–10. But each year you have an allowance that lets you make some capital gains tax-free (£10,100 in 2009–10). Try to choose the timing of your sales to keep your gains within the tax-free limit. Alternatively, check whether you can transfer newly acquired employee shares to a personal pension scheme (see Tax-saving idea 64 on page 89).

Different types of share schemes

For tax purposes, share schemes fall within five broad categories:

■ approved profit-sharing schemes

- approved share incentive plan
- approved share option schemes – either savings-related schemes, company share option schemes or enterprise management incentive options
- unapproved share option schemes
- cheap or free gifts of shares through an unapproved scheme (sometimes called share incentive schemes).

Tax-saving idea 173

> As an employee, you do not often have a choice of scheme, since employers are likely either to have just one scheme, or to have one scheme that is open to all employees and another which is open to a select few. But if you know that your employer is considering a scheme, try to make your voice heard so that the choice suits you.

You may have come across Employee Share Ownership Trusts (ESOTs) – these are a special type of trust set up to acquire shares in the company and distribute them to employees. For the employee, the shares are taxable in the same way as shares received through an unapproved scheme (p. 298).

If you received shares or share options which are taxable in 2009–10, you will need to declare them on page Ai2 unless they have already been taxed under PAYE or have been included on Form P11D. If under PAYE, you should put the taxable value of the benefit in box 1 of the Employment page, and the tax in box 2. If on Form P11D, the taxable value goes in box 15 on the Employment page.

The documents you need

You should have some correspondence from your employer concerning your scheme, including (where relevant) a share option certificate and a copy of the exercise note. You will also need to know the market price of the shares at various dates – if your employer cannot help, try a historical share price service, such as that run by the London Stock Exchange (www.londonstockexchange.com). If the company is not quoted on a recognised stock exchange, the market value has to be agreed with the Revenue.

Approved profit-sharing schemes

These were a way of transferring free shares in a company to its employees via a special trust. These schemes have been phased out. No new shares could be allocated after 31 December 2002.

The shares became taxable only if you sold them within three years of being allocated them so there should no longer be any tax changes associated with these schemes and you will not need to enter them on the share scheme pages.

Tax-saving idea 174

When you take your shares out of an approved profit-sharing scheme, savings-related share option scheme or approved share incentive plan, you can transfer them into an ISA (p. 97), providing you do so within 90 days. Alternatively, shares from any of these schemes may be transferred within 90 days to a pension scheme (p. 87). In both cases, the transfer does not trigger a capital gains tax bill at the time and any future growth in the value of the shares is free of capital gains tax.

Approved share incentive plans

Approved share incentive plans aim to give you a continuing stake in the company you work for. You can acquire shares in up to four ways:

▓ free shares – you can be awarded up to £3,000 of free shares each tax year. The award can be conditional on performance, length of service, and so on. You must normally keep the shares within the plan for a minimum holding period which can be no less than three years and no more than five years

▓ partnership shares – you can ask your employer to deduct regular sums from your pay with which to buy shares in the company. The maximum deduction is £1,500 each year and total deductions must come to no more than 10 per cent of your pay (which could be your total pay or just part of it, eg excluding overtime). The plan can set a minimum deduction but this must be no more than £10. You can withdraw these shares from the plan at any time but this may trigger a tax charge (see overleaf)

▓ matching shares – your employer can decide to award you up to two matching shares for every partnership share you buy. You must normally keep the matching shares within the plan for a minimum holding period which can be no less than three years and no more than five years

▓ dividend shares – you can opt to have cash dividends paid on any of the above shares reinvested to buy more shares. The maximum value of dividend shares you can buy in any year is £1,500. You must leave dividend shares within the plan for at least three years.

There is no tax to pay when any of these shares are acquired. You get tax relief through PAYE on any amount used to buy partnership shares. There is also no income tax due if you leave shares within the plan for at least five years (three years in the case of dividend shares).

Example

In December 2009, Lynne Harper was awarded 100 free shares in her employer's company, Treats plc, through its share incentive plan. Over the period September 2009 to February 2010, Lynne has also had £20 a month deducted from her pay to buy partnership shares in Treats plc. By February, 6 × £20 = £120 has been deducted and she has bought 24 partnership shares. As Lynne is a basic rate tax-payer in 2009–10, she gets tax relief of £4 on each £20 deduction, reducing the cost to her of £120-worth of shares to just £120 − (6 × £4) = £96.

In February 2010, Lynne takes a better job with another company. As she is leaving Treats plc, her shares cease to be subject to the share incentive plan and tax may now be due. Including the free shares, she has 124 shares in all. The share price stands at £5.50. The taxable value of the shares is 124 × £5.50 = £682. Basic rate tax on this comes to 20% × £682 = £136.40.

An income tax bill will only arise and you only need to give details on page Ai2 of the Additional information form if any free shares, partnership shares or matching shares cease to be subject to the plan (for example, on your changing job) within five years of them being awarded to you or bought by you, and the reason they ceased was not due to your leaving employment because of:

- injury or disability
- redundancy
- a job transfer covered by the Transfer of Undertakings (Protection of Employment) Regulations 1981
- transfer or sale of the company out of a group running the plan
- retirement on or after an age specified in the plan (50 or above)
- death.

If the situation above has occurred and none of the exemptions listed applies, see *How to work out the taxable amount* below and use working sheet 1 on page Ain8 of the Additional information notes to work out the taxable amount to include in box 1 on page Ai2.

There may also be income tax to pay if any dividend shares cease to be subject to the plan within three years of the date you bought them and none of the reasons listed above applies. In this case, you should enter the amount of cash dividend used to buy the shares in box 3 on page TR3 of the Main tax return (p. 198).

If you have already paid through PAYE any tax due on free shares, partnership shares, matching shares or dividend shares ceasing to be subject to the plan, enter the amount in box 2 on page Ai2 of the Additional information form.

For more information, ask the Orderline (p. 180) for booklet IR177 *Share incentive plan and your entitlement to benefits* or the un-numbered booklet *Share incentive plans – a guide for employees*.

How to work out the taxable amount

Where free shares, partnership shares or matching shares cease to be subject to the plan within three years of being granted or bought, the taxable amount is the market value of the shares at the time they leave the plan.

Where free or matching shares cease to be subject to the plan after three years but within five years of being granted or bought, the taxable amount is the lower of the market value at the time they leave the plan and their market value at the time they were awarded to you.

Where partnership shares cease to be subject to the plan after three years but within five years of being granted or bought, the taxable amount is the lower of the market value at the time they leave the plan and the total deductions in pay used to buy them.

Tax-saving idea 175

Persuade your employer to set up a share incentive plan. Your employer can give you up to £6,000 of shares a year tax-free as long as you keep them in the scheme for five years.

Approved share option schemes

For tax purposes, there are three key events in the life of an option:

▨ when you are first granted the option. If you receive the option through an approved scheme, there is never any tax to pay on the grant of the option. There could be a tax bill in the case of an unapproved scheme, but this has become less likely for options granted from 1 September 2003 onwards

▨ when you exercise your right to buy the shares. You have to pay tax on the exercise only if you fail to meet various conditions. You don't have to exercise the option (for example, where the market price has fallen below the exercise price) and there is no tax if you just let it lapse

■ if you receive some benefit for cancelling, transferring, releasing or otherwise not exercising your option. Tax is due on the value of the benefit (which may be adjusted if the value has been artificially reduced).

To work out the taxable amount (if any), you need to keep records of:

■ the date on which each key event takes place

■ the number of shares involved

■ the share price – both the price you actually have to pay, and the market value at the time of each event

■ any cash you contributed for the option, or any cash (or other benefit) you received for cancelling, transferring, releasing or otherwise not exercising it.

Approved company share options

Company share option schemes may be restricted to groups of employees. Broadly, options received under these schemes are tax-free as long as you exercise them within strict time limits (see below).

The price at which you can buy the shares under your option must not be less than the market value of the shares when the option is granted (or up to 30 days before). If you received a discounted option, it becomes an un–approved share option (p. 297).

Tax-saving idea 176

If you are granted options in an approved share option scheme, keep records of when you exercise them, and the dates by which you can next do so. For example, if you were granted options in 2000, you must exercise them by 2010 to avoid tax.

Under a company share option scheme, the maximum value of options you can be granted is £30,000.

You only have to pay tax on other options if:

■ you have received something for giving it up or not exercising it, or

■ the scheme had ceased to be approved by the time you exercised your options, or

■ you exercise the option within three years of being granted it (unless from 9 April 2003 onwards this happened because of injury, disability, redundancy or retirement as described in the list on p. 290), or

■ you exercise the option more than ten years after being granted it.

If any of these situations applies, see the box *Tax on an option* below and use Working sheet 2 on page Ain9 of the Additional information notes to work out what to put in box 1 on page Ai2.

Warning

If there is a tax charge to pay when you exercise an option, it is based on the market value of the shares at that time. The tax charge will not be reduced if the value of the shares subsequently falls. Make sure you set aside enough money to pay the tax bill. This may mean selling some of the shares as soon as you get them. If you plan to sell shares later to meet the tax bill, you are gambling that the share price will not fall in the meantime.

Tax on an option

Exercise

Step 1: take the market value of the share at the date the option was exercised and multiply by the number of shares you actually bought. This gives you the market value of all the shares you have bought.

Step 2: take the price at which you exercised the option and multiply by the number of shares you bought. This is the actual price.

Step 3: deduct the actual price (at Step 2) from the market value (at Step 1). If you paid anything for the option, you can deduct that too. The result is the taxable amount to enter in box 1 on page Ai2.

Rule changes from 1 September 2003

The meaning of 'exercise' was widened to include any acquisition of shares even if there is no actual exercise as such. For example, it includes automatically acquiring shares after a set time has passed. If someone else – say, a family member or someone you have a business connection with – benefits from your option (rather than you), you will still be taxed according to the rules here.

The grant of an option

With most unapproved share options there is no tax on the grant.

Cancellation etc. of an option

If you get any benefit in return for cancelling, transferring, releasing or otherwise not exercising your option, the taxable amount is what you received less anything you paid for the option.

Approved savings-related share options

These schemes give you the right (or 'option') to buy a set number of ordinary shares in your employer's company at some point in the future, at a price fixed now, but you must do so using savings you build up in a Save-As-You-Earn (SAYE) plan. If you meet the various conditions laid down by the Revenue, you will get your shares tax-free. For details, see the Revenue booklet *Approved SAYE (Save As You Earn) share option schemes. Guidance for employees*, available from the Revenue website at www.hmrc.gov.uk/share-schemes/employee-guidance.rtf or the Orderline (see p. 180).

Among other conditions you must agree to:

▒ save a set amount each month, with a minimum of £5 a month and a maximum of £250

▒ save for a set period – three or five years. Five-year contracts may give you the option of leaving your money invested until the seventh anniversary.

The price of the shares (the subscription price) is fixed when you are granted the option, but cannot normally be less than 80 per cent of their market value at that time (or up to 30 days before). So if, for example, shares in Horridges' plc stand at 400 pence, the lowest subscription price is 320 pence. You have no tax to pay when the option is granted to you. You will not have tax to pay when the option is exercised unless:

▒ you exercise your option when your company is taken over or sold, and you have not yet held it for three years

▒ you benefit from the option in any way other than using it to buy shares – for example, if you receive compensation for not using or agreeing not to use your option.

If either of these situations applies, see the box *Tax on an option* on p. 293 and use Working sheet 3 on page Ain10 of the Additional information notes to work out what to put in box 1 on page Ai2.

Tax-saving idea 177

Whether or not you will benefit from a savings-related share option scheme depends on the option price and the share price when you exercise your option. You do not have to exercise your option if you would make a loss (in other words, the market price has fallen below the option exercise price). You can instead simply take the tax-free cash. So, especially if you are a higher rate taxpayer, or are optimistic that you will make some profit on the shares, joining the scheme is worthwhile.

Enterprise management incentive options

This scheme is designed to help small, high-risk firms recruit and retain key employees. Independent trading companies with assets of no more than £30 million that qualify for the scheme can offer share options to any number of employees. The maximum value of shares subject to unexercised options outstanding at any time is £3 million. The shares may be quoted or unquoted. The option must be capable of being exercised within ten years. Each employee can hold a maximum of £120,000 (£100,000 before 2008–09) of unexercised options in total. (In the case of several different options, the value of each one is based on the share price on the date it was granted.)

To be an eligible employee, you must work for the company at least 25 hours a week or, if less, at least 75 per cent of your total work time, and you must control no more than 30 per cent of the company's ordinary share capital.

There is no income tax to pay when an option is granted. There is also no income tax to pay when you exercise an option unless:

■ it was a discounted option – in other words, the price you paid for the shares was less than the market value of the shares at the time the option was granted; or

■ a disqualifying event took place and you failed to exercise the option within the 40 days following the event.

If neither of these situations applies, you do not need to give any information on the Share scheme pages about your options under the scheme. If either does apply, use Working sheet 4 on page Ain11 and or Working sheet 5 on page Ain12 of the Additional information notes to work out what to put in box 1 on page Ai2.

Tax-saving idea 178

If you acquire shares on or after 6 April 2002 on the same day from more than one share scheme and you later dispose of some of them, you can elect to have the shares from each scheme treated separately and the disposal matched to the shares that show the smallest capital gain (p. 148).

Example

In August 2009, under an enterprise management incentive scheme, Sam Wright is granted an option over 50,000 shares priced at £1 each at the time the option is granted. It gives him the right to buy the shares at 75p each when he exercises the option at any time up to July 2019. There is no tax to pay when the option is granted.

In December 2009, when the shares are priced at £1.50 each, the company ceases to qualify as a trading company, having moved into the insurance business. Sam exercises his option in March 2010, when the share price is standing at £2. Income tax is due when the option is exercised because it is a discounted option and because a 'disqualifying event' took place more than 40 days earlier. The taxable amount is worked out in two stages.

First, Sam must calculate the taxable amount resulting from the discount. The market value of the shares in August 2009 when the option was granted was $50,000 \times £1 = £50,000$. The price he paid for the shares in March 2009 was $50,000 \times 75p = £37,500$. Therefore gain from the discount is $£50,000 - £37,500 = £12,500$. But Sam has agreed to pay the employer's national insurance of $12.8\% \times £12,500 = £1,600$ in respect of this gain, so the net amount on which income tax is due is $£12,500 - £1,600 = £10,900$.

Next, Sam must work out the taxable amount triggered by the disqualifying event. The market value of the shares in March 2010 when Sam exercised the option is $50,000 \times £2 = £100,000$. From this, Sam deducts the market value of the shares in December 2009 when the company changed its business ($50,000 \times £1.50 = £75,000$). This gives a gain since the disqualifying event of $£100,000 - £75,000 = £25,000$. Sam can deduct the employer's national insurance he has paid in respect of this amount ($12.8\% \times £25,000 = £3,200$) leaving a net amount on which tax is due of $£25,000 - £3,200 = £21,800$.

The total taxable amount that Sam enters in box 1 on page Ai2 is $£10,900 + £21,800 = £32,700$. Sam is a higher rate taxpayer, so pays income tax of $40\% \times £32,700 = £13,080$ as a result of exercising his option. In addition he has paid $£1,600 + £3,200 = £4,800$ in employer's national insurance contributions and must pay employee's contributions of $1\% \times £32,700 = £327$.

Your employer should be able to tell you if a disqualifying event has taken place. Disqualifying events are:

- the company becomes a 51 per cent subsidiary of another company or, in some other way, comes under the control of another company. This is not a disqualifying event if, within six months of the takeover, your original option is replaced by an equivalent option over shares in the new company

- the company ceases to count as a trading company under the scheme rules (some 'low risk' trades are in any case excluded – for example, dealing in land or shares, banking, insurance, farming, market gardening, managing woodlands, running hotels, nursing homes or residential care homes, and so on)

■ the company had been preparing to become a trading company but this failed to materialise within two years of the option being granted

■ you stop working for the company

■ you no longer work 25 hours or more (or 75 per cent or more of your time) for the company

■ the option is altered so that the market value of the option shares increases or the option ceases to meet the rules for the scheme

■ the share capital of the company is altered without prior approval from the Revenue

■ shares to which the option relates are converted to shares of a different class, unless all the shares of one class are converted to shares of one other class and certain other conditions are met

■ relating to your employment with the same company, you are granted an option under an approved company share option plan (p. 292) and together with your enterprise management incentive options this takes your holding of unexercised options above £120,000.

Unapproved share options

With unapproved option schemes, since 1 September 2003, there is normally no tax on the grant of an option. Tax is generally payable only when the option is exercised, assigned, released or you receive any benefit in connection with the option (for example, for cancelling it). However, there is no income tax to pay if this occurs after your death.

For options granted before 1 September 2003, income tax may be payable on grant if it is a 'long option'. A long option is one which can be exercised more than ten years after the date on which it was granted. Any amount already assessed for income tax can be set against income arising at a later date – for example, on exercising the option.

Example

In 2000 Edward Brough was granted an option to buy 1,000 shares at £2 which can be exercised at any time between 1 January 2007 and 1 January 2012. This counts as a long option, so he had to pay tax when it was granted. At the time the market price of the shares was £3, so their market value was £3 × 1,000 = £3,000 against the option to buy at £2 × 1,000 = £2,000. The taxable amount was therefore £3,000 − £2,000 = £1,000 on which Edward paid tax of £400.

In October 2009 Edward exercised his option. This cost him £2,000. Bucking the general stock-market trend, the market price had risen to £3.50, the market value of the shares was £3.50 × 1,000 = £3,500. The taxable amount is £3,500 − £2,000 = £1,500, less the £1,000 already taxed in 2000.

How to work out the taxable amount

In general, whatever type of share option scheme you have, and whether it is approved or unapproved, if the event (for example, the exercise or cancellation) is taxable, the amount is worked out as in the box on p. 293.

Slightly different rules apply if you have voluntarily agreed to pay any employer's national insurance contributions on the gain. When you exercise the option, your employer (and you) could be liable for national insurance contributions. The amount due will depend on the share price at the time of exercise which can't be predicted in advance. To save a company facing a large and unpredictable tax bill at some unknown future date, the company is allowed to make an agreement with you so that you pay the employer's national insurance contributions (as well as any employee's national insurance due) when you exercise the option. You can deduct any employer's (but not employee's) national insurance you pay in this way when working out the amount of income tax due.

Free or cheap shares through an unapproved scheme

Employers have many reasons for offering cheap or free shares. These count as part of your payment from the job. The exact tax treatment depends on whether the shares are counted as your earnings or treated as a fringe benefit.

The distinction is fine but significant: if the shares count as benefits, the difference is taxed as if it is an interest-free loan from your employer, which means there may be no tax to pay at all; if the shares count as earnings, the difference between their market value and the price you pay is taxed as earnings.

The following will count as benefits:

- shares you are allowed to pay for in instalments (partly-paid shares)
- shares which you buy but where part of the purchase price is deferred, for example, when a particular profit target is met
- any other exceptional cases in which cheap or free shares do not count as earnings.

All other free or cheap shares are taxed as earnings. Even after you have acquired the shares, you may be considered to receive further taxable benefits from them, for example, an increase in their value when a restriction is lifted. In that case, you may have extra tax to pay called a post-acquisition charge.

Shares taxed as earnings

You may get some benefit tax-free if the company for which you work decides to sell shares (or other securities) to the public and offers shares on special terms to its employees. You have to distinguish between:

■ a discounted price offered to employees

■ a priority allocation of the shares.

The discounted price is taxable: you pay tax on the difference between the price you pay and that paid by the general public. The calculation is very straightforward. Take the market value of the shares at the time you acquired them. Deduct anything you paid for them. The result is the taxable amount.

The benefit of the priority allocation itself is tax-free and need not be entered unless:

■ it is reserved for directors or higher-paid employees, or those who are entitled to it do not all get it on similar terms, and

■ the shares reserved for employees in their priority allocation are more than a certain percentage of the overall shares on offer – normally, more than 10 per cent of the total shares on offer.

Your employer should tell you the taxable amount, which may already have been included as part of your earnings on your P60 or P45. In that case you may already have included it in box 1 on the Employment page (p. 261) with the tax already paid included in box 2 on the Employment page. Provided there is no further tax to pay, you do not need to enter anything on page Ai2. If there is tax to pay, put the amount still to be taxed in box 1 on page Ai2.

Previously, the above rules applied only to shares and most other securities issued by companies. However, from either 16 April 2003 or 1 September 2005, depending on the type of securities involved, the scope of the rules was widened to include many other financial assets, such as government stocks, futures, units in a unit trust, and so on.

Other changes that took effect during 2003 include important elections to consider about when you might pay the income tax. This is a complicated area and you might want to seek advice from an accountant or tax specialist.

For more information, see www.hmrc.gov.uk/shareschemes.

Example

> Linden works for Good Holdings, which has just been offered for sale to the public. Using the priority allocation for employees, Linden bought 500 £1 shares, at the discounted staff price of 80p. Linden is not taxed on the benefit of the priority allocation. However, the discounted price is taxable. The market value of the 500 shares was £1 × 500 = £500, but Linden only paid 80p × 500 = £400. She is taxed on £500 − £400 = £100.

Shares as benefits

Anything entered under this category is treated as an interest-free loan. The loan is the difference between what you paid and the market value of the shares. The loan is taxable only if:

■ you count as earning at a rate of £8,500 or more or are a director (see p. 117 for how this is worked out)

■ the total amount of all the cheap or interest-free loans from your employer outstanding in the tax year comes to more than £5,000 (p. 123).

If tax is payable, it will be spread out over the whole life of the deemed loan.

The taxable value of the loan is the theoretical interest you would have paid had you been charged interest at an official rate set down by the government (see p. 125).

Your employer should have included details on the taxable amount on your P11D. Do not enter the amount here. Include it in the amount you enter at box 15 on the Employment page (p. 271).

Post-acquisition events

You are charged tax on any further benefit from securities (or an interest in them) which you acquire because of your employment. This applies even if you have since left the company. Events that may trigger a tax charge later on include:

■ restrictions attached to the securities running out or being altered

■ keeping securities in certain subsidiary companies for seven years

■ receiving special benefits as a result of owning the securities

■ the securities being converted into other securities under rights you have as a result of the employment

■ the market value of the securities being artificially increased or reduced

■ disposing of the securities in certain circumstances for more than their market value.

There may be a tax charge each time one of these events occurs and working out the tax due can be complicated. For more information, get Help Sheet 305 *Employee shares and securities – further guidance* from the Revenue website or Orderline (see p. 180). It contains worksheets to help you work out whether any tax is due. This is a complex area and you may want to get advice from an accountant or tax specialist (see Appendix E).

Warning

A change in the law in 2005 means that, where you are an owner/manager of your own company and pay yourself mainly in the form of dividends, the Revenue might seek to tax the dividends as post-acquisition event benefits if it can show that the main purpose of your mode of payment is to avoid paying tax or national insurance.

17

Self-employment

2 | **Self-employment**

2 Self-employment

Did you work for yourself (on your 'own account' or in self-employment) in the year to 5 April 2010? (Answer 'Yes' if you were a 'Name' at Lloyd's.) Fill in a separate *Self-employment* page for each business and say how many pages you are completing.

Yes ☐   No ☐   Number ☐

If any of your income for 2009–10 came from running your own business as a self-employed person, you need to fill in a separate set of Self-employment supplementary pages for each business you have.

You can fill in the new short Self-employment supplement unless one or more of the following applies:

- your turnover was £68,000 or more or would have been if you had traded for a full year. This is also the compulsory VAT registration threshold (p. 313)

- you have changed your accounting date (p. 312)

- the period to be taxed in 2009–10 (called the basis period) is not the same as your accounting period (p. 336). This is most likely in the early years of your business, when you are closing down or if you have changed your accounting date

- you are claiming overlap relief (p. 336). This may be the case if you closed down or changed your accounting date in 2009–10

- you have already given details of your accounts for this year on an earlier tax return

- you have changed the basis on which you prepare your accounts, for example from cash accounting to generally accepted accounting practice (GAAP) (p. 337)

- you are a practising barrister or advocate

- you carry on your business abroad

- you want to claim capital allowances for anything other than just plant and equipment (p. 327)

- you are a farmer, market gardener, literary or musical writer or artist who wishes to average some or all of your income over several years (p. 338).

If any of these applies, you need to fill in the full Self-employment supplement. This chapter guides you through filling in the full supplement but will also help if you are completing the short supplement. If your business is very small, with a turnover of no more than £30,000, you may instead have been sent the short tax return – see Appendix C.

Are you self-employed?

Self-employed people are able to claim more income tax reliefs than employed people and they usually pay less in national insurance, so you may need to prove to your tax office that you really are self-employed. Ask yourself the following questions:

- Do you control how your business is run? For example, do you decide what work you take on, where you do the work, what hours you keep?

- Is your own money at risk in the business? For example, have you had to pay for your own premises, do you have to finance the lag between incurring costs and receiving payments?

- Do you have to meet any losses as well as keeping any profits?

- Do you provide the major equipment necessary for your work – for example computer and photocopier for office-based work or machinery for an engineering business? It's not enough that you provide your own small tools – many employees do this too.

- Are you free to employ other people to help you fulfil the contracts you take on? Do you pay your employees yourself?

▓ If a job doesn't come up to scratch, do you have to redo it or correct it in your own time and at your expense?

The more of these questions to which you can answer 'yes', the more likely it is that you are self-employed. And if you answer 'yes' to all of them, you generally will count as self-employed. But it is the whole picture and facts of your case that determine your work status. Sometimes the decision is not clear cut – for example, if you are newly in business doing work for just one client, perhaps working at a former employer's premises on a freelance basis. Beware if you work through an agency – for example as an agency carer or temporary secretary. Even if you choose whether or not to take on a particular job, you will almost certainly count as an employee rather than self-employed.

Tax-saving idea 179

As a self-employed person, you can claim more tax reliefs than an employee. Nonetheless, small businesses can still usually save income tax and national insurance by operating as a company provided they are judged to be genuinely in business on their own account (rather than as a device for disguising employee status).

Bear in mind, too, that it is possible to be self-employed for some of your work but an employee for other jobs you do.

If you pay tax and national insurance as if you are self-employed, but later your tax office decides you are really an employee, you could face a large bill for back taxes, so it is important to get your status straight right from the start. If you're in any doubt, you can ask your tax office for a written decision about your employment status. If you don't agree with the decision, you can appeal. You can check your status and the verdict the Revenue is likely to give by using the Revenue's employment status indicator tool at www.hmrc.gov.uk/calcs/esi.htm. Print off every page as you fill in the tool, so you have a record should you need it in discussions with the Revenue.

Business details

The first part of the supplement simply deals with basic details – the name and nature of your business and the address from which you trade.

If you work from home, the Revenue already has the address and you do not need to give it again here.

| 1 | Business name – *unless it is in your own name* |

| 2 | Description of business |

Your accounting year

| 8 | Date your books or accounts start – *the beginning of your accounting period* |

| 9 | Date your books or accounts are made up to or the end of your accounting period – *read page SEFN 3 of the notes if you have filled in box 6 or 7* |

You also need to give the start and finish dates of the accounting period for which you are giving details. Normally, an accounting period is a year long, with the new accounting year starting immediately the previous year ends. But in the first and last year or two of your business, or if you change your accounting date, your accounting year might be longer or shorter (see below).

You can fill in the short supplement only if you are being taxed in 2009–10 on a standard accounting period and, on that form, all you need to tell the Revenue is the end-date.

Special arrangements

You need to put a cross in box 12 if any of several situations apply that let you draw up your accounts in an unusual way. The situations include: being a foster carer or adult placement carer (though you are more likely to be completing the short supplement rather than this full form); being a farmer, market gardener, author or artist using the averaging rules; being a barrister or advocate if you are drawing up your accounts on a cash basis; you are carrying on your business abroad and the remittance basis (p. 368) applies to you; you provide services and adjusted your accounts in 2009–10 to comply with the UITF40 rules (p. 337).

12 If special arrangements apply, put 'X' in the box - *read page SEFN 4 of the notes*

☐

13 If you provided the information about your 2009-10 profit on last year's tax return, put 'X' in the box - *read page SEFN 4 of the notes*

☐

Foster carers and adult carers are treated as if they run a business so need to complete the self-employment supplement. However, since 6 April 2003, receipts from foster caring are tax-free if they do not exceed a qualifying amount (see Tax-saving idea 180). If fostering receipts exceed this amount, you can choose either to work out your profits in the normal way or use a simplified system. Adult carers can choose to use simplified arrangements (such as fixed expense deductions) to work out their profits. In both cases, you are likely to be filling in the short supplement but you may not need to fill in all the boxes. You should put a cross in box 4 of the short supplement, so that the Revenue knows why some boxes have been left blank. For more information, get Help Sheet HS236 *Foster carers and adult placement carers*.

Tax-saving idea 180 and 181

If you take up fostering children, your receipts are tax-free up to a qualifying amount. In 2009–10, this amount is £10,000 a year per household. In addition, each foster carer can claim a week for each child under 11 and £250 a week for each child aged 11 or more. Private fostering arrangements are not eligible for this scheme.

From 6 April 2010 onwards, the simplified arrangements for adult placement carers are being replaced by a new system of tax reliefs if you are a 'shared life carer'. The tax reliefs are the same as those which currently apply to foster carers (see the tax-saving idea above). If your income from providing shared lives (and foster care) does not exceed the tax-free amounts described above, you will have no tax to pay on this income. If your income from this source comes to more than the tax-free amounts, you can choose either to pay tax on the excess income or to work out and pay tax on the profits from your caring business in the normal way. 'Shared life carers' are adult placement and other carers who provide accommodation, care and support for up to three individuals placed with them under the Shared Lives scheme.

If you carry on your business completely overseas and think you should be taxed only on the remittance basis because of your residence status, fill in only boxes 1 to 13, 65, 66, 75 and 99. You also need to complete the Non-residence supplement (see Chapter 23). Put a cross in box 12.

You might already have given information about your latest set of accounts in last year's return (for example, if your accounting periods overlap). If so, you do not need to give all the information again. Just fill in boxes 1 to 13, 65 to 81 and 99 to 101 and put a cross in 13.

What profits are taxed

This first section of the Self-employment pages establishes which profits form the basis of your tax bill for 2009–10, and what information you need to give the Revenue about them. In most cases, your tax bill for 2009–10 will be based on the profits you make during the accounting period which ended during that tax year (the current year basis). However, there are special rules if you are in the opening or closing years of the business or, have changed your accounting date.

Starting a business

6 | If your business started after 5 April 2009, enter the start date *DD MM YYYY*

If you become self-employed and liable to pay class 2 national insurance contributions, you should register with the Revenue without delay. There is a tax-related penalty for failing to do so (see p. 53). You can register by calling a helpline for the newly self-employed on 0845 915 4515, registering online at www.hmrc.gov.uk/selfemployed/register-selfemp.htm, or by completing form CWF1 in the back of Revenue leaflet SE1: *Are you thinking of working for yourself?* Registration ensures that arrangements are made for you to pay the national insurance contributions (p. 341) and that you will be sent a tax return at the appropriate time. You can also register for VAT (p. 314).

You must register – and incur the penalty if you don't – even if you are also an employee and pay enough class 1 contributions not to have to make any class 2 payments. Ask to defer the class 2 contributions (p. 343).

If you do not register, under separate rules you must tell your tax office within six months of the end of the tax year (i.e. by the following 5 October) if you have any profits on which income tax is due.

When you start a business, special rules say how you will be taxed in the first two or three years.

First tax year during which you're in business

You are taxed on your profits from the date your business started to the end of the tax year (that is the following 5 April). This can be finalised only once your first set of accounts is drawn up and is then worked out by allocating a proportion of those profits to the period up to the end of the tax year. This is usually done on the basis of days, but weeks, months or other fractions of a year are also acceptable. For example, suppose you started in business on 1 January 2010 and your first accounting period runs to 31 January 2010. Out of that first 396-day accounting period, 95 days fall between 1 January to 5 April, so your profits for 2009–10 are deemed to be 95/396ths of the profit for the whole accounting period.

Second tax year during which you're in business

In most cases, the end of an accounting period (not necessarily your first) will fall sometime during this second tax year. Provided you have been trading for at least 12 months, your tax bill will be based on profits for the 12 months up to that date. In the example above, there is an end accounting date falling within 2010–11. This is 31 January 2011 and, at that date, the business has been running for more than a year. Therefore, tax will be based on profits for the 12 months up to 31 January 2011 – that is 365/396ths of the profits for the whole accounting period.

If there is an accounting date within the tax year, but you have been trading for less than 12 months, your tax is based on the first 12 months of trading, with a proportion of the profits from your next accounting period being used to make up the full 12 months. For example, suppose you started in business on 1 March 2009 and draw up your accounts to 30 June 2009 and then to each subsequent 30 June. Tax in your second year, the 2009–10 tax year, would be based on the whole of the profits for the period 1 March to 30 June 2009 (122 days) and 243/365ths of the profits for the accounting year from 1 July 2009 to 30 June 2010.

If there is no accounting date at all during your second tax year, tax is based on the profits for the tax year itself – that is from 6 April to 5 April. For example, if you started in business on 1 March 2009 but did not draw up your first accounts until 30 June 2010, an accounting period of 487 days, you would be taxed on 365/487ths of the profits for that whole period.

Third tax year during which you're in business

Normally, an accounting period at least 12 months after you started up finishes during your second tax year. From the third year onwards, you are simply taxed on the profits for the accounting year ending during the tax year – that is normal current year basis.

Example

Jim Newall started working as a freelance computer consultant on 1 July 2007 and drew up his first accounts on 30 April 2008. 30 April is his normal accounting year end. His profit and tax position for the first few years of business was as follows:

Accounting period	*Profit for the period*
1 July 2007–30 April 2008	£ 4,000
1 May 2008–30 April 2009	£ 8,500
1 May 2009–30 April 2010	£18,500

Tax year	*Tax basis*	*Profits on which tax based*
2007–08	Profits for tax year	$280 \div 305 \times £4{,}000 = £3{,}672$
2008–09	First 12 months of trading	$£4{,}000 + (61 \div 365 \times £8{,}500)$ $= £5{,}421$
2009–10	Profits for 12 months to 30 April 2009	£8,500
2010–11	Profits for accounting year ending on 30 April 2010	£18,500

The profit for the period 1 July 2007 to 5 April 2008 is taxed twice, as is profit for the 61 days from 1 May to 30 June 2008. This gives Jim an overlap profit of $£3{,}672 + (61 \div 365 \times £8{,}500) = £3{,}672 + £1{,}421 = £5{,}093$.

Where unusually the first accounting period to end at least 12 months after start-up comes to a close in your third tax year of trading, you are taxed on profits for the 12 months to the end of that period. From the fourth year onwards, you are taxed on the normal current year basis.

Overlap profits

As you can see, the opening year rules described above mean that some profits may be taxed twice. For example, for the business which started on 1 January 2010, the profits for the first two years were as follows:

Tax year	Profits on which your tax bill is based
2009–10	95/396ths × profit for accounting period from 1 January 2010 to 31 January 2011
2010–11	365/396ths × profit for the period from 1 January 2010 to 31 January 2011

This means that $(95 + 365) - 396 = 64$ days' worth of profit have been taxed twice. This is called 'overlap profit' and the period over which it arose is called the 'overlap period'. One of the principles of the current year basis tax system is that, over the lifetime of your business, all your profits should be taxed, but only taxed once. Therefore, you are given overlap relief to compensate you for having paid tax on some profits twice in your opening year. But there is a snag: overlap relief is usually given only when you finally close the business down (see overleaf) and inflation in the meantime will reduce its value.

Businesses that started before 6 April 1994 also have overlap profit as a result of changes to the basis of taxing accounts from 6 April 1996 onwards. And a change of accounting date (see overleaf) can create overlap profit.

Fiscal accounting

You can avoid all the problems of opening year rules and overlap relief, if you opt for fiscal accounting. This means using the tax year as your accounting year. By Revenue concession, this includes having an accounting date of 31 March, rather than exactly on the tax year end of 5 April.

For example, you might have started in business on 1 September 2009, drawing up your first accounts on 31 March 2010 and on each 31 March thereafter. Your tax for 2009–10 will be based on your profits from 1 September 2009 to 31 March 2010. Your tax for the next year will be based on profits for 1 April 2010 to 31 March 2011 and so on. For further information see Help Sheet HS222 *How to calculate your taxable profits*.

Tax-saving ideas 182–184

Fiscal accounting makes accounting for tax very simple, especially in your opening years, but it has drawbacks too: you don't have long to make up your accounts and there's only a short delay between making your profits and paying tax on them (p. 34).

With fiscal accounting, by the time you have worked out your profits for the year, it is too late to tailor any pension contributions so that, for example, they eliminate a higher-rate tax bill (see p. 87) or increase your personal allowance (p. 24) or tax credits (see p. 66). You can create the time needed to use pension planning tax-efficiently if you choose an accounting year end that falls early in the tax year.

If you don't choose fiscal accounting, try to keep your profits as low as possible during the first year or two, so that your overlap profit is small.

Closing your business

7 | If your business ceased after 5 April 2009 but before
6 April 2010, enter the final date of trading

☐☐ ☐☐ ☐☐☐☐

In the tax years up to the one before closure, you are taxed on the normal
current year basis. For the tax year in which you close down, you're taxed
on profits from your last accounting date up to the date on which you
close down less any overlap profits which you have been carrying forward
(p. 310). (For how to claim relief on these overlap profits, see p. 336.) The
position for a business closing down in 2009–10 is:

Tax year	Profits on which your tax bill is based
2008–09	Profits for accounting year ending in 2008–09
2009–10	Profits from day after end of accounting year ending 2008–09 up to date of closure less overlap profits

If your normal accounting date is early in the year, your final tax bill may
be based on a long period – for example, if you closed in December 2009
and your normal accounting date was 30 April, your final tax bill will be
based on the 20 months from May 2008 to December 2009. This can mean
a large tax bill if the business is profitable even after using overlap relief.

Changing your accounting date

10 | If your accounting date has changed permanently,
put 'X' in the box

☐

11 | If your accounting date has changed more than once
since 2004, put 'X' in the box

☐

For the Revenue to accept a change of accounting date for tax purposes,
the following conditions must be met: the transitional accounting period
running up to the new accounting date (called the 'relevant period') must

not exceed 18 months; you must notify your tax office in your tax return by putting a cross in box 10; and either there must have been no previous change of accounting date in the last five years or the Revenue must be satisfied that the current change is for bona fide commercial reasons. If you have changed the date within the last five years, put a cross in box 11 and explain your reasons in box 102 (*Any other information*) on page SEF6.

If you choose a new accounting date earlier in the tax year, the relevant period will be less than 12 months. Your tax bill will be based on your profits for the 12 months up to the new accounting date. This creates some overlap profit.

If you choose a new date which is later in the tax year, your tax bill will be based on the whole relevant period which will be longer than 12 months, but you are then allowed to use some of your overlap relief (p. 336).

Reporting your figures

The taxable profits of your business are your business income less allowable expenses – that is, the expenses you are allowed to deduct under the tax rules – and after various other adjustments in accordance with the tax rules.

The starting point is your business accounts which you report in boxes 14 to 47 of the full Self-employment supplement (or boxes 8 to 21 if you are completing the short supplement). If you are registered for value added tax (VAT), you need to decide how you will report your figures in these boxes.

Warning

However small your business, the tax rules require you to prepare your business accounts in accordance with UK generally accepted accounting practice (GAAP). The GAAP rules are under constant review and change from time to time, making it hard for a lay person to keep abreast of the requirements. We recommend you use an accountant but, if you are a small business and want to prepare your own accounts, get a copy of *Financial Reporting Standards for Small Entities* (FRSSE) published by the Accounting Standards Board and downloadable free from www.frc.org.uk/asb/technical/frsse.cfm. FRSSE brings together most of the GAAP rules in one place, but you will still need to take account of recent changes not yet included in the latest version.

Value added tax (VAT)

If your turnover is £68,000 a year or more from 1 May 2009 (£70,000 from 1 April 2010), you must register for VAT. Below that threshold, you can choose whether or not to register. Registration means that you must normally charge your customers VAT on the goods and services that you sell, but you can usually reclaim VAT on the things that you buy to sell, or use, in your business. You must regularly hand over to the Revenue the net amount of VAT you have collected (or claim a refund if what you are claiming comes to more than the VAT paid by your customers). Generally this VAT does not form part of your profits and needs to be stripped out before your tax bill is calculated. You can choose how you do this. The descriptions that follow assume you are filling in the full Self-employment supplement, but the same principles apply if you have voluntarily registered for VAT and are filling in the short supplement.

Assuming you are not using the VAT flat-rate scheme (see below), you are likely to treat VAT in either of two ways. You can put in box 14 your turnover including VAT and also report in boxes 16 to 45 your costs and expenses including VAT. You then convert your profit to a VAT-exclusive amount by deducting the net amount of VAT you paid in box 29 or adding the net VAT refund you received to box 15. The VAT figure included in box 29 must be adjusted for any VAT on capital items and you should note the amount of the adjustment in the *Any other information* box on page SEF6. Alternatively, you can record VAT-exclusive amounts throughout your accounts in which case, your figures in boxes 14 to 45 will already have had the VAT stripped out.

VAT flat-rate scheme

Businesses with a yearly taxable turnover before VAT up to £150,000 can opt to join the VAT flat-rate scheme. Instead of basing your payments to the Revenue on full records of VAT on sales and purchases, under the flat-rate scheme they are a single percentage of your VAT-inclusive turnover. The percentage depends on the nature of your business. The percentages – which aim to reflect the average VAT for a business of your type – changed from 1 December 2008 in line with the temporary fall in the main rate of VAT from 17.5 per cent to 15 per cent. The then percentages increased from 1 January 2010 when the main rate reverted back to 17.5 per cent. The flat rates did not just revert to their pre-December 2008 levels. There were several changes, with the rates for some types of business increasing but falling for others. The rates range from 3.5 per cent to 13 per cent. For more information, see the Revenue website at www.hmrc.gov.uk/vat/start/schemes/flat-rate.htm or ask the VAT Helpline (0845 010 9000) to send you VAT Notice 733 *Flat rate scheme for small businesses*.

If you join the flat-rate scheme during your first year of registration for VAT, your VAT flat rate is reduced by 1 per cent for that year.

When using the flat-rate scheme, in effect the actual VAT you pay on items for your business is not recoverable. Therefore it is usually easiest to fill in the Self-employment supplement using your figures including VAT. In box 14, put your turnover including the actual VAT you charged your customers. You need to deduct the amount of flat-rate VAT you paid over to the Revenue. You can do this either as a reduction to turnover in box 14 or as an expense in box 29. You do not normally make any adjustment for VAT on capital items and, when working out capital allowances (p. 327) you should normally use the cost of the item including VAT. The exception is where the capital item costs £2,000 or more including the VAT. In that case, by concession, you can reclaim the VAT you paid on that item. There is no adjustment to the amount in box 14 or 29 but your capital allowance for the item should be worked out using the VAT-exclusive amount.

Alternatively, when using the flat-rate scheme, you can record your figures excluding VAT. You will then need to work out the amount of flat-rate VAT you paid less the amount of VAT that would have been due had you not used the flat-rate scheme (which means you are no longer saving on administration and paperwork). If using the flat-rate scheme has saved you VAT, the amount saved must be included in box 15 as other income of your business. If you have paid more VAT through using the scheme, the extra paid can be deducted as an expense in box 29.

Unregistered or partially registered

If you are not registered for VAT, you do not charge your customers VAT and the VAT you pay to your suppliers counts as a legitimate business expense. Your figures should include the VAT you have been charged. If you were registered for VAT for part of the year, but not for all, explain why, when the change occurred, and whether your figures are VAT-inclusive or not, in the *Any other information* box on page SEF6.

Tax-saving ideas 185 and 186

If your turnover is less than £70,000 in the year from 1 April 2010, you can choose whether or not to register for VAT. Being registered means you can reclaim VAT on things you buy for your business, but you must also charge your customers VAT on your whole turnover (not just the bit in excess of £70,000). Be wary of registering voluntarily if your customers cannot reclaim the VAT you charge them (because, for example, they are private individuals) – you probably won't be able to raise your prices in line with the VAT and unless you can claim back large amounts on things you buy, registration could cause your overall income to fall.

Being VAT-registered means you have the extra administration of keeping VAT accounts and dealing with payments and reclaims. But there are several schemes to reduce the administration for small businesses including the flat-rate scheme. However, you should check that the flat-rate scheme really does save on administration and that you do not end up paying more VAT as a result.

If you are VAT-registered but your supplies are partly exempt and you report your figures including the VAT, put any net VAT that you cannot reclaim as an expense in box 29 or any net refund in box 15. If you report your figures excluding VAT, make sure the VAT you cannot reclaim is included in box 29 as an allowable business expense.

Business income

14	Your turnover - *the takings, fees, sales or money earned by your business*	15	Any other business income not included in box 14 - *excluding Business Start-up Allowance*
£ · 0 0		£ · 0 0	

The starting point for working out your taxable profits is your turnover which goes in box 14 of the full supplement (box 8 of the short supplement). If you are selling something you make or items you buy in to resell, this will be mainly the money you get from sales. If you are selling your services, it will be mainly the income you get from the fees you charge. But you should include all income earned by your business, including any non-cash payment in kind that you get.

In most cases, you should be preparing your accounts on an accruals basis. This means you include income due to you during your accounting year, even if you have not received it yet. For example, include the value of invoices you have sent out even though they may be unpaid at the end of your accounting year. If you are selling your services, for example, as an accountant, solicitor or freelance journalist, you will also need to adjust your accounts for the so-called UITF40 rules. Basically, if you are working on a contract that spans your accounting year end, you need to apportion the fee for the work between the accounting years on the basis of the proportion of the work completed in each period. For more information, see Help Sheet IR238 *Revenue recognition in service contracts: UITF40*.

Do not include any business start-up allowance; this goes in box 74 of the full supplement (box 29 of the short supplement).

Put any other business income in box 15 of the full supplement (box 9 of the short form), such as rental income if you let part of your business premises to tenants and interest earned by your business bank account.

Tax-saving idea 187

Since 1 April 2009 onwards, the Revenue can visit your business premises, either at any reasonable time or on seven days' notice, for the purpose of checking your tax position (see p. 50). You can be asked to produced virtually any information and documents relating to your past, present or future tax liabilities. If your record-keeping is haphazard, this may trigger a Revenue investigation into your affairs. To lessen the chance of an enquiry and the disruption and expense it can entail, make sure that you keep proper records for your business and that they are more or less up to date at all times.

Expenses

You don't need to complete all the boxes on page SEF2 of the full Self-employment supplement (SES1 of the short supplement) if your turnover was less than £68,000. Instead, you can just put the total allowable expenses you are claiming in box 30 of the full supplement (box 19 of the short form). You should still keep proper records and accounts and be prepared to show them to your tax officer if required. (In future, the Revenue may dictate the type of records you must keep – see p. 28.) If your turnover is £68,000 or more, you need to complete all the relevant boxes in the expenses section.

Deducting an expense from your business income has the effect of giving you tax relief at your top rate(s) of tax, so it is important to claim all the expenses you can. According to tax law, you get tax relief on an expense only if it is incurred wholly and exclusively for business. Strictly speaking, this means you can't get relief at all on expenditure which is partly for your private benefit. In practice, the Revenue does allow you to claim a proportion of some costs where something – for example, your car or home – is used partly for business. However, your tax office may object to some expenses that arise because of a joint business and private purpose – for example, combining a trip abroad to see a client with a holiday.

It is difficult to lay down hard and fast rules which apply to all businesses. Different types of businesses can claim different expenses and to a different extent. It is up to you to show that any claim is justified within the context of your own line of work.

You can claim expenses you incur before you open for business if they would have been allowable anyway. Treat them as expenditure incurred on the first day of business.

Expenses that you incur after you close down can be set against any late income which comes into the closed business. However, if there is no income, tax relief on the expenditure is usually lost. With a few particular types of expense, you can get tax relief by setting the expenses against any other income or gains you have, provided the expense is incurred within seven years of the business ceasing (in box 6 of the *Other tax reliefs* section on page Ai2 of the Additional information form, see p. 236).

Tax-saving ideas 188 and 189

Claim all the allowable expenses you can. If you're not sure whether an expense is allowable, deduct it from your taxable profits but ask your tax office to confirm whether this is correct.

Unless you can claim annual investment allowance (p. 327) or other 100 per cent capital allowances (p. 328), you will get tax relief more quickly if you can claim spending as an allowable expense (a revenue expense) rather than a capital outlay. If you need to spend on something to make it fit to use, this counts as capital spending. So make sure you do the minimum work needed and defer until later any extras that can count as revenue spending.

Example

Hannah Brown has converted a room in her home into an office which is used exclusively for her computer software business. She can claim part of her household expenses as allowable expenses for business purposes and, because she uses part of the home exclusively for business, she can also claim part of her mortgage interest. She makes the following calculation:

add up total household expenses	£1,800
add up the number of rooms in the house, ignoring separate toilets, halls and landings (unless large enough to be used as rooms)	8 rooms
divide the expenses by the number of rooms to give a cost per room figure	£1,800 ÷ 8 = £225 per room
multiply the cost per room by the number of rooms used for business (or by the relevant fraction, if a room is used only partly for business)	1 × £225 = £225

She also claims one-eighth of her mortgage interest as a business expense. This comes to 1\8 × £3,600 = £450. However, Hannah may become liable for capital gains tax on the part of the proceeds. when she sells her home. If her office is no longer suited to residential use, Hannah may also be liable for business rates (see opposite).

Tax-saving idea 190

> Be wary of using part of your home exclusively for business – there may be capital gains tax on part of the proceeds when you come to sell your home. Ensuring some private use of your work space – for example, for private study, hobbies, civic duties or other voluntary work – reduces the proportion of home-related expenses you can claim as business expenses, but you should escape capital gains tax. A tribunal case in 2003 clarified the circumstances in which you may have to pay business rates if you work from home – see p. 277. (The case is relevant to both employees and the self-employed.)

The sections below describe the main expenses that you can and cannot claim for tax purposes. The box numbers relate to the full Self-employment supplement, but the rules apply equally to boxes 10 to 18 on the short supplement.

The boxes on page SEF2 of the full supplement are set out in two columns. You put the total expense (as it appears in your accounts) in the relevant box on the left. Then, put any part that is not allowable for tax purposes in the corresponding box on the right. The disallowed amounts are added back to your profits at box 60.

In the short Self-employment supplement, there is no space for disallowed expenses and you put only the allowable part in boxes 10 to 19.

Goods for resale and goods used

16 Cost of goods bought for re-sale or goods used

£ ⬚⬚⬚⬚⬚⬚⬚ · 0 0

Normally allowed

Cost of goods you buy to sell and cost of raw materials used to make things for sale, but adjusted for opening and closing stock and work in progress; direct costs of production (such as commission and sales discounts). If your business is providing transport (for example, a taxi driver or road haulier), include the cost of fuel as a direct cost here, not in box 19 below. For information on how to take stock and work in progress into account, get Helpsheet HS222 *How to calculate your taxable profits* from the Revenue Orderline (p. 180).

Not allowed

Cost of goods and materials for your private use; depreciation of equipment (which may be included as a direct cost in your accounts) – claim capital allowances instead (p. 327).

Payments to subcontractors in the construction industry

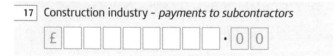

17 Construction industry - *payments to subcontractors*

£ ⬚⬚⬚⬚⬚⬚⬚⬚ · 0 0

Normally allowed

Payments you make to self-employed individuals, partnerships or companies that carry out construction work as part of your business – claim the gross amount (before taking off any tax).

Not allowed

Payments you make for work that is not part of your business.

Tax-saving idea 191

If you are involved in construction and use subcontractors, you must register with the Revenue under the Construction Industry Scheme (CIS) by calling the New Employer Helpline on 0845 607 0143. You will be responsible for deducting tax from payments to your subcontractors (unless they have arranged with the Revenue to be paid gross), handing over the tax to the Revenue and making monthly returns. Make sure you register and make the required returns – there are penalties if you don't.

Employee costs

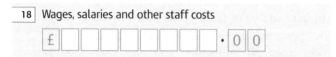

18 Wages, salaries and other staff costs

£ ⬚⬚⬚⬚⬚⬚⬚⬚ · 0 0

Normally allowed

Salaries, bonuses, overtime, commissions, etc. paid to your employees, together with the add-on costs, such as national insurance contributions, pension and insurance benefits. The costs of hiring locums to stand in for you or fees paid to people to whom you subcontract work. Training for employees. Council tax paid on behalf of employees if a genuine part of the pay package, taxed as normal through PAYE. Include the cost of employing your wife, husband or other family member in the business, provided their pay is reasonable for the work done (and bear in mind that the national minimum wage regulations may apply). Costs of entertaining staff – for example, a Christmas party.

Not allowed

Your own wages, national insurance, income tax, pension costs (though you can get personal tax relief for these), your drawings from the business. Wages to employees which remain unpaid nine months after the accounting date (although they can be deducted in the accounting period in which they are eventually paid). Payments to family members if excessive for the work done – be especially careful employing young children which might, in any case, be illegal. Cost of your own training might be allowed but claim in box 29 (p. 326).

Tax-saving idea 192

If you employ a family member in your business, there is no income tax or national insurance on their earnings if you pay them less than the 'primary threshold' (£5,715 in 2010–11). But consider paying them at least the 'lower earnings limit' (£5,044 in 2010–11), so they build up an entitlement to certain state benefits, such as state retirement pension.

Car, van and travel expenses

| 19 | Car, van and travel expenses

£ ⌈ ⌉ · 0 0

Normally allowed

Costs of running a vehicle used in your business – for example, insurance, servicing, repairs, road tax, breakdown insurance, parking charges, fuel, hiring or leasing charges. A proportion of these costs (based on mileage) if you also use the vehicle privately. Rail, air and taxi fares, hotel accommodation, cost of meals connected to an overnight stay whether included on your hotel bill or paid separately, modest additional expense of meals where your work is itinerant by nature (for example, commercial traveller) or during occasional journeys that are not part of your normal business pattern.

Not allowed

Travel between your home and business premises. Cost of buying a vehicle (but claim capital allowances – see p. 327). Cost of lunches and most other meals.

Tax-saving idea 193

If you use your car on business, you must normally keep a record of your expenses and a log of both business and private mileage so you can claim the business proportion of your total motoring costs. However, if at the time you buy the car, your turnover is no more than the VAT registration threshold (£70,000 from 1 April 2010), you can opt instead to claim a fixed mileage allowance for use of the car on business. The fixed allowance must not exceed the approved mileage allowance payments that apply to employees (p. 108). If you use the approved allowance, you cannot claim capital allowances, though you may (unlike employees) still claim relief for interest on a loan taken out to buy the car. The option to use the approved allowance is made when you buy the car and applies until you stop using that car in your business. Opting for the approved allowance could save you tax if your car is fairly cheap (perhaps second-hand) and small/fuel efficient. It also saves paperwork because the only record you need to keep is your business mileage.

Premises costs

20 Rent, rates, power and insurance costs

£ ⬚⬚⬚⬚⬚⬚⬚ . 0 0

Normally allowed

If you work from dedicated business premises, include any rent, business rates, water rates, cost of lighting, heating, power, insurance, cleaning, security, and so on. If you work from home, you can claim a proportion of your home-related expenses – for example, heating, lighting, power, cleaning, maintenance, mortgage interest, rent, water rates and Council Tax. The proportion you claim must relate to your business use of the home – for example, based on the number of rooms used or floor area and the amount of time this space is devoted to business use. You should explain the basis used in the *Any other information* box on page SEF6 of the supplement.

Not allowed

Cost of buying premises and costs relating to any part of the premises not used for business.

Repairs and renewals

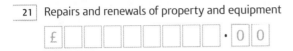

Normally allowed

General maintenance and repairs to your business premises and machinery, cost of replacing small tools.

Not allowed

Costs of alterations and improvements (see Capital allowances on p. 327 but also Tax-saving idea 189 on p. 318), costs relating to any part of the premises not used for business, general reserve for repairs.

General administrative expenses

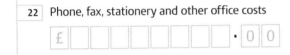

Normally allowed

Office expenses, such as postage, telephone, stationery, printing and regular expenses not included elsewhere. You can claim the cost of computer software where you pay a regular licence fee to use it or where the software has a limited lifetime (generally taken to be less than two years). In most other cases, software costs count as capital expenditure for which you can claim capital allowances (p. 327). If you work from home and use your home phone for business, you can claim your business calls and a proportion of the line rental consistent with your business use of the phone. The same approach applies to internet connections.

Not allowed

Personal expenses, payments to political parties, most donations and fees to clubs, charities and churches. Any non-business part of a cost.

Advertising, promotion and entertainment

Normally allowed

Advertising, mail-shots, free samples, gifts up to £50 a year to any client provided they promote your firm or its products or services and are not food, drink or tobacco.

Not allowed

Entertaining clients, business associates, etc. (only entertaining staff is allowed), gifts except those specifically allowed (see above).

Tax-saving idea 194

Whether interest on a loan counts as an allowable expense depends on how the money is used, not its source. Instead of overdrawing your business account or getting a business loan, a cheaper option might be extending the mortgage on your home. The part of the interest relating to business use is allowable and the Revenue assumes repayments pay off the personal debt before the business debt.

Interest

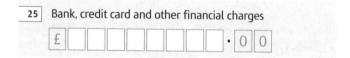

| 24 | Interest on bank and other loans |

£ ⬜⬜⬜⬜⬜⬜⬜⬜ . 0 0

Normally allowed

Interest and arrangement fees for a loan or overdraft used for business. Equivalent payments for Sharia-compliant finance arrangements.

Not allowed

The part of loan payments which represents capital repayments.

Other finance charges

| 25 | Bank, credit card and other financial charges |

£ ⬜⬜⬜⬜⬜⬜⬜⬜ . 0 0

Normally allowed

Charges on your business current account, credit card interest and fees, the interest element of hire purchase charges, leasing payments – but the amount you can claim is restricted in the case of a car where the lease began before 6 April 2009 whose retail price when new exceeded £12,000 unless it counts as environmentally friendly (p. 329). For cars that started to be leased from 6 April 2009 onwards, the rules have changed. The £12,000-restriction rule has ceased to apply and instead there is a flat-rate disallowance equal to 15 per cent of the relevant lease payments, but only for cars with CO_2 emissions that exceed 160 g/km.

Not allowed

The part of any payment which represents capital repayment.

Bad debts

26 Irrecoverable debts written off

Normally allowed

Items you have sold or amounts you have invoiced but for which you no longer expect to be paid. A proportion of a bad debt given up under a voluntary arrangement. If in a later tax year you are paid, include the amount recovered in box 74 on page SEF4 of the full supplement (or box 29 of the short supplement).

Not allowed

General reserve for bad debts. Debts that have not been included in your turnover.

Legal and professional costs

27 Accountancy, legal and other professional fees

Normally allowed

Fees charged by accountants (including extra costs due to a Revenue enquiry provided the enquiry does not reveal any negligent or fraudulent conduct), auditors, solicitors, surveyors, stocktakers, and so on, professional indemnity premiums.

Not allowed

Legal costs of buying premises, equipment, etc. (might be treated as part of their cost – see Capital allowances on p. 327), legal expenses on forming a company, cost of settling tax disputes, cost of fee protection insurance if it would cover cost of professional help in the event of tax fraud or negligence, fines, etc. as a result of acting illegally.

Depreciation and loss/profit on sale

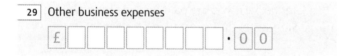

28 | Depreciation and loss/profit on sale of assets

£ ⎕⎕⎕⎕⎕⎕⎕ · 0 0

Not allowed

None of these costs is allowable – instead you claim Capital allowances (see opposite). The figure you enter at box 43 should exactly match the amount you put in box 28 – unless some of the costs relate to finance leases, in which case ask your tax office what you can deduct.

Other business expenses

29 | Other business expenses

£ ⎕⎕⎕⎕⎕⎕⎕ · 0 0

Normally allowed

Any expenses which you haven't found a place for in boxes 16 to 28. For example, any insurance premiums not included elsewhere, trade/ professional journals, contributions to approved local enterprise agencies, training and enterprise councils, local enterprise councils and business link organisations, and part or all of subscriptions to trade/professional associations which secure some benefit for your business or to societies which have an arrangement with the Revenue. Cost of your own training provided it is wholly and exclusively for business and updates your existing knowledge and skills. This is also the place to strip out VAT if applicable (p. 313).

Not allowed

The non-business element of any expenses included in box 29. This includes, for example, ordinary clothing even if you bought it specially for business and would not normally wear it otherwise, buying a patent (see Capital allowances opposite), cost of your own training if it provides you with new skills (including initial training for operating a franchise) – claim Capital allowances instead, see opposite.

Net profit or loss

46	Net profit – *if your business income is more than your expenses* (if box 14 + box 15 minus box 30 is positive)		47	Or, net loss – *if your expenses exceed your business income* (if box 30 minus (box 14 + box 15) is positive)
	£ ⬜⬜⬜⬜⬜⬜⬜⬜⬜ · 0 0			£ ⬜⬜⬜⬜⬜⬜⬜⬜⬜ · 0 0

Add together all your expenses (box 30 on the full supplement or box 19 on the short supplement) and subtract them from your business income (boxes 14 and 15 on the full supplement or boxes 8 and 9 on the short form). This gives your basic profit or loss for the year. However, there are other reliefs and adjustments to take into account before arriving at your profit for tax purposes.

Capital allowances

Your taxable profits are broadly your business income less your business expenses. But when you buy capital items for your business – that is things which will be in use for many years – you are not normally allowed to set the full cost against your business income in the year you buy the item. In your ordinary business accounts, you'll deduct depreciation each year which varies from business to business and is not allowed as an expense when working out your tax. Instead, for tax purposes, you deduct capital allowances calculated according to standard rules.

To be eligible for capital allowances, the item you have bought must be wholly or partly for business use. You can claim a proportion of the allowance if the item is used partly for business and, in part, privately.

For capital spending since 6 April 2008, capital allowances have been reformed and you may now be able to claim some or all of the annual invest-ment allowance, enhanced capital allowances and/or writing-down allowances.

Annual investment allowance

48	Annual Investment Allowance
	£ ⬜⬜⬜⬜⬜⬜⬜⬜⬜ · 0 0

All businesses have an annual investment allowance (AIA) which gives 100 per cent relief for capital spending on most plant and machinery (but not cars) up to a set limit. The limit in 2009–10 is £50,000 for a full year, but is reduced or increased pro rata if your accounting period is shorter or longer than a year. For example, if you started a business on 1 January 2010 and your first accounting year ran until 31 July 2010, a total of seven months, your AIA for that period would be $7/12 \times £50,000 = £29,167$. You do not have to use your full AIA, but unused AIA is lost and cannot be carried forward to future years. From 2010–11, the limit is increased to £100,000.

There are special rules to prevent you claiming more AIA than you are entitled to, for example, by artificially splitting your business into two or more separate entities. Broadly, businesses you own that carry on mainly the same trade or operate from the same premises count as a single business for the purpose of AIA.

Tax-saving idea 195

> You cannot set the annual investment allowance against spending on cars for your business (which, unless they count as environmentally beneficial, have to be written off gradually over a number of years by claiming writing-down allowances), but you can set the allowance against vans and motorcycles.

100 per cent first-year allowances

For some environmentally beneficial spending – for example, on combined heat-and-power systems, air-conditioning controls, solar heating, efficient toilets, water meters, and cars with very low CO_2 emissions (see table opposite for further details) – you can claim 100 per cent first-year allowances, called enhanced capital allowances (ECAs). Like the AIA, these have the effect of writing off in the first year the full amount you spend.

You cannot claim both the AIA and an ECA for the same expenditure – you have to choose one or the other. Under new rules, loss-making companies will be able to trade in ECAs for cash, but this option is not available if you are a sole trader or in partnership.

Tax-saving idea 196

> In 2010–11, you can get extra tax relief on capital spending over £50,000 if the extra spending is on items that are environmentally friendly and qualify for 100 per cent first-year capital allowances.

What counts as environmentally friendly spending?*

Date spending incurred	Item	Description
31 March 2001 onwards	Energy-saving equipment	Items such as boilers, combined heat and power, refrigeration, and so on.
17 April 2002– 31 March 2013	Low-emission cars and refuelling	Low emission cars (emitting no more than 110 g/km (120 g/km before 2008–09) of carbon equipment dioxide or electrically propelled) used in your business or by employees. Equipment for refuelling with natural gas or hydrogen fuel
17 April 2002 onwards	Environmentally friendly spending on items for leasing, letting or hiring	Items as described above. (They are not eligible for the first-year allowance if bought before 17 April 2002 for leasing, letting or hiring.)
1 April 2003 onwards	Technology to save water or improve water quality	Meters, efficient toilets and so on. For list, contact details as for energy-saving equipment above
6 April 2010	Zero-emission vans	New (not second hand)

* For further details see www.eca.gov.uk or call the Carbon Trust Customer Centre on 0800 085 2005.

Some other types of spending also qualify for 100 per cent first-year capital allowances, enabling you to write off the full costs straight away:

▪ since May 2001, spending on renovating or converting residential space above shops or other commercial premises into flats for rent. Various conditions must be met (see p. 364)

▪ since 6 April 2004, spending by residential landlords on up to £1,500 of loft and cavity wall insulation. The scheme has been extended also to include: solid wall insulation (since 7 April 2005), draught-proofing and insulation of hot water systems (since 6 April 2006) and floor insulation (since 6 April 2007). Also since 6 April 2007, the £1,500 limit applies per property, whereas previously it applied per building

▪ since 11 April 2007, spending on renovating business premises, in designated deprived areas, that have been vacant for at least a year in order to bring them back into commercial use (see p. 364 for details).

Claim these allowances either here (boxes 53 and 54) or in the UK property supplement as appropriate.

Other first-year allowances

On a temporary basis, the government often makes other first-year capital allowances available particularly to small businesses or small and medium-sized enterprises.

For spending on plant and machinery between 6 April 2009 and 5 April 2010, any business (regardless of size) can claim a 40 per cent first-year allowance on top of the AIA. Some types of spending are excluded, for example, special rate expenditure (in other words on items that would go into your special pool and attract WDA at only 10 per cent), cars and assets for leasing.

Writing-down allowances

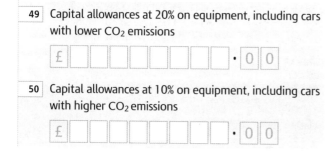

49 | Capital allowances at 20% on equipment, including cars with lower CO$_2$ emissions

£ ⬜⬜⬜⬜⬜⬜⬜⬜⬜ · 0 0

50 | Capital allowances at 10% on equipment, including cars with higher CO$_2$ emissions

£ ⬜⬜⬜⬜⬜⬜⬜⬜⬜ · 0 0

For spending that does not qualify for the AIA, ECAs or other 100 per cent allowances, or exceeds your AIA, you claim writing down allowances (WDAs). These are available for spending on plant and machinery (which covers most of your ordinary business equipment), cars and vans, patents and know-how. Capital allowances are not available for what you spend on buying business premises, such as a shop or office (though see *Transitional rules* below).

Since 2008–09 onwards, spending is allocated to two main pools – a general pool and a special-rate pool – and you can claim up to a given proportion of each every year as WDAs. (You can claim less if you want to.) The WDA for the general pool (box 49) is 20 per cent a year of the reducing balance – see Example on p. 333. From 6 April 2009, newly purchased cars with CO$_2$ emissions not exceeding 160 g/km are included in this general pool.

Some types of spending go into the special-rate pool (box 50) where they qualify for a lower writing-down allowance of 10 per cent a year:

■ integral features of your business premises. This covers, for example, spending on electrical systems (including lighting), cold water systems, space or water heating systems, various ventilation and air systems including integrated floors and ceilings, lifts, escalators, moving walkways and external solar shading

■ from 6 April 2009, newly purchased cars with CO_2 emissions exceeding 160 g/km.

Some items have their own separate pool. You can opt to have a separate pool for any short-life asset, meaning plant or machinery with an expected life of no more than five years, such as computers and many other business machines. The advantage of doing this is that you get tax relief on the full cost of the item more rapidly than if it were in your general pool (see *Buying and selling capital items* below). An item which you use partly for business and partly privately must be put in a separate pool. Only a proportion of the cost in line with the business use qualifies for capital allowances.

You do not normally get capital allowances on items you lease rather than buy. Instead the leasing charge counts as an allowable expense (see pp. 324–325). If you buy something on hire purchase, the capital element of the charges can qualify for capital allowances, but the interest element is treated as an allowable expense (pp. 324–325).

If you close down your business, in the final accounting period you cannot claim first-year allowances or WDAs. Instead, you might get a balancing allowance on the sale of the business assets (see p. 334).

Tax-saving ideas 197–199

Do not claim more capital allowances than needed to reduce your taxable profits to the level of your personal allowances – unless you have other income or gains against which you want to set a loss (p. 339).

Earmarking a capital item as a short-life asset means you can get full tax relief on the cost of the item in just five years.

A car you buy solely for business from 6 April 2009 onwards normally goes into your general or special pool. When you sell the car, whatever you get for it is deducted from the pool, but any balance of the original cost continues to be written down year by year, often well into the future – especially if the car has CO_2 emissions over 60 g/km and so is written down only at 10 per cent a year. A way round this is to make at least some private use of the car, in which case it goes into its own separate pool. Then, when you sell the car, you can immediately write off any balance left in the pool by claiming a balancing allowance (see p. 334).

Small balance pools

Where the balance left in a pool is £1,000 or less, since 6 April 2008, you can opt to write off the whole of the remaining amount (in other words you claim a capital allowance for the year equal to the remaining pool). This applies to each pool separately so, for example, if you had a balance of £800 in your general pool and £500 in your special rate pool, you could opt to write off the whole £1,300 in the same year. There is a special box (23) on the short supplement for claiming these small balances. On the full supplement, you should include the amount in box 54.

Transitional rules

Where you bought a car for your business before 6 April 2009, it will have gone into your general pool if it cost £12,000 or less. But you had to keep a separate pool for each car costing more than £12,000 and, in that case, the yearly WDA was capped at £3,000. These rules are abolished for cars acquired on or after 6 April 2009 (see above). But, for cars bought before then, the old rules will continue for around five years after which the remaining balance will shift to the general pool. However, even where you are using the old rules, the WDA is at the new rates, in other words either 20 per cent for cars with emissions up to 160 g/km and 10 per cent for cars with higher emissions.

In the past you could claim WDAs for spending on some types of business premises. But these WDAs for industrial and agricultural buildings are being phased out by April 2011 and enterprise zone allowances will also disappear from that date.

Tax-saving ideas 200–202

You choose which capital spending to set your annual investment allowance (AIA) against. If your capital spending exceeds your AIA, overall you will speed up the rate at which you get tax relief if you set the AIA against spending that qualifies for the 10 per cent writing-down allowance in preference to spending that qualifies for the 20 per cent allowance.

If possible, consider buying a large capital item in stages over two or more years so that each year's spending is within the £50,000 annual investment allowance (or pro rata amount).

From 2008–09 onwards, you can opt to write off the balance in your 20 per cent or 10 per cent capital allowance pool if it falls to £1,000 or less (see above).

Example

Joe Morris has been running a small dairy since 1979. He makes up his accounts to 31 December each year. For the year to 31 December 2009, he made the following purchases and sales of capital items:

Date	Capital item	Purchase/ sale price
10 April 2009	New van bought	£17,000
5 May 2009	Old van sold (cost £12,000 when new)	£5,000
2 November 2009	Second-hand cream separator bought	£38,000
30 November 2009	New lighting system for the dairy	£16,000

On 31 December 2008, after claiming writing-down allowances (WDAs), Joe's general pool of capital expenditure stood at £158,000. He does not have a special-rate pool.

Joe has an AIA of £50,000 for his 2009 accounting year. All of his capital spending is eligible for the AIA and he can choose how to use it. The lighting system (which counts as an integral feature) would qualify for lower WDAs than the other spending, so Joe sets his AIA first against the lighting and the remainder against the van and cream separator. This immediately writes off £16,000 + £17,000 + £17,000 = £50,000.

The remaining cost of the cream separator is £38,000 − £17,000 = £21,000. Since he spent on this item between 6 April 2009 and 5 April 2010, he can claim a first-year allowance of 40 per cent which writes off a further 40% × £21,000 = £8,400 of the cost. This leaves just £38,000 − £17,000 − £8,400 = £12,600 to be carried forward in his general pool. Assuming Joe claims the full AIA and first-year allowance, and taking into account the sale of the old van, at 31 December 2009, his general pool becomes:

Pool at 31 December 2008		£158,000
plus Lighting system	£16,000	
less Annual Investment Allowance	(£16,000)	
plus New van	£17,000	
less Annual Investment Allowance	(£17,000)	
plus Cream separator	£38,000	
less Annual Investment Allowance	(£17,000)	
less First-year allowance	(£8,400)	
		£12,600
less Sale of van		(£5,000)
Pool at 31 December 2009 before WDA		£165,600

Expenditure in his general pool qualifies for WDA at 20 per cent, in other words: 20% × £165,600 = £33,120. This gives maximum total capital allowances of £50,000 + £8,400 + £33,120 = £91,520 to set gainst his taxable profit for the year. In fact, he has only enough profits to justify using £80,000 of the allowance. So he claims the full AIA and first-year allowance but only £21,600 of the WDA. His capital pool at 31 December 2009 becomes £165,600 − £21,600 = £144,000.

Buying and selling capital items

When you buy an item of capital, it is added to the appropriate pool of expenditure. This usually increases the year-end value of the pool in subsequent years on which the writing-down allowance is worked out. However, even spending that has had tax relief because of the AIA is added to the pool and, in that case, it goes in at nil cost, so there is no increase in the value of the pool. The reason for this is so that any proceeds from selling the item later can be taken into account (see below). Slightly different rules ensure that the sale proceeds for any item on which you had first-year allowances are also taken into account.

When you first start in business, you might take into the business capital equipment you already own – for example, a desk, shelving, a computer. Although no money changes hands, you are treated as having sold the item to your business and you can claim WDAs (but not the AIA or first-year allowances) in the normal way. Value each item at its second-hand market value given its age, state of repair, and so on.

When you sell a capital item, the amount you get for it (up to its original cost) is deducted from the expenditure pool. Occasionally, this may be more than the total value of the pool, in which case, the excess (called a balancing charge) is added to your profits or (taxable income) for the year, increasing your tax bill. It is entered in box 58 (or in a few cases, box 57) on the full Self-employment supplement or box 25 of the short supplement.

If you sell the item for less than its written-down value – at the extreme, you might scrap it for nothing – the shortfall remains in your pool of expenditure and continues to be written down. So you could be claiming allowances on an item for many years after you have sold it. Only when you finally close down the business can you claim a balancing allowance for any remaining value of the pool. This is where short-life assets come into their own.

If you scrap a short-life asset within five years, you can claim tax relief on the difference between what you get (if anything) for the asset and its written-down value. The relief is given in the tax year in which you scrap it – you don't have to wait until the business closes down. To claim relief, put the shortfall in box 55 on the full Self-employment supplement or box 24 of the short form. If, having declared an asset as short life, you actually go on using it beyond five years, it is transferred into your general pool of expenditure and treated like any other capital item.

If you are registered for VAT, the amount you put in your expenditure pools should not include VAT (unless you are unable to recover the VAT through your VAT returns or, in some cases, where you are using the VAT flat-rate scheme – see p. 314). If you are not registered for VAT, you claim capital allowances on the cost including VAT.

Claiming capital allowance

Add up all the figures you have entered in boxes 48 to 55 and write the total in box 56. This will be deducted at box 62.

Taxable profit or loss

In boxes 59 to 64 of the full supplement you make adjustments to arrive at your profit or loss for tax purposes. In many cases, there is no equivalent box on the short supplement, because many of these adjustments relate to the sort of complex situations that rule out using the short supplement (p. 303).

Goods and services for own use

59 Goods and services for your own use - *read page SEFN 15 of the notes*

£ ⬜⬜⬜⬜⬜⬜⬜⬜ • 0 0

If you take stock out of your business for your own use or for your family or friends, the Revenue treats this as a sale at market value and the deemed proceeds have to be added back to your profits. Put the figure in box 59 of the full supplement (box 26 of the short form) unless you have already included it in box 14 (or 8) – see p. 316. If you provide services to yourself, family or friends free, for example, building work, financial advice, or meals if you run a restaurant, the cost of providing these services is not an allowable expense. Add back the cost in box 59 (or 26) unless you have already put the relevant amounts in boxes 31 to 45 of the full supplement or excluded them from the amounts you put in boxes 10 to 19 of the short supplement.

Identifying profits for the correct period

65 Date your basis period began *DD MM YYYY*

☐☐ ☐☐ ☐☐☐☐

66 Date your basis period ended

☐☐ ☐☐ ☐☐☐☐

67 If your basis period is not the same as your accounting period, enter the adjustment needed to arrive at the profit or loss for the basis period - *if the adjustment needs to be taken off the profit figure put a minus sign (-) in the box*

£ ▭ ☐☐☐☐☐☐☐☐ • 0 0

So far, in completing the Self-employment supplement, you have entered figures for one particular accounting period. As explained on p. 308 this may not be the same as the period over which you are actually taxed, which is known to the Revenue as your basis period. After the first two or three years in business, your basis period (and the dates you enter in boxes 65 and 66) will normally be the same as your accounting period. But in the early years of the business, or if you change your accounting date, you may have to enter different dates.

If your basis period does differ from your accounting period, you have to make an adjustment in box 67. Work this out by adding together and/or dividing the profits or losses for the relevant accounting periods. This is explained on pp. 308–310 and in Help Sheet HS222 *How to calculate your taxable profits*. Take care to put a minus sign in the box if the adjustment reduces your profit or increases a loss.

Overlap relief

68 Overlap relief used this year - *read page SEFN 17 of the notes*

£ ☐☐☐☐☐☐☐☐☐ • 0 0

69 Overlap profit carried forward

£ ☐☐☐☐☐☐☐☐☐ • 0 0

On p. 310 we explained how overlap profit can be created. If you have changed your accounting date or your business closed down in 2009–10, you may be able to claim some or all of this overlap profit to reduce your profit or create a loss. Put the amount being claimed in box 68. If you are continuing in business and you have not been able to claim relief for the whole amount, put the overlap profit that you are continuing to carry forward in box 69. See HS222 *How to calculate your taxable profits.*

Example

Sam started his business as a self-employed landscape gardener on 6 July 2009. His basis period for the tax year ending 5 April 2010 is the period between 6 July 2009 and 5 April 2010. He draws up his first set of accounts on 5 July 2010. In all the boxes up to 64, he enters the figures for his first accounting period, running to 5 July 2010. His profit in this accounting period was £8,000. Because he was only in business for 274 of the 365 days in the year to 5 April 2010, his profits for the tax year were 274/365 × £8,000 = £6,005. At box 67 he enters an adjustment of £6,005 − £8,000 = −£1,995.

Change of accounting practice

70 Adjustment for change of accounting practice - *read page SEFN 17 of the notes*

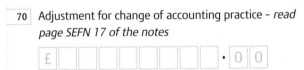

Use box 70 to report any increase or decrease in your profits for 2009–10 as a result of a change in the basis on which you draw up your accounts. This may apply to you if you provide professional or other services (for example, as an accountant or solicitor) and you are affected by the accounting guidance known as 'UITF40'. This guidance, which took effect for accounting periods covering 22 June 2005 (but could voluntarily be adopted earlier), requires you to account for the income notionally accrued on part-completion of contracts instead of including the full amount only on completion. For most people, this will have affected the accounts they reported in their 2005–06 or 2006–07 tax returns. But, unless you elected to make a one-off adjustment at the time, the adjustment is automatically spread over a period of up to six years. Enter the appropriate adjustment in box 70.

Tax-saving idea 203

If you adjusted your accounts to the UITF40 basis, you had to restate your balance sheet at the start of your accounting period as if UITF40 had applied in the previous year. This is likely to have resulted in an increase in your balance sheet total which counts as a 'prior period adjustment' and is taxable. Tax due on this adjustment is automatically spread over a period of three to six tax years, unless you elect for the relief not to apply. When deciding whether or not to continue spreading the relief, consider your whole tax position for the year and whether you might obtain tax relief instead by, say, making pension contributions.

Income averaging

71 | Averaging adjustment (only for farmers, market gardeners and creators of literary or artistic works) - *if the adjustment needs to be taken off the profit figure put a minus sign (-) in the box*

£ [   ] · [0][0]

Farmers and creative workers (such as authors and artists) whose income varies substantially from year to year can make a claim to be taxed on the average of their earnings from consecutive years. In box 71 enter the increase or reduction in your income as a result of the claim. See Help Sheets HS224 *Farmers and market gardeners* or HS234 *Averaging for creators of literary or artistic works*.

Tax-saving ideas 204 and 205

You do not have to make up your mind about how to get tax relief for your losses straightaway. You have a while to wait and see how your business affairs turn out. But the time limits for each option are strict, so don't delay so long that you miss them.

As a temporary measure to help businesses affected by the credit crunch and ensuing recession, in addition to the usual loss relief rules, you can set a loss for the 2009–10 tax year against profits from the same business made in the previous three tax years, in other words, 2007–08, 2006–07 and 2005–06. You must set the loss against the most recent year first and there is a cap of £50,000 in total on the amount you can set off against the profits for 2006–07 and 2005–06. To make a claim, either write to your tax office or claim through box 78 on the full supplement (box 33 of the short supplement). The same relief was also allowed for a loss for 2008–09.

Losses

73 Loss brought forward from earlier years set-off against
this year's profits - *up to the amount in box 63 or
box 72 whichever is greater*

In box 73 of the full Self-employment supplement (box 28 of the short supplement), you claim any losses you have brought forward from earlier years
(see p. 341) that you want to use now to reduce your profits for this year.

If you have made a loss this year, there are ways you can get tax relief on
it, which are described below. For more information, see Help Sheet HS277
Losses.

Other income or gains for this year

77 Loss from this tax year set off against other income
for 2009-10

Complete box 77 (32 on the short supplement) to set the loss against other
income you have during 2009–10 – for example, from working for an
employer or from your savings. If this does not use up all the loss, you can
ask for the rest to be set against any taxable capital gains for 2009–10 – use
box 14 on the Capital gains summary (p. 400). If any loss still remains, you
can ask for relief on it to be given in some other way. The time limit for
making this choice with respect to losses made in the accounting period
being declared for 2009–10 is 31 January 2012.

Tax-saving ideas 206 and 207

Regardless of how you use a loss to claim tax relief, you may also be able to use it
to make or increase a claim for tax credits (p. 66).

In 2010–11, if your income is in the range £100,000 to £112,950, you will be losing
personal allowance (see p. 24). If claiming loss relief either reduces your taxable profits
or your other taxable income for the year and so restores part (or all) of your personal
allowance, you will in effect get tax relief on the loss at a rate of 60 per cent.

Example

Sonja Frisk has been an antiques dealer for the last ten years. Normally, she makes a reasonable living but, in 2009, the sale of some expensive artifacts fell through and Sonja made a £7,000 loss for the 2009–10 tax year.

Sonja could set the remaining loss against other income which she had in the tax year ending 5 April 2010 from her savings. Alternatively, she can carry back her loss to the tax year ending 5 April 2009, or carry it forward to set against future profits from her antiques business. She doesn't want to use her loss in 2009–10, because she paid only 10 per cent tax on her savings income, compared with the 20 per cent top rate of tax she paid the year before; nor is she keen to carry forward her loss because she does not expect to pay a higher rate of tax in future. She claims to carry back her loss to the year ending 5 April 2009. qualifying for tax relief of 20 per cent × £7,000 = £1,400.

Warning

Setting losses against other income or gains for either this or the previous tax year is sometimes referred to as 'sideways loss relief'. In rules aimed at curbing tax avoidance, since 12 March 2008, sideways loss relief for the self-employed is restricted to a maximum of £25,000 a year if you devote on average less than 10 hours a week to your business and disallowed altogether if the losses derive from tax avoidance. The restriction on relief does not apply where you are carrying on a film-related trade (which is subject to other anti-avoidance rules). From 21 October 2009 onwards, sideways loss relief is derived completely where the loss arises directly or indirectly through arrangements a main purpose of which is to avoid tax.

Other income and gains for the previous year

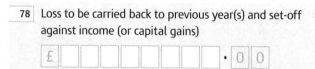

78 | Loss to be carried back to previous year(s) and set-off against income (or capital gains)

Complete box 78 (or 33 on the short supplement) to carry back the loss to 2008–09 to set against your income from any source for that year. If this does not use up the full loss, you can ask for the rest to be set against any capital gains for 2008–09. If some loss still remains, you can ask for relief on it to be given in some other way. The time limit for making this choice is 31 January 2013.

Other income for earlier years

See Tax-saving idea 205 for temporary relief available to all businesses.

You can ask for a loss made in the first four years of the business to be carried back and set against income (but not gains) for the previous three tax years – that is, 2006–07, 2007–08 and 2008–09. The loss is set against the earliest year first. The time limit for this choice is also 31 January 2013.

Put the amount of the loss in box 78 (or 33 of the short return) and give details of how much is to be set off against which year's income in the *Any other information* box on page SEF6 of the full supplement. There is no space on the short supplement for additional information, so use box 19 on page TR6 of the Main tax return.

Future profits

79	Total loss to carry forward after all other set-offs

- including unused losses brought forward

£ ⬜⬜⬜⬜⬜⬜⬜⬜⬜ • 0 0

Complete box 79 (34 on the short supplement) to carry the loss forward to set against your future profits from the same business. It will be set against the next profits you make with any remaining loss being rolled forward to set against the next profits and so on until the loss is completely used up. You will have until 5 April 2014 to make this choice.

Closing down

If your business closed down during 2009–10, you have a further option. A loss you made during your last 12 months of trading can be set against your profits for the three previous tax years – that is you can go back to 2006–07. The time limit for this choice is also 5 April 2014. Use box 78 (or 33) to make this claim now and give details of how much is to be set off against which year's income in the *Any other information* box on page SEF6 of the full supplement (or box 19 on page TR6 of the Main tax return if you are completing the short Self-employment supplement).

National insurance

99	If you are exempt from paying Class 4 NICs, put 'X' in the box - *read page SEFN 20 of the notes*

⬜

100	If you have been given a 2009-10 Class 4 NICs deferment certificate, put 'X' in the box - *read page SEFN 20 of the notes*

⬜

101	Adjustment to profits chargeable to Class 4 NICs - *read page SEFN 20 of the notes*

£ ⬜⬜⬜⬜⬜⬜⬜⬜ • 0 0

Running your own business, you will usually have to pay national insurance contributions (NICs) both for yourself and for any people you employ. You will have to pay: class 2 contributions at a flat-rate of £2.40 a week in 2009–10 (unchanged in 2010–11). If your profits are less than £5,075 in 2009–10 or 2010–11, you can opt not to pay.

Class 2 NICs help you to qualify for certain state benefits, such as retirement pension and employment and support allowance, so it might be better to carry on paying even if your profits are low. Class 2 contributions are paid direct to the Revenue, usually by direct debit.

Tax-saving idea 208

At £2.40 a week, class 2 national insurance contributions are a good value way of building up rights to state benefits such as state basic pension. If your profits are low, think carefully before deciding not to pay these contributions. However, people reaching state pension age on or after 6 April 2010 need only 30 years' worth of contributions to qualify for the full state basic pension. If you already have 30 years' contributions, you get less value from continuing to pay Class 2 contributions.

You may also have to pay class 4 contributions. Unlike other types of national insurance, class 4 contributions do not entitle you to any state benefits – they are simply a tax on profits which is collected along with your income tax. In 2009–10, class 4 NICs were payable at a rate of 8 per cent on profits over £5,715 up to £43,875 and at a rate of 1 per cent on profits above £40,040. (In 2009–10, these thresholds and rates are unchanged. However, the government has announced from April 2011, each of the rates will rise by 1 per cent.) If your profits are less than the lower limit, you do not pay any class 4 NICs at all.

Example

Jim Newall has profits for income tax purposes of £18,500 for 2009–10. These are also the profits on which his Class 4 NICs are based. They are calculated as follows:

Profit for Class 4 NICs purposes	=	£18,500
Less lower profit limit	=	£5,715
Amount chargeable (£18,500 − £5,715)	=	£12,785
Class 4 NICs at 8 per cent × £12,785	=	£1,022.80

Tax-saving ideas 209 and 210

Losses can be used to reduce your class 4 national insurance contributions as well as your income tax bill. (Enter the amount you are claiming in box 101.) And the treatment of losses is not necessarily identical: where, for income tax purposes, you elect for a loss to be set against income or gains other than profits from your business, that amount of loss is carried forward and set against future profits for class 4 purposes.

If you're paying both class 1 and class 4 national insurance on some of your income, ask to have the class 4 liability deferred until you know precisely how much is due. Otherwise, you could end up paying too much in contributions. (If you have done this, put a cross in box 100.)

A few groups of people are excluded from having to pay class 4 NICs. They include people over state pension age (around 60 for women and 65 for men), people under age 16 if they have been granted an exemption by the Revenue (ask for form CA2835U available from HM Revenue & Customs, NICO Deferment Services, Brenton Park View, Newcastle upon Tyne, NE98 1ZZ) and people who are not resident in the UK.

In some circumstances, you may have earnings that count as profits of your business but which have already had class 1 NICs deducted. In other cases, you may have earnings both as an employee (on which class 1 contributions are payable) and from self-employment. There is a cap on the overall amount you have to pay in national insurance, so it may be that class 4 NICs won't be payable after all. However, you usually don't know whether this is the case until after part of the class 4 NICs would have become payable, so you can ask to have payment deferred until the position is known by filling in form CA72B from www.hmrc.gov.uk or tax offices.

If you are either excluded from paying class 4 NICs or your tax office has agreed that you can defer paying them, put a cross in box 99 or 100, as appropriate. If you have any losses from 2009–10 or previous years which have not yet been set against profits chargeable to class 4 contributions enter them in box 101 because they can reduce your profits used for working out class 4 NICs (as well as reducing your income tax liability). If you have paid interest for business purposes but it has not been deducted in working out your profits for income tax purposes, you might be able to deduct it for class 4 NICs purposes. If this applies enter the amount of interest also in box 101.

Class 2 and class 4 contributions are not allowable expenses and can't be deducted when working out your profits for income tax purposes. If you have employees, you have to pay employer's class 1 NICs for them if they earn more than the primary threshold (£110 a week for 2009–10 and 2010–11). In this case, the amount you pay counts as an allowable expense (p. 320).

If you employ someone, you are responsible for collecting income tax and national insurance on their pay and for paying employer's national insurance contributions. You do this by operating the Pay-As-You-Earn (PAYE) system – see Chapter 3. This involves keeping records and filing returns after the end of each tax year. Since 6 April 2009, nearly all employers, regardless of how few employees you have, must file these end-of-year returns online. There is an exception where you employ only 'domestic employees' – for example, you have a disability and technically employ someone who comes into your home to help you with personal care.

Tax-saving idea 211

If you are an employer in business and prefer to avoid the administration involved in operating PAYE, consider contracting a payroll bureau or accountant to do the job for you. The fees you pay can be deducated as expenses of your business (through box 18 or 27 of the full self-employment pages or box 12 or 15 of the short form).

18

Partnership

3 **Partnership**

Were you in partnership? Fill in a separate *Partnership* page
for each partnership you were a partner in and say how
many pages you are completing.

Yes ☐   No ☐   Number ☐

If you are in business with one or more partners, you should fill in the
Partnership supplement. There are two versions:

- short version. Use this if the partnership income is from trading profits
  or interest from bank or building society accounts which has already
  been taxed at the savings rate. This version will be adequate for most
  partners

- full version. If your partnership earnings are more complex because
  you have untaxed investment income, foreign income or income from
  land and property, for example, you'll need to complete this longer
  supplement.

The partnership should already have provided you with a Partnership
Statement summarising your share of the profits, losses and other income.
If you received the full statement, you need the full version of the supplementary pages; if you received a short statement, you need only the short
supplement. If you haven't received a Partnership supplement or you need
the full version, contact the Revenue Orderline (p. 180).

You and your fellow partners are jointly responsible for the partnership tax
return, although one partner may be nominated to deal with it. This is a

separate document from the partnership supplement that you personally fill in. Profits are calculated on the return as if the partnership were a single person using largely the same rules as for a self-employed person (see Chapter 17). How profits are shared between partners depends on your partnership agreement. Note that if you personally pay some of the expenses of the partnership business, you need either to reclaim these from the partnership so that they are included in the partnership return or to negotiate an adjustment to your share of the profits in recognition of the expenses you bear. You cannot claim such expenses through your partnership supplement.

Once the partner dealing with the tax return has worked out the taxable profits for the partnership as a whole, he or she must show each partner's share of the profits, losses and tax suffered on the Partnership statement at the end of the Partnership return. The Partnership statement gives each individual partner the information needed to complete their own Partnership supplement. Each partner is then responsible for the tax on their own share of the profits.

Each partner is treated as if they were carrying on a business on their own, and the short version of the Partnership supplement is very similar to the Adjustments to arrive at taxable profit and loss and class 4 national insurance sections of the Self-employment supplement (pp. 335–344). The other sections of the supplement simply summarise your share of any tax that the partnership has already suffered. For this reason, we have not gone through the Partnership supplement in detail.

Becoming a partner

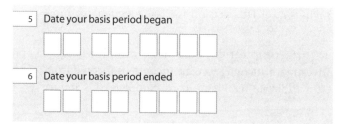

When you join a partnership, the normal opening rules described on pp. 308–311 apply. The period on which your tax is based is likely to be different from the accounting year for the partnership. The dates you put in boxes 5 and 6 should reflect how the opening year rules apply to you.

The opening year rules may result in overlap profits (p. 310) on which you can eventually claim tax relief either when you leave the partnership or, possibly, if the partnership accounting date is changed.

Once the special opening year rules have worked through, you are taxed on the normal current year basis. The period on which your tax is based will then be the same as the accounting year of the partnership, so you put the start date of the partnership year in box 5 and the end date in box 6.

Ceasing to be a partner

If you leave a partnership you are treated as if you are closing down your own business. The normal closing rules apply (p. 312), including the claiming of tax relief on any overlap profits carried forward from the opening years or a change of accounting date.

Partnerships providing personal services

If your partnership hires out your services to client companies and, in the absence of the partnership, your work would effectively amount to that of an employee, you may be caught by the 'IR35 rules' described on p. 256. Similarly, it is possible for partnership earnings to be caught by the managed service company rules, described on p. 259. Ask the Orderline (p. 180) to send you Help Sheet HS222 *How to calculate your taxable profits*, which explains the adjustments you need to make.

Tax-saving idea 212

Partnerships providing services need to comply with the UITF40 rule. This means the accounts must recognise revenue from projects that are only part-completed at the end of an accounting year. Switching to the UITF40 basis is likely to have resulted in a prior period adjustment (p. 337). Tax on this will usually automatically be spread over three to six years. If a partner leaves, all the tax remaining to be collected is normally the responsibility of the remaining partners and any new partners who join, even though it relates to an earlier period. You may want to adjust your partnership agreement so you can charge leaving partners their share of the tax. Alternatively, consider electing not to use the spreading provisions so that all the tax is paid now.

Losses

Since 10 February 2004, if you are a partner but do not yourself spend a significant amount of time running the business, the amount of losses for which you can claim 'sideways loss relief' is limited to the amount you have contributed to the partnership. For example, if you paid £20,000 into the partnership, the loss relief is limited to a maximum of £20,000. 'Sideways loss relief' means the setting of losses against other income and gains (pp. 339–340), setting losses against profits for earlier years (p. 340) and claiming relief for interest on a loan used to buy into the partnership (p. 239). From 21 October 2009 onwards, sideways loss relief is denied completely where a loss arises directly or indirectly because of any arrangement with a main purpose of avoiding tax. You can still claim relief without any restriction by carrying losses forward to set against future profits from the same business.

Warning

For investments you make from 2 March 2007 onwards, sideways loss relief for a non-active partner is restricted to the lower of the eligible amount as described above and £25,000. You will count as a non-active partner if you devote on average less than 10 hours a week to the business. There is an exception: the £25,000 limit will not apply where you are investing in a partnership carrying on a film-related trade (but then other anti-avoidance rules apply).

19

UK property

4	**UK property**

UK property

Did you receive any income from UK property (including rents and other income from land you own or lease out)?

Yes ☐   No ☐

If you put a cross in the Yes box against question 4 on page TR2 of the Main tax return, you will need the UK property supplementary pages. Many people renting out the odd room in their home may have to do little more than tick one box on the first page. But there is also space for details of more substantial lettings businesses and for income from holiday homes.

If you take in lodgers in your home, providing meals and other services, this may amount to a form of business (but see the Rent a Room scheme overleaf) and details should be entered on the Self-employment supplementary pages (see Chapter 17). Income from property abroad is entered on the Foreign pages (see Chapter 20). Do not enter property income dividends from real estate investment trusts (REITs) or property authorised investment funds (PAIFs) here – they go in box 15 on page TR3 of the Main tax return (p. 211).

Warning

The Revenue is cracking down on people who fail to declare and pay tax on foreign sources of income. If you rent out a property abroad – say, a holiday home – you must in most cases declare this income even if you leave it in a bank account abroad and use it only for the upkeep and running of the property. Do not declare such income here – use the Foreign supplement (see Chapter 20). The Revenue is also tracking down owners of holiday homes and buy-to-let properties who fail to declare capital gains when they sell. These gains should be declared on the Capital Gains supplement (see Chapter 22).

The documents you need

You will need details of the rents you have received and any receipts or invoices for expenses. With furnished holiday lettings, you will also need records of the periods the properties were available for letting out.

If any of these properties is jointly owned, remember to enter only your share from these documents when filling in the tax return.

Tax-saving idea 213

Where you own a rental property with your spouse or civil partner, you must split the taxable income between you in the same shares as you own the property (usually equal shares unless you have made a declaration specifying some other split). But if you own property jointly with anyone else, you can agree to divide the income in different shares from those in which you own the property provided the actual shares you receive are the same as those agreed. For example, an unmarried couple who pay tax at different rates can agree to have more of the rent paid to the lower taxpayer.

The Rent a Room scheme

> **4** If you are claiming Rent a Room relief and your rents are £4,250 or less (or £2,125 if let jointly), put 'X' in the box

The Rent a Room scheme applies to rent from letting out furnished accommodation in your home and income from providing any related services, such as providing meals or doing your lodger's laundry. In the normal way you would pay tax on any profit you make – in other words, the income you get less allowable expenses you incur. If instead you opt for the Rent a Room scheme, the first slice of the income is tax-free, but you are not allowed to deduct any expenses.

Tax-saving idea 214

If you make a profit from taking in lodgers and your income from the lettings is £4,250 or less in 2009–10, there will be no tax to pay on this income if you opt for the Rent a Room scheme. If your gross income from the lettings is more than £4,250 but the expenses and allowances you can claim come to £4,250 or less, you will pay less tax if you opt for the Rent a Room scheme. Using the Rent a Room scheme can save you administration because, for tax purposes, you need only keep records of your income not any expenses.

The scheme can apply only to rooms you let in your only or main home (see Chapter 6). It doesn't matter whether you own the home or you yourself are a tenant (though bear in mind that you may need permission from a mortgage lender or landlord before taking in lodgers). The scheme is not intended to apply to rooms let as offices or for other business purposes. And you cannot claim Rent a Room relief if you yourself are not living in the property because, say, you have gone abroad or moved into job-related accommodation.

Under the scheme, in 2009–10, the first £4,250 of such income (without any expenses deducted) is tax-free. If anyone else living in the same home is letting out another room or you are jointly letting out room(s) with one or more other people, you each get £2,125 tax-free. The amount of Rent a Room relief has been unchanged since April 1997.

Example

Natalie Lean lets out three rooms in her house, bringing in a total of £150 a week in rent. This means her gross rental income for 2009–10 is £7,800, on which she could claim expenses and allowances of £2,350.

If the rental income is taxed as normal property income, she will pay tax on £7,800 − £2,350 = £5,450. But if she claims the Rent a Room relief, she will pay tax on the excess of the gross rental income of £7,800 over £4,250 – that is, on £3,550.

Rent a Room relief means Natalie will pay tax on £1,900 less income.

Unless you made a loss on the letting (in other words, your expenses came to more than the income), it will be worth claiming Rent a Room relief if your gross income from the letting(s) is £4,250 or less. All you need to do is put a cross in box 4 on page UKP1 if this is your only letting income. There is nothing more to enter – leave the rest of the UK property pages blank.

In all other cases, which boxes you complete depends on how much profit or loss you made from the letting(s) in 2009–10:

■ if you made a loss, follow the instructions for *Property income* (p. 265)

■ if the expenses and allowances you can deduct from your letting income come to more than £4,250 (or £2,125 if you are sharing the relief), follow the instructions for *Property income* (p. 361)

■ if the deductions you can make from your letting income come to £4,250 (£2,125) or less, opt for the Rent a Room scheme by putting your income in box 18 on page UKP2 and the Rent a Room relief you are claiming (either £4,250 or £2,125) in box 35. Don't enter any expenses in boxes 22 to 27 and don't claim any other deductions in boxes 30 (annual investment allowance) or 34 (wear and tear allowance).

Warning

It is commonly claimed that taking in lodgers through the Rent a Room scheme will not mean losing any of the private residence relief which prevents a capital gains tax bill when you sell your home (see Chapter 6). This is not correct. The Revenue's view is that if you have a single lodger (whether you use the Rent a Room scheme or not), you do not lose private residence relief. But if you have two or more lodgers (again, regardless of whether you have opted for the Rent a Room scheme), you are effectively running a business and so lose some of the capital gains tax relief on your home. However, you may instead claim lettings relief (p. 77).

Furnished holiday lettings

If you have no income from short-term furnished lettings, turn over to page UKP2 of the supplement and to p. 359 of this book.

Tax benefits of furnished holiday lettings

Income from furnished holiday lettings is treated differently from other forms of property income, to reflect the fact that it is a form of business for many owners. This offers several tax benefits:

- you can claim the annual investment allowance and other capital allowances (p. 327) for items (such as furniture and kitchen appliances) used in the property, as well as other capital spending. This contrasts with other types of property rental, where spending on items used in a residential property are not eligible for capital allowances
- losses can be set off against other income or gains for the same or previous tax year and losses in the first four years can be deducted from other income from the previous three years (p. 358)
- it counts as relevant earnings for tax relief on pension contributions (p. 88)
- you can claim entrepreneur's relief when you dispose of the business (p. 156).

To take advantage of these benefits, you have to work out your profit or loss from furnished holiday lettings separately from that for other rental properties you own.

Tax-saving ideas 215 and 216

From 2010–11, the special rules for furnished holiday lettings are due to be abolished. However, until 5 April 2010, the rules were extended to such properties anywhere in the European Economic Area (p. 424) and this treatment is backdated to the latest of the date the property was first used as a furnished holiday letting, the date the country joined the EEA or 1 January 1994. Check the advantages opposite to see if you can reduce your tax bill for previous years, for example by claiming capital allowances, loss relief or, for 2007–08 and earlier years, capital gains tax taper relief (see p. 144). Provided you submit your claim by 5 April 2011, you can go back as far as the 2006–07 tax year to change the way your property income was taxed.

Since 6 April 2008, a new annual investment allowance (AIA) has been introduced. The AIA gives you 100 per cent relief for capital spending on plant and equipment (other than cars) up to £50,000 for each 'qualifying activity' that you have. Each of the following counts as a separate qualifying activity and so qualifies for its own £50,000 AIA:

▓ a furnished holiday lettings business (in other words, all the EEA properties of this description that you have)

▓ an ordinary property business (made up of all your UK rental properties other than those that qualify as furnished holiday lettings – see p. 359), and

▓ an overseas property business (see Chapter 20).

Therefore you may be able to increase tax relief on capital spending by holding a mix of types of rental property.

What income is taxed?

Income from land and property (other than that dealt with under the Rent a Room scheme) is all taxed in the same way – irrespective of its type. All income from land and property in the UK is added together. You pay tax on the income after deduction of allowable expenses, interest paid on loans to buy or improve the properties and losses from letting out property in the past. You can also claim allowances for some equipment you buy.

The tax you pay in a tax year is based on the property income and expenditure during that year. If you make up accounts for your property business for the year ending 5 April, the figures in your accounts will be the ones to use in filling in your tax return.

But if your accounting year runs to different dates, you will have to use two sets of accounts to work out what your property income and expenditure was for the tax year.

To count as furnished holiday lettings, the property must normally meet all the following conditions for 2009–10:

▓ be available for letting to the general public on a commercial basis (that is, with a view to a profit) for at least 140 days

▓ actually let commercially for at least 70 of those days

- periods when the property was occupied for more than 31 days in a row by the same person (called periods of longer-term occupation) do not count towards the 70 days. The total of any periods of longer term occupation (which need not be consecutive) must not exceed 155 days.

These conditions must be satisfied for at least 12 months so, if you first started letting your property after 6 April 2009, there will not be time to satisfy the conditions before the scheme is abolished. If you finished letting the property during that tax year, the conditions must have been met for the 12 months ending with the last letting. If you own more than one furnished holiday letting, you can average out the letting for the 70 days rule between all of them.

The property need not be a fixed building. It could, for example, be a caravan. But whatever its structure you will have to convince the Revenue that you are genuinely letting on a commercial basis not simply trying to offset some of the costs of your holiday home. For example, you should be able to produce a business plan and properly drawn-up accounts.

Tax-saving ideas 217 and 218

Furnished holiday lettings, as such, do not count as business property for the purpose of inheritance tax. But, if they are serviced lettings (for example, providing meals and laundry), they may qualify. You can employ someone else to provide these services. Provided certain conditions are met, gifts of business property qualify for 100 per cent business property relief which means they can be passed on or given away free of inheritance tax.

From 6 April 2010 onwards, the special treatment for furnished holiday lettings is due to be abolished. If the abolition goes ahead, from 2010–11 onwards, income from letting your property will be treated in the same way as other property income (see p. 359). However, where you have claimed capital allowances before 5 April 2010 for spending on items used within a furnished holiday letting, you can continue to claim writing down and other capital allowances in the normal way (see p. 363). For spending on items for use within the property from 6 April 2010 onwards, you cannot claim capital allowances but can claim wear-and-tear allowance instead. Losses on a furnished holiday letting made before 6 April 2010 will be treated as made in 2009–10 and can be set against future income from let property. Exceptionally, if you provide services as well as accommodation, you may be able to show that your property activities amount to a business. If this applies, you will be able to carry on claiming capital allowances, a wider range of loss relief, and so on, but you will also have to start paying Class 2 and Class 4 national insurance in the same way as any other sole trader or partner (see p. 341).

Income

Enter the total income from all your furnished holiday lettings in the UK for 2009–10 – before any deductions such as agents' commission. Include any income for services provided to tenants, such as cleaning, linen hire and use of additional facilities. Also include any money received from insurance policies for loss of rent.

Expenses

If your total property income, including that from furnished holiday lettings, is less than £15,000, enter your total expenses in box 9, as *Other allowable property expenses* – you don't need to give details of individual expenses. If your total property income is over this limit, you need to list expenses separately.

Rent, rates, insurance, etc.

Enter the amount of rent, business rates, council tax, water rates, ground rent and insurance premiums on the furnished holiday lettings (including for insurance against loss of rents) in box 6.

Also claim in box 6 for any work that prevents the property deteriorating that counts as a repair – such as painting and damp treatment. You can't claim here the cost of improvements, additions or extensive alterations even if such work makes repairs unnecessary.

If you aren't claiming capital allowances for the furniture, fixtures and fittings, you can claim a renewals deduction for the cost of replacing them. If the new items are better, you cannot claim the full cost. And if any of the old items are sold, the proceeds should be deducted from the amount you claim.

Tax-saving idea 219

> The Revenue accepts that work which once counted as an improvement to a property may over time and due to technological advances now be accepted as a repair and so count as an allowable expense. The example it gives is replacing old windows with double glazing. If you are replacing an old feature with a modern equivalent, try claiming and ask your tax office to confirm that the expense is allowable.

Loan interest and other financial costs

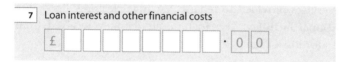

Enter in box 7 the cost of any loan you took out to buy the property – including interest paid, any Sharia-compliant equivalent payments and charges for setting up the loan.

Legal, management and professional costs

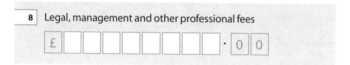

You can claim legal and professional expenses for a letting of less than a year, including fees for agents, surveyors and accountants and commission. You can also claim such costs when renewing the lease for a longer letting provided it is for less than 50 years. But you cannot claim expenses incurred in the first letting of a property for more than a year. Nor can you claim costs of registering title to land, getting planning permission or in connection with the payment of a premium on renewal of a lease. Enter the total in box 8. Also claim here any legal and professional costs for evicting an unsatisfactory tenant.

Other expenses

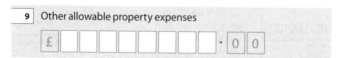

Other expenses include advertising costs, stationery, telephone calls, rent collection and travel to the property when solely for the letting.

You can also claim as an expense the cost of services such as gardening, cleaning and porterage. You can't claim the cost of your own time, but you can claim the cost of paying other people, such as a member of your family.

Tax adjustments

You need to make a couple more adjustments to arrive at your profit or loss for the year.

Private use

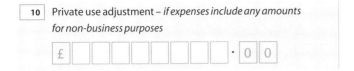

10 Private use adjustment – *if expenses include any amounts for non-business purposes*

£ [   ] . [0][0]

If a furnished holiday letting is partly used for your own enjoyment or that of friends staying cheaply or rent-free, this counts as private use. Part of the costs must be apportioned to this private use, and cannot be claimed as an expense. For example, if it was available for letting for nine months of the year and used by you for the rest of the time, you can claim only three-quarters of the costs of owning it. (You can still claim the full costs of letting it out as expenses.)

There are two ways to make an adjustment to reflect private use. You can enter the appropriately reduced share of the costs in boxes 6 to 9, but let your tax inspector know what you've done. Or, better, you enter the costs in full in these boxes and enter in box 10 a figure for private use which is deducted from the total.

Capital allowances and balancing charges

11 Balancing charges – *read page UKPN 4 of the notes*

£ [   ] . [0][0]

12 Capital allowances - *read page UKPN 5 of the notes*

£ [   ] . [0][0]

You can claim capital allowances for the cost of buying furniture, machinery such as a lawnmower or equipment such as tools, ladders and a computer.

If you get rid of an item on which you have claimed capital allowances, a balancing charge may be added to your profits, reflecting the sale proceeds or the second-hand value. There's more on p. 327 about capital allowances and balancing charges. You might also find it useful to get Help Sheet HS250 *Capital allowances and balancing charges in a rental business* from the Orderline (p. 180).

Enter the amount of any capital allowances you are claiming for the tax year ending 5 April 2010 in box 12 and the amount of any balancing charge in box 11.

Losses for the year

14 Loss for the year (if boxes 6 to 9 + box 12 minus (box 5 + box 10 + box 11) is positive) £ · 0 0	**16** Loss set off against 2009-10 total income £ · 0 0
15 Loss set off against other income from property £ · 0 0	**17** Loss carried back to earlier years £ · 0 0

Follow the instructions for boxes 13 or 14. If the answer is a minus figure it goes in box 14.

Any loss in box 14 can be used to reduce the amount of tax you pay on other income or capital gains in 2009–10 or earlier tax years:

- other income for 2009–10 (enter the amount you wish to claim in box 16)

- capital gains for the same tax year – include the amount you wish to claim in box 14 on the Capital gains summary (p. 400)

- income and gains for earlier tax years – enter the amount you wish to claim in box 17. If you have already claimed to offset this loss, still include it here but make a note of the amount in the *Any other information* box on page TR6 of the Main tax return.

If you haven't used all the loss in box 14, you can set off what remains against other property income for 2009–10. Enter what is left in box 15. This amount will be carried forward and reflected in the figure that goes in box 39 on page UKP2 of this supplement.

44444

Tax-saving ideas 220 and 221

Keep careful and detailed records so that you can claim for all your expenses. Don't forget to claim the interest on any mortgage used to finance the purchase of the property as an expense against letting income. The mortgage does not have to be secured against the let property in order to be allowable – it could be secured, for example, against your own home. (But, in that case, you should make clear to the lender the purpose of the loan. It could be deemed fraudulent if you apply for a residential mortgage but your intention is to repay it out of the income from a buy-to-let business.)

As a temporary measure to help businesses affected by the credit crunch and ensuing recession, including providers of furnished holiday lettings, in addition to the usual loss relief rules, you can set a loss for the 2009–10 tax year against profits from the same business made in the previous three tax years, in other words, 2008–09, 2007–08 and 2006–07. You must set the loss against the most recent year first and there is a cap of £50,000 in total on the amount you can set off against the profits for 2007–08 and 2006–07. To make a claim, either write to your tax office or claim through box 17. This relief also applied to a loss made in 2008–09.

Property income

All your rental and other income from property, including from furnished holiday lettings (except rents within the Rent a Room scheme – see p. 350) is added together and treated as the proceeds of a single rental business. You are treated in this way whether you have, say, a single buy-to-let property or a whole string of flats and houses.

Income

Rents and other income from property

18 Total rents and other income from property (including any furnished holiday lettings profits in box 13)

£ ⬚⬚⬚⬚⬚⬚⬚⬚ · 0 0

In box 18, put the sum of your net profit (if any) from furnished holiday lettings from box 13 plus all your income from any other property rentals before deductions. In addition to rental income for 2009–10, include the following:

■ rent you will receive after 5 April 2010 that is payment in arrears for 2009–10 (equally, leave out any rent received in arrears this year that was included in last year's return, and any rent received on or before

5 April 2010 which is payment in advance for rent for periods after 5 April 2010)

- any income for services provided to tenants, such as cleaning, gardening or porterage
- any money received from insurance policies for loss of rent
- ground rent and feu duties
- grants from local authorities for repairs (you can claim the cost of repairs as an expense)
- payments for using your land – for example, to shoot or graze.

If any tax has been deducted from the income before you get it, enter the total in box 19. The figure you enter in box 18 should be the before-tax amounts – so should include the amount in box 19.

If you own and let the property jointly with someone else, enter only your share of the income in box 18, and your share of the expenses lower down.

Chargeable premiums, reverse premiums

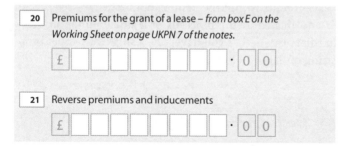

If you receive a premium from a tenant in return for granting a lease, you will have to pay income tax on part of it if the lease lasts 50 years or less (and capital gains tax on the rest). Any work the tenant agrees to do for you on being granted a lease counts as a premium.

If you are paid the premium in instalments, the total premium is still taxable in the year the lease is granted. But if paying in one go would cause you hardship, you can ask your tax inspector to allow you to pay by yearly instalments. The maximum number of instalments is eight (or the number of years you are getting the premium over, if less).

The proportion on which you will have to pay income tax is calculated as follows:

$$\frac{51 - \text{number of years of the lease}}{50}$$

So if the lease is a 20-year one, the proportion of the premium which is taxable as income is:

$$\frac{51 - 20}{50} = \frac{31}{50}$$

Enter the taxable amount in box 20.

A lease for more than 50 years is treated as capital rather than business income. There is no income tax to pay, but capital gains tax may be due (see Chapter 9).

You might have received a lump sum payment or other benefit (such as a contribution towards fitting out the property) from a landlord to persuade you to take out a lease on a property. This may be a property you live in yourself as a tenant or it could be a property you sublet to someone else. The payment or benefit is called a reverse premium and you have to pay tax on it as if it is income from a property business. Give the amount in box 21 – if you are not sure whether you have received a reverse premium, ask your tax inspector or your business adviser.

Expenses

22 Rent, rates, insurance, ground rents etc.	25 Legal, management and other professional fees
£ · 0 0	£ · 0 0
23 Property repairs, maintenance and renewals	26 Costs of services provided, including wages
£ · 0 0	£ · 0 0
24 Loan interest and other financial costs	27 Other allowable property expenses
£ · 0 0	£ · 0 0

If your total property income, including income from furnished holiday lettings, for 2009–10 is less than £15,000, go to box 27 and enter your total expenses in it (but excluding any expenses relating to furnished holiday letting because these have already been deducted from the figure you included in box 18). If your total property income is over this limit, you need to list the expenses incurred in 2009–10 separately.

The details of what expenses you can claim in boxes 22 to 27 are the same as those given under Furnished holiday lettings on pp. 335–357. Note that with furnished property, you can claim a renewals deduction in box 23 for the cost of replacing furniture, fixtures and fittings, but not if you are already claiming a wear and tear allowance on the property (see overleaf).

Don't include any expenses you have already claimed in boxes 5 to 13.

Example

Miriam Patel has divided most of her house into furnished rooms which she lets out, providing cleaning. The total yearly income is £9,640 but she can deduct these expenses:

■ a proportion of the outgoings on the house (council tax, water rates, gas, electricity and insurance) which add up to £3,400 a year. Miriam is letting out three-quarters of the house and claims this proportion

■ the cost of cleaning (cleaner's wages plus materials) – £1,300 a year

■ an allowance for wear and tear of the furniture and furnishings – Miriam claims the actual cost of replacement (£500 for this year).

Thus Miriam's tax bill would be calculated as follows:

Total rent received		£9,640
Less expenses		
Three-quarters of the outgoings of £3,400 a year	£2,550	
Cost of cleaning	£1,300	
Cost of replacing furniture and furnishings	£500	
Total allowable expenses		£4,350
Taxable rental income		£5,290

If Miriam does the cleaning, no allowance can be made for her time. But if she pays someone else to do the work (her mum, say), she can claim this cost as an allowable expense.

Tax adjustments

Box 28 is where you enter a figure for any private use of the property, in the same way as for furnished holiday lettings (p. 357).

Any balancing charges (p. 358) should be put in box 29. See overleaf for details of capital and other allowances you can claim.

Enter in box 35 any tax-free amount you are claiming under the Rent a Room scheme (p. 350). Otherwise leave it empty.

Capital and other allowances

30 Annual Investment Allowance

£ ⬜⬜⬜⬜⬜⬜⬜⬜⬜ • 0 0

31 Business Premises Renovation Allowance (Assisted Areas only) – *read page UKPN 9 and UKPN 10 of the notes*

£ ⬜⬜⬜⬜⬜⬜⬜⬜⬜ • 0 0

32 All other capital allowances

£ ⬜⬜⬜⬜⬜⬜⬜⬜⬜ • 0 0

33 Landlord's Energy Saving Allowance

£ ⬜⬜⬜⬜⬜⬜⬜⬜⬜ • 0 0

34 10% wear and tear allowance – *for furnished residential accommodation only*

£ ⬜⬜⬜⬜⬜⬜⬜⬜⬜ • 0 0

Capital allowances and wear and tear allowance

If you want to claim the annual investment allowance (p. 327), enter the amount in box 30. Apart from any business premises renovation allowance (see opposite), other capital allowances (see pp. 328–335) go in box 32. You can't claim capital allowances on items used in a property let as a furnished home (unless it is a furnished holiday letting). You can instead claim a renewals deduction for the cost of replacing such items (in box 23 on p. 361). Or you can claim a wear and tear allowance in box 34 of 10 per cent of the rent less service charges and local taxes. Once you have chosen a method, you can't switch. And if you have been using a different method of allowing for wear and tear agreed with your tax inspector before 6 April 1976, you can carry on using it.

Tax-saving idea 222

> Unless you let furnished holiday properties, you cannot claim the annual invstment allowance (AIA) for spending on items inside the property you let, but you can use the AIA to get full relief on what you spend on many other items, such as equipment you use to maintain the garden, ladders and tools you use maintaining the property, office equipment used in the administration of the business, a van you use to visit the property, and so on. On some types of spending you can claim 100 per cent first-year allowances (see page 328) instead, leaving you free to use your AIA on other items.

Flats over shops and businesses

You can claim a 100 per cent capital allowance to cover in full any amount you have spent in 2009–10 renovating or converting the space over a shop or other commercial property into flats for rent, provided certain conditions are met. The property must have been built before 1980; all or most of the ground floor must be for business use; it must have no more than five floors; and the upstairs part must originally have been constructed primarily for residential use. The flats must pass a value test with the rents not exceeding given limits. The limits are set at £350 a week for a two-room flat in Greater London and £150 a week elsewhere rising to £480 a week for a four-room flat in Greater London and £300 a week elsewhere. Flats with five or more rooms do not qualify. 'Room' does not include kitchens, bathrooms and small hallways. Include any 100 per cent allowance for this type of spending in the figure you enter at box 32.

Business premises renovation allowance

You can claim 100 per cent capital allowances on the cost of renovating, converting or repairing a property in a deprived area to bring it back into commercial use. It must be a commercial building or structure (or part of one) that has been unused for at least a year and the spending must occur on or after 11 April 2007 and before 11 April 2012. Renovating, converting and repairing does not include buying land or extending the building (for example, adding another storey).

To qualify for the scheme, after renovation, the building must be available for commercial use but not in any of the following excluded trades: fisheries and aquaculture, shipbuilding, coal industry, steel industry, synthetic fibres, certain agricultural products or products that imitate or substitute for milk or milk products.

For the purpose of this scheme, the whole of Northern Ireland counts as a deprived area. See www.dtistats.net/regional-aa/aa2007.asp to check which other parts of the UK qualify.

Put any amount you are claiming under the scheme in box 31.

Environmentally beneficial spending

The 100 per cent first-year capital allowances are also available for specified types of environmentally beneficial spending (p. 329). Include these amounts in box 32.

There is also a separate scheme giving residential landlords 100 per cent relief on up to £1,500 of spending on each let property on: loft, floor, cavity wall or solid wall insulation; and draft proofing and insulation for hot water systems. Put any amounts you are claiming under this scheme in box 33.

Profit or loss for the year

Use the working sheet on page UKPN14 of the notes that come with the UK property supplement to work out the adjusted profit figure to help you work out:

- rental income from box 18
- plus any premiums, reverse premiums, private use adjustments and balancing charges
- less any furnished holiday letting losses, capital and other allowances and any Rent a Room scheme exemption.

If the answer is positive, you have made a profit for the year, which goes in box 36. This is not quite the figure you pay tax on because you may be able to claim some relief for losses – see opposite. If the answer is less than zero, you have made a loss, which goes in box 39.

Losses

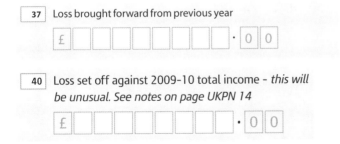

| 37 | Loss brought forward from previous year |

£ ⬚⬚⬚⬚⬚⬚⬚⬚ · 0 0

| 40 | Loss set off against 2009-10 total income - *this will be unusual. See notes on page UKPN 14* |

£ ⬚⬚⬚⬚⬚⬚⬚⬚ · 0 0

| 41 | Loss to carry forward to following year, including unused losses brought forward |

£ ⬚⬚⬚⬚⬚⬚⬚⬚ . 0 0

Any loss on furnished holiday lettings in 2009–10 has already been taken into account in working out the amount to go in either box 36 or 39.

If you have made a profit in 2009–10 (you have an entry in box 36), you can now deduct any losses brought forward from earlier years. Put the amount you are claiming in box 37. (This will be part or all of the figure from box 41 of your 2008–09 tax return.)

If you have made a loss overall from your property business in 2009–10 (in other words, you have an entry in box 39), normally you get relief by carrying the loss forward to set against future profits from your property business. Exceptionally, you can deduct a property income loss from other forms of income for 2007–08 but only in certain circumstances:

■ if you have claimed capital allowances in boxes 30 and 32. Even then, the maximum loss you can set off in this way is restricted. See the notes accompanying the UK property supplement for details

■ if you have land used for agriculture and the loss is due to certain agricultural expenses. If this applies, see Help Sheet HS251 *Agricultural land*.

Enter the amount of loss you wish to deduct in this way in box 40. Alternatively, a loss which reflects an excess of capital allowances over balancing charges can be carried over to next year and set against your income for 2010–11. If this is what you would like to do, make a note of the figure to enter in the 2011 tax return.

Finally, any other unused losses can be carried over to deduct from future profits from property – enter these in box 41.

20

Foreign income

5 | **Foreign**

If you:

- were entitled to any foreign income, or income gains
- have, or could have, received (directly or indirectly) income, or a capital payment or benefit from a person abroad as a result of any transfer of assets
- want to claim relief for foreign tax paid

please read the notes on page TRG 4 to decide if you have to fill in the *Foreign* pages.

Do you need to complete the *Foreign* pages?

Yes ☐   No ☐

If you put a cross in the Yes box at question 5 on page TR2 of the Main tax return, you will need the supplementary pages called Foreign. These have space to give details about your foreign savings, pensions and benefits, property income and other investment income from abroad. Earnings from work abroad should be entered in the Employment, Self-Employment or Partnership pages of the tax return as appropriate, though you will need to use page F6 of the Foreign pages to claim any tax credit relief (p. 370). Similarly, details of capital gains on overseas transactions should be entered in the Capital gains supplement, though you will need to use page F6 of the Foreign pages to claim any tax credit relief (p. 370).

Note that anywhere other than England, Scotland, Wales and Northern Ireland counts as 'foreign', so you should include, for example, interest from accounts held in the Channel Islands, Isle of Man or Republic of Ireland on the Foreign pages.

This chapter tells you how to fill in the Foreign pages, and about the expenses and allowances you can claim. But the tax treatment of people who live abroad is beyond the scope of this guide. If this applies to you, seek professional advice from your bank, accountant or tax adviser.

Warning

The Revenue is conducting a sustained campaign to track down people who fail to declare and pay tax on foreign income. It has been given permission to require banks, building societies and other overseas financial assets to hand over details of customers with foreign accounts, credit cards linked to foreign accounts and other financial institutions. The data goes back six years, so will also cover people who have had foreign accounts in the past even though they might not have them now. If you are domiciled and resident in the UK, you are liable for UK tax on your income from anywhere in the world. This includes, for example, interest from a foreign bank account that you have simply to help you run a holiday home abroad as well as income from any offshore investments you might make. Although it is now too late to take advantage of any specially disclosure opportunities offered by the Revenue (except where you wish to disclose offshore holdings in Liechtenstein), you will still pay less in penalties if you voluntarily tell the Revenue about your foreign income than if you are found out later (see Chapter 4).

What income is taxed

The instructions below are for people who are domiciled in the UK and resident or ordinarily resident here. Their foreign income is taxed on an arising basis – when they get it or it is credited to them, regardless of whether or when it is brought back to the UK. You should enter the amounts you got in sterling, using the exchange rate on the date the income arose.

There are different rules for people who are not domiciled or not ordinarily resident in the UK – see Chapter 23 for how this is determined. If either applies, you will need to fill in the Non-residence supplementary pages (see Chapter 23). And your foreign income can be taxed on a remittance basis (i.e. only when income is brought into the UK rather than when it arose) – on the Foreign pages, put a cross in box 1 and enter the amounts of income received in the UK and the equivalent share of any foreign tax deducted from it.

Tax-free foreign income

The following types of foreign income are tax-free in the UK:

- pensions paid by Germany or Austria to the victims of Nazi persecution and to pensioners who have fled from persecution

- the extra foreign pension paid to you if you have been retired because you were disabled by injury on duty or by a work-related illness

■ any part of a pension from overseas that reduces the amount of tax-free UK war widows' and dependants' pensions

■ social security benefits which are similar to UK benefits that are tax-free – child benefit, maternity allowance, guardian's allowance, child's special allowance, bereavement payments, incapacity benefit (only for the first six months if it began on or after 13 April 1996), attendance allowance, disability living allowance and severe disablement allowance.

A tenth of overseas pensions funded by an overseas employer or pension fund is tax-free in the UK unless it is taxed on a remittance basis (see opposite).

Income stuck in a foreign country

| 1 | If you were unable to transfer any of your overseas income to the UK, put 'X' in the box - *read page FN 3 of the notes and give details in the 'Any other information' box on your tax return or on a separate sheet* |

If you are taxed on an arising basis, in some cases, you will be unable to remit foreign income to the UK because it arises in a country that has exchange controls or is short of foreign exchange. If so, you can claim that the income should not after all be taxed in 2009–10. If income is unremittable, put a cross in box 1 and give details in the *Any other information* box on page TR6 of the Main tax return or on a separate sheet.

If previously unremittable income has become remittable during 2009–10, you must include it in this tax return even if you have chosen not to bring the income into the UK.

How foreign income is taxed

| 2 | If you are calculating your tax, enter the total foreign tax credit relief on your income |

£

Income from abroad is taxable in the UK, even if you have already paid foreign tax on it. You can deduct any foreign tax paid from the income before working out your UK tax bill – so you pay UK tax only on the net amount of income you receive.

But, in most cases, you can instead claim a deduction from your UK tax bill to reflect the foreign tax paid, known as foreign tax credit relief. This is likely to mean paying less in UK tax than if you simply deduct the foreign tax from the gross income before working out the UK tax bill.

Foreign tax credit relief is not available for all foreign tax and the maximum relief cannot exceed the amount of UK tax due on the gross income or gains. Note, in particular:

- double-taxation agreements. These are arrangements between the UK and many other countries to reduce the amount of tax collectively paid under both regimes. Where an agreement exists with the country from which your income arises, the maximum tax credit relief you can claim is for the minimum foreign tax payable under the agreement

- no agreement. You can get foreign tax credit relief only for taxes that correspond to UK income tax or capital gains tax (and not, for example, for any annual wealth tax or purchase tax)

- dividends. You can claim tax credit relief for foreign tax on dividends in these countries: Antigua, Australia (where they are paid net with a credit in respect of tax already paid by the company), Belize, Cyprus, The Gambia, Guernsey, Isle of Man, Jersey, Kiribati, Malaysia, Malta, Singapore. But you can deduct the tax from the dividend income before working out the UK tax due.

Example

Bill Livingstone made £2,500 after expenses in 2009–10 letting out his villa in Freedonia. He paid the equivalent of £400 tax on this to the Freedonian tax authorities.

In calculating his UK tax, he could have simply deducted the £400 of Freedonian tax from the £2,500 and paid UK tax on £2,100. Since he paid tax on the income at the basic rate of 20 per cent, the tax bill would have been 20% × £2,100 = £420.

But he claimed tax credit relief, so the full £2,500 was taxable at 20 per cent – which gives an initial UK tax bill of £500. He could then deduct the £400 of Freedonian tax, making his UK tax bill just £100.

Working out the amount of tax credit relief can be complicated and this guide assumes you are leaving the calculations to your tax office. In that case, leave box 2 blank. If you do feel up to making the calculations your-self, use the working sheet in Help Sheet HS263 *Foreign tax credit relief* available from the Revenue Orderline (p. 180) and put the amount of relief you are claiming on your income in box 2. Tax credit relief on gains goes in box 39.

Special withholding tax

If you receive income from a European Union member state or some other related territories, it may be paid after deduction of special withholding tax (SWT). This is treated as a payment on account of UK tax. If the SWT deducted comes to more than your UK tax bill, the excess is refunded.

The documents you need

You will need to gather together dividend vouchers for overseas shares, bank statements for overseas bank accounts, pension advice notes, foreign property bills – as well as details of any foreign tax paid.

Foreign income other than property income

A Country or territory code	B Amount of income arising or received before any tax taken off	C Foreign tax taken off or paid

Interest and other income from overseas savings

A	B	C
£	£

D Special Withholding Tax and any UK tax taken off	E To claim foreign tax credit relief put 'X' in the box	F Taxable amount – *if you are claiming foreign tax credit relief, copy column B here. If not, enter column B minus column C*
£		£

On pages F2 to F3, give details of income from foreign savings, dividends, pensions and benefits, and trusts and other sources, except property (which goes on page F4 – p. 374). Enter all amounts in sterling. Convert foreign currency to sterling at the exchange rate on the date the income arose if you are taxed on an arising basis or the date the income was received in the UK if you are taxed on a remittance basis.

Pages F2 to F3 give you separate sections for each type of income. Within each section, add together income of the same type from the same country and then use a separate line for the total from each country as follows:

- column A. Put the code for the country concerned. The codes are listed in the notes that come with the Foreign supplement, starting on page FN17

- column B. Put the gross amount of income before taking off any foreign or UK tax or SWT

- column C. The amount of foreign tax you have paid but not any SWT. If there is a double taxation agreement between the UK and the country concerned, tax should have been deducted at a reduced rate. If the amount you put in this column is more than you should have paid, you need to reclaim the excess from the foreign tax authority

- column D. Any SWT and UK tax you have already paid on the income

- column E. Put a cross in this column if you are claiming foreign tax credit relief (which will usually be the best option) – see p. 370

- column F. Put the taxable amount of the income here. If you are claiming foreign tax credit relief, this will be the same as the gross amount you entered in column B. If you are not claiming tax credit relief, it will be the income net of the foreign tax paid – in other words, column B minus column C.

At the end of each section, work out the totals for each income type of SWT and UK tax paid (column D) and the taxable amount (column F). If you have too many sources of foreign income to fit on pages F2 and F3, put the rest on a second Foreign supplement and just fill in boxes 4 and 5 on the second form. You can get an extra supplement from the Revenue Orderline (p. 180) or www.hmrc.gov.uk/sa.

Foreign savings

In this section, include interest from foreign bank and building society accounts, income from foreign bonds, interest distributions from overseas unit trusts and other investment funds, the taxable part of income from annuities other than those bought through a pension scheme.

If you have some foreign bonds and the value of all the fixed-interest securities you hold, including your UK holdings, comes to more than £5,000, you will need to make an adjustment for accrued income – see p. 216 for details of the scheme. If your holdings do not exceed £5,000, you can ignore the scheme.

Tax-saving idea 223 and 224

Some countries, such as Jersey, Guernsey and the Isle of Man, pay gross interest on savings (in other words, without deducting any tax). If you are a UK taxpayer, you must declare this interest and pay UK tax on it. But there can be a delay between earning the interest and paying the tax. For example, if interest was paid or credited on 30 April 2010 and you pay tax through self-assessment, the tax is not due until 31 January 2012. In the meantime, you can earn extra interest on the uncollected tax.

If you received dividends before 6 April 2008 from companies based in Finland, Greece or Ireland, you may be entitled to claim back some tax. Due to a change in the interpretation of the law, the Revenue states that you should have been entitled to a tax credit equal to one-ninth of the dividend you received. Provided you claim by 5 April 2011, you can go back as far as 2006–07 to claim back tax. If this may apply to you, contact your tax office.

Foreign dividends

Include dividends and other distributions from shares in foreign countries and dividend distributions from overseas unit trusts and investment funds (see p. 378 for taxation of funds). But do not include:

- distributions by a foreign company in the form of shares (but enter any cash alternative you took instead)
- stock dividends from foreign companies
- bonus shares from a scrip issue by a foreign company
- capital distributions – for example, the return of your capital or distributions in the course of liquidation.

Pensions and social security benefits

Exclude pensions and benefits which are free of UK tax – see pp. 368–369. If only part of a payment is free of UK tax, give the amount which is not exempt in columns B and F.

Income received by trusts or companies abroad

You may have transferred assets with the result that income becomes payable to a company, trust or other entity based abroad. If you or your husband or wife may at any time enjoy that income (say, because you are shareholders of the company or beneficiaries of the trust), or you receive or are entitled to receive a capital sum (including a loan) in connection with the transfer, the income or capital sum is taxable as income and should normally be included on pages F2 and F3 in boxes 10 and 11 if it is dividend income or box 42 for other income. These rules are designed to stop you benefiting from tax avoidance arrangements. However, you can claim an exemption from UK tax if the transaction can objectively be shown not to be tax motivated. In that case, do not include these amounts as income on pages F2 and F3, but put the amount you have omitted in box 46 on page F6 of this supplement. Give full details of the arrangement in the *Any other information* box on page TR6 of the Main tax return.

Similarly, if someone else makes a transfer to the company, trust or other entity described above, you are taxed on the income or other benefit to the extent that the company has 'unexpended income'. This means income that has not already passed to someone else or been spent by the company, trust or other entity. You should put the value of any such benefits in box 42 on page F6 of this Foreign supplement. But, again, if the arrangement can objectively be shown not to be tax motivated, you can claim an exemption from UK tax. In that case, do not put the amount in box 42 but include in box 46 the amount you have omitted and give details in the *Any other information* box on page TR6 of the Main tax return.

For further information, see Help Sheet HS262 *Income and benefits from transfers of assets abroad or from non-resident trusts* available from the Revenue Orderline (p. 180).

If you have these complex types of arrangement, you should take specialised tax advice.

Income from land and property abroad

14	Total rents and other receipts (excluding taxable premiums for the grant of a lease)	17	Property expenses (rent, repairs, legal fees, cost of services provided) - *enter the total amount*
	£		£
15	Number of overseas let properties	18	Net profit or loss (box 14 + box 16 minus box 17) - *if this is a negative figure (a loss) put a minus sign in the box*
			£
16	Premiums paid for the grant of a lease		
	£		

Income from overseas property is taxed in much the same way as that from UK property (see Chapter 19). You can deduct expenses including the cost of managing the property and collecting the income (for example, paying an agent). If you buy equipment, you may be able to claim a capital allowance or some other form of deduction (p. 327). And you can deduct loan interest on the property.

As for UK property, there are certain expenses you cannot claim. These include personal expenses – such as the costs incurred while the property is not let – and capital allowances for items used within a residential property.

You give details in boxes 14 to 24 on pages F4 to F5 if you have just one overseas rental property; you have several but they are all in the same country and all the income is remittable; or you have several across more than one country but no foreign tax has been deducted and all the income is remittable. If other circumstances apply, you need to copy pages F4 to F5 and fill in one set for each property.

Next fill in columns A to F, which follow the same format as page F2 (p. 371). Complete this section by filling in boxes 25 to 32 as appropriate to claim tax relief for losses – see p. 366 for information on claiming property income losses.

Tax-saving ideas 225 and 226

Following a reinterpretation of the law, until 5 April 2010, if you let out a furnished holiday home anywhere in the European Economic Area (p. 424), it qualifies for the special tax treatment previously thought applicable only to UK furnished holiday lettings – see p. 352. This treatment is backdated to the later of the date the property was first used as a furnished holiday letting, the date the country joined the EEA or 1 January 1994. Check the advantages listed on p. 352 to see if you can now claim a reduction in your tax bill for previous years, for example by claiming capital allowances, loss relief or, for 2007–08 and earlier years, capital gains tax taper relief (see p. 144).

To avoid problems with, for example, foreign inheritance laws, it is common to own an overseas property through a company. If the owners (who are usually directors of the company) spent time at the property, technically they received a benefit in kind which was taxable under normal employment income rules (see Chapter 8). From 2008–09, the law exempted this situation from tax and the change was backdated as if it had always applied. If you paid tax on the benefit in kind in any year before 2008–09, you can claim a refund. See www.hmrc.gov.uk/news/hol-home-abroad.htm for details.

Warning

If you are UK-domiciled and resident, you must pay tax on the overseas rents you received in 2009–10 whether or not you brought this income into the UK.

Foreign tax credit relief

As described on pp. 369–371, you can just pay UK tax on the net foreign income you get after foreign tax has been deducted, but you'll usually pay less tax overall if you claim foreign tax credit relief. For most types of foreign income, you make your claim by putting a cross in the appropriate boxes on pages F3 and F5 of this supplement. You use page F6 to claim tax credit relief on income and gains reported elsewhere in your tax return.

Employment, self-employment and other income

A Country or territory code	C Foreign tax paid	E To claim foreign tax credit relief put 'X' in the box	F Taxable amount - read page FN 18 of the notes
☐☐☐	£ ☐☐☐☐☐☐☐☐	☐	£ ☐☐☐☐☐☐☐☐

Use this section if you want to claim foreign tax credit relief on any income you entered on the Employment supplement or Self-employment supplement. All amounts should be given in sterling. Complete the columns as follows:

■ column A. Put the code for the country concerned. The codes are listed in the notes that come with the Foreign supplement, starting on page FN21

■ column C. The amount of foreign tax you have paid

■ column E. Put a cross in this column if you are claiming foreign tax credit relief (which will usually be the best option) – see pp. 369–371

■ column F. Put the taxable amount of the income here – in other words, the gross amount before any tax was taken off. In the case of self-employment where part of your business income was earned overseas, you may need to apportion your expenses and other adjustments in some reasonable way to work out how much of your profit should go in column F.

Capital gains

Complete boxes 33 to 40 on page F6 if you have been taxed on a capital gain from a foreign country and you want relief for foreign tax paid on the gain. Enter all amounts in sterling. If you have more than one gain, copy page F6 and fill in a copy for each gain, then put the totals in boxes 33 to 40 on page F6 of the supplement. For help making these entries, get Help Sheet HS261 *Foreign tax credit relief: capital gains* from the Revenue Orderline (p. 180).

Other overseas income and gains

This is where you give details of miscellaneous other types of overseas income. If you have these complex investments, you should take specialised tax advice.

Offshore funds and non-resident trusts

| 41 | Gains on disposals of holdings in offshore funds (excluding the amounts entered in box 13) and discretionary income from non-resident trusts - *enter the amount of the gain or payment* |

£ ☐☐☐☐☐☐☐☐

The income from an offshore fund should be entered as savings income on pages F2 to F3 of the Foreign pages. Here you must give details of any gain made on cashing in part or all of your investment unless the fund qualifies as a distributor fund – one which distributes most of its income as dividends. This is to stop investors rolling up income in offshore funds to create capital gains and so reduce their tax bills (see overleaf for details).

If the fund does not count as a distributor fund, enter the gain in box 41. If you have received an equalisation payment from a distributor fund, you should enter the part of the gain taxable as income in box 41. The taxable amount will be shown on the voucher given to you by the fund manager.

Any income paid to you from a non-resident trust at the discretion of the trustees should be entered in box 41.

Tax-saving idea 227

Since 2009–10, the rules for offshore-fund 'distributor status' have been relaxed. Funds are treated as meeting the rules if, instead of distributing most of their income, they report it each year to investors so they in turn can report the income and pay tax on it (see overleaf). As relatively few offshore funds applied for distributor status, this should increase the investment choice available.

Foreign life insurance policies

| 43 | Gains on foreign life insurance policies etc. (excluding the amounts entered in box 13) – *enter the amount of the gain* |

£ ⬜⬜⬜⬜⬜⬜⬜⬜

Give details here of any gains you have made on foreign life insurance policies – whether because the policy has come to an end or because you have
drawn some benefit from it. Enter the number of years you have held the
policy in box 44 and the gain in box 43.

Most such gains are simply added to your taxable income because no
foreign tax has been paid on them. If foreign tax has been deducted, you
may be able to get a 'credit for notional savings rate tax' which means
the gain will be taxed only at the difference between the basic and higher
rates in the same way as a UK life insurance policy gain (p. 217). Enter the
amount of any notional income tax credit in box 45.

Changes to the taxation of offshore funds

Offshore funds are often located in areas where tax treatment is more
favourable than in the UK. The UK authorities cannot control how non-UK
funds are taxed, but can determine how your return from such funds is
treated. The main aim of the offshore funds tax regime, which has operated
since 1984, is to prevent you rolling up income tax-free offshore and then
paying tax only at the capital gains tax rate when you eventually cash in
the investment. This principle is retained, following a major review of the
regime. Key changes came into effect during 2009:

■ from 2009–10 onwards, offshore funds may be reporting funds or non-
reporting. (This replaces the earlier distinction between distributing
and non-distributing funds.) A reporting fund declares its income each
year – some or all of the income may be paid out to investors or it
may be reinvested. To be a reporting fund, the fund must get advance
certification from the Revenue, so you will know at the time you
invest whether or not the fund has this status

■ if you invest in a reporting fund, you must declare your share of the
income on the Foreign income pages of the tax return and pay income
tax on it. This applies whether the income is paid out or reinvested.
When you eventually cash in your investment, any gain or loss comes
within the capital gains tax regime. Any reinvested income that has
already been taxed is deducted in working out your gain or loss

■ if you invest in a non-reporting fund, you do not pay tax on any income while it is rolling up within the fund but, when you eventually cash in the investment, you pay income tax on the full amount of the return, even any part that is really a capital gain

■ from 22 April 2009, dividend distributions from offshore funds come with a non-refundable 10 per cent tax credit in the same way as foreign dividends from shares (see p. 84). Where more than 60 per cent of the fund's assets are bonds and cash, you will instead get an interest distribution

■ from 1 December 2009, these rules apply to all funds that match the characteristics of an offshore fund, regardless of the precise structure (trust, company, and so on).

21

Trusts

6 **Trusts etc.**
Did you receive, or are you treated as having received, income from a trust, settlement or the residue of a deceased person's estate?

Yes ☐   No ☐

If you put a cross in the Yes box at question 6 on page TR2 of the Main tax return, you will need the supplement called Trusts etc. You should give details about taxable income from trusts and other forms of settlement such as a transfer of assets, and from the estates of people who have died. In some cases, you may have to give details of income from trusts you have set up. Even though the money has been paid to someone else, it may be treated as yours.

Do not enter any details in this supplement about income from a 'bare trust' – a trust to which you have an absolute right to both the income and assets. You are treated as the owner of the assets and any income or gains from them. You should enter income from a bare trust in the appropriate sections of the Main tax return and other supplements that deal with the particular type of income concerned.

The documents you need

With a payment from a trust or an estate, the trustees or personal representatives should have given you a form R185 setting out the details. There are different versions of the forms for interest in possession trusts, for other trusts and for estates.

If you have directly or indirectly provided funds for a settlement and are not sure whether the income will be treated as yours, Help Sheet IR270 *Trusts and settlements – income treated as the settlor's* should help. Ask the Orderline (p. 180).

Income from trusts and settlements

Income paid out by trusts and other forms of settlement in 2009–10 comes with a tax credit which reflects the amount of tax already deducted from it or deemed to have been paid on it. What you receive is the net (after-tax) amount of income. To find the gross (before-tax) amount, you need to add back the tax credit. You can find out the amount of the tax credit from certificate R185 or similar statement the trustees should give you.

How trust income is taxed

The amount of the tax credit depends on the type of trust:

- trust with an interest in possession where you have the 'absolute right' to the income from the trust. The tax credit will be at the rate of 20 per cent of the grossed-up amount of interest; 10 per cent of the grossed-up amount of share dividends and unit trust dividend distributions; and for other sorts of income, such as rents or royalties, it will be at the basic rate of tax – 20 per cent for 2009–10

- a discretionary trust where the trustees have discretion about paying out the income. The tax credit will be at the 'rate applicable to trusts', which in 2009–10 is 40 per cent of the grossed-up income or 32.5 per cent for share dividends and distributions. (From 2010–11 the rates applicable to trusts will rise to 50 per cent and 42.5 per cent.)

- accumulation and maintenance trusts – the income also comes with a tax credit of 40 per cent or 32.5 per cent in 2009–10

- trust for a disabled person or minor child following death of a parent – the income may be taxed on the basis of the beneficiary's personal circumstances taking into account their allowances and tax bands.

Review of trust taxation

The government is considering, in future, taxing income from a discretionary trust at 10 or 20 per cent as appropriate rather than 40 per cent (or 50 per cent) where the income is paid out to beneficiaries by 31 December following the year in which the income arose.

If the tax credit, other than the 10 per cent credit on share dividends and similar income, is more than the amount of tax you would have paid if the grossed-up income had come direct to you, you can claim a rebate. For example, if you get interest from a trust and your income – including the grossed-up trust income – is too low to pay tax, you could reclaim all the tax credit which comes with it. With a discretionary trust, anyone not liable to higher rate tax can reclaim part of the tax credits.

Tax-saving idea 228

Reclaim some or all of the tax credit that comes with income from trusts if it is more than you would have paid if the income had come straight to you. Unless you pay tax at the higher rate, you will always be entitled to a rebate on income from a discretionary trust.

Trust income that might be treated as yours

If you have directly or indirectly provided funds for a settlement, the income from those funds may be treated as yours – even though you haven't received it.

Example

Jimmy Hall received £250 from a discretionary trust in 2009–10, which comes with a tax credit of £166.67. He pays tax at no more than the basic rate (even when the grossed-up trust payment of £416.67 is added to his income). So he should have paid tax on the payment at the basic rate of 20 per cent only – a tax bill of 20 per cent of £416.67, or £83.33. He is thus entitled to a rebate of: £166.67 – £83.33 = £83.34.

The sorts of arrangement that may produce an income that would be treated as yours (called 'settlor-interested trusts') include:

■ a trust from which you, your spouse, civil partner or children can benefit

■ a trust that has lent or repaid money to you or your spouse or civil partner

■ a trust where the capital would come back to you if the beneficiaries died before becoming entitled to it.

For more information, get Help Sheet HS270 *Trust and settlements – income treated as the settlor's* from the Revenue Orderline (p. 180).

When your child's income might be treated as yours

This treatment may also apply if you make investments on behalf of your children unless they have reached 18 or they are married – for example, opening a savings account in their names. Any income from such investments is treated as yours unless it is £100 a year or less before tax. This exception applies to gifts from each parent, so a child can have up to £200 a year before tax in income from gifts from both parents without a problem. This treatment does not apply to money you put into child trust funds.

Tax-saving idea 229

If you want to give a child more capital and their income is approaching the limit at which it will be treated as yours, think about gifts in investments such as National Savings & Investments (NS&I) Children's Bonus Bonds, NS&I Certificates which produce a tax-free return or paying into a stakeholder pension scheme for your child. Income produced by sums you pay into your son's or daughter's child trust fund (p. 100) will not be treated as your income.

You can't get round this by giving the funds to someone else who passes them on to your child. You would still have indirectly provided the funds and the income would be yours. The same would be true if you settled some money on a friend's child in return for him doing the same for you.

This income should be included as your own on page TR3 of the Main tax return and not entered on the Trusts etc. pages unless you create a proper trust.

What to enter

Enter the income from trusts in 2009–10 in boxes 1 to 15. Also include here any income from trusts or settlements that is treated as yours, even though you haven't received it.

You don't need to enter the following here:

- scrip dividends or foreign income dividends received from a trust with an interest in possession and paid by UK companies, authorised unit trusts or open-ended investment companies – give details of these on page TR3 of the Main tax return (p. 198)

- income from foreign sources paid to you by a trust with an interest in possession – give details on the Foreign supplementary pages (p. 373)

■ income from a discretionary trust where the trustees are not resident in the UK – this should also go on the Foreign pages.

Discretionary income payment

Discretionary income payment from a trust	
1 Net amount – *after tax taken off* £ ⬚⬚⬚⬚⬚⬚⬚⬚ · 0 0	2 Total payments from settlor-interested trusts £ ⬚⬚⬚⬚⬚⬚⬚⬚ · 0 0

Put the actual income you received – in other words, after deducting tax and ignoring the tax credit – in box 1.

Do not include in box 1 any amounts you received from a settlor-interested trust (the trustees can tell you if this is the case). If you are not the settlor of the settlor-interested trust, put the amounts you receive in box 2. If you are the settlor as well as being a beneficiary, leave boxes 1 and 2 blank and complete boxes 7 to 15.

Non-discretionary income entitlement

Non-discretionary income entitlement from a trust	
3 Net amount of non-savings income - *after tax taken off* £ ⬚⬚⬚⬚⬚⬚⬚⬚ · 0 0	5 Net amount of dividend income - *after tax taken off* £ ⬚⬚⬚⬚⬚⬚⬚⬚ · 0 0
4 Net amount of savings income - *after tax taken off* £ ⬚⬚⬚⬚⬚⬚⬚⬚ · 0 0	6 If you have included in your tax return income from trusts or settlements whose trustees are not resident in the UK for tax purposes, put 'X' in the box ⬚

For income from a trust with an interest in possession on which the tax credit is 20 per cent, put the amount you actually receive in boxes 3 and 4, as appropriate, and dividend income in box 5.

Income chargeable on settlors

If you are the settlor of a settlor-interested trust (or similar non-trust arrangement), income received by the trust will usually be treated as your personal taxable income even if the income is not paid out to you. Give details in boxes 7 to 15. The trustees should be able to give you the figures you need. For more information, get Help Sheet HS270 *Trust and settlements – income treated as the settlor's* from the Revenue Orderline (p. 180).

Income from estates

Income from UK estates

16 Non savings income - *after tax taken off*

£ . 0 0

17 Savings income - *after tax taken off*

£ . 0 0

18 Dividend income - *after tax taken off*

£ . 0 0

19 Non savings income taxed at non-repayable basic rate - *after tax taken off*

£ . 0 0

20 Income taxed at 22% - *after tax taken off* Read page TN X of the notes

£ . 0 0

21 Dividend income taxed at non-payable dividend rate - *after tax taken off*

£ . 0 0

You do not pay income tax on anything you inherit from a dead person. And if you have inherited something which then produces an income, such as money in a bank savings account or properties that produce rent, you should enter the interest or other income in the appropriate part of the Main tax return. You might receive interest along with a legacy because, say, there has been a delay between your inheriting the item and it being handed over. Do not include the interest on these pages – it should be entered in box 1 on the Main tax return.

However, you should give details in this section of the tax return of any income you receive from the estate that has been accrued while the estate is being wound up by the personal representatives – the executors or administrators. You would be entitled to this income if you were a residuary beneficiary – the person or one of the people who gets what is left after all the specific bequests and legacies have been made.

Such income will come with a tax credit in the same way as a trust with an interest in possession. For most types of income, this tax will be repayable if it is more than you would have paid; but the tax is not repayable for some types of income such as gains on life insurance policies and UK dividends.

The statement supplied by the personal representatives – tax certificate R185 (Estate income) – will show you the rate the income has been taxed at and whether it is repayable. Enter the details for 2009–10 in boxes 16 to 21. Give the name of the estate and the total amount paid to you in box 25 (*Any other information*) on the same page.

In some cases, income accrued during the life of the dead person and paid into the estate after their death will come to you after being taken into account in calculating the inheritance tax bill on the estate. There is a special tax relief that stops you having to pay higher rate tax on such income – ask your tax inspector for details.

Income from foreign estates

22	Foreign estate income		23	Relief for UK tax already accounted for
£ · 0 0			£ · 0 0	

If you get income from a foreign estate, it will not have borne full UK tax – either because the personal representatives are outside the UK tax net or because the estate is that of someone who died while domiciled outside the UK and has income from non-UK sources. Enter the full amount of such income in box 22.

If the foreign estate has some income from UK sources, it will have paid some UK tax. You can claim relief for this UK tax. Use the working sheet on pages TN5 or TN6 to work out the amount you can reclaim and enter it in box 23.

Foreign tax paid

24	Foreign tax for which foreign tax credit relief has not been claimed
£ · 0 0	

If you have been paid income from an estate which has already been taxed in a foreign country, you may end up paying two lots of tax on it: tax in the foreign country and tax in the UK. You may be able to reduce the amount of UK tax you pay on the income to reflect the foreign tax paid – this is known as tax credit relief.

To claim tax credit relief – which will usually be worthwhile – leave box 24 blank and make your claim on the Foreign supplementary pages (p. 376).

If you don't want to claim tax credit relief – which can be complicated – you can instead deduct the foreign tax you have paid from the income. Enter the amount in box 24.

22

Capital gains

| 7 | Capital gains summary |

> If you disposed of any chargeable assets (including, for example, stocks, shares, units in a unit trust, land and property, goodwill in a business), or had any chargeable gains, or you wish to claim an allowable loss or make any other claim or election, read pages TRG 5 of the guide to decide if you have to fill in the *Capital gains summary* page.
>
> Do you need to complete the *Capital gains summary* page?
>
> Yes ☐ No ☐

If you made capital gains of more than £10,100 in 2009–10, disposed of chargeable assets worth more than £40,400 or want to claim capital gains tax reliefs, you should have put a cross in the Yes box on page TR2 of the Main tax return and you need the supplement called Capital gains summary. This supplement asks you about taxable gains you have made on selling assets, such as shares, unit trusts and property. You may also have to report a gain even though you haven't sold something – for example, if you gave it away or it was lost or stolen. If you have made a loss on such assets, you should also give details here, since it may reduce your overall tax bill now or in the future.

You do not have to report any gains that are exempt from capital gains tax – see the list in Chapter 9 on pp. 128–129 – and they do not count towards the £40,400 limit for deciding whether or not you need this supplement.

This supplement is deceptively short. There are now just two pages to complete with summary information about all your gains and losses. But you must also send the Revenue a copy of your calculations for every transaction included in the summary. There is a working sheet on page CGN19 of the notes that come with the supplement. Using this is optional and it is suitable only for simpler transactions – for example, it does not cover all the calculations you need to make if you are disposing of just part of a holding of shares or unit trusts.

In this chapter, we guide you through the calculations you need to make and what to enter in the boxes on the Capital gains summary. The capital gains tax rules were greatly changed from 6 April 2008 (see Chapter 9) and completing this supplement is now far less daunting than in the past. However, we suggest you still refer back to Chapter 9 for additional information on claiming reliefs and allowances to minimise your capital gains tax bill.

The documents you need

You will need details of anything you have spent on buying or selling or maintaining the value of assets. With shares and unit trusts, you also need any paperwork relating to share issues while you owned them or company reorganisations.

For assets owned on 31 March 1982, you will also need details of their value on that date (p. 133). Use catalogues, press advertisements or stock market share price records to value them.

If you do not buy or sell an asset, but acquire or dispose of it in some other way (for example, a gift), you will usually need to use the market value of the asset in your calculations. Where there is a formal market, for example shares traded on a stock exchange, you can usually get the exact market value from a historical valuation service (see, for example, www.london stockexchange.com for shares traded on the London Stock Exchange). If there is no formal market for buying and selling an asset, it may be difficult to arrive at the correct value. You will need to tell the Revenue how you have valued the asset and the Revenue, which uses its own specialist valuers, may challenge your figures. We strongly advise that you get an independent, professional valuation whenever possible. The cost of getting a valuation can be deducted as an allowable expense when you work out the tax due.

With assets that are jointly owned, you need enter only your share of any gains. With a husband and wife or civil partners, the gain or loss is split 50:50 between them unless they have told their tax inspectors that the asset is not owned equally (p. 58).

Tax-saving idea 230

If you include estimates or valuations in your tax return, try to get a proper valuation from an independent, professional valuer. Give full details in the Additional information box explaining who carried out the valuation, their qualifications and the basis on which the valuation was made. This should be sufficient to stave off a discovery enquiry following the rules established in the *Langham* v *Veltema* case (p. 48). This will give you the certainty that your tax affairs for 2009–10 are finalised once a year has passed from the date you filed the return.

The working sheet

You will find a working sheet on page CGN19 of the notes accompanying the Capital gains supplement. Using the sheet is optional. You may prefer to write out your own calculations, but you will still need to follow the same steps in the same order. Alternatively, you can send in printouts from any spreadsheet or software that you or your tax adviser use, provided it clearly contains all the information the Revenue requires.

If you use the working sheet, you need a copy for each transaction that you are reporting. The sheet covers only straightforward calculations. In particular, it does not deal with the extra sums you need if you are disposing of part of a holding of shares or unit trusts. See p. 145 for details of these rules and the calculations you need.

Description of the asset

Description of asset *for example, type and number of shares sold or address of property*

In this box, you need to give a detailed description of the asset including:

- ▓ what it is, for example, Tesco plc ordinary shares or Schroder UK Mid-250 Fund Retail A Accumulation Units. If you are selling a property, give the address and whether it is freehold or leasehold

- ▓ how many. Unless it is a single asset, such as a property, the number you are selling, for example, the number of shares

- ▓ any other relevant information. For example, if shares are unquoted, if you disposed of the asset to a connected person (p. 132) and who this person is, or if this is a gain or loss by a settlor-interested trust that is treated as yours (p. 381).

Where you disposed of shares or similar assets, you should normally count all the disposals of the same class of shares on the same day as a single disposal (but if some were, say, to a connected person, you will need to treat these separately).

Disposal details

Date of sale *DD MM YYYY*

Disposal/sale proceeds or market value *if appropriate*   A £

Incidental costs of disposal/sale   B £

Net disposal proceeds *box A minus box B*   C £

Give the date you sold, gave away or otherwise disposed of the asset and the disposal proceeds (final value). If you sold it on the open market to an unconnected person, enter the amount you received. In other cases, you need to enter the market value. If the amount you put in box A is an estimate, write 'estimate' beside the box and describe how you have reached this value, including a description of the independence and qualifications of anyone you asked to provide a valuation. Attach a copy of any formal valuation you were given.

If you have been given the right to something in the future in return for the disposal, this should be included as part of the proceeds unless it would be taxed as income (for example, dividends or royalties). If it is not clear what you will get in future – as with a share of any future profits – include an estimate in the disposal proceeds and explain what you have done. When that uncertain part is finally paid, this will count as another disposal (because, for example, the right to a share of profits will have been converted to real cash). There will then be another capital gain or loss to report at that time. If a loss, you can claim repayment of part of the earlier tax bill.

See p. 132 for examples of the incidental costs you can claim as allowable expenses. Deduct box B from box A and write the answer in box C.

Acquisition details

Cost or 31 March 1982 value *see page CGN 5*	D £
Incidental costs of acquisition	E £
Improvement costs	F £
Total costs *boxes D + E + F*	G £

Give the date you acquired the asset and the cost (initial value). If you bought it on the open market from an unconnected person, this is the amount you paid. In other cases, you need to enter the market value. Once again, you need to make clear if this is an estimate, how it was arrived at and to attach a copy of any formal valuation. Chapter 9 (p. 132) explains the allowable expenses you can deduct in boxes E and F.

Follow the instructions to arrive at your gain or loss in box H of the worksheet.

Elections and reliefs

Capital gains elections or reliefs *not the annual exempt amount* and description	I £

In box I, you need to put any amount that you are claiming should be tax-free or on which tax should be deferred because of any of a variety of elections and reliefs that you can claim. Do not include here any allowable losses or your annual capital gains tax allowance (which is deducted on the Capital gains summary pages). Reliefs you can claim here include:

■ private residence relief on your only or main home (see Chapter 6). If the relief applies to your whole home, you do not need to report the gain at all. But if, for example, you have used you home partly for business, you may need to enter the relevant amount of this relief in box I

■ hold-over relief (p. 155). You may claim this if you are making a lifetime gift to a trust or of business assets

■ deferral relief (p. 153) if you are reinvesting the gain in shares through the enterprise investment scheme

- letting relief (p. 77) if you are disposing of a property that has at some time been your main home, which you let out

- dependent relative relief (p. 73) if you have disposed of a home that you provided for an eligible relative since before 6 April 1988

- negligible value claim on shares or units that the Revenue has declared are eligible for this treatment

- entrepreneurs' relief (p. 156) if you have sold a business or shares in it, or assets used in a business you have closed down

- roll-over relief (p. 157) if this is a gain on an asset used in your business, including a furnished holiday letting business and you have replaced or intend to replace it with another business asset. Give full details by completing the form in Help Sheet HS290 *Business asset roll-over relief* and attach it to your Capital gains summary.

The maximum amount you can put in box I is the value in box H. Deduct the amount in box I from the amount in box H to find your net gain or loss on the disposal.

The Capital gains supplement

There are four main sections to the Capital gains supplement plus an *Any other information* box. You are asked to complete the second, third and fourth sections before filling in the *Summary of your enclosed computations* at the start of the form.

Listed shares and securities

16 Number of disposals	19 Gains in the year, before losses
17 Disposal proceeds	20 If you are making any claim or election, put 'X' in the box
18 Allowable costs (including purchase price)	21 If your computations include any estimates or valuations, put 'X' in the box

In this section summarise the details from your working sheets (or equivalent calculations) that relate to disposals of listed shares or securities, which means:

■ shares or securities of a company that are quoted on the London Stock Exchange (including its subsidiary techMARK) or the quoted section of the PLUS-Listed market throughout the period you held them. This does not include UK shares quoted on the Alternative Investment Market or the PLUS-quoted market

■ shares or securities of a company listed on an overseas recognised stock exchange throughout the period you held them. This includes Nasdaq. It does not include shares quoted on some European junior markets, such as the Nouveau Marché and Neue Markt Frankfurt which should go in the Unlisted shares and securities section on page CG2 of the supplement. For a list of recognised exchanges, see www.hmrc.gov.uk/fid/rse.htm

■ units in a unit trust or shares in a company that was an open-ended investment company (OEIC) that was UK authorised throughout the period you held them.

If you have been using the working sheets in the notes that come with the supplement, your entries should be:

■ box 16: number of disposals. The number of working sheets you completed for listed shares and securities

■ box 17: disposal proceeds. The sum of the entries at box A on the relevant working sheets

■ box 18: allowable costs. The sum of boxes B, D, E and F on the relevant working sheets

■ box 19: gains before losses. The sum of box H on the relevant working sheets (but in each case only where box H is greater than zero) less the sum of any reliefs claimed in box I

■ box 20: claims or elections. If you have filled in box I on any of the relevant working sheets put a cross in this box

■ box 21: estimates or valuations. Put a cross here if any of the figures on the relevant working sheets has been estimated or is based on a valuation. Make sure you have included details on the working sheets concerned.

Unlisted shares and securities

Now give exactly the same details as described above for *Listed shares and securities* for shares, bonds and so on that do not fit the description of listed securities opposite in boxes 22 to 27.

Property and other assets and gains

| 32 | Attributed gains where personal losses cannot be set-off |

£ [   ] . [0][0]

Give exactly the same details as described above for *Listed shares and securities* for property and any other assets in boxes 28 to 31 and 33 to 34.

There is also space in this section (box 32) for certain gains made by a trust that are being treated as your personal gains but which are not eligible to be reduced by any capital losses that you personally have made. You may have gains of this type if you are the settlor of a settlor-interest trust (p. 381) or if you are the beneficiary of an offshore trust. For more information, see Revenue Help Sheets HS294 *Trusts and capital gains tax* and HS299 *Non-resident trusts and capital gains tax.*

Summary of your enclosed computations

Finally, you can return to page CG1 of the supplement to summarise your gains and losses for the year and complete the calculation of your taxable gains.

Gains and losses

| 3 | Total gains in the year, before losses |

£ [   ] . [0][0]

| 4 | Total losses of the year – *enter '0' if there are none* |

£ [   ] . [0][0]

| 5 | Losses brought forward and used in the year |

£ [   ] . [0][0]

In box 3 put the total of the amounts you have entered in boxes 19, 25, 31 and 32 on this supplement.

Note that if you have made a loss on an asset you sold or gave to a connected person, you can set that loss only against gains on disposals to the same person. This is called a 'clogged loss'. For capital gains tax purposes, a connected person is broadly your spouse, civil partner, your business partner and their spouse or civil partner, a relative of you or these other people (meaning a sister, brother, parents, grandparents and other ancestors, children, grandchildren and other descendants), the spouse or civil partner of any of these relatives, the trustees of a trust where you are the settlor.

You must set any losses you made in 2009–10 against gains for the year (but if your losses exceed you gains, the excess is carried forward to use in future years). You must also deduct any carried-forward losses but only to the extent that they reduce your total net gains for the year to no more than £10,100 (the amount of your tax-free allowance). See Chapter 9 for more information.

Tax-saving idea 231

Normally a capital loss must be set against gains made in the same tax year even if that means some or all of your tax-free allowance (£10,100 in 2009–10) is wasted. However, a loss made on a disposal to a 'connected person' (see opposite) must be carried forward until it can be set against gains on disposals to the same connected person. Therefore, you can avoid wasting your tax-free allowance by selling or giving the loss-making asset to a connected person (which could include a trust of which you are the settlor).

In box 4 put the total of all the amounts you entered at box 8 on the working sheets you completed or your equivalent calculations if they showed a loss. Include any clogged losses to connected people here in box 4, but keep your own note of the clogged losses you are carrying forward so that, in future, you set them only against gains on disposals to the same person.

In box 5, put the amount of losses made in earlier years that you are now claiming relief for.

Your tax-free allowance

6 | Total gains, after losses but before the annual exempt amount

£ [   ] . [0][0]

7 | Annual exempt amount

£ [   ] . [0][0]

8 | Net chargeable gains (box 6 minus box 7) – but if box 7 is more than box 6, leave blank

£ [   ] . [0][0]

The amount you put in box 6 will normally be box 3 less boxes 4 and 5. The first part of your taxable gains each year is tax-free (£10,100 in 2009–10) so deduct this from box 6. If the answer is less than zero, leave box 8 blank – you have no capital gains tax to pay. Otherwise, put the answer in box 8 and, for most people, this is the taxable amount for 2009–10.

The exception is where you have received or are treated as having received gains from an offshore trust or a trust with dual residency. If this applies to you, you will be taxed on the sum of the gains in boxes 8 and 9.

Capital losses carried forward or used in other ways

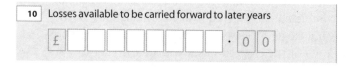

10 | Losses available to be carried forward to later years

£ [   ] . [0][0]

If your losses for 2009–10 come to more than your gains or you have been unable to use up all of the losses you were carrying forward from earlier years, you will have unused losses to carry forward to 2010–11 and beyond. The figure you put in box 10 should be the total of all your unused losses but keep your own note of the following losses so that they can be used correctly in following years:

■ disposals to connected persons (p. 132). These losses can be set only against gains on disposals to the same person

■ assets transferred to you after 15 June 1999 by trustees when you become absolutely entitled to settled property. These losses can be set only against gains on the same asset or an asset derived from that asset and have to be used before any other losses

■ unused losses claimed for 1996–97 and later years. These can be carried forward indefinitely but have to be claimed within four years after the end of the tax year in which they arise. In practice, if the losses are reported in your tax return, that amounts to a claim and you do not need to take any further action. These losses are used first in preference to losses made in earlier years

■ unused losses claimed for 1995–96 and earlier years. These can be carried forward indefinitely but, in addition, there are no rules about formally claiming them with any time limit – they can be claimed at any time.

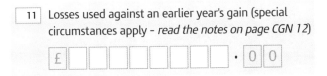

11 Losses used against an earlier year's gain (special circumstances apply - *read the notes on page CGN 12*)

£ [   ] · [0][0]

You cannot normally carry losses back to set against gains in earlier tax years (box 11). The main exception is where personal representatives, clearing up the estate of someone who has died and completing the deceased's tax return for the part of a tax year up to the date of death, can carry unused losses back to earlier tax years and effectively claim a tax rebate for the estate. For further information, see Help Sheet HS282 *Death, personal representatives and legatees.*

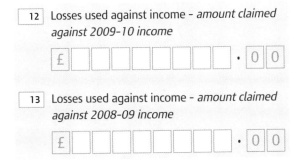

12 Losses used against income - *amount claimed against 2009-10 income*

£ [   ] · [0][0]

13 Losses used against income - *amount claimed against 2008-09 income*

£ [   ] · [0][0]

If you have made losses on shares in unquoted trading companies (see p. 102), you can set them off against income from the same tax year or the previous tax year by putting the appropriate amount in box 12 and/or 13. For more information, see Help Sheet HS286 *Negligible value claims and income tax losses for shares you have subscribed for in qualifying trading companies and IR297 Enterprise investment scheme and capital gains tax.*

Income losses set against gains

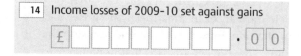

In box 14, enter the amount of any losses from your business, partnership or furnished holiday lettings (pp. 339, 347 and 358), post-cessation losses (p. 239) or post-employment deductions (p. 240) reported elsewhere in this tax return that you are setting against your capital gains for 2009–10.

Entrepreneurs' relief

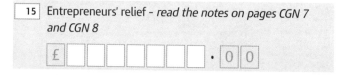

Finally, if you have claimed any entrepreneurs' relief in 2009–10 note the amount here in box 15 (maximum £1 million up to 5 April 2010). From 6 April 2010, you have a lifetime limit of £2 million (see p. 156) so keep your own running total of the amounts you claim over the year so you can see how much unused relief you have left. For more information, see Help Sheet HS275 *Entrepreneurs' relief.*

23

Non-residence

Residence, remittance basis etc.
Were you, for all or part of the year to 5 April 2010, one or more of the following - not resident, not ordinarily resident or not domiciled in the UK and claiming the remittance basis; or dual resident in the UK and another country?

Yes ☐   No ☐

If you are a resident of the UK, you are usually liable for UK tax on all your income whether it comes from within the UK or abroad. But, if you count as a non-resident, there is no UK tax on your income from abroad, only on any income which originates in the UK. And if you are resident but non-domiciled or not-ordinarily resident, you may be able to claim the remittance basis (p. 368), which in the past has let you escape tax on your foreign income and gains unless you bring them into the UK – but see *Changes since 6 April 2008* overleaf.

If you want to claim non-residence (or non-domicile) for 2009–10, you need to fill in the Non-residence supplement which you can get through the Orderline (p. 180). You are likely to need this if:

- you are normally a UK resident but you are working abroad for an extended period
- you have been a UK resident but you are going to live abroad permanently or indefinitely – for example because you are retiring abroad
- you have been resident elsewhere but you are based in the UK for now or you have returned for permanent residence.

This guide cannot give you all the detail you may need so you should consult a professional adviser. See also Revenue booklet HMRC6 *Residence, Domicile and the Remittance Basis* which applies from 6 April 2009 onwards or IR20 *Residents and non-residents etc*, if you need to review your position in earlier tax years. Important changes to the rules regarding domicile and residence came into effect from 6 April 2008. They are summarised in the box below.

Residency is not defined in the tax legislation, but it has been the subject of much case law. Broadly, it means the place where you usually live. Because different countries use different criteria to decide who is resident, it is possible to count as a resident of more than one country at the same time, in which case you could pay two lots of tax on the same income. However, the UK has double-taxation agreements with many countries to avoid this situation.

In general, payment of UK taxes depends on whether or not you were resident during the particular tax year in question. Occasionally, it may hinge on where you are ordinarily resident. Again, there is no hard and fast definition, but basically your ordinary residence is the country you are resident in year after year, which you use as your base, returning to it for extended periods, and probably where you have an established home.

Your domicile can be the key to whether or not there is tax on foreign income and gains you receive and any inheritance tax to pay on your estate when you die. Your country of domicile is the place which you consider to be your permanent home and where you would intend to end your days. You can have only one country of domicile and it is not necessarily the country in which you are resident or ordinarily resident. Claims for foreign domicile should be made as soon as possible on form DOM1.

Note that even if you are non-resident for tax purposes, you might still be able to claim the UK personal tax allowances to set against your income from UK sources, for example, if you are a citizen of a country within the European Economic Area (this includes the UK), a Crown employee (or a widow or widower of someone who was a Crown employee) or employed by a UK missionary service. However, the personal allowance is no longer available to Commonwealth citizens from 6 April 2010.

Changes since 6 April 2008

> ▪ Days when you are present at midnight in the UK count towards the 183-day and 91-day tests – see pp. 404–405. (Up to 5 April 2008, days of travel were not included.) But there is an exception for passengers in transit.

■ If you are resident in the UK but not domiciled or ordinarily resident here, you face extra tax charges if you want to use the remittance basis (p. 368) and your unremitted foreign income and gains come to £2,000 a year or more. You do not qualify for a personal allowance against income tax or the yearly tax-free allowance for capital gains tax. In addition, if you are aged 18 or over and have been UK resident for more than seven out of the past ten years, you have to pay an extra yearly tax charge of £30,000, which is collected through self assessment in the usual way. You can choose which foreign income or gains are the subject of the £30,000 charge and set the charge against any foreign tax due.

Tax-saving idea 232

If you are a long-term UK resident but not UK domiciled (for example, you have married and settled in the UK but still consider another country to be your permanent home), from 2008–09 onwards, you may have to choose between:

■ paying UK tax each year on your foreign income and gains as they arise whether or not you bring the income and gains into the UK, or

■ paying no UK tax on your foreign income and gains but losing your personal allowance (worth up to £2,590 to a higher-rate taxpayer in tax savings in 2010–11); losing your capital gains tax allowance (worth up to £1,818 in tax savings in 2010–11); and paying an extra tax bill of £30,000.

Choose the option which results in the lower tax bill. You can choose a different option each year and this may be worth doing if your foreign income and gains vary a lot or you have a big gain in one year only (say, from the sale of a property abroad). Members of a couple each make their own choice – they do not have to be the same.

How do you count as being non-resident?

If you have generally been considered as a UK resident, to count as non-resident for tax purposes, you need to pass all four of the following tests:

■ the motive test

■ the absent for a whole tax year test

■ the 183 days' test

■ the 91 days' test.

The notes with the Non-residence supplement include a calculator to help you to work out whether you pass all these tests.

The motive test

You will pass this test if you leave the UK to work full-time, providing the other tests are also met. Whether or not your job is full-time is judged, first, by comparing your hours with the norm in the UK, but if your job is less structured it will be assessed on its own merits and in the light of what is normal for your type of work and the country you are going to. You could also count as working full-time if you have two or more part-time jobs.

If you count as non-resident because of your work abroad, your wife or husband, if they go with you, will also count as non-resident, providing they pass the other tests.

Another way to pass the test is if you go abroad to live permanently or at least indefinitely. The Revenue will want evidence that this is your intention – for example, that you have bought a home abroad or you are going to marry someone in another country. If you still have a UK home, it wants to know how that fits with your plans to live overseas. Once you've lived abroad for three years, it will be accepted that you are non-resident.

If you can't pass this test at the time you go away, the situation can be reviewed later on, if new evidence of your motive becomes available or once you have been abroad for three years.

The absent for a whole tax year test

To count as non-resident for a tax year, if you work abroad, your job must last for at least a whole tax year and you must be out of the country for the whole tax year or longer, except for visits within the other rules (see opposite). Similarly, if you go to live abroad permanently or indefinitely, you must be out of the country for at least a whole tax year.

In the year you leave and the year you return, you can count as non-resident for just part of the year, provided that year is part of a longer period of non-residency. If you want to claim this split-year treatment, put a cross in box 3 on page NR1 of the Non-residence supplement.

The 183 days' test

You will always count as resident for the tax year if you spend 183 days or more in the UK. There are no exceptions to this rule. For example, if you make visits back home during a period working abroad, the total of your visits during any tax year must come to less than 183 days if you are not to lose your status as a non-resident. For the purposes of this rule and the next, the days on which you travel do not count as days spent in the UK if they occurred before 6 April 2008, but your day of arrival does count from that day onwards.

The 91 days' test

In addition to the 183 days' test, the average time you spend in the UK must come to less than 91 days in a tax year. This is worked out over the period since you left until you have been away for four tax years. After that it is worked out over the most recent four tax years. You are allowed to ignore periods you had to spend in the UK for reasons beyond your control – for example, because someone in your family was ill. As with the 183-day test, days of travel do not count if they occurred before 6 April 2008 but the day you arrive does count towards the 91 days from that date onwards (though there is no statutory basis for this practice).

Warning

Bear in mind that you have to pass all four of the above tests. For example, the 91-day and 183-day rules apply only to temporary visits back to the UK where the Revenue is satisfied that the motive test has been met and you have permanently left the UK. In a recent case (*Gaines-Cooper* v *Revenue & Customs* [2006]), the Special Commissioners decided that a businessman who had a permanent home in the Seychelles was still UK resident as well because, for example, he maintained a home and club memberships in the UK, his son had attended school in the UK and he made regular trips to the UK to socialise and take part in sporting activities. Taking all the evidence as a whole, the Revenue successfully argued that Mr Gaines-Cooper had not left the UK and therefore the 91-day test was not relevant. The Court of Appeal subsequently upheld this approach.

Mobile workers

You may have the sort of job that takes you on frequent trips abroad, possibly working abroad all week and just returning home to the UK for weekends. Even if you pass the 183 and 91 days' tests, the Revenue takes the view that you are unlikely to count as non-resident, if your home and domestic life continue to be UK-based. It argues that, in these circumstances, you have not genuinely left the UK. In the past, the Revenue might have granted non-resident status to people in these circumstances and it has indicated that it might review these cases if there is reason to believe that the earlier decision was not based on a full disclosure of all the relevant facts. Even if you do succeed in being classed as non-resident, bear in mind that since 6 April 2008, days when you are in the UK at midnight count towards the 183- and 91-day tests.

How do you count as being non-domiciled in the UK?

Your domicile is relevant only if it will affect the tax you must pay, so unless you fall into one of the following categories, you do not need to fill in boxes 22 to 26. The tax areas that may be affected are where:

- you have income or gains from foreign investments that you will not be bringing in full into the UK

- you are claiming UK tax relief on contributions to a foreign pension scheme made out of earnings from a non-UK resident employer

- the costs of travelling between the UK and your normal home have been paid by your employer

- you worked abroad for a non-UK employer and have not brought all the earnings into the UK.

Tax-saving ideas 233–235

If you go to work or live abroad, make sure your trips back home average less than 91 days a year and come to less than 183 days in any single tax year to avoid paying UK taxes on your overseas income.

Taking a long lease of three years on a home abroad would help to show that you intended to live abroad permanently.

If you are returning permanently to the UK after a period of non-residence abroad and you have been saving through an offshore roll-up fund, make sure you sell your investment before you become a UK resident again. If you don't, you will become liable for tax on the rolled-up income.

You can have only one domicile at a time and there are three ways in which it can be established: by birth, by dependency or by choice. From birth, you normally have the domicile of your father – that is not necessarily the same as the country in which you were born. If the domicile of the person on whom you are dependent changes, so will yours. Similarly, if you become dependent on someone else of a different domicile, your own domicile will fall into line with that. Women no longer acquire their husbands' domicile on marriage. Once you reach the age of 16, you have the right to choose a new domicile but the change is not easily made. You would need to show that you had settled in the new country of domicile with a view to staying there permanently. Your home, business interests, social and family ties, and the form of any will would all be relevant, but other factors could also be just as important.

If you are a woman who married before 1 January 1974, you automatically acquired the domicile of your husband. This is unaffected by subsequent divorce or bereavement.

Appendix A

Tax-free income

Income from a job

Check with your employer if you are uncertain about whether any of these forms of income is taxable:

- work-related expenses reimbursed to you by your employer and covered by an agreement with the Revenue that they do not need to be declared

- some fringe benefits, such as canteen meals, mileage allowance up to the authorised rates if you use your own transport for business and certain help with childcare costs

- foreign service allowances paid to diplomats and other servants of the Crown

- goods and services your employer lets you have cheaply

- miners' free coal or cash allowances in lieu of coal

- long-service awards as long as they are not in cash and are within set limits

- awards from approved suggestions schemes

- payments for moving because of your job, within set limits

- genuine personal gifts – for example, wedding presents

- compensation due to medical reasons linked to service in the armed forces, whether or not you continue in service

- armed forces operational allowance paid to members of the armed forces serving in some areas, such as Iraq and Afghanistan

- payments under the Armed Forces Council Tax Relief scheme.

Income on leaving a job

Check with your ex-employer

■ gratuities from the armed forces

■ payments relating to certain foreign service

■ lump-sum compensation for an injury or disability that means you can no longer do the job

■ tax-free lump sum instead of part of a pension and certain other *ex gratia* payments on retirement or death

■ up to £30,000 of other compensation on leaving a job, including statutory redundancy payments, pay in lieu of notice (provided receiving it was not part of your contract of employment or customary) and counselling and outplacement services.

Pensions and benefits

Check with the organisation paying the pension or benefit

■ pension credit, Christmas bonus with state pension, winter fuel payment, cold weather payment

■ war widows' and orphans' pensions and equivalent overseas pensions

■ bereavement payment

■ certain compensation payments and pensions paid to victims of Nazi persecution

■ war disablement pensions

■ additional pensions paid to holders of some bravery awards, such as the Victoria Cross

■ the part of a pension paid to a former employee who retires because of a disability caused by injury at work or a work-related illness that is in excess of the pension paid to an employee who retires on normal ill-health grounds

■ income support paid to single parents with a young child and those staying at home to look after a severely disabled person. Part of income support paid to unemployed people may be tax-free – see your statement of taxable benefits

■ jobfinder's grant, most youth training scheme allowances, employment rehabilitation and training allowances, back to work bonus, return to work credit, in work credit, in work emergency discretionary fund payments and in work emergency fund payments

■ housing benefit and council tax benefit

■ improvement and renovation grants for your home

■ payments from the social fund

■ maternity allowance (but statutory maternity pay is taxable)

■ child benefit, health in pregnancy grant, school uniform grants

■ additions for dependent children paid with a state pension or social security benefit

■ guardian's allowance

■ student grants and educational maintenance allowance

■ income-related employment and support allowance

■ industrial disablement benefits

■ disability living allowance

■ attendance allowance

■ working tax credit and child tax credit, although the amount you get is reduced if your before-tax income exceeds certain thresholds.

Investment income

If in doubt, check with the organisation paying the income

■ interest on National Savings & Investment (NS&I) Certificates (and Ulster Savings Certificates, if you normally live in Northern Ireland), NS&I Children's Bonus Bonds

■ interest and terminal bonuses on bank and building society Save-As-You-Earn (SAYE) schemes

■ income from savings accounts and bond-based investments held in an individual savings account (ISA) or child trust fund (CTF)

■ income from share-based ISAs, CTFs and certain friendly society plans counts as tax-free and does not have to be included on your tax return but, since 6 April 2004, the income has in effect been taxed at 10 per cent

■ dividends on ordinary shares in a venture capital trust

■ part of the income paid by an annuity (other than a pension annuity)

■ saving gateway interest and bonus

■ loan interest paid to members of a credit union.

Other tax-free income

If in doubt, check with the organisation paying out the money

■ what you receive in maintenance payments from a former spouse

■ up to £4,250 a year of income from letting out a furnished room in your only or main home – the Rent a Room scheme

■ gambling winnings (as long as you are not a bookmaker or similar)

■ lottery winnings

■ premium bond prizes

■ income from qualifying life insurance policies that pay out on death – for example, mortgage protection policies, family income benefit policies

■ income from insurance policies to cover mortgage payments if you are sick or unemployed

■ income from income protection policies you yourself pay for, creditor insurance and some long-term care policies

■ pay-outs under some accident insurance policies (usually group ones)

■ interest on a delayed settlement for damages for personal injury or death

■ compensation for being wrongly sold a personal pension (but not any interest element of compensation for endowment mis-selling)

■ compensation from UK and foreign banks to Holocaust victims and their heirs for assets frozen during World War Two

■ interest on a tax rebate

■ foster carer's and Shared Lives carer's receipts up to £10,000 a year per household plus £200 a week per child under 11 and £250 a week for children over age 11 and adults

■ providing you are not carrying on a trade, income you make from putting into the national grid surplus power from domestic solar panels, wind turbines and other microgeneration methods.

Appendix B

Converting net income to gross

Some forms of income are paid net – after some tax has been deducted from them. For example, 20 per cent tax is normally deducted from the interest on savings accounts in banks and building societies before it is paid out to you or added to your account (unless it is a tax-exempt special savings account or individual savings account). In working out your tax bill, you may need to know how much the income was before the tax was deducted – the gross income.

You can find the gross income by grossing-up the net income using the ready reckoners overleaf. The first is for grossing-up income which comes with a tax credit of 10 per cent – share dividends and most unit trust distributions. From 2008–9, the basic rate fell to 20 per cent and this is also the rate of tax deducted from most savings income in 2009–10 and earlier years, so that is the rate in the second ready reckoner. The third is for grossing-up income where tax has been deducted in 2007–08 or earlier years at the basic rate of 22 per cent (or payments where tax relief has been deducted at 22 per cent).

If the tax rates change the tables here will not apply, but you can use the following formula to work out the grossed-up income:

$$\text{Amount paid to you net} \times \left(\frac{100}{100\% - \text{rate of tax}} \right)$$

So, looking forward to the tax changes from 2010–11, if you might receive income from a discretionary trust with tax at 50 per cent deducted and if you receive £1,000 after tax, you could find the grossed-up amount as follows:

$$£1,000 \times 100/(100 - 50) = £2,000$$

Grossing-up at 10 per cent

Net amount £	Gross amount £	Net amount £	Gross amount £	Net amount £	Gross amount £
1	1.11	10	11.11	100	111.11
2	2.22	20	22.22	200	222.22
3	3.33	30	33.33	300	333.33
4	4.44	40	44.44	400	444.44
5	5.56	50	55.56	500	555.56
6	6.67	60	66.67	600	666.67
7	7.78	70	77.78	700	777.78
8	8.89	80	88.89	800	888.89
9	10.00	90	100.00	900	1,000.00
				1,000	1,111.11

Grossing-up at 20 per cent

Net amount £	Gross amount £	Net amount £	Gross amount £	Net amount £	Gross amount £
1	1.25	10	12.50	100	125.00
2	2.50	20	25.00	200	250.00
3	3.75	30	37.50	300	375.00
4	5.00	40	50.00	400	500.00
5	6.25	50	62.50	500	625.00
6	7.50	60	75.00	600	750.00
7	8.75	70	87.50	700	875.00
8	10.00	80	100.00	800	1,000.00
9	11.25	90	112.50	900	1,125.00
				1,000	1,250.00

Grossing-up at 22 per cent

Net amount £	Gross amount £	Net amount £	Gross amount £	Net amount £	Gross amount £
1	1.28	10	12.82	100	128.21
2	2.56	20	25.64	200	256.41
3	3.85	30	38.46	300	384.61
4	5.13	40	51.28	400	512.82
5	6.41	50	64.10	500	641.03
6	7.69	60	76.92	600	769.23
7	8.97	70	89.74	700	897.44
8	10.26	80	102.56	800	1,025.64
9	11.54	90	115.38	900	1,153.85
				1,000	1,282.0

Appendix C

The short tax return

You may be one of the 1.5 million people invited to complete a short four-page tax return for 2009–10 instead of the normal full return.

Check you have the right form

The short return is designed for people with relatively straightforward tax affairs. The Revenue will have selected you on the basis of your previous tax returns, but the onus is on you to check that this is correct. If your tax affairs have become more complicated since last year, you may need a full return instead which you can get from the Revenue Orderline (p. 180).

For example, you cannot use the short return if in 2009–10 you:

- were repaying a student loan (p. 186) or want to send in your own tax calculation
- received a state pension lump sum (p. 206)
- received a lump sum from your employer or on a leaving a job unless it counts as a tax-free payment under £30,000 (p. 278)
- were a company director
- received shares from an employee share scheme or exercised share options (see Chapter 16)
- were self-employed and your turnover was more than £30,000, you had more than one business, you changed your accounting date or you want to claim businesses losses against non-business income or income for an earlier year (see Chapter 17)
- were in partnership (see Chapter 18)

- had income from property of more than £15,000, from more than one property or from furnished holiday lettings (see Chapter 19)

- received life insurance gains (p. 217), had income from abroad (see Chapter 20), from a trust, from the estate of someone who has died (see Chapter 21)

- you are not both resident and domiciled in the UK (see Chapter 23).

You can still use the short return if you have any capital gains or losses to declare. In that case, you will also need to complete the normal capital gains supplement that goes with the full return (see Chapter 22). You can either download the supplement from the Revenue website (www.hmrc. gov.uk/sa) or get it from the Revenue Orderline (p. 180).

Filing the short tax return

You will need to complete the full return if you prefer to file by internet since there is no internet version of the short return. Submit the short return by post.

You must send in your short return by 31 October 2010 so that the Revenue can work out your tax bill for you in good time to settle any outstanding bill by the 31 January 2011 deadline. (You are not expected to work out your tax yourself.) If you miss this deadline, you will either have to file online (which is based on the full tax return) or pay a penalty of £100 or the amount of tax you owe if less – see Chapters 3 and 4 for details.

Completing the short tax return

Take care completing the return. It will be read by an electronic scanner so it is important that you keep to the boxes, leave blank boxes that do not apply to you, follow the instructions for mistakes and do not fold the form. If you need a replacement, call the helpline number given in the guidance notes.

Although Part 2 of this book deals with the full tax return, the information and guidance is just as relevant if you are filling in the short return. The table overleaf shows which sections of this guide to read for each set of questions on the short return.

Where to find help in this book when filling in the short return

Section of short tax return	Sections of this book which you may find helpful
Employment income	Chapter 15 (income, benefits and allowable expenses), Chapter 8 (fringe benefits)
Self-employment income	Chapter 17 (turnover, capital allowances, allowable expenses, losses, class 4 national insurance)
UK pensions and state benefits received	Chapter 12 (pensions – see p. 202)
UK interest and dividends	Chapter 12 (p. 192), Chapter 7 (savings, investments)
UK land and property	Chapter 19 (income, expenses, losses)
Other UK income for 2009–10	Chapter 12 (p. 210)
Gift Aid	Chapter 13 (p. 231)
Paying into registered pension schemes	Chapter 13 (p. 226), Chapter 7 (p. 87)
Blind person's allowance	Chapter 14 (p. 248)
Married couple's allowance	Chapter 14 (p. 249), Chapter 5 (p. 59)
If you have paid too much or too little tax?	Chapter 11 (p. 187)

Appendix D

Tax deadlines

Within 30 days

- Appeal an assessment issued by the Revenue

Within 60 days

- Tell your tax office if you disagree with the statement of taxable social security benefits you receive from Jobcentre Plus or The Pension Service

On or before 31 May 2010

- Form P60 should have been given to all employees by employer

On or before 4 June 2010

- Choose to pay tax in instalments on exercise of option in 2009–10 to acquire shares through an approved scheme

On or before 5 July 2010

- Send in your first tax credit claim form to get credits for the full year ending 5 April 2011

On or before 6 July 2010

- Form P9D (or Form P11D) should have been given to employees receiving fringe benefits, plus details of other benefits provided by someone else

On or before 31 July 2010

- Second interim payment of tax due for 2009–10
- Send in renewal form for tax credits to finalise award to 5 April 2010 and renew claim for 2010–11 without any break in payments

On or before 5 October 2010

- Tell your tax inspector about any new source of income or capital gain for the 2009–10 tax year

On or before 31 October 2010

- Send in paper tax return to avoid penalty if you do not want to file online

On or before 30 December 2010

- Employees who owe less than £2,000 should file their tax return by internet, if they want the tax to be collected through the PAYE system

On or before 31 January 2011

- File online tax return to avoid a penalty
- Pay any outstanding tax for 2009–10
- Claim to reduce payments on account for the 2010–11
- Make first interim payment on account of tax due for 2010–11 (statement received from Revenue based on previous year's tax bill or your own self-assessment calculation)
- Choose to carry back Gift Aid donations made in 2010–11 to previous year (unless you have already sent in your tax return)
- Send in actual income details for 2009–10 if, for tax credits, you could provide only estimates by 31 July 2010

On or before 5 April 2011

- Last chance to claim allowances and deductions for 2006–07

On or before 31 January 2012

- Set losses made in a new business for 2009–10 against other income for the previous three tax years
- Set business losses made in 2009–10 against other income
- Claim entrepreneurs' allowance for disposal of a business in 2009–10

Appendix E

Useful leaflets, forms and contacts

You can get these leaflets from any tax office (look in the phone book under HM Revenue & Customs). Most are also available from www.hmrc.gov.uk or by calling 08459 000 404.

Increasingly, the Revenue is ceasing to publish printed leaflets and instead putting information on its website where it can easily be kept up to date. If you do not have access to the internet, phone the helplines listed in this Appendix and ask to be sent a print-out of the information on the website.

Introductions to self-assessment

SA/BK4   Self-assessment. A general guide to keeping records
SA/BK8   Self-assessment. Your guide

General guides to the Revenue

Tax appeals
IR160   Enquiries under self-assessment
AO1   The Adjudicator's Office for complaints
C/FS   Complaints and putting things right
COP10   Information and advice (online only)

Income tax for particular groups

IR121   Approaching retirement – a guide to tax and National Insurance contributions
ICU1   Tax and your new pension – what you need to know

Pride 1   Taxes and benefits – information for our lesbian, gay, bisexual and transgender customers

CA5603   To pay voluntary national insurance contributions

Tax credits

WTC1   Child tax credit and working tax credit. An introduction

WTC5   Help with the cost of childcare

WTC8   Child tax credit and working tax credit (overpayments)

WTC10   Tax credits. Help us to help you get it right

WTC/AP   Child tax credit and working tax credit: how to appeal against a tax credit decision or award

(no ref.) Tax credits: how HMRC handle exit credit overpayments

COP26   What happens if we have paid you too much tax credit

WTC/FS1   Tax credits enquiry

Income tax and international issues

HMRC6   Residence, domicile and the remittance basis

Savings and investments

IR111   Bank and building society interest. Are you paying tax when you don't need to?

(no ref.) ISA factsheet

Employees

480   Expenses and benefits. A tax guide

IR115   Payment for childcare. Getting help from your employer

IR177   Share incentive plans and your entitlement to benefits

Self-employed

SE1   Are you thinking of working for yourself?

ES/FS1   Employed or self-employed for tax and National Insurance contributions

CA72B   Deferring self-employed National Insurance contributions

Employers (also see *Employees* above)

490   Employee travel. A tax and NICs guide for employers

P11DX   How to cut down on your paperwork: dispensations

Capital gains tax

CGT1/FS1   Capital Gains Tax. A quick guide for 2007–8 and earlier. (See website for information for 2008–9 onwards.)

Inheritance tax

HM Revenue & Customs no longer publishes any leaflets about inheritance tax. Instead see its customer guide to inheritance tax at www.hmrc.gov.uk/inheritancetax

Inheritance tax is not dealt with by your usual tax office. Instead contact HMRC Inheritance Tax at:

England and Wales: Ferrers House, PO Box 38, Castle Meadow Road, Nottingham, NG2 1BB

Scotland: Meldrum House, 15 Drumsheugh Gardens, Edinburgh EH3 7UG

Northern Ireland: Level 5, Millennium House, 17–25 Great Victoria Street, Belfast BT2 7BN

Probate and Inheritance Tax Helpline: 0845 302 0900

Revenue background notes on businesses

The Revenue publishes Business Economic Notes (BEN) on its website at www.hmrc.gov.uk/bens/index.htm but these are very out of date. The Revenue had started to publish more recent Tactical and Information Packages (TIPs) but, following a review of its publications policy, decided to withdraw them. If you are the subject of an enquiry, ask the officer dealing with your case whether they are drawing on information from a TIP and, if so, ask for a copy.

Useful Revenue forms

You can get these forms from tax offices, the Revenue website www.hmrc.gov.uk (follow the link to 'Find a form') or by calling 08459 000 404.

CWF1   To register if you are newly self-employed
IHT100   To report a taxable lifetime gift for inheritance tax*
IHT205   Simplified return of estate where no inheritance tax due*
IHT400   Inheritance tax account*
P11D   Summary of your taxable fringe benefits (from your employer)
P2   Notice of coding**
P38S   For students working in holidays who want to be paid gross
P50   Claiming tax back when you have stopped working

P60   End of year certificate of PAYE deductions (from your employer)

P86   To determine residence and domicile issues

P810   Tax review form if you pay tax through PAYE**

R40   To claim a tax repayment

R85   To register to receive savings interest gross

SA100   The full tax return (main form). You may need supplements as well

SA200   Short tax return (not available from website)**

SA300   Self assessment statement if you pay tax under self assessment**

SA303   To claim to reduce payments on account

VAT1   To register for VAT

* From website or Probate and Inheritance Tax Helpline 0845 302 0900.

** Your tax office sends you this form if relevant to you.

Revenue helplines

Here are a few examples. For a full list visit www.hmrc.gov.uk and click on 'Contact us' at the top of the screen

Helpline for newly Self-Employed: 0845 915 4515

Individual Savings Accounts Helpline: 0845 604 1701

National insurance enquiries: 0845 302 1479

New Employer Helpline (NESI): 0845 60 70 143

Probate and Inheritance Tax Helpline: 0845 302 0900

Self Assessment Helpline: 0845 900 0444

Self Assessment Forms Orderline: 0845 900 0404

Taxation of bank and building society interest: 0845 980 0645

Tax Credits: 0845 300 3900

VAT Helpline: 0845 010 9000

Advice about tax

Chartered Institute of Taxation

First Floor, 11–19 Artillery Row, London SW1P 1RT

Tel: 020 7340 0550/0844 579 6700

www.tax.org.uk

For list of members who give professional tax advice for a fee

Tax Aid

Room 304, Linton House, 164–180 Union Street, London SE1 0LH

Tel: 0845 120 3779

www.taxaid.org.uk

Free tax help for people on a low income

Tax Help for Older People (TOP)
Pineapple Business Park, Salway Ash, Bridport, Dorset DT6 5DB
Tel: 0845 601 3321/01308 488 066
www.taxvol.org.uk
Free tax help for older people on a low income

Tax-saving idea 236

> Whenever you contact HM Revenue & Customs, make sure you make a note of the conversation for your records in case of dispute later on.

European Economic Area (EEA) countries

Austria	Liechtenstein
Belgium	Latvia (since May 2004)
Bulgaria (since January 2007)	Lithuania (since May 2004)
Cyprus (since May 2004)	Luxembourg
Czech Republic (since May 2004)	Malta (since May 2004)
Denmark	Netherlands
Estonia (since May 2004)	Norway
Finland	Poland (since May 2004)
France	Portugal
Germany	Romania (since January 2007)
Greece	Slovakia (since May 2004)
Hungary (since May 2004)	Slovenia (since May 2004)
Iceland	Spain
Ireland	Sweden
Italy	United Kingdom

Index

Note: Bold numbers indicate page extents for **chapters** *and* numbered **tax-saving ideas**

absence from home 75–6
absent for year test of non-residence 404
accommodation *see* homes
accounting
  date, changing (self-employed) 312–13
  fiscal 311
  practice, changing 337
  year 306
accrued income scheme 215–16
accumulated unit trusts, income tax on 150
acquisition details and capital gains 393
Adjudicator's Office 56
administration expenses 323
adoption pay 264
advertising/promotion expenses 323–4
Advice about Tax 423–4
  see also leaflets
age-related allowances 247–8, 249
  see also older people
allowable expenses 132–3
  see also expenses
allowances 7, 24–6, **247–52**, 416
  age-related 247–8, 249
  blind person's 248
  details of 26
  marriage or civil partnership 59–61, 62,
    64, 249, 251–2
  pension 91
  personal 59, 247–8
  sharing 250–1
  tax-saving ideas 25, 139, 247
  transfer of 61, 252
annuities
  interest from 197
  retirement 228–9
  see also main tax return
anti-tax-avoidance rule 148
appeals *see* penalties, appeals and
    complaints
assets
  capital gains 143–5, 396
  description of 391–2
  disposal *see under* businesses

jointly owned 58–9, 193
pre-owned 174–6, 213–14
provided, tax-saving and 270
as taxable fringe benefits 113–15
wasting 134
working out bill for capital gains tax
    143–5
see also pre-owned assets
Austria 424
authorised unit trusts and investment
    companies 201
averaging, income 338
avoidance of tax 148, 246

banks
  interest from 81, 83, 197, 324
  offshore account 82
  transferred to public ownership 286
Belgium 424
benefits
  and capital gains tax 132–3
  dependants' 243
  employment 255
  and expenses 266–76
    and capital allowances 276–7
    payments 266–8
      see also company cars and vans
    tax-saving ideas 108–13, 117–18,
      269–71
      fringe benefits (no. **162**) 267
      zero emission vehicle (no. **163**) 269
  incapacity 208–9
  retirement 213
  schemes, employer-financed retirement
    213
  social security 373
  tax-saving 408–9
    see also under expenses *above*
  see also fringe benefits; main tax return;
    pensions
bereavement 64
blind person's allowances 248
bonds, corporate, income from 83, 215

bonus securities or shares, redemption of
243–4
building industry 320
building society interest 197
Bulgaria 424
businesses 11–12
capital gains tax and assets (before 2008)
143–5
disposal of assets 155–8
entrepreneur's relief 156–7, 400
roll-over relief 157–8
flats over and renovation allowance
364–5
income 316–17
premises inspected 51–2
receipts taxed as income of earlier year
221
run from home 71–2
see also farms; self-employment

calculation
of code for PAYE system 44–5
of tax 33–4, 145
capital allowance 276–7
property lettings 357–8, 363
capital gains **389–400**
capital losses carried forward or used in
other ways 398–400
documents needed 390
entrepreneur's relief 156–7, 400
inheritance tax 78
investing for 85–6
summary 185
supplement 394–7
listed shares and securities 394–5
property and other assets and gains
396
summary of enclosed computations
396–7
unlisted shares and securities 395
tax on see capital gains tax
working sheet 391–4
acquisition details 393
description of asset 391–2
disposable details 392
elections and reliefs 393
see also gain or loss
capital gains tax 10, 85
and assets 143–5
bill see reducing or delaying
on businesses 143
or farms, disposal of 155–8
calculation (before 2008–9) 145
and capital losses 142
deferral relief 155
foreign relief 376

on homes 72–8
absence from 75–6
gardens 73
inheritance 78
lettings 77–8
more than one 73
private residence relief on main home
72–3
regular property dealings 78
sale of 72
working from 75
leaflets, forms and contacts 422
minimising see minimising capital gains
tax
on separation and divorce 64
on shares see under shares
tax-free allowance 398
tax-saving ideas 73, 74, 75, 76–7, 86–7,
391, 397
see also businesses and farms; gain or
loss
capital losses 137, 142, 398–400
carbon dioxide emissions 119–21
cars see company cars and vans
cash ISAs 97
cashbacks 212
changes to tax return 47–52
discovery assessments 49–50
estimates, mistakes and corrections 47–8
information checks 50–1
inspection of business premises 51–2
interventions 48–9
tax-saving ideas 50, 52, 53, 54
charges
balancing and furnished holiday lettings
357–8
chargeable estate 159–60
chargeable income 360–1
surcharges on tax payments 37–9
charitable giving and reliefs 231–6
Gift Aid 69, 70, 231
shares, unit trusts and property 234
tax refund given to 189–90
tax-saving ideas 231–4, 235–6
charity
property gifted to 234
tax refund given to 189–90
Chartered Institute of Taxation 56
chattels, selling 134–6
children and household 65
Child Trust Fund (CTF) 100
low income and tax credits for 69–70
tax-saving ideas **36–8**, 66
civil partnerships see marriage and civil
partnerships
closing business 312

income tax relief on 239–41
taxable profit and loss and self-
        employment 341
coding notice, PAYE system 40–1, 43
Community Investment tax relief 106, 238
company cars and vans 117, 118–23
    fuel 122, 268
    list price when new 118–19
    mileage allowance 116, 269–70
    tax-saving ideas **89–92**, 119–21
        CO_2 emissions 119–20
        nos. **93–5** 121–3
compensation payments 278–9, 281
complaints *see* penalties, appeals and
        complaints
compulsory scheme for dependants'
        benefits 243
computer as tax-saving idea 272
construction industry subcontractors 320
contacts *see* leaflets, forms and contacts
corporate bonds, income from 83, 215
corrections, problems of 47–8
credit
    cards 116, 269–70
    tax 9, 18, 69–70, 376, 421
CTF (Child Trust Fund) 100
Cyprus 424
Czech Republic 424

date income is taxable 256
deadlines, tax 31, 417–19
death 64, 161–3
debts, bad 325
deductions
    claimable 225–6
    excessive 81
    fixed 275
    foreign service 281
    interest paid after 79–80
    seafarers' 282
    of tax from pay 264
deed of variation 171
deeply discounted securities 214–17
deferral relief 155
deficiency relief 220
Denmark 424
dental insurance, private 125, 269
dependants' benefits, compulsory scheme
        for 243
depreciation 326
disability 212, 281
discounted securities 214–17
discovery assessment in tax return 49–50
discretionary income payment 385
discretionary trust 168
disposals 146–8, 392

see also sales and *under* businesses *and*
        farms
dividends
    foreign 202, 373
    income from 198–202
    open-ended investment companies 201
    stock 150, 220–1
    UK companies 199–201
    unit trusts 150, 197, 201
divorce *see* separation and divorce
due time for tax 127–8

earnings *see* money from employment
EEA *see* European Economic Area
EIS (Enterprise Investment Scheme) 103–4,
        237
elections and reliefs 393
emissions, carbon dioxide 119–21
employees *see* employment
employers
    compulsory scheme for dependants'
        benefits 243
    contribution to overseas pension
        schemes 283
    leaflets, forms and contacts 421
    and money from employment 265
    retirement benefits schemes financed by
        213
employment/employees 11, 182, **253–83**,
        416
    basics 254–61
        benefits 255
        lump sums 255
    date income is taxable 256
    example 257–8
    expenses 272–8
        and capital allowances 276–7
        fixed deductions 275
        professional fees and subscriptions
            276, 325–6
        travel and subsistence 273–5
    foreign earnings 184, 194, 282–3
    leaflets, forms and contacts 421
    lump sums and compensation 278–9,
        281
        terms and payment expected 279–81
        unregistered pension schemes 280
    MSCs (managed service companies)
        259–60
    other payments 281
    P60, P11D or P9D forms 260–1
    pension schemes, unregistered 280
    personal service companies 256, 347
    shares and share schemes 149, 278,
        286–7
    tax credit relief 376

tax-saving ideas (Nos. **161**, **169** and **171**)
256–7, 277–8
see also benefits and expenses;
employees; employers; money
from employment
Enterprise Investment Scheme (EIS) 103–4,
237
enterprise management incentive options
and share schemes 295
entertainment expenses 323–4
entrepreneur's relief 156–7, 400
environmentally beneficial spending 365
estates
chargeable 159–60
freezing 170, 171
minimising capital gains tax 131
estimates and tax return 47–8
Estonia 424
European Economic Area: countries listed
424
expenses
furnished holiday lettings 355
self-employment *see under* self-
employment
UK property, renting out 361–2
see also under benefits

farms, disposal of 155–8
entrepreneur's relief 156–7, 400
inheritance tax planning 170
rollover relief 157–8
fees, professional 276, 325–6
final enquiry into tax return 48
final payment of tax 34–5
final value and capital gains tax 132
Finland 424
First-Tier Tribunal 49, 51–2, 55–6
flat-rate scheme of VAT 314–15
flats over shops and businesses 364
foreign income 184, 194, 281–2, **367–79**
dividends 202, 373
employer's contribution to pension
schemes 283
land and property 374–5
life-insurance policies, foreign 378
not taxable in UK 282–3
offshore funds and non-resident trusts
377
pensions 373
savings 372
Seafarers' earnings deduction 282
social security benefits 373
stuck in foreign countries 369
tax 283, 369–71
credit relief 376
-free 368–9

-savings and ideas 372, 373, 375
trusts and companies abroad 373–4
foreign service deduction 281
forms *see* leaflets, forms and contacts
France 424
free loans 123–4
freezing estates 170, 171
fringe benefits **107–26**, 267, 416
HM Revenue and Customs official
interest rate 125
medical or dental insurance, private 125,
269
and tax 113–16, 267
salary sacrifice to save 107–8
tax-free for all 108–13, 117–18
see also company cars and vans
furnished holiday lettings 352–9
income and expenses 355
losses for year 358
tax adjustments 357–8, 362
capital allowances and balancing
charges 357–8
private use 357
tax-saving ideas 356–7, 359
future profit 341

gain or loss, working out 131–6
allowable expenses 132–3
chattels, selling 134
initial and final value 132
personal belongings (wasting assets) 134
special rules 133–4
see also capital gains tax; losses
gardens 73
gateway, savings 101
Germany 424
getting started *see* starting a business
Gift Aid 69, 70, 231, 233–4
gifts and passing money on **159–76**
and capital gains tax bill 153–5
free of inheritance tax 162–3, 164, 165
Gift Aid 69, 70, 231, 233–4
and PETS 164
pre-owned assets tax (POAT) 174–5
with reservations 171–2
tax-free
always 162
on death only 162–3
in lifetime only 163
unit trusts and property 234
within seven years of death 161–2
see also gifts free of inheritance tax;
inheritance tax; planning pitfalls
gilts/gilt-edged stock
and income tax 83
interest from 214–17

strips 216–17
goods 335
    provided and tax-saving 270
    for sale and goods used 319–20
Greece 424
grossing up 80–1
growing businesses, investing in 101–5
    Enterprise Investment Scheme 103–4,
        237
    reliefs on 236–8
        Community Investment tax relief 106,
            238
    unquoted trading companies 102–3
    venture capital trusts (VCTs) 105, 236

help
    Inland Revenue helplines 423
    Tax Help for Older People (TOP) 42, 56,
        424
'high-income individuals': restricted
        pension reliefs 226–8
HM Revenue and Customs official interest
        rate 125
home income schemes 71
homes and tax 9–10, **71–8**, 116, 270–1
    capital gains *see under* capital gains tax
    income schemes 71
    income tax on investments 79–85
    inheritance 78
    letting *see* letting home
    living accommodation provided 116,
        270–1
    mortgage interest relief tax 71–2
    paying less 9–10
    see also household and tax; property *and*
        under capital gains tax
household and tax **57–70**
    bereavement 64
    Community Investment tax relief 106,
        238
    saving gateway 101
    unmarried but living together 65–6
    warning 105
    see also children and household; growing
        businesses; homes and tax; ISAs;
        marriage and civil partnerships;
        pensions; separation and divorce/
        dissolving of partnership
hundred and 83 days test of non-residence
        404
Hungary 424

Iceland 424
incapacity benefits 208–9
incentives 212, 263–4
income 19–21, **191–221**

averaging 338
    chargeable and reverse premiums
        360–1
    dividends 198–202
    from property 183, 355, 359–61
    interest-accrued scheme 215–16
    main types of (2010–11) 19–20
    net converting to gross **411–13**
    payments 20, 21
    scheme, accrued 215–16
    tax *see* income tax
    see also foreign income; low income;
        pensions *and under* dividends;
        interest; other UK income; profit;
        savings and investments
income tax
    and allowances 7
    on investments 79–85
        bank and building societies 81, 197
        bond-based unit trusts 83
        gilt-edged stock 83
        grossing up 80–1
        interest paid after deduction of tax
            79–80
        non-taxpayers and 81–2
        offshore bank accounts 82
        shares-based unit trusts 83–4
        Sharia-compliant products 83
        tax-saving ideas 81, 83
        too much tax deducted 81
        see also overview of income tax *and*
            under property funds
    paying less 7
    reliefs *see* reliefs, income tax
indexation allowance 140–1
individual savings accounts *see* ISAs
informal 'intervention' 48
information
    checks of tax return 50–1
    'information notice' 50
    on losses 244–5
    on pensions and savings 245
inheritance tax 159–74
    capital gains 78
    chargeable estate 159–60
    farms 170
    gifts free of 161–3, 164, 165
    on inherited home 78
    leaflets, forms and contacts 422
    limits on 160, 161
    payment 11, 172–4
    pitfalls, planning 171–2
    pre-owned assets tax (POAT) 174–6
    separation and divorce/dissolving of
        partnership 64
    tax-free allowance 160, 161

tax-saving ideas 161, 164, 169, 171, 175, 176
and trusts 168–9
see also planning for inheritance tax
initial value and capital gains tax 132
Inland Revenue 50–1
  background notes on businesses 422
  contacting 180–1
  general guide to 420
  helplines 423
  IR35 special rules for personal service companies 256
  useful forms 422–3
  see also leaflets
inspection of business premises 51–2
instalments, paying tax in 151
insurance
  disability 212
  policies, income from 212
  private medical 125, 269
  see also life insurance; National Insurance
interest
  accrued income scheme 215–16
  after tax deduction 79–80
  on annuities 197
  bank 81, 83, 197, 324
  building society 197
  from financial institutions 196–8
  gilts and securities 214–17
  on investments paid after tax deduction 79–80
  on loans 71, 239, 271, 324
  mortgage, tax relief on 71–2
  official rate 125
  in possession trust 168
  -reduced tax on low income 81
  on tax payments 37–9
  unit trusts 197, 201
  untaxed 198
interim payment of tax 34–5
international issues and income tax 421
internet filing of tax return 33
interventions and tax return changes 48–9
investment *see* savings and investments
Ireland 424
ISAs (individual savings accounts)
  amount you can invest 98
  cash ISAs 97
  stocks and shares 97–8
  tax 98, 99, 100
Italy 424

jobseeker's allowance (JSA) 209
jointly owned assets 58–9, 193

Lanham v. Veltema case 48
Latvia 424
law and legislation 172, 325–6
leaflets, forms and contacts (Inland Revenue) 420–4
  Advice about Tax 423–4
  background notes on businesses 422
  capital gains tax 422
  employees 421
  employers 421
  Forms P60, P11D or P9D 260–1
  general guide 420
  helplines 423
  inheritance tax 422
  Inland Revenue, useful forms 422–3
  international issues 421
  particular groups 420–1
  savings and investments 421
  self-assessment 420
  self-employed 421
  tax credits 421
  tax-saving idea 237
legal matters 172, 325–6
less tax, paying *see* paying less tax
letting property 71–2, 77–8
Liechtenstein 424
life insurance 169
  foreign 378
  gains 217–21
    non-qualifying policies 218–20
    qualifying policies 217
  and pension schemes 94–5
life insurance policies
  non-qualifying 218–20
  tax-saving ideas and 58–61, 86–7
lifetime allowance (pensions) 91, 93–4
Lithuania 424
living accommodation *see* homes
loans
  cheap or free 123–4
  interest 71, 239, 271, 324
  student, repayment of 186–8, 265–6
losses 244–5, 339
  capital 137, 142, 398–400
  making best use of 153
  net 327
  partnership, working 347–8
  property letting 365–6
  and tax saving 365–6
  see also gain or loss, working out; taxable profit and loss
low income
  and children 69–70
  interest-reduced tax for 81
  transfer of allowances and 61
lump sums 255, 278–9, 281

Luxembourg 424

main home, private residence relief on
        72–3
main tax return and pensions, annuities
        and state benefits 202–10
    incapacity benefit 208–9
    jobseeker's allowance 209
    pensions 205–10
        not state 209–10
        state 97, 205–6
    should not be included 203–4
    support allowance 208–9
    see also tax return
maintenance payments on separation and
        divorce 63
    income tax relief on 241–2
Malta 424
managed service companies (MSCs) 259–60
marriage and civil partnerships 57–62
    allowances 59–61, 62, 64, 249
        after April 2009 251–2
        transfer because of low income 61
    capital gains tax *see* reducing or delaying
    dissolved *see* separation and divorce
    jointly owned assets 58–9, 193
    tax-saving ideas 61, 62, 69
        minimising capital gains tax 130–1
maternity pay 264
medical insurance, private 125, 269
mergers and capital gains tax 150
mileage allowance 116, 269–70
minimising capital gains tax **127–58**
    due time 127–8
    payers 130–1
    tax saving ideas (98 and 107) 133, 150–2
    see also gain or loss; reducing or delaying
        capital gains tax bill; shares and
        unit trusts and capital gains tax;
        working out bill for capital gains
mistakes, problems of 47–8
money from employment 255, 261–6, 281
    adoption pay 264
    employer and 265
    foreign earnings 184, 194, 281–2
    incentive awards 263–4
    maternity pay 264
    occupational pension 228, 263
    payroll giving schemes 263
    sacrifice to save tax 107–8
    sick pay 264
    student loan replacement 186–8, 265–6
    tax deducted 264
    tips and other payments 265
    see also fringe benefits
monthly savings schemes 151

more than one home 73
more than one source of income 45
mortgage interest tax relief 71–2
    home income schemes 71
    running business or letting home 71–2
motive test of non-residence 403–4
MSCs (managed service companies) 259–60
mutuals becoming PLCs 151

National Insurance contributions 12–13,
        342, 343–4
net income converted to gross **411–13**
Netherlands 424
ninety-one days test of non-residence 405
non-active partner 348
non-domiciled definition of non-residence
        405–6
non-income payments 20
non-qualifying distribution of dividends
        221
non-qualifying life insurance policies
        218–20
non-residence **401–6**
    change since April 2008 402–3
    mobile workers 405
    non-domiciled definition 405–6
    tax form, filling in 185–6
    tax-saving idea **232**, 403
    tests to prove 403–5
        91 days test 405
        183 days test 404
        absent for whole year test 404
        motive test 403–4
    trusts 377
    warning 405
non-taxpayers
    and investments 81–2
    and pensions 90–1
Northern Rock shares 152
Norway 424

obligations when paying and reclaiming
        tax 27–33
    new source of income or capital 27–8
    records 28–9
    see also tax return; tax-savings
occupational pensions 89, 228, 263
offshore funds
    changes to taxation on 378–9
    and income tax on investments 82
    and non-resident trusts 377
older people
    age-related allowances 247–8, 249
    Tax Help for 42, 56, 424
    see also age-related allowances; pensions;
        retirement

open-ended investment companies'
    dividends 201
options, share 92–3, 295
    tax on 293
    unapproved 297–301
other UK income 210–21
    business receipts taxed as income of
        earlier year 221
    cashbacks and incentives 212
    deficiency relief 220
    employer-financed retirement benefits
        schemes 213
    from service companies 214
    gilts and securities, interest from 214–17
    insurance policies 212
    pre-owned assets 174–6, 213–14
    self-employment 339
    stock dividends 150, 220–1
    taxable profit and loss 339
    see also gains under life insurance
overlap profits 310–11
overlap relief 336–7
overpaid tax, repayment of 47–8
overseas see foreign
overview of income tax **15–26**
    see also allowances; quick guide to
        income tax; reliefs

P60, P11D or P9D Forms 260–1
PAIFs (property authorised investment
    funds) 85
partnership, civil see marriage and civil
    partnerships
partnership, working 183, **345–8**
    becoming partner 346–7
    ceasing to be partner 347
    losses 347–8
    non-active partner 348
    personal services supplied by 347
    tax-saving idea no. 212 347
pay see money from employment
PAYE system: and paying and reclaiming
        tax 39–46
    claiming tax refund 40–1, 43, 45–6
    code
        calculating 44–5
        coding notice 40–1, 43
    examples 42–4, 45
    more than one source of income 45
    review form 179
    tax-saving ideas 40, 41–2
paying less tax and tax changes for
        2010–11 **5–13**
    businesses 11–12
    capital gains tax 10
    credits, tax 9, 19, 69–70, 376, 421

    employees 11
    homes and property 9–10
    income tax and allowances 7
    inheritance tax 11
    National Insurance 12–13
    savings and investments 10
    trusts 13
    see also reliefs
paying and reclaiming tax 9, **27–48**, 34–9
    calculation of tax 33–4, 145
    interest and surcharges 37–9
    interim and final 34–5
    records 28–9
    reducing payments on account 36
    repayment of overpaid tax 47–8
    statement 36
        self-assessment 35
    tax-saving ideas 35, 37, 39
    see also obligations; PAYE; paying less
        tax
payroll giving schemes 263
penalties, appeals and complaints 52–6
    getting help 56
    tax-saving ideas 53, 54–6
pensions 87–97, 206–8
    additional information 245
    allowances 91
    and benefits 209–10
    foreign income 373
    and life insurance 94–5
    lifetime allowance 91, 93–4
    and non-taxpayers 90–1
    occupational schemes 89, 228, 263
    overseas, employer's contribution to 283
    personal plans 228
    and reliefs 226–30
        income tax (2011–12) 87–90, 228
        occupational schemes 228
        restricted 87–8, 226–8
    retirement annuity 228–9
    rights (pre-April 2006) protected 96
    savings
        additional information form 245
        how much one can save 88–9
    unregistered schemes 280
    see also benefits; ISAs; retirement; state
        pension and under savings and
        investments and tax-saving ideas
personal allowances 59, 247–8
personal belongings (wasting assets) 134
personal pension plans 228
personal services companies 256, 347
PETS (potentially exempt transfers) 164
planning for inheritance tax 160, 161,
        163–71
    estate freezing 170, 171

farm 170
home 166–7
life insurance 169
own business 170
problems *see* planning pitfalls
shares 170
tax-saving ideas 164, 169, 171
and trusts 168–9
wealth sharing 165
will trusts 167–9
see also inheritance tax
planning pitfalls of inheritance planning
        171–2
associated operations 172
gifts with reservations 171–2
legislation, retroactive/retrospective 172
related property 172
PLCs, mutuals becoming 151
POAT (pre-owned assets tax) 174–6
Poland 424
possession trust, interest in 168
potentially exempt transfers (PETS) 164
poverty *see* low income
premiums, chargeable and reverse 360–1
pre-owned assets 213–14
tax (POAT) 174–6
private medical or dental insurance 125,
        269
private residence relief on main home
        72–3
private use of furnished holiday lettings
        357
problems, tax, dealing with **47–56**
getting help 56
see also changes to tax return; penalties,
        appeals and complaints
professional fees 276, 325–6
profits 326
for correct period identified 336
net 327
overlap 310–11
property letting and tax saving 365–6
see also income; taxable profit and loss
promotion expenses 323–4
property
authorised investment funds (PAIFs) 85
and capital gains supplement 396
gifted to charity 234
income in UK 183
letting and tax saving 365–8
real estate investment trust (REITS) funds
        85
regular dealings 78
see also homes; household; renting; UK
        property
public ownership, bank transferred to 286

qualifying distribution on redemption of
        bonus securities or shares 243–4
qualifying life insurance policies 217
quick guide to income tax 15–18
rates of tax 16–18
tax credits 18
tax saving ideas 18

real estate investment trusts (REITs) 85
receipts taxed as income of earlier year 221
reclaiming tax *see* obligations; PAYE
        system: paying and reclaiming tax
records when paying and reclaiming tax
        28–9
redemption of bonus securities or shares
        243–4
reducing or delaying capital gains tax bill
        152–8
gifts 153–5
husbands, wives and civil partners 153
losses, making best use of 153
tax-saving idea no. **108** 153
tax-saving idea no. **109** 155
reducing tax payments on account 36
refund, tax
claiming 40–1, 43, 45–6
to be given to charity 189–90
REITs (real estate investment trusts) 85
reliefs, income tax 8, 21–5, **223–46**, 416
basic rate on contributions 229
closing business 239–41
Community Investment 106, 238
deductions claimable 225–6
deferral 155
deficiency 220
documents needed 223–4
employers' compulsory scheme for
        dependants' benefits 243
entrepreneur's 156–7, 400
full, payments made in 230
how to get 21–2
investment in growing businesses 236–8
loan interest 239
losses, additional information from
        244–5
main types for 2010–11 tax year 23–4
maintenance payments 241–2
and pensions *see under* pensions
qualifying distribution on redemption of
        bonus securities or shares 243–4
roll-over 157–8
tax-savings ideas **143–145** 224–5, 230
on trade union payments 242
see also charitable giving; tax-saving
        ideas *and under* growing
        businesses

renovation allowance 364–5
renting property
    capital allowances 357–8, 363
    Rent a Room scheme 350
    see also UK property
repairs and renewals expenses 323
repayment
    of overpaid tax 47–8
    of student loan 186–7, 265–6
reporting figures 313–16
    value added tax (VAT) 313–16
        flat-rate scheme 314–15
        unregistered or partially registered 315
        warning 313
reservations, gifts with 171–2
retirement
    annuity 228–9
    benefits schemes, employer-financed 213
    tax-saving ideas 92–3
    see also pensions
Revenue *see* Inland Revenue
reverse premiums and chargeable income
    360–1
rights issues 150
rights, pension 96
roll-over relief 157–8
Romania 424

salary *see* money from employment
sales
    costs of loss on 326
    and disposals and capital gains tax
        146–8
    of goods 319–20
    of home, capital gains tax on 72
saving gateway 101
savings and investments 10
    capital gains, investing for 85–6
    Community Investment tax relief 106,
        238
    companies, open-ended, dividends from
        201
    examples 80
    in growing businesses 236–8
    income from 192–6
        jointly owned 193
        see also ISAs
    interest paid after tax deduction 79–80
    leaflets, forms and contacts 421
    life insurance policies 58–61, 86–7
    monthly schemes 151
    and pensions 10, **79–106**
    and tax return 81, 83
    and tax-free income 192–3, 409–10
    and tax-saving ideas 58–61, 86–7, 193,
        195, 202

treated as yours 193–5
trusts 146
see also income tax on investments;
    pensions
Seafarers' earnings deduction 282
securities, deeply discounted 214–17
self-assessment 35, 420
self-employment 182, **303–44**, 416
    accounting date, changing 312–13
    business details 305–8
        accounting year 306
        income 316–17
        special arrangements 307
    expenses 317–26
        bad debts 325
        car, van and travel 321–2
        depreciation and loss on sale 326
        employees 320–1
        goods for sale and goods used 319–20
        interest on loans 324
        legal and professional 325–6
        premises 322–3
        subcontractors in construction
            industry 320
    leaflets, forms and contacts 421
    National Insurance and tax-saving ideas
        341–4
    profit and loss, net 327
    see also taxable profit and loss
    tax credit relief 376
    tax-saving ideas **179–187** 305, 307–8,
        311, 315–16, 317, 318, 319,
        320
    see also reporting figures; starting a
        business
separation and divorce/dissolving of
    partnership 62–4
    Capital Gains tax 64
    inheritance tax 64
    maintenance payments 63
    married couple's allowance 64
    National Insurance contribution 63
service companies, income from 214
share schemes 83, 278, **285–301**
    bank transferred to public ownership
        286
    different types of 287–94
    employee 149, 286–7
    enterprise management incentive
        options 295
    tax-saving ideas 148, 287–97
        no. **172** 287
        no. **173** 288
        no. **174** 289
        no. **175** 291
        no. **176** 292–3

no. **177** 294–5
no. **178** 295–7
unapproved options 297–301
shares and unit trusts 394–5
  buying in instalments 151
  and capital gains tax 83, 145–52
    anti-tax-avoidance rule 148
    employee share schemes 149, 286–7
    investment trusts 146
    paying in instalments 151
    rights issues 150
    sales and disposals 146–8
    stock dividends and accumulated unit
      trusts 150, 220–1
    takeovers and mergers 150
    tax-saving idea 106, 148
    valuing shares 146
  employee share schemes, basics of 149,
    278, 286–7
  gifted to charity 234
  income tax on 83–4
  ISAs 97–8
  and planning for inheritance tax 170
  schemes *see* share schemes
Sharia-compliant products 83
sharing allowances 250–1
shops, flats over 364
short tax return 414–16
  checking 414–15
  completing and filing 415
  sources of help 416
sick pay 264
sickness insurance policy 212
Slovakia and Slovenia 424
social security benefits 373
Society for Motor Manufacturers and
    Traders 119
Spain 424
special rules
  capital gains tax 133–4
  personal service companies 256
starting a business **179–90**, 308–11, 416
  first tax year 309
  second tax year 309–10
  third tax year 310
  fiscal accounting 311
  overlap profits 310–11
  see also self-employment
starting rate taxpayer 90–1
starting to fill in tax form
  capital gains summary 185
  contacting Inland Revenue 180–1
  employment 182
  foreign income 184
  non-resident 185–6
  partnership 183

property income in UK 183
  refund to be given to charity 189–90
  self-employment 182
  student loan repayments 186–7
  tax-saving ideas (nos. 132 and 133) 189,
    190
  trusts 184
state pension
  increase 97
  and main tax return 205–6
  see also pensions *and under* tax-saving
    ideas
statements, tax 35, 36
stocks
  dividends 150, 220–1
  gilt-edged 83
  and shares ISAs 97–8
  see also shares
strips, gilt 216–17
students
  loan repayments 186–7, 265–6
  and PAYE system 46
subcontractors in construction industry
    320
subscriptions 276
support allowance 208–9
surcharges on tax payments 37–8
Sweden 424

takeovers and capital gains tax 150
taper relief 142–3, 144
tax
  adjustments
    and furnished holiday lettings 362
      capital allowances and balancing
        charges 357–8
  allowances **7–10**, 25, 139, 140
  avoidance 148, 246
  benefits 108–13, 117–18, 352
  and businesses 11–12
  capital gains *see* capital gains tax
  charitable giving 189–90, 231–4, 235–6
  computer 272
  credit 9, 18, 421
    relief 376
  deducted from pay 264
  foreign *see* foreign tax
  on fringe benefits *see under* fringe
    benefits
  and homes *see* under homes
  and household *see* household and tax
  income *see* income tax
  inheritance *see* inheritance tax
  interest on 37–9
  investment 192–3, 409–10
  on ISAs 98, 99, 100

and marriage and civil partnerships 61,
    62, 69, 130–1
on option 293
overpaid, repayment of 47–8
PAYE 40, 41–2
paying less *see* paying less tax
paying and reclaiming 35, 37, 39
  example 30
  internet filing 33
  not sent in 33
problems, dealing with *see* problems, tax,
    dealing with
refund *see* refund, tax
relief *see* reliefs, income tax
return *see* tax return
savings 81, 83
  furnished holiday lettings 219, 356–7
  see also tax-saving ideas
Tax Help for Older People (TOP) 42, 56,
    424
TaxAid 56
on working out bill for capital gains tax
    (before 2008–09) 145
tax return 29–33
  deadlines 31, 417–19
  example 30
  internet filing 33
  not sent 33
  see also changes to tax return; main tax
      return; short tax return
taxable profit and loss and self-
    employment 335–41
  accounting practice, change of 337
  closing down 341
  future profit 341
  goods and services for own use 335
  income averaging 338
  losses 339
  other income or gains 339
    for previous year 340–1
  overlap relief 336–7
  profits for correct period identified 336
tax-free allowance 139, 160
  capital gains 398
tax-free benefits 108–13, 117–18, 408–9
tax-free foreign income 368–9
tax-free gifts (inheritance) 164
tax-free income 20, **407–10**
tax-free limits on inheritance tax 161
tax-saving ideas
  No. **1** 18
  No. **2** 21
  No. **3–4** 22
  No. **5–6** 23
  No. **7–10** 25
  No. **11** 29

No. **12** 31
No. **13** 31–2
No. **14–15** 33
No. **16** 34
No. **17–18** 35
No. **19** 37
No. **20–22** 39
No. **23** 40
No. **24** 41–2
No. **25–6** 46
No. **27** 50
No. **28** 52
No. **29** 53
No. **30** 54
No. **31–2** 58
No. **33** 61
No. **34–5** 62
No. **36–41** 66–7
No. **42–4** 69–70
No. **45–6** 73
No. **47–8** 74
No. **49–50** 75
No. **51** 76–7
No. **52** 77
No. **53–4** 81
No. **55** 83
No. **56** 85
No. **57–61** 86
No. **62–4** 89
No. **65** 90
No. **66** 91
No. **67–9** 93
No. **70** 95
No. **71** 96
No. **72** 97
No. **73–5** 98
No. **76** 99
No. **77** 101
No. **78–9** 105
No. **80–4** 109
No. **85–6** 111
No. **87–8** 113
No. **89–92** 119
No. **93** 121–3
No. **94–5** 123
No. **96** 128
No. **97** 130
No. **98** 133
No. **99** 134–6
No. **100** 137
No. **101** 138
No. **102–3** 139
No. **104–5** 145
No. **106** 148
No. **107** 150
No. **108** 153

No. **109** 155
No. **110–14** 157
No. **115–17** 161
No. **118–20** 164
No. **121–3** 169
No. **124–6** 171
No. **127–9** 175
No. **130–1** 176
No. **132** 189
No. **133** 190
No. **134** 193
No. **135–6** 195
No. **137** 201
No. **138** 202
No. **139–40** 206
No. **141** 214
No. **142** 215
No. **143–5** 224
No. **146** 226
No. **147–8** 230
No. **149–52** 231
No. **153–5** 233–4
No. **156–7** 235
No. **158** 236
No. **159** 247
No. **160** 255
No. **161** 256–7
No. **162** 267
No. **163** 269
No. **164** 270–1
No. **165** 272
No. **166–8** 275
No. **169–70** 277–8
No. **171** 278
No. **172** 287
No. **173** 288
No. **174** 289
No. **175** 291
No. **176** 292–3
No. **177** 294
No. **178** 295
No. **179** 305
No. **180–1** 307
No. **182–4** 311
No. **185–6** 315
No. **187** 317
No. **188–9** 318
No. **190** 319
No. **191** 320
No. **192** 321
No. **193** 322
No. **194** 324
No. **195–6** 328
No. **197–9** 331
No. **200–202** 332
No. **203–5** 338

No. **206–7** 339
No. **208** 342
No. **209–10** 343
No. **211** 344
No. **212** 347
No. **213–14** 350
No. **215–16** 353
No. **217–18** 354
No. **219** 356
No. **220–1** 359
No. **222** 364
No. **223–4** 373
No. **225–6** 375
No. **227** 377
No. **228** 383
No. **229** 384
No. **230** 391
No. **231** 397
No. **232** 403
No. **233–5** 406
No. **236** 424
tips and other payments 265
TOP (Tax Help for Older People) 42, 56, 424
trade union payments 242
transfers
  of allowances 61, 252
  banks to public ownership 286
  potentially exempt (PETS) 164
  surplus allowances 252
travel and subsistence 273–5
Tribunal System
  First-Tier 49, 51–2, 55–6
  Upper Tribunal 51, 55, 56
trusts 13, 184, **381–7**
  documents needed 351–2
  income from estates
    foreign 387
    UK 386–7
  and inheritance tax 168–9
  minimising capital gains tax 131
  and planning for inheritance tax 168–9
  and settlements, income from 382–5
    chargeable 385
    child's income counted as yours 384
    discretionary income payment 385
    example 383
    taxation of 382–3
    tax-saving idea no. **228** 383
    tax-saving idea no. **229** 384
    trust income 382–3
  see also unit trusts

UK companies, dividends from 199–201
UK property, renting out **349–66**, 416

business premises renovation allowance 364–5
capital and other allowances 363
chargeable and reverse premiums 360–1
documents needed 350
expenses 361–2
flats over shops and businesses 364
income from 355, 359–61
Rent a Room scheme 350
tax-saving ideas 364–6
  flats over shops and businesses 364
  no. **213** 350
  no. **214** 350–2
  no. **222** 364–6
warning 349
see also furnished holiday lettings
unapproved share options 297–301
unit trusts
  assets 201
  bond-based, income tax on 83
  gifted to charity 234
  interest/dividends 150, 197, 201
  tax on, accumulated 150
  see also trusts
United Kingdom *see* UK
unlisted shares and securities, and capital gains supplement 395
unmarried people living together 65–6
unquoted trading companies, investing in 102–3
unregistered pension schemes 280
untaxed interest 198
Upper Tribunal 51, 55, 56

value added tax (VAT) 313–16
  flat-rate scheme 314–15
  unregistered or partially registered 315
vans *see* company cars and vans
variation, deed of 171
VAT *see* value added tax
VCTs (venture capital trusts) 105, 236
vehicles
  mileage allowance 116, 269–70

Vehicle Certification Agency 119
  see also company cars and vans
venture capital trusts 105, 236
vouchers 116, 269–70

wasting assets (personal belongings) 134
wealth sharing and inheritance tax 165
will trusts 167–9
working out bill for capital gains tax (before 2008–9) 140–5
  business assets 143–5
  calculations 145
  capital losses 142
  indexation allowance 140–1
  taper relief 142–3, 144
  tax-saving ideas 145
working out bill for capital gains tax (2008–9 onwards) 136–40
  capital losses 137
  tax-free allowance 139
  tax-saving ideas 137–9
  and pensions 89–97
    annual allowance 91
    investments, pension scheme 95–6
    life cover provided by pension schemes 94–5
    lifetime allowance 91, 93–4
    non-taxpayer 90–1
    occupational schemes 89
    pension rights pre-April 2006 protected 96
    retirement, options at 92–3
    small pensions 94
    starting rate taxpayer 90–1
    state pension increase 97
    topping up pension 92
    see also pensions *under* savings and investments
  property let 364–6
  share schemes 287–96
  taxable profit and loss and self-employment **203–5**, 338
zero emissions as tax-saving idea 269

Comprehensive. Authoritative. Trusted.

FT Guides will tell you everything you need to know about your chosen subject area

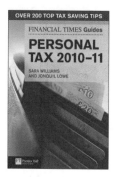

9780273735694

9780273724520

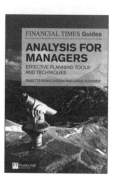

9780273722014

9780273729846

9780273712671

9780273723967

9780273727835

9780273730293

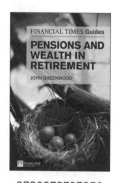

9780273727859

9780273723745

9780273727873

9780273729105

Change your business life today

FT Prentice Hall
FINANCIAL TIMES